Barcode in Back

W9-ADG-213

The Great War and German Memory

Under Weimar Germany and the Third Reich, the mentally disabled survivors of the trenches became a focus of debate between competing social and political groups, each attempting to construct their own versions of the national community and the memory of the war experience. Conceptions of class, war, masculinity and social deviance were shaped and in some cases altered by the popularized debates involving these traumatized members of society.

Through the tortured words of these men and women, Jason Crouthamel reveals a current of protest against prevailing institutions and official memory—and especially the Nazi celebration of war as the cornerstone of the 'healthy' male psyche—that has remained hidden until now. By examining the psychological effects of war on ordinary Germans and the way these war victims have shaped perceptions of madness and mass violence, Crouthamel illuminates potent and universal problems faced by societies coping with war and interrogates the politics of how we care for our veterans today.

Jason Crouthamel is Assistant Professor of History at Grand Valley State University, Michigan. He has published several articles on war neurosis and psychological trauma in inter-war Germany and has presented papers on the subject at conferences including those of the American Historical Association, the German Studies Association and the German Historical Institute.

Twentieth-century history
from University of Exeter Press

Nazism 1919–1945
edited by J. Noakes and G. Pridham

Volume 1: *The Rise to Power 1919–1934* (new edition 1998)
Volume 2: *State, Economy and Society 1933–1939* (new edition 2000)
Volume 3: *Foreign Policy, War and Racial Extermination* (new edition 2001)
Volume 4: *The German Home Front in World War II* (1998)

The Soviet Union: A Documentary History
by Edward Acton and Tom Stableford

Volume 1: *1917–1940* (2005)
Volume 2: *1939–1991* (2007)

*The Civilian in War: The Home Front in Europe, Japan and the USA
in World War II*
edited by Jeremy Noakes (1980)

*The Last Years of Austria-Hungary: A Multi-National Experiment
in Early Twentieth-Century Europe*
edited by Mark Cornwall (new edition 2002)

*Nazism, War and Genocide: New Perspectives on the History
of the Third Reich*
edited by Neil Gregor (2008)

The Great War and German Memory

Society, Politics and Psychological Trauma, 1914–1945

Jason Crouthamel

UNIVERSITY
of
EXETER
PRESS

First published in 2009 by
University of Exeter Press
Reed Hall, Streatham Drive
Exeter EX4 4QR
UK

www.exeterpress.co.uk

British Library Cataloguing in Publication Data
A catalogue record for this book is available
from the British Library.

ISBN 978 0 85989 842 3

Typeset in Sabon, 10 on 12 by
Carnegie Book Production, Lancaster
Printed in Great Britain by
Short Run Press Ltd, Exeter

FSC
Mixed Sources
Product group from well-managed
forests and other controlled sources

Cert no. SA-COC-002112
www.fsc.org
© 1996 Forest Stewardship Council

For Grace and Max

Contents

Acknowledgements

It is a pleasure to thank the numerous individuals who have provided such generous support during the completion of this project. When I began working on the Great War at Indiana University, my *Doktorvater* Jim Diehl gave me tremendous encouragement as I pursued the history of psychologically traumatized veterans. The project has led to a never-ending conversation that has been one of the great joys of doing research under his expert direction, and I would like to thank him for helping me keep a sense of humor while working on the horrifying effects of mass violence. The original manuscript and multiple revisions were made possible by the very generous support of the DAAD (German Academic Exchange Service), whose grants allowed me to pursue and develop my research. My current institution, Grand Valley State University, has been very kind in providing several research and development grants that have given me the chance to keep digging in Germany's archives for the writings of lost war victims.

I would like to thank the many colleagues who gave their time and expertise to help me improve this book. At different stages of the project Robert Whalen, Andreas Killen, Gary Stark, David Bielanski, David Pace, Ann Carmichael, Albrecht Holschuh and Bill Cohen read drafts and chapters and provided invaluable feedback. Robert Whalen's advice in particular encouraged me to further pursue the stories of traumatized men and let their voices, especially those struggling after 1933, cut through the labyrinthine policy debates and bureaucracy. The anonymous reviewers for the University of Exeter Press helped me make final revisions that were essential to sharpening my ideas and analysis. I have greatly enjoyed the ongoing conversations with scholars whom I very much admire and who have helped me to clarify my ideas. I would like to thank Roger Chickering for inviting me to share my work at the German Historical Institute (GHI) in Washington, D.C. and Flemming Just for allowing me to join the Centre for European Conflict and Identity History (CONIH) seminar on war and sexuality in twentieth century Europe. At various conferences I received questions and comments from colleagues that have been enormously helpful in looking at my work from different perspectives. In particular, I would like to thank Tony Kaes, Paul Lerner, Richard Wetzell, Sace Elder, Heather R. Perry, Warren Rosenblum, Richard Fogerty, Wolfgang Eckart, Jane Caplan, Hans-Georg Hofer, Dagmar Herzog, Daniel Walther, Clayton Whisnant and Erika Kuhlman. Most recently, my colleagues Cay-Rüdiger Prüll, Petra Peckl and Philipp Rauh at the Institute for the History of Medicine at the University of Freiburg welcomed me with expert advice and insightful questions that helped me sharpen my thinking at the final stages of writing the book.

Some of the friendliest individuals that German historians get to work with include the librarians and archivists who make it possible to explore sources. Herr Lange's humor and unfailing patience at the Bundesarchiv Berlin-Lichterfelde helped make the archive feel like home. Petra Prietzl at the Archiv der Parteien und Massenorganisationen der DDR in Berlin-Lichterfelde helped me locate some fascinating documents that were crucial to the book. My colleague Joseph Perry made it possible to leap right into the files by sharing his experience at the Bundesarchiv in Berlin. The archivists and staff at the Bundesarchiv Koblenz, the Deutsche Bücherei Leipzig, Berlin's Staatsbibliothek and the Bayerisches Hauptstaatsarchiv in Munich also provided constant help and advice.

I would also like to thank the University of Exeter Press for helping see through the book's publication. The press's editor, Anna Henderson, has generously given considerable patience and support that made the project possible. I would also like to thank the editors at the *Journal of Contemporary History, Peace and Change: A Journal of Peace Research* (Blackwell) and *War and Society* for their permission in allowing me to publish elements from my articles for those journals in this book. Thanks also to Brandon Moblo for his obsession with detail that helped greatly with the editing.

Finally, I would like to thank friends and family whose humor and love kept me sane over the years. Sean Quinlan and Sandra Reineke provided my family with a model for how to keep one's priorities straight. At Grand Valley State University, Bill Morison, Gary Stark, David Eick and Maria Fidalgo-Eick not only provided useful feedback, but they also helped show by example how to value both teaching and research. Thanks to my parents for laying the foundations by taking me to every museum and library on the map. The greatest joy of my life has been sharing Berlin with Grace Coolidge and my son Max. Grace has brought existential living to new heights, and Max's enthusiasm for being part of both our academic careers has inspired me in ways I could not have imagined. We have been able to carve out 'our own private Germany', and it is to them that I dedicate this book.

Jason Crouthamel
March 2009

Introduction

In 1928, taxi driver Konrad D., tortured by what he described as feelings of aggression, moodiness and a 'high level of nervousness', navigated with difficulty through the streets of Berlin. These problems had plagued him for years and made it impossible for him to hold down his previous job as a bank clerk, where he was fired for his 'quarrelsome personality'.[1] One night only a few weeks after he took his job driving taxis, he collided with another car and killed a passenger. Investigators concluded that he was too 'mentally unstable' to operate a car. The doctor who examined him recommended that, though he suffered from nervousness, anxiety and depression, he was able to hold a job, as long as it did not involve driving taxis.[2]

Konrad D. believed that his problems stemmed from war-related stress. He wrote vivid letters to the Labor Ministry and his welfare office about the 'crashing artillery fire' that caused nightmares and depression.[3] He had been proud that since the end of the war he was able to work, but now he found it impossible to control his worsening psychological problems. Konrad D. had been examined by doctors in 1916, when he first showed signs of mental illness, but they concluded that he suffered from inborn psychological disorders that were not war-related, and thus did not entitle him to a pension.[4] Doctors reexamined him in 1930 only to confirm earlier reports that his problems were hereditary, and they informed the welfare office that D. was 'irritable, whiny' and prone to 'grumbling'.[5]

As the Great Depression shattered Germany's already precarious political and economic institutions, Konrad D. set up his typewriter and began a relentless assault against the Weimar Republic, firing off several lengthy letters every month. He mocked the republic's finance ministers, whom he called 'rabid animals ... who sinned against the German spirit', and he predicted they would subvert the democracy and pave the way for Hitler's success.[6] The collapse of his nerves paralleled the collapse of the republic, he wrote, and he predicted that, with Hitler, Germany's nerves would fall completely to ruin. He introduced himself to the Nazi government with letters signed with sardonic pride, 'Germany's main whiner and grumbler',

1

and he cast himself in the role of an agitator against those he believed persecuted him. He mocked the Nazis' celebration of war and the front experience, and he wrote extensive essays on the 'authentic' war experience, full of terror, dehumanization and psychological destruction, to contrast with Nazi propaganda. True 'heroism', he wrote, meant providing support for war victims, and he asserted that 'only by granting justice can the national psyche avoid becoming sick and the spirit of truth not fall into decay'.[7] In his last letters in 1935, Konrad D. accused Nazi leaders of being the real psychopaths who traumatized the nation by inflicting violence on its most vulnerable citizens: 'A state that simply kills all of its sick annihilates the spirit and preparedness of sacrifice. It digs its own grave!'[8]

Konrad D.'s story is a vivid example of the extent to which individuals traumatized by World War I connected their own nervous collapse with the collapse of Germany's political and economic systems. Kaiser Wilhelm II's 1914 prediction that the war would be a 'war of nerves' was prophetic in ways that probably could not have been imagined at the time.[9] The collapse of the *Kaiserreich*, the myriad tensions that afflicted the Weimar Republic, and the subsequent collapse of Germany's first democracy and the rise of Nazism were all perceived through the lens of 'nerves' and psychological trauma. This book examines the history of shell shock, or 'war neurosis' as it was labeled in Germany, primarily from the perspective of war victims. Shattered war victims filled the bus-stops, train stations, and other public spaces, where they generated fear, resentment, sympathy and contempt from Germans reeling from the national trauma of total war.

The social history of mental wounds is essential to understanding how trauma and memory were defined and contested on a popular level, in the lines at welfare offices, at work, in political demonstrations, and in the streets. The experiences of war neurotics shed light on interwar Germany's fierce debates over the psychological impact of the war, blame for defeat, and the politicization of mental trauma through the 1920s and into the Nazi era. As they attempted to reintegrate into work, politics, and family life, mentally disabled veterans put pressure on Weimar and Nazi Germany's capacity for remembering, and healing, the trauma of the war. The structure of this book revolves around several interrelated questions. What were the psychological effects of the war on men, women and their families? Who determined the causes of these wounds, and who ultimately held authority over the bodies and minds of traumatized veterans? How did different social and political groups construct theories of brutalization and psychological trauma vis-à-vis disabled veterans? How were the different theories of psychological trauma used to shape memory and define future visions of war?

The book concentrates on the experiences of victims of the First World War, but it is a history that stretches through 1945. The main argument is that traumatized survivors of the First World War became a central site of debates over politics, memory and welfare throughout the Weimar and National Socialist periods. One of the major tensions that fragmented German society during the era of total war was the question of who controlled the postwar narratives on trauma. Control over the narrative of traumatic neurosis and memory of the war was essential to larger contests over the politics of welfare and debates over who would pay for the costs of the war. Focusing on the history of mental trauma from the perspective of war victims not only fills a gap in the story of this 'war of nerves', but also complicates the narrative. The perspectives of traumatized German war victims have generally been relegated to secondary status in the scholarship on war neurosis, perhaps because they present a number of problems. It is, for example, difficult to discern who was telling the 'truth' about the origins and nature of psychological wounds. Despite this problem, it is more telling to analyze the different ways in which competing groups – doctors, veterans, politicians – *perceived* these injuries and related them to political and economic conditions. War victims reveal that the definitions of mental trauma were much more fragmented and politicized than medical accounts imply. In their attempts to take control over the narrative of mental trauma, veterans battled over broader issues concerning the nature of brutalization and society, the political origins and biases in the construction of trauma, and the significance of wounds in defining a dominant memory of the war. By looking at competing perspectives on the effects of mass violence, constructions of memory and the politics of trauma, it is possible to reconstruct just how central the idea of 'neurosis' was in Germany's experience of total war.

Brutalization and the First World War

Modern industrial warfare inflicted horrifying injuries on people's bodies and minds. Machine guns, high-explosive artillery, poison gas and trench warfare created unprecedented levels of stress and a whole range of physical and psychological symptoms that puzzled doctors and terrified civilians at home. Men described being buried alive under mud with debris and the body parts of friends torn to pieces by shellfire. Many were tormented by the prolonged waiting before bombardments and the experience of killing other human beings. Survivors endured haunting nightmares years after the war. Immersion into what veterans often described as the 'other-worldly landscape' of the front – where the living and the dead mingled in a twisted landscape of mechanized violence and brutalized humans – shattered their minds and made it impossible for some to return home. Mental trauma represented for many a desperate path of escape from an unbearable reality – a kind of numbing of self to one's environment.[10] During the course of the war, over 600,000 German soldiers in the regular and reserve army were treated for a wide range of symptoms, including tics, tremors, shaking, paralysis, nightmares, and other physical and mental problems.[11] Though it would later be diagnosed as 'war neurosis' or 'war hysteria', many veterans give a sense of the deep psychological destruction in their letters after the war by using the phrase 'shaking of the soul (psyche)' (seelische Erschütterung) to describe these wounds.

Veterans defined the meaning of these psychological wounds in dramatically different ways. Their interpretations of mental trauma, both its origins and effects, highlight fundamental conflicts over the memory of the war. Some veterans saw modern war as essentially liberating and strengthening for the human psyche, with primitive instincts towards violence and self-preservation taking precedence over the allegedly weakening effects of peace, bourgeois civilization and modernity. Front fighter turned writer-philosopher Ernst Jünger fed a 'myth of the war experience' perpetuated by the political right in particular, which cultivated an image of psychologically emboldened veterans in its publications and political mobilization. Ernst Röhm, the front veteran who would later become the head of the SA (Sturmabteilung – 'Storm detatchment' or Stormtroopers), described the trenches as the 'spiritual father' of the Nazi movement, which he believed derived its 'mental powers' from the front experience.[12] One Nazi commentator wrote glowingly about the war in a journal for disabled veterans: 'the unshaken faith of the simple soldier [remained intact] despite the incredible violence of the front ... all events of our time emerge from the psychological effects of the most profound experience of the century: the World War'.[13]

For other veterans, the war was a psychologically destructive experience. Most famously, Erich Maria Remarque wrote in the preface to his antiwar masterpiece, All Quiet on the Western Front, '[This book] will tell simply of a generation of men who, even though they may have escaped its shells, were destroyed by the war'.[14] Remarque's account of a young idealist who loses his faith in nationalism and militarism sold millions and was adopted by the moderate left as the authentic representation of most soldiers' experiences. Remarque's depiction of shell-shocked soldiers as sympathetic victims of stress and unimaginable violence was one of the most controversial elements of his novel. Veterans' groups on the political right denounced the novel, and later the film, for falsely portraying German soldiers as quivering wrecks. One writer for the right-wing veterans' organization, the 'Steel Helmet' (Der Stahlhelm), criticized the film version of All Quiet in this way: '[The film's release] must infuriate every nationalist, every front soldier ... These are supposed to have been the German front soldiers, these gallows-faced men who eat like animals, ... who at the first shellfire soil their own pants and in the buried dug-out know of nothing better to do than howl hysterically'.[15] A veteran in the Social Democratic Party shot back: '[T]he film shows the true face of war and the physical suffering and psychological shock of the front soldier'.[16]

Gender and Class Politics

The image of the 'war neurotic' was the central site – at the medical, political, and popular level – for debates over the memory of the war and its larger significance. These debates were articulated through the prism of gender and class politics. Berlin's federal archives contain hundreds of letters from mentally ill veterans whose rantings, sometimes at the rate of several ten-page letters every month for up to ten years, were stuffed into files labeled 'individual problems' by labor ministers. These letters are a cornerstone of this book, as they provide a history of war neurosis from the perspective of these mentally ill individuals themselves, many of whom saw their experiences under the Weimar Republic and the Third Reich as a continuation of the violence they experienced in the trenches.

Many of these letters, especially those written by mentally disabled veterans after 1933, have previously been overlooked by historians focusing on doctors' perspectives, but they are crucial to reconstructing the history of mental trauma from below. These letters highlight the complex ways in which veterans defined masculinity in relation to the war. The interwar period was dominated by a discourse on 'martial masculinity', found especially in the rhetoric of veterans' political organizations on the right, that envisioned the soldier as a hardened 'real man' who conquered weakness with 'comradeship' and 'sacrifice'.[17] However, based on their letters, we find that this conception of veterans' masculinity was heavily critiqued by traumatized men who had very different interpretations of the front experience. As historian Thomas Kühne has demonstrated, 'comradeship' was defined in more nuanced ways and even had a 'soft' side linked to concepts of nurturing and supportive roles between men.[18] This 'softer side' to the comradeship ideal can be found in interwar letters from veterans struggling with the meaning of their nightmares, tremors and other symptoms of mental illness. Traumatized men often asserted that there was nothing 'unmanly' about breaking down under the stress of modern war. Instead, they often associated 'weakness' with civilians who escaped the trauma of the war, but refused to accept the reality of traumatic neurosis experienced by men in the trenches.

Veterans appropriated concepts of 'comradeship' and 'sacrifice' to demand empathy for war victims' hidden traumas and commitment to long-term welfare and health care. 'True comradeship' and 'spirit of sacrifice', they observed, were characterized by an acknowledgement of war's psychological horror and willingness to pay for its costs. Civilians could partake in the comradeship experienced in the trenches by showing solidarity for veterans and supporting welfare programs. As masculinity in the age of total war came to be defined more closely with the soldierly image, war neurotics symbolized a critique against this shift. By claiming to be 'normal men' despite breaking down under stress, traumatized veterans contested the idea that only hardened soldiers who suppressed their emotions in combat were truly men. The stoic, dispassionate soldier who calmly 'held through' was lambasted as a denier of war's reality, and real men, war neurotics insisted, confronted the nightmarish true horrors and their long-term effects.

Veterans' voices were often consumed by the political organizations and medical interests invested in the war neurosis debate. The shell-shocked veteran provided ammunition for opposing social and political groups to discuss the psychological foundations for social conflicts in German society, including class war and changing constructions of masculinity, madness, and social deviance. Psychiatric discourse on 'psychosis' and 'hysteria' took on a wider role in political discourse and theories after 1918. Left-wing groups appropriated ideas about mental trauma to articulate their views on the psychological origins of the war and the causes of Germany's defeat and social and political fragmentation. Social democratic war victims argued that war neurosis was the perfect wound for understanding the trauma inflicted by total war – mental injuries united soldiers and civilians, men and women, shattered by combat, poverty, and other ills inflicted in the modern industrial age. However, attempts at forging a unified consciousness were short-lived, as welfare cuts radicalized many social democratic veterans and civilian activists, who began to theorize that Germany's neurosis was class-specific, namely an affliction of the middle classes who refused to pay for the long-term human costs of the war. Communists took this to another level, claiming that the middle class was irretrievably psychotic as long as capitalism remained intact, and that the propertied classes used psychiatrists to repress the memory of the war by denying the reality of psychological injuries in order to prepare Germany for a new world conflict.

The political left lost credibility among mentally disabled veterans when it lost the pension wars in the wake of the Great Depression. During these years when the already polarized Weimar democracy completely broke down, the Nazi party seized the opportunity and appealed to war victims, whom they called the 'first citizens of the Reich'. War neurosis was a key component of the Nazis' memory of 1914–18. The front experience allegedly anointed veterans like Ernst Röhm and Adolf Hitler with superhuman psychological powers and entitled them to lead the nation. War neurotics threatened this myth of the war experience, and the Nazis portrayed them as enemies of the nation who weakened the community of veterans and the burdened the welfare system with their degenerate and unmanly views of work, war, and the *Volksgemeinschaft* (national community). Borrowing from pre-1933 psychiatrists who were hired into the Nazi Labor Ministry and welfare administration, Nazi leaders asserted that the origin of 'war neurosis' was not the war at all, but defeat, revolution, the rise of democracy and the welfare state. The Nazis continued the reaction against modernity that characterized the backlash against the welfare state, but they retooled this resentment in a popularized psychiatric discourse intertwined with their racial and social ideologies.[19] Traumatized men were merely pension neurotics, addicted to sponging off the state rather than seeking work and self-sufficiency, the Nazis asserted, and they drained the *Völkisch* (national) community, threatened Germany's racial fitness, and contaminated the memory of 'true' veterans who were hardened by the war experience. The Nazis' promise to grant greater respect to disabled veterans at first expanded their popularity with this constituency. However, wider pension cuts under the new 1934 pension laws triggered widespread disillusionment with the regime.

After the Nazis shut down any possibility of regaining a pension, war neurotics turned from pension battles to battles over memory. In this vein, they became ardent critics of the Nazi portrayal of the front experience. When Hitler plunged Germany into another war, men with psychological wounds from 1914 to 1918 appointed themselves as desperate defenders of the 'truth' about war. They criticized the Nazi regime for sterilizing and idealizing the war's violence, and they asserted that it was normal, not unmanly, for men to break down under the stress of modern war. Soon after the taxi driver named Konrad D. crashed his car on the streets of Berlin, he gave up on ever receiving a pension. He proclaimed himself a 'dog who howls at the moon', and correctly predicted that his diatribes would have no effect on the regime. Though mentally disabled veterans like Konrad D. could not be described as a concerted movement – they were successfully atomized as were other voices of dissent in the regime – these men represent a hidden layer of protest, as they prophetically warned that the Nazis would inflict traumatic injuries from which the nation would never recover.

Psychiatry, Welfare and Modernity

War neurotics were also a lightning rod for perceptions of the welfare system as pathogenic. Those already critical of the welfare system, in particular, conservatives, held war neurotics up as 'proof' of welfare's allegedly degenerative effects. Further, for political groups like the Social Democratic Party who had defended the welfare system as the basis for recovery and sociopolitical stability, in particular providing security for the working class, war neurosis created numerous problems that complicated their goals for building a welfare system and a 'social state' (*Volksstaat*). Ground-level battles between employers and welfare officials suggested that the backlash against welfare was fueled by widespread fear of disabled veterans, particularly men suffering from mental trauma. Mentally disabled veterans were perceived, especially by middle-class employers resentful of social leveling and job quotas, as proof of an unrealistic welfare system that protected as socially dysfunctional, sexually deviant, and unproductive men as dangerous 'pension neurotics'.

Recent scholarship on the history of mental illness has uncovered the complex ways in which ideas about 'nerves' played a role in Germany's national recovery. The concept of 'nervousness' in Germany became ubiquitous within discourse on militarism, politics, and constructions of social outsiders.[20] Andreas Killen convincingly argues that the discourse on nerves became 'one of the master narratives of the *Kaiserreich*'.[21] I contend that a 'language of nerves' also evolved after 1918 to become an ever more popularized 'master narrative' as it was appropriated by competing groups to articulate their memories of the war, perceptions of welfare, and theories of class politics. Scholarship on traumatic neurosis in Germany focuses mainly on medicopolitical debates over war neurosis, tracing the process in which psychiatric medicine became increasingly militarized and rationalized in the context of total war.[22] This link between modernity and rationalization has been a dominant issue in German history.[23] Scientific and medical approaches to social problems became central to Weimar Germany's experiment with creating the most progressive welfare state in the world, as a symbol of modernity and its ability to improve the quality of life for wider social groups. The downfall of Weimar's welfare state symbolized the collapse of this attempt to channel the forces of rationalization towards progressive social change, and the beginning of a crisis in modernity signaled by the rise of the Nazi movement.

A number of scholars have examined the collapse of Germany's welfare system as a symptom of socioeconomic crisis. As Robert W. Whalen effectively demonstrates, Weimar faced the catastrophe of having to heal the nation's wounds at a historical moment in which the economic pie had shrunk, just as more groups were organizing themselves to claim it. Weimar's experiment with the Western world's most progressive welfare system was doomed by financial realities.[24] The welfare system's dependence on the struggling economy, and its over-bureaucratization, which fostered resentment from veterans who identified it as a symbol of Weimar's alleged disrespect for veterans, undermined this social experiment.[25]

Recent scholarship has also emphasized the sociopolitical tensions within Weimar's welfare system, and the conservative backlash against welfare which contributed to the rise of National Socialism.[26] Greg Eghigian has traced the widespread perceptions of social welfare as pathogenic, guilty of fostering a system of 'pension neurosis'. War neurotics, in Eghigian's analysis, were treated as victims of welfare rather than victims of war.[27] Andreas Killen puts these social and economic problems into a larger theoretical framework in which he sees the collapse of Weimar's social welfare state as part of a rejection of modernity. Killen traces a shift in the view of neurosis in Imperial Germany as rooted in the effects of modern technological developments to the construction of neurosis as rooted in individual pathologies. He persuasively demonstrates that this change developed as a result of ambivalence towards social insurance and its alleged degenerative effects, symbolized in Berlin's social and economic landscape during the imperial and Weimar years.[28]

Fears about the spread of war neurosis were an integral part of Germany's ambivalence towards welfare. War neurotics became the nexus for all that conservatives hated about Weimar's expanded welfare state. Welfare was perceived by the middle class, themselves traumatized by the war, economic disaster and social leveling, as the nest of social democracy, which in their minds coddled the psychologically weak with a cult of victimhood and pension-dependence. War neurotics symbolized the alleged evils of social welfare and its beneficiaries: its long-term costs, unproductive citizens, difficulties in assimilating the economically destitute into work and family, and alleged 'antisocial' tendencies. For conservatives trying to explain Germany's crisis, war neurotics came to represent everything that was most demonized – the democratic welfare state and the 'November Criminals,' who included Jews, socialists and other 'social outsiders' allegedly responsible for betraying the nation and causing defeat in 1918.[29]

War Neurosis and Memory

Battles over welfare were closely linked to battles over the memory of the war. At the heart of this was a struggle over the master narrative on the impact of mass violence and responsibility for defeat. The flashpoint of this wider debate can be found in the conflict between veterans and doctors over the origins of traumatic neurosis. Their battles expanded into a war over who had authority over bodies and minds, and eventually who had authority over the authentic memory of the war. Paul Lerner analyzes how psychiatrists and veterans struggled over the narrative of war memories, with both groups motivated by their interests in saving or winning the state's precious resources.[30] In their effort to cut the pension budget, psychiatrists engaged in a process of denying individuals their war memories, which 'led doctors to deny the traumatizing impact of war as a whole'.[31] The question of whether or not these memories of the trenches were real or constructed becomes difficult to discern, and the reality of the war experience is submerged in the contest between psychiatrists and patients over pensions.

This book does not attempt to untangle the question of whether or not men are telling the truth about their war experiences. Instead, the focus here is on the meaning of this constructed reality, and the role played by veterans in shaping national memory through the lens of psychological trauma. Pensions were not always the primary driving force behind veterans' war narratives. Traumatized men also obsessed over their versions of the war for the purpose of cultivating and defending what they saw as the 'authentic' memory of the front experience. Veterans and their patrons in political organizations constructed a range of theories concerning militarism, class war, welfare and social 'outsiders' that appropriated the language of psychiatry yet also existed independently of medical institutions. By the mid-1920s, the image of the war neurotic took on greater sociopolitical rather than medical significance in the public consciousness. In the popular and political press, debates were focused on the place of the mentally disabled veteran in society and his meaning as a reminder of the reality of war. Whether the war neurotic was 'proof' of war's brutalizing, destructive effects, or symbolic of a national obsession with victimhood that threatened to abolish a memory of war as ennobling and invigorating, depended on one's social, political, and cultural interests.

Scholars have recently identified the war neurotic as the central 'haunting' image who reminded Weimar society of the deeply destructive effects of the war as evidenced in Weimar's cultural production.[32] This haunting image, I argue, resonated most dramatically in the political sphere as different groups sought symbols of the war to articulate their interests, and locked on to the ubiquitous figure of 'quiverers' and 'shakers' in the streets. Competing sociopolitical groups across Weimar's spectrum attempted to appropriate the mentally ill veteran to articulate their different memories of the war. Their efforts often objectified actual veterans in ways that sparked resentment against and disillusionment with the major parties.

Neither the political right nor the left were able to control the image of the war neurotic successfully. One of this book's aims is to discern how veterans beyond those organized along clear political lines defined traumatic neurosis. Though veterans' organizations produced the most visible traces of debate over the significance of the trenches, the memory of World War I was contested in settings that are often much more elusive: in the welfare lines, on the streets, and in doctors' offices. This layer of debate over the meaning of the war reveals much more complex patterns in thinking about trauma and violence than is found in the political discourse. The voices of mentally traumatized veterans are abundant in the archives, yet they do not often fit clearly into any of the narratives constructed by political groups claiming to represent an 'authentic' memory of the war. Memories of the war do not conform clearly to a dichotomy of the left (brutalization) and the right (celebration of war). More often, one encounters an overlap of apparently contradictory world views. Veterans suffering from mental trauma often idealized their sacrifices for the nation and their notions of 'heroism' and 'comradeship', while at the same time condemning war and its brutalizing effects. They often rejected both the conservatives' cult of militarism, which they believed sterilized the traumatic memory of the war, and the left's reluctance to foster a cult of memory that idealized front veterans as unique members of the community.

The wealth of scholarship on German veterans' history focuses on men who were organized and politically mobilized and thus left a vast amount of printed material for historians to analyze. These groups, especially those on the right, played a key role in the weakening and ultimate collapse of the Weimar Republic.[33] Studies of veterans' memories of the war have focused primarily on these right-wing organizations. George L. Mosse argues that the political right nurtured a 'myth of the war experience', which he defined as a sacred, quasi-religious celebration of war 'designed to mask war and legitimize the war experience; it was meant to displace the reality of war'.[34] This myth was popular within wide sectors of German society, in particular with veterans who became part of the Nazi movement. The largest veterans' groups in the Weimar Republic, in particular the 'Steel Helmet' (Der Stahlhelm) with over 600,000 members, were right-wing organizations who cultivated this image of war as an ennobling, hardening, and regenerative experience for the individual and society.[35] This myth also found wide currency among mainstream psychiatrists, most of whom were politically conservative, and who before the war expressed their hopes for increased military discipline that would heal the nation's nerves, which had allegedly been strained by the speed, materialism, and mass politics brought on by modernity.[36] War neurotics, who broke down under the terror and stress of modern war, posed a threat to this cult of memory, and traumatized men were targeted as unmanly, degenerate shirkers who stood outside the sacred community of veterans.

Ten years after the war, the appearance of All Quiet on the Western Front signaled a sudden readiness in German society to confront long-repressed memories of the war's effects.[37] However, long before the emergence of popular war literature, the war's psychological legacy was already a central feature of popular debate about the memory of the war. This debate was spearheaded by the political left, like the social democratic-oriented National Association of War Victims and the communist International Association of War Victims. Both groups were convinced that war neurotics were the symbols of a national failure to come to terms with the hidden, mental effects of the war. Though they often drew support from mentally disabled veterans for their assertion that these were real wounds, their failure to win pensions was disastrous. By the onset of the Great Depression, Social Democrats were reduced to pledging their support for the dignity, if not financial security, of war neurotics, while communist ideologues were content with war neurotics as a wedge against 'capitalist psychiatrists' and conservative political parties, as long as these 'hysterical' men remained outside the realm of the communist party's image of a militant, masculine revolutionary movement.

Fears of war neurotics crossed sociopolitical lines, and there was general anxiety that war had negatively altered the psychological condition of the nation. Even among conservative groups who expected the war to heal national and individual nerves, there was tremendous anxiety that it actually had the opposite effect. Modern industrial war left even 'healthy' men emotionally shattered, sexually dysfunctional, and addicted to violence. Some conservative journalists and critics reassured the public that men who succumbed to this violence were traditional 'deviants', including socialists, Jews, and others responsible for the 'stab-in-the-back', the widely held myth that 'enemies' on the home front had caused defeat, yet they also expressed anxiety that 'normal', middle-class, racially 'pure' front fighters were permanently damaged by the psychosocial effects of violence.

Nazism, Trauma, and the Memory of the Great War

Finally, it is important to consider the question of continuity and change between Imperial Germany, Weimar, and the rise of National Socialism with regard to war neurosis. Did psychiatrists' perceptions of war neurotics before 1933 represent a 'special path' (*Sonderweg*) that carved the way towards National Socialism's extermination of the mentally ill?[38] National Socialist conceptions of war neurosis did not inevitably triumph over competing interpretations of trauma. However, the Nazi critique of war neurotics had roots in pre-1933 medical and popular perceptions of the mentally ill. Views of mentally disabled veterans as social outsiders found their way into more widespread public perceptions of these men as threats to the national community. Furthermore, conservatives' arguments in 1918 that the revolution and democracy caused more damage to the nation's nerves than war and violence found their way into Nazi discourse on traumatic neurosis.

The Nazi regime did its best to mobilize society into forgetting the traumatized survivors of the First World War. But, as a lingering issue for the regime the history of war neurosis helps clarify some of the more recent historiographical debates on everyday life in Nazi Germany, including the complexities of conformity and the role of the 'Hitler Myth' in building consent, and larger questions about the relationship between the state and everyday Germans. Letters from mentally disabled veterans of the First World War to the Nazi regime reflect a phenomenon recently highlighted by a number of scholars, the manipulation of the regime at a local level.[39] Men deemed 'social outsiders', that is, 'hysterical' men, attempted to rehabilitate themselves as members of the national community by manipulating local officials to persuade the Nazi elite that they were vital members of society. The year 1933 marked a turning point in which many individuals were able to reconstruct a narrative of their own past (whether it was true or not) as traumatized, yet fervent and racially pure nationalists. By doing so in a way that was consistent with Nazi ideology, they reaped economic benefits, in this case war victims' pensions. Many of these men believed that, since Hitler took part in the war, he would share their interpretation of traumatic neurosis as a real wound that damaged 'normal' men.

The regime created a strange paradox for veterans of the First World War, and inadvertently empowered them to dissent. Nazi leaders portrayed war victims as the 'first citizens' of the Reich, but carefully controlled who was entitled to this status. Many veterans felt empowered by this new status, even if they were technically denied it because they were mentally traumatized. They claimed 'first citizen' status to assert power over long-hated doctors and bureaucrats. Many were successful in gaining pensions, especially when they convinced local officials that they were traumatized more by the defeat, revolution, and democracy than the war – an approach that was consistent with Nazi ideology. This element of National Socialist ideology, namely the myth of the war experience, was to some degree a working model that could be flexible depending on the political stripe of the mentally disabled veteran. Those who insisted the war, rather than Weimar, was the source of their trauma in some cases found support from old war buddies in their local party system, but not from Nazi leadership. When, ultimately, they were rejected as pariahs rather than heroes, these men tried to take control of their own diagnoses, case histories, bodies and minds, and they continued to characterize themselves as both legitimate victims of war and genuine members of the national community.

These cases of 'hysterical men' in Nazi Germany add further knowledge to our understanding of the limits of the 'Hitler Myth'.[40] Where many historians have located the onset of the war as the turning point in which the dissonance between image and reality in the Third Reich became apparent, the regime had been at war with its own 'first citizens' since its inception. Long before the Second World War broke out, the traumatic realities of mass violence were still vivid for those haunted by nightmares from the years 1914 to 1918. Their critique of the Nazi myth of the war experience represented a hidden layer of dissent from within. They were not a form of organized 'resistance' in any threatening fashion, but a symbolic group that revealed the Nazis had not really been able to control the memories of a constituency it considered the backbone of the movement. As Germany plunged into another war in 1939, men with psychological wounds from World War I attacked the regime's sterilized view of war. Thus within the ranks of veterans, where the Nazis claimed to base their support, we find dissent from men who prophetically warned that Hitler's war would inflict traumatic injuries from which the nation would never recover. Survivors such as Konrad D. announced that though the state might try to define their bodies and minds, it could not control what they thought about the war.

This book is organized chronologically, with themes of politics, welfare, and memory connecting the chapters. The first chapter examines the origins of war neurosis as a medical, social and political problem during the First World War, with particular focus on the appropriation of psychiatric discourse by conservative and social democratic groups as they articulated their explanations for the war, defeat and revolution. Chapter two looks at the immediate postwar period and interactions between returning veterans and civilians, both of whom were skeptical about the psychological health of the nation and its capacity for recovery. Chapter three examines the rise of Weimar's sweeping 1920 National Pension Law and its aim to heal the psychological wounds of war. Lingering perceptions of disabled veterans in general as too violent, dangerous, and unstable to reintegrate into work and society undermined the successful implementation of the law and weakened Weimar's attempts at integrating these men into society.

The fourth chapter investigates the political left's construction of war neurosis and its defense of mentally disabled war victims. This chapter compares and contrasts social democratic and communist definitions of mental trauma in war, their use of psychiatric discourse to promote their political visions, and reasons for their failure to win the hearts and minds of war neurotics in their ranks. Nazi Germany's construction of war neurosis, memory, and social welfare for veterans is the topic of chapter five. The regime carefully delineated the difference between 'legitimate' psychologically disabled men and 'hysterics' who were outside the 'national community'. Case studies of traumatized First World War veterans living under the Third Reich are the centerpiece of chapter six, which examines the ways in which veterans retaliated against the regime's treatment of mentally ill veterans, and their critique of National Socialist myths of the war experience.

Chapter 1

Healing the Nation's Nerves
Imperial Germany at War

I learned that there are two types of sick people: the harmless ones, who lie in cells with bars on the windows and no handle on the door, are called 'insane'. The others, the dangerous ones, who argue that hunger educates people, found societies 'for the defeat of England', and are allowed to lock the harmless ones up.
— Ernst Toller, *Eine Jugend in Deutschland*[1]

The horrific images of mass death produced by trench warfare left an indelible, haunting imprint on the minds of German soldiers. Wilhelm Pfuhl, a physician's assistant diagnosed with nervous problems in the wake of the battle of the Somme in 1916, wrote:

I believe it is not so much the strain as it is the horrors that I experienced in the last few months that shook my health. It seems completely incomprehensible how humanity can tear itself to pieces in mutual mass murder. I can't boast that I was especially able to resist against the repugnance and horror, but now I'm at the end of my rope. I'm so tired and spent. What I want most is to fall asleep and never wake up until there is peace in the land, otherwise never wake up at all.[2]

Pfuhl was careful to assert that while he could endure much of the strain of the front experience, he had a breaking point. The unimaginable horror of the trenches pushed him over the edge, and he hoped for a peaceful death as an escape from the psychological stress of life at the front.

Before the First World War, many in German medicine and politics saw war as a psychologically healthy experience. Peace, it was widely believed, was potentially traumatic, and many longed for war as an antidote to possible degeneration. Instead of reversing psychological decay, the trench experience was the epicenter of an earthquake that would shake German society's foundations. Psychological wounds caused by this catastrophe rippled from the trenches to the home front, and these wounds became a source of debate about controlling the mental health, and sociopolitical status quo, of the nation. Trench combat accelerated the popularization of a discourse on trauma, nerves, and hysteria to explain the catastrophe of 1914–18. A language dealing with mental illness spread from medical circles to political organizations and the general public by the end of the war, giving German society a new way to describe psychological, social, and political crises.

Doctors and politicians expressed great anxiety about Germany's psychological health before 1914. Conservative critics and doctors targeted the rise of industrialization, urbanization, and mass politics – specifically the success of the Social Democratic Party (SPD), which in 1912 became Germany's largest political party – as threats to the health of the nation.[3] Conservative groups embraced the idea of war as a potential healing agent for Germany's allegedly strained nerves, and they predicted that a mass burst of patriotism would unify the nation and restore what they saw as a collective 'national psyche' (*Volksseele*), which would bind together both working- and middle-class Germans, and provide the foundation for victory.[4]

The war that unfolded after 1914 was unlike anything imagined by those who predicted it would solve the nation's problems. This long-term, stalemated war of industrial attrition, with millions killed and wounded, caused catastrophic social, political and economic dislocation in German society.[5] Thousands of men responded to the horrors of trench combat by breaking down psychologically, exhibiting a wide range of symptoms that psychiatrists would diagnose as 'war neurosis' or 'war hysteria'. Over 600,000 men suffering from some form of 'nervous illness', a term that was highly debated, flooded military hospitals between 1914 and 1918.[6] The number of men experiencing these symptoms provoked great alarm for the increasingly centralized military government, which enlisted psychiatrists to stave off disaster by controlling further breakdowns and restoring those already traumatized to fighting fitness. Psychiatrists approached war neurosis with prewar assumptions about the origins and treatment of mental illness. The war was less to blame for the outbreak of neurosis in the trenches, psychiatrists claimed, than the inferior moral character of the bulk of men who claimed to be shattered by the psychological stress of the war, the working class. Though not all diagnosed war neurotics were from working-class backgrounds, the wound became associated with allegedly working-class characteristics, including social deviance, welfare dependence or 'pension neurosis', disloyalty to the nation, and an inferior work ethic.[7] Under pressure from the state to control the pension budget, most doctors argued that war neurotics were shirkers who required disciplinary action and rapid treatment for their temporary breakdown. The medical establishment set out to contain the spread of neurotic symptoms, which they claimed was contagious and posed a danger to the psychological strength of other recovering disabled veterans and front-line troops. As part of treatment, neurotic men were returned to the supposedly healing properties of combat or labor, where they would be restored as disciplined, productive components of the war effort.

In this chapter, I argue that war neurosis became the central question for competing social and political groups to debate the psychological causes of Germany's defeat. As the war dragged on, doctors failed to stem the outbreak of neurosis in front-line troops. With the growing fear that it would spread to the home front, the social and political dimensions of war neurosis become more evident. Psychiatrists equated left-wing, revolutionary politics with hysterical behavior, and interpreted the collapse of November 1918 as a symptom of psychosis spreading at home, betraying those whose nerves remained steadfast throughout the war. Social Democrats came to the defense of mentally ill veterans as legitimately disabled, loyal soldiers unjustly brutalized by the state and denied pensions. Working-class Germans, Social Democrats argued, were not inherently weak and not at fault for the spread of war neurosis and Germany's defeat. By the end of the war, the political left adapted the version of the war experience touted by many mentally disabled veterans themselves: the origins of war neurosis lay in the shattering experience of the war itself, not in the inherently deficient moral character of 'hysterical men'. The goal of this chapter is to trace emerging battle-lines, as military, medical, and political interests argued over the well-being of the nation and the psychological significance of the war. In order to understand these debates, it is first necessary to examine 1914 expectations about the war experience.

Revitalizing the Nation's Health on the Brink of War

At the outbreak of the war in August 1914, Kaiser Wilhelm II proclaimed that those with the strongest nerves would emerge victorious.[8] Psychiatrists echoed this view, and characterized the war as one that would ultimately pit Germany's nerves against those of other nations. In this vein, many psychiatrists feared that decades of peace – the last war had been fought a generation before, against France in 1870–71 – eroded the fighting capacity of German men, and that the events of the last thirty years that had contributed to this decline would have to be dramatically reversed in order to win. The majority of Germany's psychiatrists articulated the conservative, nationalist sentiments consistent with their elite social class. They identified the rise of industrial society and democratic politics as threatening not only to middle-class status, but also the entire nation's psychological fitness.[9] With the rise of the primarily working-class Social Democratic Party, Germany's largest political organization with over a million members by 1914,[10] psychiatrists lamented the erosion of traditional values and authority. Doctors linked SPD politics with urbanization and technological revolutions that strained the nation's nerves and threatened to overload the senses, with increased speed, more crowded living conditions, and greater mobility. Modern industrial culture also altered social roles and behavior; its materialism and individualism encouraged people to reject traditional values and ultimately led to psychological degeneration. Cities, critics feared, became repositories for crime, alcoholism, disease and a rise in mental illness.[11] While conservative interest groups argued that Germany's nerves were better prepared for the challenge of war than those of other belligerents, these critics also expressed concern that some segments of German society, particularly the urban working class, which was the most profoundly affected by modern industrial conditions, were likely to give up their loyalty to the nation in exchange for the modern values of city life and social democracy. If these values and ideas spread, critics argued, the nation would not be psychologically or morally up to making the sacrifice necessary to win a war.

In the spring of 1914, just before the outbreak of the war, the province of Thuringia assembled some of the nation's medical experts at the University of Jena to take part in a conference on Germany's health. Dr Otto Binswanger, a city councilman and psychiatrist at the university, led a panel on the specific question of mental and nervous illness. Three months after mobilization in August 1914, Binswanger published his conclusions from the meeting and characterized this conference as a unique investigation of 'psychological-nervous illnesses in the present generation', the one that went into the trenches. Binswanger touted his authority in assessing Germany's mental health:

> It does not lie in the circle of my expertise or inclination to talk about the political consequences of this murderous national struggle, but I am glad to be given the chance to talk about the psychological effects of the war. I would like to consider in particular, as I have been doing for some time in the years of peace, the modern path of development of our nation's psychological strength.[12]

The question of Germany's psychological health was purely scientific, Binswanger claimed. The nation was on the verge of nervous collapse before the war broke out, and psychological disorders ran rampant 'in all social classes'. Binswanger's reactionary politics were evident throughout his writings, despite claims to strict scientific analysis. The most prominent cause of psychological stress, he wrote, was 'the almost revolutionary dislocation of our traditional life conditions and relationships that has taken place in the second half of this polytechnical 19th century'.[13] At the root of Germany's mental deterioration lay the concentration of populations in cities, the growing noise level, the 'restless lifestyle led by many in this technical society', music that caused over-excitement, 'tension-inducing reading material', the rise of alcoholism, the theater, and changing fashions for women. All of these factors contributed to a culture of 'increasing sickliness and degeneration', in which individuals, particularly those already predisposed to mental illness, had little chance of resisting complete nervous collapse. To solve this epidemic, Binswanger argued, Germans would have to change their lifestyles and the modern industrial environment in which they lived or risk the downfall of German culture.[14]

Binswanger's conclusions reflected the general view of psychiatrists in 1914.[15] The war, Binswanger found, was a godsend that brought psychological regeneration to a nation in mental decline. Germany's prewar psychological decay was only superficial, he optimistically predicted, and the population was ultimately prepared for the struggle ahead. The Kaiser's announcement of a *Burgfrieden* ('peace within the fortress'), or truce in which he promised to recognize no social or political divisions, was seized upon by conservatives like Binswanger as an opportunity to heal the nation's prewar conflicts.[16] He believed the *Burgfrieden* combined with the patriotic spirit of August 1914 would heal the psychological decay that characterized prewar society, bringing previously antagonistic social groups together in the unified struggle against the nation's enemies. The demands of the war gave idle minds a 'deeper purpose' in which to direct mental energy. War also stimulated the collective national psyche (*Volksseele*) that had been too-long dormant:

> Nowhere are there any complaints or grumbling, but rather there is a blaze of excitement and a lively consciousness ... The weak throw the mental quiverers down and the strong raise them up ... The condition of the *Volksseele* is not the condition of a special social class, but the collective internal and external mental condition and strength of the entire nation.[17]

The notion of a 'national psyche' that transcended class boundaries permeated Binswanger's writings. He was convinced that the weak-minded, who fixated on their own individual needs, would finally give in to 'a new, idealistic, philosophical movement that will place the highest mental and moral values of existence again at the center of a world view'.[18] The sacrifices demanded by war thus bonded Germans together and eradicated prewar social and political tensions.

After nine weeks of war, Binswanger saw concrete evidence of the nation's new-found psychological strength. He listed the enthusiastic, orderly march to war, crowded churches, the return of women to the home to pack their husbands' suitcases for the front, and the absence of alcohol consumption at troop debarkation points as examples of the war's ability to restore traditional values. The war 'awoke the mental and moral strength of the human mind' and healed neurotic individuals through the regenerative effects of sacrifice and fatherland-worship. Binswanger used case studies to prove his points, including one 'cowardly, anxiety-ridden, weak-willed man-child' whose neurotic condition evaporated 'like a sudden blow'. In depriving men of food and sleep, and inflicting 'extreme violence on soldiers' nerves', the war provided 'superhuman' (*übermenschlichen*) challenges needed to shock men out of a neurotically self-centered state. Men diagnosed as neurotics should not be turned away from the army, Binswanger argued. On the contrary, the war was a godsend to them, and at the front he believed that 'the strong raised up the weak, who are inspired to cast away their mental shakiness'.[19] The war thus healed not only social and political fragmentation, but also the unmanly character of individual men weakened by cultural decay.

While combat easily healed prewar neuroses, the home front, it was feared, was more susceptible to mass hysteria and breakdown. Binswanger compared the war to the Black Death and its 'epidemic proportions of psychological reactions'.[20] Binswanger treated cases of 'hysterical' civilians who 'fantasized' that they saw spies in city streets, which were already filled with what the doctor described as disorder, paranoia, and almost unbearable excitement. However, Binswanger claimed, German civilians were essentially unified despite the spontaneous, mild hysteria that swept through the already nervous cities. In contrast, Germany's enemies were stricken with 'mass psychosis', evidenced by the 'hysterical lies that sweep through the foreign press about German barbarism and atrocities'. The tendency of irrational English and French readers to believe these stories, he concluded, revealed their deep mental sickness, and made it all the more urgent that German culture and morality should triumph.[21] The German home front proved that it was stronger because it did not need propaganda to motivate itself and because those at home concentrated on their primary task, which was to provide care and support for front-line soldiers at Germany's moment of crisis. Though civilians were not in close touch with the psychologically invigorating front lines, Binswanger optimistically predicted that Germany would win the war because its soldiers 'had the strongest nerves' and its civilians 'had the strongest moral fiber'.[22]

Conservative social critics echoed the conclusions of doctors regarding the war's potential for psychological and moral regeneration. The *Burgfrieden* tested Germany's inner resolve to win, wrote Ernst Schultze, who published regularly with the right-wing journal *Deutsche Kriegsschriften*. The Kaiser's call for sociopolitical cooperation challenged 'those divisive elements', which he defined as groups who challenged the Kaiser's authority, and who had to 'overcome their bitter experiences in order for Germany to win the war'.[23] Schultze hoped that the war signaled a return to the Bismarck-era when, he claimed, war effectively contained Social Democrats and integrated the working class into a state 'led by bourgeois political parties'.[24] Victory, according to Schultze, depended on the mobilization of more than just weapons and the economy, but also the mind. All Germans had to set aside their individuality and 'find deep within themselves their selflessness and will to sacrifice'.[25] Class divisions, specifically, had to be suspended: 'All promises [for unity] at this time have greater significance than usual. Those belonging to social classes that until now have stood far apart from one another must take these promises to heart'. Schultze expressed certainty that the nation was psychologically united: 'All mental energy is unified in this war. We see a picture of everyone, soldiers and non-combatants, men and women, old men and even our children formed along a battlefront in which there is no gap'. Schultze optimistically concluded that while Germans were mentally fit, the populations of other nations were too preoccupied with the causes and consequences of the war to form a unified front.[26] Throughout the war, the portrayal of enemy combatants as neurotic and near defeat, especially the 'nervous Parisians', appeared in the popular press.[27]

Though conservatives expressed faith in the 'spirit of 1914' and the authenticity of the *Burgfrieden*, they had less confidence in the troops themselves. Controlling and maintaining the nerves of front-line soldiers, especially as the duration of the war stretched on, became a priority for doctors enlisted by the War Ministry. Some of the earliest fears articulated by doctors involved increased alcohol abuse among soldiers. At a medical conference in Berlin in December 1918, Dr F. Gonser argued that alcoholism, which he believed was spreading as the war bogged down into a stalemate, was an immediate danger to the combat readiness of the troops as it weakened the strength of their nerves.[28] This line of reasoning was adopted by the military, which banned, as much as possible, the use of alcohol during mobilization, especially in the public eye at parades, train stations, and in troop areas on the way to the front.[29] The military aimed not only at orderly and efficient mobilization, but also preserving a positive image of the troops. Temperance unions took advantage of the ban to claim that this was the chance to promote abstinence in the army. One temperance organization specifically noted that a stress on abstinence was vital because the bulk of the troops came from working-class backgrounds, where alcohol abuse was allegedly rampant.[30] With the unique conditions of trench warfare becoming apparent, Gonser had to acknowledge that the war produced terrifying levels of stress. It was clear to him that restraint was not going to last in the stressful environment of the front lines, and he led a study of the degree to which alcohol consumption could be controlled so that it calmed men's fears without reducing their mental strength. The most weak-willed men would break down first, but he also predicted that, if the war lasted beyond Christmas, even the most stalwart individuals would seek solace in drinking, thus reducing the army's fighting capability.[31] The tendency of many to turn to alcohol as a means of combating frayed nerves alarmed Gonser, who speculated that even the most loyal, patriotic recruits were not immune and that cracks were already appearing in the initial August 1914 spirit.

Within only a few months of the outbreak of the war, a number of doctors questioned whether the nerves of even middle-class men could hold up for long in the trenches. State medical representative W. Fuchs feared that the nation's elite pampered its sons, and that they did not possess the 'desire for war' (*Kriegslust*) essential for surviving a prolonged war of attrition.[32] Fuchs complained that industrialization produced great wealth, but it had softened the youth that were destined to lead the nation through war. Mobilization demanded more than just material sacrifice: 'The call for duty is not only a challenge to one's wallet, but also a sharp, hard and loud call to one's mind and emotions. But recently, under the guise of German ethics, the mind has been made completely wretched through pampering'. Fuchs was convinced that the nation's youth who were in a position to lead as officers were not psychologically prepared for the demands of war. Authority figures, he wrote, needed to make greater efforts to condition their children with fanatical hatred:

> And thus the challenge of the day is the education of the *Volksseele*!
> First the family, then the state and next the schools, and then off
> to do foreign policy! Educate to hate! Teach the admiration of hate!
> We should not hesitate to blaspheme: We are given faith, hope and
> hate! But the greatest of these is hate.[33]

Prewar decadence weakened the nation's warrior spirit, and prosperity, success and overly permissive parents deprived their children of the psychological edge that bolstered Germany in past wars.[34] Like other conservative critics, Fuchs imagined that the war would heal the national, collective psyche, as long as Germans remained focused on their patriotic duty to destroy the nation's enemies.

Both working- and middle-class Germans, conservatives argued, were susceptible to perceived psychological deterioration brought on by modern society, including mass politics and urbanization, deviant social behavior, and the erosion of discipline and traditional authority after a prolonged period of industrialization and the absence of a reinvigorating war. The war, critics predicted, came just in time to revitalize the nation's strained nerves. In the outpouring of patriotism of August 1914, conservatives saw proof that the nation was still essentially intact. However, as historians have recently noted, the spirit of 1914 existed more in the conservative imagination than reality, and it eroded quickly under the strain of modern industrial war.[35] Contrary to expectations, this war sparked an epidemic of mental breakdown, which so alarmed military circles that they enlisted a battery of doctors to fight 'war neurosis' from behind the lines and control its spread before it became a serious threat to the nation's victory.

The Spread of War Neurosis – From Trauma to Diagnosis, Treatment and Recovery

War neurosis became more than a wound. It was also a site of intense political controversy, and it accelerated prewar tensions. As it spread, doctors were the first to assign blame to the social and political groups that were traditionally viewed as the greatest threat to the nation's mental health. Psychiatrists viewed war neurosis through the prism of long-existing assumptions about which groups were the most socially reliable, well-adjusted, morally fit, and patriotic. In the first weeks of the war, reports of mental breakdown in the army caused alarm among military leaders, who feared that it would spread first through the trenches and then behind the lines, to the home front, weakening Germany's war effort. Leading military psychiatrists concluded that weakness of will power and moral deficiency rather than the terror of the trench experience were the primary reasons for the outbreak of neurosis in men. War neurosis, and subsequently a weakened war effort, was often blamed on working-class men, who were long-suspected by doctors for their moral inferiority, lack of self-control, and failure to fully integrate into the national ideal.

Germany's psychiatrists, as historian George L. Mosse has argued, were exceptional in their labeling of prewar 'outsiders' as most prone to war neurosis, though it has been demonstrated that in Great Britain the 'hysteria' diagnosis was often reserved for working-class men while doctors granted middle-class officers the label 'exhausted'.[36] In Germany, prewar conceptions of 'outsiders', including working-class and so called 'effiminate' or 'hysterical' men, served as a foundation for a medical establishment in crisis over how to deal with the dramatic explosion of mentally disabled soldiers at the front. War neurosis challenged existing theories of hysteria and neurosis held by mainstream neurologists and psychiatrists as the influx of complex psychological wounds and the failure of traditional forms of treatment pushed doctors to reevaluate the ways in which they defined and explained this new type of wound. As doctors worked to control and cure the rise of war neurosis, they began to play an increasingly important role in the government's management of the war. Employing what historian Paul Lerner has described as a 'rationalized', industrialized approach to health care, psychiatric medicine served the state's needs by restoring mentally disabled soldiers to the war effort, whether in munitions work or the trenches.[37]

Psychiatrists echoed conservatives' views that the war would reinvigorate the nation and heal a long period of sociopolitical division and psychological deterioration that threatened the *Kaiserreich*. Two of Germany's most prominent psychiatrists, Karl Bonhoeffer and Robert Gaupp, who would become leading experts on what they would characterize as 'war hysteria', wrote extensively before the war on what they believed was a sharp rise in mental illness. They located this in the effects of industrialization and urbanization, which they believed exacerbated inborn mental disorders in the masses of individuals who flooded into Berlin, Hamburg, and other urban centers. 'Hysteria', according to Bonhoeffer and Gaupp, was the response of predisposed individuals who lacked will and broke down under stress. Psychiatrists were increasingly alarmed by the presence of hysterical tendencies in not only working-class individuals but also middle-class Germans, both of whom suffered from a deficiency of will power that was all the more dangerous because it was difficult to detect. Nevertheless, this generation of psychiatrists optimistically predicted that most men would be able to make the mental adjustments needed for Germany to win a war.[38]

The outbreak of a wide range of psychological wounds, however, challenged doctors' assumptions about the regenerative effects of combat. Official army records indicate that just over 313,000 cases of neurological disorders were treated during the course of the war, only about 2% of all war-disabled cases.[39] The total number of men treated for various forms of 'nervous illness', however, reached over 600,000.[40] These numbers were constantly contested, as doctors and, later, political organizations argued over how many men actually experienced a form of 'war neurosis' or 'hysteria', manifested a wide range of symptoms sometimes long after men were out of the trenches. The causes of these injuries were also a source of tremendous debate among doctors, who battled over the question of whether or not 'normal' men broke down in combat, and whether the origins of mental disorders were found on the battlefield or in the individual's predisposition towards weakness.

Doctors encountered a wide range of symptoms that became associated with the newly identified, and highly debated, 'war neurosis' or 'war hysteria'. Throughout the war, case studies of war neurotics were published in one of Germany's most respected medical periodicals, *The Journal for Neurology and Psychology* (*Zeitschrift für die gesamte Neurologie und Psychiatrie*). In these accounts, doctors noted that the extreme violence produced by modern weapons seemed to trigger psychological and neurological disorders on an unprecedented scale. In a 1915 case detailed by Dr W. Schmidt at the psychiatric clinic in Freiburg, where thousands of cases were treated, the complex symptoms resulting from modern combat were produced as evidence:

> Joseph B., head waiter, 25 years old, Rhinelander ... B. was transported directly from the [front lines] into the local clinic on May 5, 1915. According to statements made by comrades in his unit who were in the same transport, B. was buried alive by a mine explosion and finally pulled out after two hours ... Upon checking into the clinic B. is completely disoriented, confused, and

his motor system is disturbed. B. collapses into fetal position at every noise, and begins to jabber and cry when he is brought into the examination room. In bed he shows further signs of anxiety, crawls under his bed, and seeks cover against enemy fire ... At night B. is very agitated, screams and weeps, rushes out of bed, crawls around and heads out of the room ... According to his wife, B. had once been a peaceful, matter-of-fact, and diligent man who lacked any psychological problems.[41]

The experience of being buried alive and the symptoms described above were frequently mentioned in both doctors' and soldiers' accounts. Doctors highlighted the social class background of their patients, yet their descriptions of symptoms indicate that the intense anxiety, nightmares, lack of control, paralysis, and what one doctor described as 'the fixed stare' crossed ranks. Dr Friedländer, psychiatrist for the 16th and 21st army corps, detailed 'case 501', a twenty-five-year-old officer:

Upper arm shot through. Bunker buried by a direct hit. Attempted to dig himself out with his comrades. The latter gradually lost their strength and they died of suffocation ... a second bomb opened the buried bunker and he was thus saved. Subsequent nervous state of anxiety, sleeplessness, nightmares, irritability. Feelings of 'breathing crisis' [Atemnot] constantly return, feelings of suffocation, three-month treatment brings no results ... strong, once healthy, industrious man.[42]

Just as alarming as the symptoms and the failure to treat them was the fact that 'case 501' came from an elite background, '[a] once healthy, industrious man'. This account also exemplifies the links doctors saw between traumatic experiences and symptoms. Thus men buried alive continued to experience feelings of suffocation, and soldiers who bayoneted men in the face developed facial tics. The memory of a particularly stressful event continued to be played out in physical behaviors and nightmares, as veterans hallucinated they were under attack when at home, or revisited their dead comrades in dreams.[43]

The specific threshold at which individuals deteriorated and began to show signs of mental illness varied, and sources that provide a glimpse into war neurosis from a soldier's perspective are limited. One of the most interesting collections of German soldiers' narratives, *German Students' War Letters*, went through a publication history that reflected controversies over memory and war narratives. Edited by literary historian Philip Witkop, this anthology was commissioned by the Foreign Office and first published in 1916, when censorship laws allowed only the release of soldiers' letters that celebrated the 'spirit of 1914' and nationalist ideals.

In versions published after the war, Witkop included letters by students that were much more complex in their sense of disillusionment and their discussion of physical and psychological brutality. In the 1920s, *German Students' War Letters* was used by some pacifist groups to support their political views. However, after the Nazi takeover in 1933, the book was again published but with accounts by Jewish soldiers and pacifists removed. *German Student's War Letters* was censored to emphasize a nationalistic, constructed memory, and it focused primarily on men from middle-class backgrounds, but nevertheless it provides an interesting perspective on the ways in which a discourse on nervous disorders and mental illness permeated war narratives.[44]

Men often experienced psychological breakdown as a result of a combination of events at the front: the pervasive images of other-worldly horror and brutal violence, disillusionment following the collision of prewar romantic assumptions about 'heroic' experiences versus the impersonal reality of mechanized warfare, and the resulting sense of emotional numbness that on one hand allowed men to cope with these experiences, but on the other drove them into a psychological state that many referred to as a form of 'madness'. For many, the repetitious, mechanical nature of industrial warfare replaced the romanticism and idealism that some described in August 1914.[45] Soldiers often referred to a sense of numbness in coping with the dehumanizing effects of trench combat. Some veterans, like H. Hellwich, described a condition of psychological distance that was more than just 'hardening of the heart', and was also 'purifying and deepening' because it led him to appreciate life more. But at the same time, it was not in the romantic sense that he expected. Rather, he noted, 'one gets into a peculiar state in the trenches, physically and psychologically'.[46] In this environment, one's sense of autonomy or agency was gradually replaced by a jaded repetition of mass killing. As theology student Friedrich Georg Steinbrecher described it: 'Stern duty has taken the place of a keenness sometimes amounting to passion – a frigid, mechanical doing of one's duty'.[47]

Men at the front often referred to themselves as sinking into a sense of 'callousness' that was necessary to endure both the monotony and sudden horror experienced in the trenches. Hugo Müller identified this numb state as the only alternative to breaking down into mental illness: 'I am still feeling shaky after yesterday afternoon, when the English battered our trench with shrapnel and shells. More than one water-hole was dyed purple with the blood of those who were killed ... We all become callous and unfeeling out here in this horrible war; whoever does not goes mad in the most real and awful sense of the word'.[48] This 'unfeeling' state allowed Müller to maintain his self-control while surrounded by nightmarish images. After describing the psychological distance from reality he felt he needed, he relates the following episode:

I have just written a letter to the father of one of my Platoon Corporals, who was killed the day before yesterday. If the poor parents could have seen their son! A shell had torn off his head and we literally scraped up his brains with a spade. Such incidents are by no means uncommon in trench life! The wagon which brings up the rations tonight will take back these pitiful fragments of once proud manhood.[49]

In contrast, many individuals were unable to protect themselves by maintaining a psychological distance from their surroundings. These encounters with scenes of unimaginable horror served as a trigger for many men to break down, sometimes immediately but more often over a long period of time, even weeks after the event as nightmares began to overwhelm them when they were behind the lines and had time to dwell on their memories.

While veterans complained that those at home could never comprehend the horror of the trenches, many still tried to convey their experiences and subsequent feelings to the home front. This has recently been documented by historian Bernd Ulrich, who demonstrates that soldiers frequently used the term 'nerves' to define both their psychological health and their different interpretations of the trench experience as an ennobling, or brutalizing, event. The idea that modern combat strengthened and improved the human condition circulated in veterans' accounts published for popular consumption. In 1915, Erich Everth, a journalist who served briefly as a lieutenant on the Eastern front, created a stylized image of the war experience, which he believed generated a unique consciousness, developing instincts towards primitive survival and psychological strength. This experience was ultimately healing and rejuvenating. Everth edited a volume of veterans' letters, *From the Psyche [Seele] of Soldiers in the Field – Observations of a War Veteran*, in which he claimed to define the 'strength of nerves at the front', in particular in officers who worked to infuse an iron will into infantrymen. Only men at the front, Everth argued, possessed authentic knowledge of war's effects on one's nerves.[50]

The letters of front-line infantrymen, however, often conveyed a much more complex view of the psychological effects of the war than Everth portrayed. In fact, Everth received letters of criticism from both veterans and doctors for his one-sided view of the war experience that ignored the more negative psychological experiences caused by combat.[51] In their own descriptions of combat and psychological breakdown, soldiers stressed the close link between experiences in the trenches and psychological violence. In these letters, men detailed the incredible stress caused by encounters with new forms of weaponry, in particular high-explosive heavy artillery. Individuals often waited for days under brutal bombardments for the order to 'go over the top' and attack an enemy trench. Thus, some broke down before they even saw the enemy. From his hospital bed in Berlin, Franz Müller wrote in January 1915:

> Because of tremendous strains, especially in the last three days, during which time our trenches were completely ripped apart by heavy artillery, I was afflicted with a nervous illness. Thus on November 8, two days before the general offensive on the entire front, I was sent back ... I'm able to stand up only a few hours each day, because this cursed illness has taken over my legs, so that because of pains and paralysis through my legs and left arm, my progress is hindered.[52]

For many men writing about their experiences at the front, it was important to emphasize the unique character of this war and how it affected their psychological condition. Soldiers' letters often noted that most could endure the general strain of life at the front, but the unique fear and terror found in modern industrial combat pushed them over the edge. The evisceration of human bodies under shell and machine-gun fire, living with corpses there was no time to bury, and the other-worldly environment of trench warfare produced indelible images in the minds of survivors. Some celebrated these as intoxicating or even joyful experiences, while others felt burdened by guilt and disgust from their memories of the war.[53]

While soldiers stricken with psychological disorders emphatically claimed that traumatic war experiences were the primary cause of their mental injuries, psychiatrists entered into fierce debates over the link between combat and psychological trauma. The central question for psychiatrists was whether or not these wounds were caused by war experiences or a predisposition towards mental illness that led individuals to break down under stress. The origins of war neurosis were at first thought to be located in anatomical damage, or shock, caused by exploding shells – hence the term 'shell shock' used by British psychiatrists. One of Germany's leading theorists on trauma, Hermann Oppenheim was at the center of debates over organic versus psychological causes of this illness. Though he modified his findings at different stages in the war, in 1915 he argued that, as in prewar cases of trauma caused by industrial accidents – in particular railway collisions – traumatic neurosis in the trenches involved physical damage to the neurological system caused by the concussive effects of exploding shells, which in turn produced visible symptoms ranging from paralysis to tics and tremors, as well as emotional excitability, and loss of speech and hearing.[54]

The diagnosis of war neurosis was closely linked to the pension question. If war neuroses were defined as legitimate wounds, men were then categorized as war victims and entitled to a pension. Oppenheim's theory of traumatic neurosis made pensions an academic question. If contusions or lesions could be identified in a patient's neurological system, their symptoms were then diagnosed as 'war-service related wounds' or 'DB' (*Dienstbeschädigung*), and they were eligible for compensation like any other war-disabled individual. The 'DB' status was essential to gaining a pension. Once a veteran secured a DB diagnosis from a doctor he became eligible for social assistance set according to rank and prewar occupation. By 1916, this system was administered by the National Committee for War Victims' Care (*Reichsausschuss für Kriegsbeschädigten- und Kriegshinterbliebenen-Fürsorge*), which was formed as an advisory body to the War Ministry and the National Finance Office in order to cope with the overwhelming number of disabled veterans that were being funneled through existing local insurance and disability offices. According to Dr Franz Schweyer, a Bavarian Interior Minister who outlined the National Committee's policy in the journal, *War Victims' Care* (*Die Kriegsbeschädigten- und Kriegshinterbliebenen-Fürsorge*), pensions were not a legal right, but rather a means of restoring the economic welfare of a war victim and preserving prewar social and economic structures:

> [A pension] is not compensation for military service. A pension is compensation for any economic disadvantage the disabled person suffers in his civilian position ... This compensation can only be based on the principle that each person be assisted in staying in the social position he occupied before the war ... A pension is certainly not any type of legal restitution for injury for which the nation is obliged; war victims' care is simply a question of wartime social welfare.
>
> ... No one can demand that a pension free him from all responsibility to engage in work; indeed, the duty of veterans to work must be constantly stressed.[55]

In this system, the state was not obligated to compensate men for their sacrifices. Instead, war victims were obligated to prove that their wounds limited their ability to work.

Doctors played an increasingly instrumental role as intermediaries between disabled veterans and the state. They determined the war-related status of the wound and its potential damage to that individual's capacity for work, which, combined with the person's rank, determined the pension rate. Economic pressures compromised scientific objectivity. With the skyrocketing numbers of disabled men flooding the welfare system, representatives from the Interior Ministry urged the National Committee for War Victims and the Reichstag to limit pensions in order to stave off economic disaster.[56] These economic pressures had a direct effect on how psychiatrists diagnosed psychological wounds. Alfred Sänger, a neurologist from Hamburg, summed up the way in which economic concerns influenced doctors: 'In view of the enormous economic damage to the state, this concept [traumatic neurosis] should be jettisoned not only for scientific, but also practical reasons'.[57] Before the war, pensioners began to assume entitlement for compensation from an expanding welfare state that provided social insurance for disability, injury, and old age.[58] But Germany's welfare state and war economy were unable to cope with the overwhelming flood of men entitled to compensation as victims of traumatic neurosis.

These tensions between medical diagnosis, individual health, and welfare status formed the backdrop for debates over the cause of war neurosis. These debates reached a fever pitch in the wake of the Somme and Verdun battles in 1916. In a series of congresses on war neurosis, psychiatrists shifted their focus towards the diagnosis of hysteria, rather than traumatic injury, which pointed towards a patient's alleged lack of will, rather than the war.[59] Oppenheim's earlier theory of traumatic neurosis, which incorporated both physical and psychological trauma on the battlefield as causes of mental breakdown, lost out against advocates of the hysteria diagnosis.[60] Many of these doctors suspected that a majority of these men, even if they legitimately broke down in fear of combat, gradually learned to fake their wounds, or simply did not will themselves to heal.

One of the most famous psychiatrists to enter this debate was Dr Karl Bonhoeffer. Bonhoeffer's son, Dietrich, would later gain fame for his role in the Confessional Church and his resistance against Nazism that led to his execution at the Flossenbürg concentration camp in April 1945.[61] In the years just before 1914, Karl Bonhoeffer became chair of the psychiatric and neurologic hospital at the royal Charité clinic in Berlin, where he was active in clinical and scientific work until 1938. After the apparent epidemic of psychological trauma emerged from the trenches, Bonhoeffer argued that whether it was called 'war neurosis' or 'war hysteria', it was a legitimate wound caused by the mental stress and terror of trench warfare. He also warned, however, that if men who suffered from war neurosis were told that their wounds inflicted actual neurological damage, they would become 'fixated' and unwilling to overcome what Bonhoeffer believed were temporary, hysterical reactions to fear.[62] At a 1916 conference of leading German psychiatrists, Bonhoeffer's theory of war hysteria found support from a wide contingent of psychiatrists who believed that the army was on the verge of an epidemic of soldiers who discovered hysterical tics, tremors and other symptoms to be the best means of escaping from the front lines. 'The war neurotics are mostly not wounded', allies of Bonhoeffer argued at the conference, but rather they were expressing reactions to the fear of combat, and their symptoms arose from the wish to escape at all costs.[63] The question of will power, rather than the trench experience, became the focal point for military psychiatrists. Men who were deemed morally unfit, doctors alleged, broke down, while those with greater character, self-control, manliness and will power withstood the stress of combat.[64]

By 1917, the number of men suffering from various mental disorders reached such crisis proportions that the military's health care infrastructure stretched to the breaking point. Military hospitals complained to the War Ministry that war neurosis was the most pressing problem in health care for soldiers. The Baden Regional Committee (*Landesausschuss*) for war disabled, for example, reported at a 26 October 1917 meeting that mentally disabled war victims had become the single largest group of war wounded at the Karlsruhe military hospital. Of 251 war disabled, including men undergoing orthopedic, internal and psychiatric care, 84 cases suffered from a form of war neurosis. Doctors reported that for a number of reasons, 'special attention is given by the health office to the care of neurotics'. Complex mental and motor disturbances, which often appeared and disappeared at unpredictable intervals made occupational retraining uniquely difficult. Even worse, doctors complained, war neurotics grew increasingly worse while out of the trenches. It was felt that even in cases of genuine 'terror neurosis' (*Schreckneurose*), as they labeled men who were psychologically traumatized by a single shocking traumatic event at the front, hysterical symptoms emerged while at home and in the hospital, where doctors believed these men were coddled until their temporary psychological injuries became chronic conditions.[65] Freiburg psychiatrist Alfred Hoche, in a 1916 speech to the National Committee on War Victims' Care, set up by the Reichstag to mediate between state welfare and medical institutions, placed the blame for the rise of war neurosis on the rise of social democracy. War neurotics, he argued, were driven by the idea that they were entitled to compensation for any economic damage, creating a 'lust for pensions' that stemmed from the 'historical psychological sickness [*Seelenerkrankung*] of the proletarian class'.[66]

Doctors believed that the front was the best place for stressed soldiers to maintain their composure, while outside the trenches they were in danger of falling prey to forces that drained their hardened psyches. The period of two to three months after leaving the front was considered the crucial window in which individuals were most vulnerable to breaking down. While away from comrades and the healing powers of the 'spirit of the front' (*Frontgeist*), doctors claimed, men were tempted by self-interest, and dwelled on the idea of getting out of their duties as fighting soldiers and future workers. If temporarily separated from the values of national sacrifice and selflessness that doctors claimed prevailed in the front lines, men developed 'unclear desires and imaginings' that sapped them of the will to recover, and formed the basis for 'pension psychosis', or dependence on welfare and pensions. Thus the best treatment for men who displayed hysterical symptoms while behind the lines was a return to the trenches where men would be exposed to the positive example of 'a fighting comrade who embodies the spirit of the front'.[67] Most doctors believed that the front was psychologically more healthy than behind the lines. Military discipline, the pressure of enemy fire, and the influence of mentally fit comrades were considered by leading psychiatrists to be the most effective 'rapid cures' for men who broke down. Their temporary symptoms, doctors believed, would only be exacerbated and made chronic if exposed to the pity of those on the home front.[68]

Doctors also feared that the purity of the 'spirit of the front' would eventually be corrupted by the contagion of war neurosis. Therefore hysterical men had to be treated behind the lines before being sent in, side-by-side with still healthy, but fragile and dangerously stressed, front soldiers. The treatment of hysterical men took on three general phases: the correction of physical symptoms through electrotherapy and suggestion, immersion in a stable environment that promoted self-discipline and a sense of military and civic duties, and finally the return to the front or, in most cases, war-related industrial labor. Labor was considered the best alternative to returning potentially dangerous men to the front, in that it fulfilled the wartime needs of the nation while at the same time restoring in hysterical men the masculine virtues of hard work, patriotism, and a sense of will power.

The process of healing began with separating hysterics from genuine war neurotics and applying treatment. In 1914, the use of hypnosis and other psychotherapeutic techniques, including psychoanalysis, was widely rejected in established psychiatric circles as 'unscientific'.[69] Frustration with traditional forms of treatment (including electrotherapy) based on theories of neuro-psychiatry, which generally failed to solve the war neurosis problem, resulted in a greater interest in experimental techniques that had not been accepted within the psychiatric profession, which was dominated by neurologists who focused on the organic origins of neurosis. An established neurologist, Max Nonne developed a method of psychotherapy that was seen as respectable by wartime psychiatrists. He argued that war neuroses were indeed essentially psychological in origin, and rooted in the individual's loss of will and self-control. Using suggestive therapy with patients placed under hypnosis, Nonne claimed up to a 90% success rate in restoring the will power of war neurotics.[70] After placing them in a hypnotic trance, Nonne assured traumatized soldiers that their symptoms would disappear as long as they wanted to heal themselves. Nonne suggested to patients that they should assert themselves and exert control over their physical disorders. Nonne claimed that the majority of his patients ultimately returned to normal. However, his technique proved difficult for other psychiatrists to reproduce successfully. Patients reacted differently to hypnosis and suggestion therapy. Not all doctors had the personality and charisma needed to hypnotize individuals effectively, and it required more time and patience than many psychiatrists had, particularly with the overwhelming numbers of patients arriving in field hospitals.[71]

While many doctors found only mixed success with Nonne's hypnosis technique, another method was introduced that gained popularity among psychiatrists and proved to be easier and less time-consuming for doctors to reproduce with relatively little training. This was the Kaufmann method, developed by neurologist Fritz Kaufmann. It was characterized by a combination of electrotherapy and verbal assault, carried out, as one of Kaufmann's adherents described it, with aggressive discipline 'according to the specific needs and values of the military'.[72] The Kaufmann method was widely publicized and demonstrated, and psychiatrists claimed that it produced a high rate of success in curing the various symptoms of war neurosis, including tremors, stuttering, paralysis and other physical disorders. In his first application of the technique, Kaufmann claimed to have cured forty cases in short order, and he recommended that doctors first apply the method on men who lingered around hospitals as chronic, supposedly incurable, cases.[73]

Kaufmann described his method as having four essential steps. The first step was a psychological procedure. The patient was given constant assurance from doctors and hospital staff that he suffered from a simple physical condition which doctors were able to cure completely as long as the patient cooperated. The second step involved what Kaufmann characterized as an aggressive physical treatment, or 'surprise attack'. While directing increasingly intense verbal suggestion at the patient, the doctor applied electrical current directly to the parts of the body where tremors and paralysis existed. These electrical streams had minimal physiological effects, he wrote, but rather they had a psychological impact on patients who became convinced that their symptoms were essentially physical and could be cured with the electrotherapy.[74]

The third and fourth components of Kaufmann's method were, he explained, key to its success. The entire session, Kaufmann insisted, 'was to be conducted with strict adherence to military form in respect to discipline, treatment of patients as subordinates, and the application of suggestion in the form of orders'. While patients were handled as subordinates carrying out military orders, 'as in the barracks', they were also to be encouraged with 'optimistic phrases' that they were 'winning the fight' against their illness.[75] Finally, Kaufmann emphasized, the session was under no circumstances to be disrupted or abandoned until the patient was completely cured, otherwise the patient would imagine that his symptoms were incurable and he would return to malingering in hospitals, convinced that he would never recover. Kaufmann's advocates also stressed the importance of seeing the session all the way through to a cure.[76]

Though many doctors expressed reservations about the medical and ethical problems they saw in the Kaufmann technique, it was one of the most widely adopted forms of treatment because it was suitable to existing military needs. The treatment itself, with the 'surprise attack' on the patient, the coercive methods employed by doctors, the patient's fight to heal and survive the intense, even brutal nature of the electrical current specially modified for a more intense shock to internal organs gave the whole procedure a military-like quality suitable to disciplining the enlisted men who made up the bulk of the patients. When Kaufmann introduced and demonstrated his technique in a series of lectures in 1916, it won widespread support from psychiatrists struggling to find a technique that would cure war neurosis. However, some protested the Kaufmann method as cruel and medically without basis, particularly after several patients were killed during the course of treatment.[77] Because the technique was so brutal, some doctors were concerned that the Kaufmann method was possibly a threat to the *Burgfrieden* as it would spark conflicts with working-class organizations who might view it as biased. Psychiatrist Kurt Mendel asserted that soldiers deserved greater compassion in view of their sacrifices for the fatherland.[78] Patient resistance to the Kaufmann method escalated, especially as it became known that men died while undergoing treatment. Disabled men circulated sketches that portrayed military doctors as sadists inflicting shocks to half-dead, screaming patients, suggesting that the violence of the trenches was being reproduced in the hospitals.[79]

Though a number of psychiatrists grew critical of the Kaufmann method, and psychotherapeutic theories and techniques gradually gained currency, leading doctors in the medical establishment continued to justify electrotherapy as long as it produced successful results. One of psychiatry's most respected doctors, Robert Gaupp, went on lecture tours to promote electrotherapy and suggestion techniques. Gaupp countered public and professional criticism about the brutality of electrotherapy by asserting that in the conditions of war, the first goal of doctors was to make patients healthy so they could once again serve the fatherland.[80] Kaufmann's method was used through the end of the war and remained the most popular technique among military psychiatrists. Kaufmann claimed to have healed 95% of the 1,500 war neurotics he treated.[81] The Kaufmann method was also touted in the popular press, which detailed the symptoms of war neurosis and the process of electrotherapy. One Berlin newspaper reassured the public that 'hysteria is indeed curable; the means are suggestion and electricity'.[82]

The military and psychiatric professions formed a close alliance during the course of the war. The first priority of military doctors was healing the physical symptoms of war neurosis in order to make men once again useful to the nation's war effort. Though doctors claimed high success rates using electrotherapy and suggestion, they complained that recovery was hindered by the social background of patients. Men who failed to recover, doctors argued, lacked the self-discipline and work ethic necessary for recovery.

Medical and military interests had to be ironed out when it came to long-term recovery. Doctors thought the structured, disciplined environment offered by the front lines provided the most effective opportunity for training men to regain control over their bodies and minds. But it was too dangerous, from a military point of view, to put neurotic men back in the trenches, where they were at best unreliable, or at worst dangerous, to their fellow soldiers. Yet doctors warned that dismissing the most hopeless cases from military service would stigmatize these men, obliterate the last vestiges of self-trust and motivation needed to recover, and, perhaps worst of all, pander to their selfish desires to get out of the war at all costs. This would only turn these men into over-dependent, unproductive burdens in civil society. War hysterics therefore had to be immersed in another strictly controlled environment outside the trenches where they could 'recover the self-discipline that is necessary to develop the entire physical and mental strength required to be useful for civil activities'.[83] The most suitable environment for recovery, doctors determined, was in the activity of work itself.

For doctors, reintegrating war hysterics into the labor system constituted another battle going on behind the lines. War neurotics found the labor market structured similarly to the military. In occupational therapy programs for mentally disabled war victims, social class played a central role. Paths of recovery, work, and productivity were defined differently for enlisted men and officers. Different social groups were resegregated once they left the trenches. Officers were labeled 'exhausted' rather than 'hysterical', and paths of recovery and retraining followed class lines.[84] The type of work considered suitable for mentally disabled veterans depended on both the origins and nature of the wound and the socioeconomic status of the patient. The National Committee on War Victims' Care concluded that those suffering from 'nervousness', including hysteria, neurosis and other psychological disorders were not suitable for work in clerical or other white-collar jobs for which the War Ministry was funding occupational therapy programs.[85] Mentally disabled veterans suffering from 'wounds to the nervous system', that is, physiological nervous disorders that were directly war-related ('DB'), were eligible, along with other disabled veterans from middle-class backgrounds, to enter job retraining programs for work as clerks and other industries as 'laborers who do mental work' (Kopfarbeiter).[86] In the case of war hysterics, if doctors determined that they could not be sufficiently healed and it was too dangerous to send them back to the front lines, they were evaluated on a case-by-case basis for industrial and agricultural labor or, if totally incapable of work, family care. Thus middle-class and working-class men, given different diagnoses, were channeled into their traditional occupations. While doctors were under pressure to make men once again productive in industrialized war, they also protected traditional social hierarchies.

Recovery was not just a medical or social issue. It was subordinate to the needs of the nation. Even as wounded men returning to work and family, disabled veterans still lived under the expectation to fulfill their patriotic duty by obeying paths of recovery dictated by doctors. At the same time, civil society was being increasingly militarized as it was expected to cooperate with the army's programs for reintegrating war victims. In February 1916, the National Committee on War Victims' Care assembled hundreds of medical specialists in occupational therapy and rehabilitation for a conference to discuss reemployment. Werner Hartwich, a staff officer and doctor from the reserve field hospital at Paderborn, echoed arguments made by his colleagues when he asserted, 'Our experiences have demonstrated that in the area of occupational therapy, civil and military care must go hand in hand, and that civil society must open up opportunities for employment suitable to war victims.[87] Hartwich and his fellow doctors argued that employees in civil society now needed to cooperate with the military to make jobs available, particularly jobs in industries that contributed directly to the war effort. Their major goal was to determine which types of occupations were suitable to particular injuries, and then bring employers in these industries into the process of occupational therapy, with on-site training closely managed by military doctors.

The issue of war neurosis dominated much of the conference. A sharp distinction was made between men with psychological injuries and those whose mental disorders originated in physical trauma, namely injuries to the central nervous system. Frankfurt am Main psychiatrist Kurt Goldstein emphasized that this distinction was decisive in determining a patient's potential reemployment. Goldstein, a neurologist and leading advocate in the profession for Kaufmann's electrotherapy technique, argued that men suffering from war hysteria were, in contrast to men with physical head wounds, exceptionally difficult to retrain for the world of work: 'Alongside those with organic disturbances are persistent hysterical disturbances, which are unique and often require completely different forms of treatment'.[88] War hysterics were difficult to work with in occupational therapy, he noted, because they displayed unpredictable mental disturbances, 'excitability', and a lack of will to work. They were not easy to reassimilate into the social environment. In contrast, Goldstein wrote, men with actual brain damage (*Hirnverletzte*) could 'like children' be retaught the skills they needed to return to work. The disorders of veterans suffering from brain damage involved a combination of psychological and physiological disorders. But, in contrast to war hysterics, these could be precisely diagnosed and a curriculum of reeducation could be developed accordingly.[89]

Doctors at the conference expressed their preference for working with men with head-shot wounds over war hysterics. Dr W. Poppelreuter, a specialist in 'head-shot wound invalids' (*Kopfschussinvaliden*), outlined the pedagogical programs he designed for disabled veterans in Cologne. Poppelreuter focused on retraining men with the speech, writing, and motor skills needed to perform as factory workers, craftsmen and white-collar workers. He placed men in different courses according to their particular needs with learning how to once again read, write, and speak effectively. Within these courses, men were divided according to social status and profession. Men returning to lower-middle-class jobs underwent therapy in 'schools', while working-class disabled veterans retrained in 'work stations'. In these different settings, Poppelreuter noted, specialists could concentrate on precisely what men needed to perform in their predesignated professions again.[90] Poppelreuter's colleague, Dr Gutzmann, emphasized in his panel that therapy for men from working-class backgrounds was much less extensive, because 'while officers who lost their speech as a result of head wounds were often robbed of the most important skill necessary to their profession, workers in the same circumstances have not lost nearly so much, since they still perform the labor with which they are familiar and already trained in just as well as before they suffered their head wounds'.[91] Therapy that aimed at restoring speech, writing and other skills was thus carefully rationed according to social class. Individuals were only given the training needed to be productive workers again. Poppelreuter's techniques received praise from the mainstream press, which touted his approach as patriotic and one of Cologne's most significant contributions to the war effort.[92]

War hysterics were not placed in the same schools and workshops designed for reeducating veterans with physical brain damage. Though their symptoms were similar, doctors admitted, with various speech, hearing, and motor disturbances, they were considered completely different cases. In particular, doctors believed that hysteria was contagious, and they saw psychiatric hospitals as breeding grounds for malingerers who would potentially infect psychologically healthy soldiers. It was further suspected that hysterical men would never heal as long they were around each other, as they 'infected each other' with their low morale, lack of discipline, and 'self absorption and hopelessness'.[93] The best cure for these men, doctors argued, was a return to vigorous, carefully structured work.

The recovery of manly virtues like hard work and discipline, doctors predicted, would eventually restore the will of hysterical men. Lack of will was their central 'disorder', and its restoration would make them once again eligible for trench duty and the postwar world of work. Psychiatrists saw work itself as a form of therapy. They developed a rationalized, highly controlled work routine as an extension of electrotherapy and suggestion therapy. Work resuscitated patriotism, a sense of discipline, and masculine virtues. The blind, gas victims, and other physically disabled veterans were assigned basket-weaving and other handcraft skills as part of occupational therapy. But war hysterics were placed into agricultural and industrial labor, which doctors considered more appropriate as 'masculine', and intensive forms of work. Further, rehabilitation through agricultural and industrial labor made these men once again directly useful to the war machine while not endangering the will power of comrades at the front. The goal was thus two-fold, to maintain war production and instill in war neurotics a sense of sacrifice and national purpose. As one doctor treating both physically and psychologically disabled veterans wrote in the pamphlet *Die Hilfe*, men recovered most effectively through 'purposeful work that discouraged dilly-dallying ... in which we produce hard, serious, thinking men'.[94] Agricultural and industrial labor provided men with a type of work that restored 'specific German virtues' like 'hard work and orderliness', reflected in 'the more orderly and technically advanced German trenches, which were the product of superior German gardening and landscaping skills'. At the *Kriegs-Invalidenschule* in Potsdam, traumatized men recovered their 'mental energy' after a day of field work by building a scale model of the Verdun battlefield, 'the importance of which was not so much the display itself as the spirit that went into it'. The relationship between work and rebuilding the soldierly spirit 'went hand in hand'.[95]

Separate work-therapy stations designed specifically for war neurotics sprang up in 1916–17 as doctors tried to cope with the growing numbers of mentally disabled patients. In Baden, neuro-psychiatrists developed programs that became widely adopted by doctors throughout Germany. At a work station in Hornberg founded by Dr Ferdinand Kehrer, neurotics who had just completed Kaufmann's electrotherapy method were first given a daily regimen of exercises and work in the station's gardens. If men cooperated well and showed an increased will to work, their routine was made more rigorous and they performed a full day's work on the assembly line of a munitions plant located near the station. As part of the effort to remove these men from the pension system and integrate them into civilian work, patients were given wages and time to spend with their families and outside the hospital. Men who were unreliable in factory labor and continued to suffer from nervous breakdowns were kept under close supervision in an environment in which strict military discipline was enforced. Though they were not sent back to the trenches for fear of spreading their contagious nervous disorders, men were formed into 'neurotic battalions', where they continued to wear uniforms and performed labor useful to the war effort. Men who continued to display symptoms of hysteria were sent back to electrotherapy. The Hornberg station claimed a nearly 100% rehabilitation rate, and it was used as a model for other war neurotic work-therapy programs throughout Germany.[96]

Personal health was constantly being deemphasized as secondary to the war effort, and guilt was imposed on those who did not recover quickly enough. Posters in hospitals exhorted: Everyone is capable of returning to service 'if only he has enough will'.[97] For physically disabled veterans, the primary goal of industrial and agricultural labor was to rehabilitate the body, often with help from prosthetics and occupational training for postwar work, with the recovery of will as the secondary part of the physical regimen. The psyches of physically disabled veterans, doctors feared, were as vulnerable to 'pension hysteria' as those of war hysterics if they were not given a strictly controlled routine and vigorous work environment.[98] But mentally disabled men were believed to be most in need of will power repair compared to the physically injured, and for this reason work programs for war neurotics focused on restoring their will and spirit of sacrifice allegedly shattered by the war.

War neurotics experienced a wide variety of complex symptoms, yet doctors simplified treatment by concentrating on one factor – the will of the patient. Thus doctors eliminated any discussion of the war experience itself, instead placing all attention on the patient's character. Psychiatrists interpreted war neurosis through the prism of prewar assumptions concerning the moral constitution, discipline and will power to work and make sacrifices for the nation. Collaborating with the War Ministry to stem the overwhelming numbers of mentally ill soldiers emerging from the trenches, psychiatrists developed a system of managing and redisciplining these men through a rapid, aggressive, military-like regimen of therapy, closely-supervised industrial and agricultural labor, and then cautious reintegration into the army or work geared towards the war effort. The success of this system of controlling war neurosis, doctors predicted, was essential to preventing the spread of it behind the lines.

The Home Front and War Neurosis

At the end of 1915, a columnist for Berlin's *Borsen-Courier* suggested that civilians could alleviate nervous tension with escapist entertainment:

> Variety show treats in wartime are perhaps not to every person's taste. God knows, there is much preaching about the seriousness of our times, that the carefree singsong of the dance troops and the dizzying agility of the acrobats do not seem to fit in. On the other hand: many people believe that occasional diversion is needed precisely for nerves that have been stretched to their limits, that are hounded from one excitement to another.[99]

This was an unusually candid acknowledgement that the home front's nerves were strained by the war. Anxiety about widespread stress manifested itself in the popular media, where prescriptions for the public's mental health circulated. However, conservative groups would have challenged the *Borsen-Courier's* depiction of a home front in need of escape. According to critics organized in nationalist groups and conservative religious circles, many Germans found in their patriotism and faith the healing agents they needed to endure the psychological stress of modern industrial war. Those who broke down behind the lines were defined as grumblers and outsiders who weakened the national psyche at this moment of crisis. For conservative critics, Germany's traditional 'enemies', in particular Social Democrats and Jews, long constructed as threats to the nation.[100] lurked behind the image of the war neurotics. As the war put increased human and economic strain on German society by 1917–18, war neurosis on the home front became conflated with pathological social and political groups. Conservatives explained the collapse and revolution of 1918 as a symptom of socialist revolutionaries spreading psychosis at home and betraying the groups whose nerves allegedly remained steadfast until the bitter end.

War neurosis was not confined to the combat front. According to doctors, psychological breakdown spread through already susceptible social groups who were unwilling to make the necessary sacrifices required by total war. Kurt Walter Dix, a doctor who before the war specialized in the mental and physical development of children, found that intense excitement created by the war triggered mental breakdown in many already 'weak individuals'. Beginning as early as the long wait for mobilization in July 1914, compounded with the onslaught of fears about social and economic security, civilians who succumbed to 'hysteria' presented 'a tremendous danger to the general good'.[101] This home front war hysteria, Dix explained, was characterized by a pathological fixation on one's own needs above the needs of the nation. Dix uncovered many layers of behavior that destabilized home front resolve and unity. These included panic-stricken runs on banks, disorder among those waiting in line for scarce daily provisions, and public displays of anguish over lost loved ones.[102]

Dix placed most of the blame on women. He cited cases of women who remained obsessed with their own problems. He also criticized women for using wartime anxieties to bring attention to themselves, including cases of women spreading false stories about spies carrying bombs in their gardens. Men, Dix argued, also slipped into these 'hysterical', feminine behaviors when they grumbled about sacrifices on the home front, especially those who wanted their prewar comforts to remain undisturbed. Dix alluded to cases of neurotic men, whom he described as extreme hypochondriacs and chronic complainers so focused on themselves that they failed to see the higher purpose that demanded the individual subsume himself into the patriotic national effort. Dix described these individuals as 'anxiety-ridden, cowardly, man-children (*Menschenkinder*)', who complained incessantly. They could only be 'cured' when they joined the army and were delivered to the front, where they discovered something more important than their own needs. For the self-absorbed hysterics on the home front, both men and women, Dix prescribed faith in the army and the nation, and he optimistically predicted that Germany would inevitably experience a postwar psychological resurgence based on the spirit of 1914.[103]

In order to cure the home front of neurotic symptoms, many doctors prescribed a strict regimen of propaganda, which was to be administered through cooperation between state, military, and medical authorities. Psychiatric techniques they developed with individuals, psychiatrists contended, could be applied to the nation as a whole through the mass power of propaganda. The boundaries between medical information and propaganda overlapped as psychiatrists pitched their recommendations for healing the public and managing the war effort. In a 1916 pamphlet aimed at a civilian audience and titled '*We must and will win!*', Dr Felix Muche argued that during wartime, techniques like suggestion and hypnosis should be turned to controlling the morale of the nation and ensuring victory. He wrote: 'In the current world war, suggestion also plays in important role. Not only are individuals influenced through suggestion, but *also entire nations* [*Völker*, literally 'populations' – emphasis in the original text]'.[104] Muche called on Chancellor Bethmann-Hollweg and patriotic Reichstag representatives to lead the press and officers at the front by hammering home that Germany would win the war. This should be a coordinated effort at 'mass suggestion', Muche emphasized, and it would convince a hard-pressed home front and front-line troops that victory was imminent and sacrifices were not in vain. Suggestion and propaganda were essentially the same, based on the common goal of motivating people to remain steadfast in the face of stress. As suggestion motivated soldiers to go over the top, propaganda purged the nation of 'grumblers ... who are never satisfied with our great victories and the results of our campaigns on water and land'.[105] Muche warned that the government had to immediately make use of mass suggestion, otherwise defeatist Reichstag representatives on the political left and other 'grumblers' would poison morale and weaken the nation's strength. Suggestion was thus a powerful tool for mobilizing the masses, Muche found, but it could also be used by the nation's internal 'enemies' to sap the spirit of a fragile population.[106]

The psychologically traumatic effects of the war also alarmed conservative religious leaders. From their pulpits, pastors preached about buttressing the nerves of both front soldiers and Germans at home with faith in Jesus Christ. In a 1917 sermon in Stettin titled *Strong Nerves*, Pastor Hans Schulze heralded what he saw as the collapse of the 'nervous age' (*nervöse Zeitalter*) and called for a new epoch of psychological strength led by Christian soldiers in the trenches and on the home front:

Is it not true that we consider it part of our Christian duty to possess strong nerves? ... In peacetime, one knew how necessary it was to have strong nerves. They were a sign of especially good health. One admired those with strong nerves, while excusing those

who displayed nervousness. We live in a nervous age. The stressful
work in all occupations, and with it the life of pleasure, alcohol
consumption, nightly revelry ... worries and lost hopes connected to
the limitations and intoxications of the big city ... it rings across our
lips with a heavy sigh: God protect us from nervousness! Nervous
individuals are in peacetime a tremendous hindrance to the growth
of community life. In our now three long years of world war we
must ask for protection against nervousness from God. Everything
has become so much more violent and stressful both at home and
on the front ... Look, my dear ones, for us Christians the secret to
strong nerves and inner peace in these hard times is deep-rooted,
soaring faith. That is the difference between God's children and the
children of the world.[107]

Here Pastor Schulze conflated religious and medical discourse by equating
spiritual health and nerves. Through Christian faith, Schulze theorized,
Germans would win the war and conquer prewar enemies: modernity,
immorality, atheism. He portrayed the war as horrifying and violent, yet at
the same time an agent of restoration because it pushed Germans towards
their spiritual foundations of Christian piety and patriotic spirit in order
to make the sacrifices necessary for victory.

Publications by evangelical organizations portrayed the war, though a
necessary 'defensive war' that Germany was forced to fight, as a cataclysmic
struggle between 'material culture and the religious spirit'.[108] The trenches
represented to some religious Germans the ultimate manifestation of all
that was wrong with modernity. Modern industrial warfare, wrote Elsa
Hasse in *The Great War and the German Soul – Pictures from the Inner
Life of our People* [*Volk*], eroded the 'inner purity' of Germans with its
'cold technology and the illusion of order and strength'. This kind of
combat had the potential to seduce Germans into thinking that industrialization and modern weapons were the most powerful forces ever known.
Hasse was confident, however, that the German nation would prevail
because of its 'spirit of sacrifice and idealism, and the belief in truth and
faith' that would conquer both the enemy and the 'materialistic world view'
that possessed other nations and threatened to take over Germany.[109] A
Protestant pamphleteer named Federmann predicted that Germany would
win the war because its 'unified German soul' healed prewar social and
political divisions and turned the home front into an invincible spiritual
bulwark.[110] Many of these religious critics, however, showed signs of
pessimism about the long-term psychological effects of the war. Hasse,
for example, confidently predicted final victory, but feared the effects of
the war on Germany's postwar psyche. Karl Lindenberg, who wrote *The
German Soldier's Inner Experience*, announced gleefully that the spirit
of 1914 was closely connected to religious ecstasy and marked a return to

God, but at the same time he asked whether or not Germany could recover after the war from the 'soulless murder machine' and unprecedented cruelty that characterized trench warfare.[111]

In expressing fears about the psychological and social effects of the war at home, conservative critics were most adamant about the alleged mental deterioration of women, leading to 'immoral behavior' and the breakdown of families. During the war, the Ministry of the Interior intervened with trained social workers assigned to counsel girls 'to be judged in moral danger', especially those involved in prostitution.[112] Church groups were instrumental in spreading alarm over the alleged epidemic of moral collapse, and characterized the erosion of traditional norms as the home front's version of war neurosis. In a series of pamphlets edited in 1916 by Paul Haffner, a crusader for social reform on behalf of the Catholic Church, the tendency of women to 'lose their dignity' under the pressures of life on the home front was a symptom of 'psychological wounds' (*Seelenwunden*).[113] While most women, Haffner argued, were able to protect the 'purity and honor' of their families while their husbands were away at the front, a disturbing number of women could not endure the strain of worrying about their men while managing the home, without giving in to the temptation of sexual infidelity. Haffner narrated several cases of women, mentioning only their first names, who were deeply traumatized by the long wait for their husbands and fathers and the fear that they might be killed or return crippled. He attributed their breakdown to the 'intense sensations' unleashed by fear, and the difficulty women had coming to terms with the enormous sacrifices needed to win the war.[114] Women were already naturally inclined to lose control of their sexual desires, Haffner argued, and the dislocation caused by the war made it possible for them to act on these latent urges.

It was most shocking, Haffner argued, that these women who became prostitutes and 'night owls' came from all social classes. The war brought women into 'unnatural contact with men', as women found themselves in close proximity to soldiers in their roles as nurses, cooks, and volunteers for the war effort. Further, Haffner lamented, the war accelerated the breakdown of the family and religious values, which were already deteriorating due to rampant materialism and a prewar decline in faith, as the long absence of men in the home and unbearable human losses caused many to question traditional values. Haffner prescribed a return to Catholic moral values and a renewed sense of urgency in educating young women 'in their primary duty as mothers'.[115] He expressed anxiety that if the war continued much longer, it would be impossible to return to traditional values and codes of behavior, as the strains and fears produced by the war would permanently dislocate the psychological condition of women and their social environment.

As the war continued to cause huge losses with no end in sight, conservative critics and doctors writing for a general audience assured the home front populace that front soldiers were still psychologically intact and on the brink of victory. Some doctors criticized psychiatrists working for the War Ministry for exaggerating the number of war neurotics and spreading general anxiety about the health of the nation's nerves. Alfred Hoche, while continuing his work on war neurotics as the director of the psychiatric clinic at the University of Freiburg, was one of these doctors who wrote essays aimed at a popular audience, and he analyzed what he described as Germany's 'collective psyche' in his 1915 treatise, *War and Psychological Life*. Here he complained that some psychiatrists played into the hands of defeatists and wrongly characterized the nation as on the verge of nervous collapse:

> For a long time there has been a lot made of the mental and nervous health problems of our people. Some have spoken of this decaying *Kultur*, of this degenerate nervous age that indicates we are in a stage of decline ... For some years I have taken a position against this pessimistic view and set forth some general foundations that will make it possible to believe in the future of our people. Right now Germany is putting itself to the test on a grand scale. For the psychiatrists there appears an unwanted but important task they have placed upon themselves to study the effects of the great war on the mental life of individuals as well as the nation, and I ask that they listen to my suggestions on this subject.[116]

Hoche asserted that psychiatrists carried a tremendous responsibility as loyal to both medicine and the interests of the nation. Psychiatrists were concerned with not only the nerves of soldiers, but also the nerves of the home front, and he asked that doctors weigh the implications of their findings for home front morale. In this vein, Hoche warned against alarmist interpretations of the home front psyche, which he diagnosed as intact: 'Today is the time for heroes! Whoever is bold enough to talk of the nervous disposition in today's population would not only be wrong, but he would also be perpetrating a great falsehood'. Hoche concluded that doctors should chime in with the unifying spirit of the war and offer a more optimistic diagnosis of the nation's mental health.[117]

Hoche was a primary example of psychiatrists who devoted themselves to diagnosing the collective national psyche. Despite the stressful conditions of attritional, stalemated warfare, he concluded that individual strains dissolved into the collective sense of purpose and unity, with each German forming their own niche in the central nervous system of the nation:

> Our subjective claims to anything for the individual has collectively shriveled; there is no longer any right to individual joy, no right to

individual mourning. The entire *Volk* is converted into a unified, locked-on organism of a higher order, not only in the political-military sense, but also in terms of the consciousness of each individual. The nerve strings of this new, gigantic body are telephone wires through which identical feelings, identical streams of will raise themselves from space and time in the same glance, and oscillate in the same vibration.[118]

The unity and resilience of the population was more than an abstraction. Self-sacrifice and patriotism had the power to strengthen nerves. The above passage was a response to a French newspaper's accusation that Germany experienced 'mass psychosis' when it went to war. Hoche argued that the war actually produced a 'mass psyche' (*Masssenseele*), in which the 'spirit of 1914' intertwined the nation's nerves into a common organism against the external enemy.[119]

Nevertheless, not everyone was plugged into this national nervous system. Hoche alluded to hysterical women and the congenital mentally ill as chronic outsiders. But the war did not produce new forms of mental illness. Hoche insisted that if neuroses appeared on the combat or home fronts, these were at the same rates as under prewar conditions. He noted that in a conscripted army consisting of millions of men, the appearance of mental disturbances was inevitable, and it was not the cause for speculation that Germany was on the verge of collapse. Hoche argued that war psychosis existed 'in all past wars', and could even be found in the wars Germany won, including the Franco-Prussian War, where mentally unfit conscripted soldiers who were either too young or too old contributed to the appearance of widespread breakdown. In the more recent Russo-Japanese and Balkan Wars, he found higher rates of war psychosis, particularly in 'Russian officers who exhibited a high degree of alcohol psychosis'. High levels could also be measured in colonial south-west Africa, where heat, thirst and stress imposed psychological strain in even the most healthy European troops.[120] In fact, war neurosis was to be expected as normal.

Hoche indicated that the rates of war neurosis on the Western front had been exaggerated. He called for a revision in the way in which war neurosis was defined and counted, and suggested that psychiatrists contextualize outbreaks of neurosis in order to better understand it. For example, he pointed to the older reservists in the Landwehr troops on the trains to France in 1914, whom he said over-indulged in Schnapps to alleviate their anxieties in these exciting, but uncertain, first days of the war. Psychiatrists, Hoche argued, overreacted to the tremors and uncooperative behavior exhibited by these men who were uniquely stressed by being the first to leave their families and endure the long wait en route to the opening battles. These men were restless and worried, but healthy, and should be separated from men who suffered from actual psychoses. New conscripts, mostly younger, less emotionally mature men who came into the war with little life experience were least prepared to deal with mobilization. In these younger recruits, Hoche observed, one also found higher incidence of prewar mental illness, and their symptoms of 'war neurosis' actually sprang from preexisting inclinations towards hysteria. Thus the uncontrollable fear and extreme resistance to military discipline displayed by the younger recruits should not be confused with symptoms brought on by alcohol used by older men coping naturally with extreme pressure. The men who drank were normal soldiers. But the prewar hysterics, Hoche emphasized, were a danger to their comrades and militarily useless because they were unfit to carry weapons.[121]

Despite his claims that the bulk of men at the front held up under fire, Hoche gave in to pessimism as the war dragged on. Like many other psychiatrists, he saw war as a natural and healthy experience that weeded out the inherently neurotic, but this particular war, which dragged out into industrialized attrition, weakened even the most resilient, normal men. Hoche warned that this environment at the front in which both officers and enlisted men were forced into a state of passivity and prolonged loss of control over their physical and psychological condition would eventually spill over into the home front. In response to this forced passivity, men developed unfocused rage and a potential for violence that could be unleashed long after they were removed from the constraints of the front environment. Hoche described cases of men on leave haunted by hallucinations of the dead. One patient he treated suffered from horrifying nightmares so vivid that he woke up believing he was under fire and remained in 'a condition in which he lived in a half-dream world'. These nightmares often brought the front home: 'For a brief time I treated a neurasthenic officer who was in such a state when he returned to Germany that he used a revolver to shoot a lamp on his table because he believed it was a French lantern at the front'.[122]

More dangerous to the national body was the defeatism and deterioration of patriotic spirit that mentally wounded veterans allegedly brought to the home front. Hoche warned that the frustrations caused by immobile, attritional warfare turned soldiers against the war. Mentally ill soldiers were dangerous to home front morale: 'With these returning neurotic soldiers one finds an acute sense of depression characterized by gloomy attitudes towards our military and political situation'. Hoche feared that a 'front pessimism' was taking root, in which frustrated soldiers with too much time for introspection conveyed an exaggerated picture of problems at the front, and an overly critical view of the military. As long as this stalemated, machine-driven warfare continued, Hoche concluded, soldiers would break down further into cynical, depressed, and potentially violent men, and the patriotic spirit of August of 1914 would dissolve. Hoche saw himself in a battle to resuscitate this spirit of unity and sacrifice.[123]

A member of the conservative Pan-German League before the war, Hoche supported the Fatherland Party in 1918, when he feared that the national community was in disarray, threatened by pacifists, the political left, and defeatists at home.[124] The breakdown of soldiers and civilians, Hoche predicted, threatened to bring not only defeat, but also social, political and economic ruin. Most alarming was the tendency of disabled soldiers to sink into a state of passivity, and many lost their sense of will to become active participants in the fabric of work, family, and community. Responsibility for this fell on the individuals, according to Hoche, who found that the majority of veterans were capable of 'exerting their energies towards becoming healthy', but a significant number of 'weak willed' individuals did not display a normal level of interest in recovery. These men would pose the greatest threat to the postwar order, Hoche feared, as they would become dependent on their wounds as a means of holding on to their status and pensions:

> Many returning veterans will hold on to their feelings of demoralization, especially if they have difficulty retaining their social position. These men will not show any sign of positive energy when their invalid condition is their key to compensation ... this is especially possible with the high number of nervous disorders that are appearing in the colossal number of disabled veterans.[125]

If the postwar welfare system made it easier to maintain one's social and economic status as a disabled person, Hoche suggested, men inclined towards nervous illnesses would benefit, and the legitimately disabled would follow their lead and hesitate to recover. Thus the pension system, he argued, was the cause of a disproportionately high number of nervous disorders. After the war, Hoche and many other psychiatrists working for the War Ministry before 1918, argued for the development of a state-run 'euthanasia' program in order to save postwar society from enormous welfare costs needed to support the mentally ill. He recommended that the state put an end to the lives of an estimated 500,000 'idiots' and 10,000 hereditarily ill on Germany's welfare rolls, and he later played a leading role in the Nazi 'euthanasia' program.[126]

Psychiatrists like Hoche were typical in blaming the mentally disabled for their symptoms. But as the war dragged on and the numbers of neurotics continued to increase, doctors targeted a new traditional enemy for responsibility in the nation's mental breakdown: the political left. Social Democrats actively portrayed themselves as defenders of mentally disabled war veterans and made the case that psychological problems in soldiers stemmed directly from the traumatic war experience rather than preexisting deficiencies. In contrast with doctors, the SPD focused less on the character of war neurotics and more on the war experience itself when seeking blame for psychological trauma. Further, the Social Democrats were interested in not only the potential of war victims to recover their economic or military productivity, but also the war's long-term effects from the perspective of war victims themselves, in particular their faith in the future and reintegration into the community, work and family.

Like the doctors whom Social Democrats often constructed as enemies of war victims, the SPD's diagnosis of war neurosis was shaped by their political interests. Social Democrats themselves highlighted these competing agendas and characterized the debate over psychological trauma as more than just a struggle between doctors, patients, and the state, but also as a battle between opposing social and political groups. Early in the war, activists published articles on war neurosis in the social democratic *Vorwärts*, where they accused employers of disrupting the social truce and national unity if they refused to hire traumatized men out of mistrust of character.[127] By 1917, the Social Democrats openly criticized the government's perception of mentally disabled veterans as cowards and pension neurotics who were unwilling to fight or work. SPD representatives conceded that some men may indeed have lost their will power.[128] This, however, was due to the war experience, not their social background or inherent character flaws. The state was thus responsible, SPD critics argued, to bear the financial costs associated with helping physically and psychologically disabled veterans recover their damaged wills:

> How do you expect soldiers who have suffered terrible wounds to their bodies and their minds to return to work if they have lost all joy in life (*Lebensfreude*), all hope, all trust, all faith in the future? The fact is that with the explosive rise of war disabled, there is also a significant rise in the number of disoriented men who are psychologically lost, sunk in a quagmire ... A reality that we must confront, for better or for worse, is that these psychologically lost men, who are socially and economically completely disoriented, may never be able to find their way back to their families, society, occupations and livings. It does not do anything for them to demand that they have the proper will. For war disabled there is only one thing left: the state must act as a representative of the entire nation and take care of them, not just with a pension, but in all possible ways, with emphasis on social and economic care.[129]

According to Social Democrats, the state was responsible for the recovery of war victims and acted on behalf of a society that desired to give thanks for their sacrifices. The question of will power raised by doctors, they argued, was short-sighted and concealed the reality that the war was psychologically devastating, and that the nation faced the crisis of a whole generation of men who would not be able to mentally reassimilate into work, family and social life. Pensions for men who could prove directly war-related wounds, the SPD asserted, did not adequately cover the psychological and social costs incurred by the war. According to Social Democrats, doctors and the state failed to recognize the deeper psychological effects of the war, which had caused them to lose a sense of self-trust and confidence to reintegrate into postwar social and economic life and healthy, productive individuals. *Vorwärts* columnists subsequently demanded that the state set up war invalid homes (*Kriegsinvalidenheime*) where it could care for the symptoms of psychological stress, including long-term effects like depression, alcoholism and domestic violence. In addition, Social Democrats demanded that traumatized men deserved to be returned to their old occupations, or at least given a choice if they were no longer capable of performing their former jobs. This 'free choice in activities and paths of recovery', they argued, would heal the will of these veterans by restoring their confidence, self-trust, and the joy for life lost in the trenches. In turn, they would become productive citizens.[130]

When the state failed to meet these demands, left-wing war-disabled organizations became more radicalized and concentrated even greater focus on war neurotics.[131] The war neurosis question also intensified in the context of political radicalization in the wake of labor strikes, protests over food shortages, and increasingly open opposition to the war by 1917–18.[132] In the fall of 1917, *Vorwärts* editor and disabled veteran Erich Kuttner, along with Erich Roßmann, who would become a leading SPD Reichstag representative after the war, and Karl Tiedt, who in 1919 would break off to form the communist *Internationaler Bund der Opfer des Krieges und der Arbeit* (International Association of Victims of War and Work), founded the *Reichsbund der Kriegsbeschädigten und Kriegsteilnehmer* (National Association of War Disabled and their Dependents), which by 1918 would emerge as the largest organization representing war victims.[133] Kuttner and his colleagues formed the *Reichsbund* both as a response to what they perceived as the government's failure to provide for the social and economic rehabilitation of physically and psychologically disabled veterans, and because they feared that, without a socialist war-disabled organization, working-class veterans would be drawn into conservative veterans' groups.

Social Democrats actively criticized the techniques used to treat psychologically disabled war victims. In the summer of 1918, a series of debates over war neurosis took place in the Reichstag, where the SPD, and the more radical Independent Social Democrats (USPD), who had recently split from the SPD, took a leading role in voicing the frustration of war neurotics. These complaints focused on the brutal effects of electrotherapy. SPD deputy Georg Davidsohn, himself a disabled veteran and one of the founders of the *Reichsbund*, took the floor of parliament:

'[T]he majority of soldiers who are subjected to this [electrical] treatment come out of the institution terribly bitter ... they consider suicide during the treatment ... They ultimately take an enormous amount of bitterness, rage and hate with them from this treatment into their families'.[134] These Reichstag representatives generally did not question the authority of medical practitioners or the need for active treatment, but rather the short-sighted system in which it was applied, and the subordination of health and individual interests to the military and the economy.[135] In saving the state pensions and getting men back into the trenches by any means necessary, they complained, the state risked brutalizing these men in such a way that they would be incapable of long-term reintegration into postwar social and economic life.

According to conservative groups, the Social Democrats pandered to disabled men, particularly war neurotics, and helped spread pension psychosis through the ranks of veterans. Carl Schneider, a member of the right-wing *Vaterlandspartei* (Fatherland Party) and supporter of the nationalist *Essen-Verband* portrayed himself as a defender of veterans who was above party politics, a 'neutral, patriotic advocate for the strictly economic welfare of war victims'. Meanwhile, he called for the dissolution of the social democratic *Reichsbund*, which he complained turned wounded veterans over to biased social and political interest groups. The *Reichsbund*, Schneider argued, 'exploited disabled veterans', and eroded their patriotic spirit with 'the divisive character of party politics'.[136] Though the government was officially opposed to organized disabled veterans groups on the basis that they interfered with the National Committee's administration of disabled veterans, the *Essen-Verband* gained the support of conservative politicians, and General Ludendorff as their honorary chairman. *Essen-Verband* organizer Hans Adorf argued that his organization was the state's most effective bulwark against the radical-ization of war victims and their absorption into 'bolshevik' organizations like the *Reichsbund*. As a result, the *Essen-Verband* swayed further to the right until it became openly associated with the Fatherland Party, but by the end of 1918 the organization came apart in the wake of repeated scandals, including Adorf's embezzlement of funds.[137]

By early 1918, after the 'turnip winter' and the further deterioration of Germany's economic situation, it became clear that Germany's capacity for mobilizing support for the war was deteriorating.[138] The Social Democrats and more radical leftist organizations continued to benefit, and according to a 1921 Labor Ministry report, the *Reichsbund* ranked by far as the most popular war victims' association with over 600,000 members. This represented half of all veterans who joined war-disabled organizations, and easily outpaced leading right-wing organizations like the *Kyffhäuser Bund* (Kyffhäuser Association), with over 225,000 members, and the *Einheitsverband* (Unity Party) with over 200,000 members.[139]

Interestingly, a small minority of psychiatrists claimed that revolutionary movements actually helped to eradicate the war neurosis problem. Working-class veterans, some psychiatrists believed, became so empowered by their organizational activities that they ceased to fear doctors and a return to the front, and instead developed the confidence needed to lead revolution. After the war, psychiatrist Kurt Singer argued in a lecture to the Berlin Society for Psychiatry and Nervous Illness that 'the revolution brought the class which comprised the main contingent of neurotics, that is, the working proletariat, with one stroke into a position in which neurotic complexes, as the expression of protest of inferiors, the oppressed, and the subordinate were ruled out'. Though Singer believed that the 'higher self-esteem' of the organized working class was based on the fiction of a promised rise in status and a change in power relationships, he nevertheless believed that this, along with the evaporation of fears about returning to the front, contributed to the decrease in neuroses observed in his patients.[140]

Most psychiatrists, however, believed that Germany's defeat and the revolution signaled a rise in nervous disorders. According to the War Ministry's doctors, the increase in disabled veterans joining organizations on the political left represented a crisis in military-medical efforts to control the spread of war neurosis. Specifically, left wing politics and revolution accelerated, or even created, more cases of war neurotics. Psychiatrists Robert Gaupp and Hermann Oppenheim linked revolutionary activity and neurosis directly, observing that their patients in war neurosis stations embraced the formation of soldier's councils in November 1918. The activities of leftist radicals, Gaupp argued, more than the war, contributed to the psychological collapse of soldiers and ultimate defeat:

Among these young [soldier] reinforcements, moral degeneration and political proselytizing were the cause of the 'collapse', not the difficult experience of combat or the wearing down of the nerves through excessive exhaustion. Today they are the fellow-travelers of the Spartacists, whose motivations are less clear political conviction than the joy in destroying and rabble-rousing and living out of primitive and crude instincts.[141]

The revolution itself, Gaupp contended, was really the triumph of the psychopaths. Psychiatrist Karl Hildebrandt concluded that his patient, a war hysteric turned Spartacist revolutionary, was driven by both self-gain and the need for power in his attempts to escape his duty in the war.[142] Thus the revolution was the ultimate expression of hysterical selfishness and self-obsession. In this vein, psychiatrists generated their own 'stab-in-the-back' myth, conflating hysterics, political enemies and defeatism.

Racial antisemitism also shaped medical constructions of the mentally ill at the end of the war. Munich psychiatrist Eugen Kahn, for example, found in revolutionaries like Ernst Toller and Kurt Eisner examples of moral-psychological degneration and 'hysterical' behavior particular to Jews.[143] The role of Jews in spurring revolution and hysteria was also marked by psychiatrist Emil Kraepelin, who argued that a number of radicals were Jews, whom he believed possessed inherently psychopathological characteristics. In particular, Kraepelin noted, Jews, revolutionaries, and war hysterics shared weak wills and an unhealthy obsession with their instincts rather than reason. Thus psychiatrists blamed long-suspected *Reichsfeinde* ('national enemies') for the revolution, which they believed marked the victory of not only inferior social groups and suppressed political ideologies, but also the loss of control, rationality, and the potential destruction of the traditional order.

*   *   *

The outbreak of war neurosis in front-line troops had an impact that went beyond mental medicine. It also shaped debates over the causes of Germany's deteriorating military, socioeconomic and political situation. Blame for war neurosis fell on pre-1914 'enemies' constructed by those in power, particularly the political left, which allegedly incited working-class veterans and civilians to betray the 'spirit of 1914' by their lack of will to make the sacrifices necessary to winning the war. In this way, doctors and the military shifted the problem from the war to the character and background of allegedly unmanly and undisciplined men. The latter could only be healed by being reintegrated into the official version of the war experience, in which individual health was subsumed into the collective body of the nation, and weak nerves were reinvigorated by the cleansing effects of war, sacrifice, and the 'spirit of 1914'.

War victims responded vociferously with their own explanations for the war neurosis problem. Marginalized as social pariahs, war neurotics found status with the 'outsider' political groups that gradually stepped up their critique of the war. The Social Democratic Party embraced the cause of war neurotics, whom they integrated into a larger pacifist agenda. The SPD asserted that war neurosis was not a symptom of inherently deficient moral character, but rather caused by the traumatic experience of modern industrial combat. War neurosis, they claimed, was endemic to a larger psychological breakdown spreading through German society that would weaken the nation's capacity for long-term social and economic recovery. One thing both the political left and the right agreed upon was that war neurosis was not just a phenomenon of front-line combat, but it also appeared in civilians dislocated by the effects of total war. Blame for the cause of this epidemic differed: conservatives scapegoated the combined effects of modernity and the loss of traditional values and social structures ushered in by the war. In contrast, progressive groups believed the war shattered most Germans' faith in the idea that the nation represented their interests, resulting in a traumatized populace alienated from work and community. After the war, debates over which social and political groups caused the nation's collapse intensified, and conflict over responsibility, compensation and the psychological legacy of the war further divided German society. As will be seen in the next chapter, both critics and advocates for mentally disabled veterans would mobilize their resources to heal the trauma they saw in individuals and the nation.

Chapter 2

The War Neurotics Return Home

Psychologically Disabled Veterans and Postwar Society, 1918–1920

> These war quiverers (*Kriegszitterer*) are the living documents of our time.
>
> – Magnus Hirschfeld, *The Moral History of the World War*[1]

> In the image of the so-called 'war neurotics' … we are reminded of the monstrous psychological stress and the great catastrophe under whose violence we still breathe with great difficulty today.
>
> – Prof. J.H. Schultz, *Berliner Tageblatt*, Oct. 5, 1921.[2]

Shortly after the February 1920 release of the classic expressionist film *The Cabinet of Dr Caligari*, German psychiatrists noticed a rise in murders that mimicked the hypnosis and psychological torture depicted in the controversial film.[3] Berlin's most famous psychiatrists treating war neurosis attributed this rash of copycat crimes to the postwar environment, where fragile nerves were endemic, making individuals easily susceptible to criminal coercion and hysterical behavior. Under pressure from psychiatrists, the Ministry of National Health, and the Ministry of the Interior, the film censorship board banned *Caligari* and a series of other films that depicted murderous crimes carried out by psychopaths under the influence of fraudulent hypnotists. Dr Karl Bonhoeffer, director of Berlin University's psychiatric clinic, warned that quack hypnotists, imitating the evil Dr Caligari in the film, were 'without a doubt contributing to the hystericalization (*Hysterisierung*) of a specific portion of the population'.[4] In their justification for censorship, state officials argued that the shaken postwar public could not withstand the psychological violence that appeared onscreen: 'Unhinged persons in this postwar period, where nervousness and excitability are on the rise, could be extremely vulnerable to hypnotic influences that stimulate certain criminal tendencies'.[5]

The sense that the world had been inverted and the irrational had become commonplace was famously described by writer Albrecht Mendelssohn-Bartholdy. Looking back on the 1920s, after Hitler had come to power, he described the 'end of causality', a state of being in which rational behavior, hard work, and obedience to authority no longer led to prosperity and progress in the wake of war and economic devastation.[6] Survivors debated whether or not Germany could be restored to its prewar moral standards and social relationships. As historian Richard Bessel has observed, the effort to return to prewar norms was all the more difficult because it was based on an illusionary past that existed mainly in the minds of Germany's middle classes, who were traumatized by social leveling, the erosion of social and political authority, and economic crisis.[7]

As Germans at home were traumatized by the erosion of the prewar moral universe, they feared the return of men from the trenches. 1918 marked the beginning, rather than the end, of the war neurosis problem. What would be the effect of millions of men coming home from the brutalizing experience of the trenches? Were German men permanently psychologically damaged by the war or could they return to prewar norms? Would these men bring the psychopathologies of their front experience home with them and inflict the violence and horror of the trenches on postwar society? In this chapter, I argue that war neurosis shifted from a primarily medical issue to a social one, immediately after the war. Though doctors claimed to have 'solved' the question of its origins and treatment, debates about the long-term effects of mental trauma on soldiers and civilians intensified. Returning veterans, particularly men diagnosed with psychological trauma but also veterans in general, were viewed by psychiatrists and the public with suspicion as criminal, deviant and potentially dangerous to postwar society.

Traumatized men were scapegoated for a whole range of perceived postwar catastrophes. Former military psychiatrists consulted by state officials in the first months after the war correlated the rise of the new democratic republic with the spread of war neurosis, with 'criminal psychopaths' – including socialists and Jews – inciting political revolution just as the military and home front, though exhausted, was on the brink of victory.[8] According to psychiatrists and conservative interest groups, democracy itself worsened Germany's beleaguered national psyche by legitimizing long suppressed working-class organizations, including unions and the Social Democratic Party, and negating middle-class values regarding property, work, and sexual behavior.

War neurotics were a tremendous source of fear for people at home. The return of psychologically disabled veterans represented a second trauma that shook both front soldiers and civilians.[9] As veterans returned to the world of work and family life, they often encountered rejection and stigmatization from groups who were expected to facilitate healing, resulting in a number of men describing a continuance or even intensification of traumatic stress and associated symptoms. Returning veterans after 1918 were treated with suspicion by civilians anxious about the psychological destruction caused by the war. Using war neurotics as their primary evidence, survivors on the home front, particularly Germans resentful that their own sacrifices were in vain, feared that veterans would weaken postwar society by transmitting degenerate, pathological attitudes about the nation, work ethic, traditional authority and sexual behavior to the already shaken middle class.[10] Former military psychiatrists, now working for the Labor Ministry and Weimar's emerging social welfare system, assured the state and society that they could help stabilize the problem by containing the spread of these social diseases and root out frauds and psychotic criminals from the welfare system.[11] Increasingly, even authentic war neurotics were conflated with criminality and disease allegedly spreading at home.

In contrast to military psychiatrists, a number of psychiatrists outside the military and state-employed medical establishment argued that psychologically disabled veterans did not inflict the brutality of the trenches on postwar society. Rather, they claimed, an equally psychologically shattered home front traumatized veterans further by treating them as criminals rather than victims. This perspective was echoed by veterans primarily on the political left, who argued that the home front was as psychologically disabled by total war as front veterans. These veterans stressed that doctors and a public that did not want to acknowledge the psychological wounds caused by the war further brutalized veterans and their families. Thus life at home began to replicate the trauma of the front, and tensions between survivors of trauma and systems of authority responsible for the war intensified.

Military Defeat, Revolution, and the War Neurosis Epidemic

The German military's last bid for victory failed by the end of the summer of 1918. General Erich Ludendorff, who had been running the nation under a virtual military dictatorship with Field Marshal von Hindenburg since 1916, experienced a mild nervous breakdown at the end of September, when it became clear that Germany's situation on the Western front was on the verge of collapse. Instead of publicly acknowledging their responsibility for defeat, Ludendorff orchestrated the handover of the government to the Social Democrats and other political parties, placing the responsibility on them to end the war and sue for peace.[12]

In October 1918, news that the government was seeking peace terms came as a shock to a public that widely believed propaganda that Germany was on the verge of victory. Revolutionary groups gained increasing support from soldiers and demonstrators at home. Radical left-wing soldiers' and workers' councils held power in Berlin and elected officials they wanted to appoint to a new government. The moderate left-wing majority Social Democratic Party recognized that it would have to form an agreement with the radical Independent Socialist Party (USPD) that drew support from the revolutionary councils. In early November, these groups set up a new provisional government that abolished the monarchy, and on 9 November 1918, Kaiser Wilhelm II abdicated. For the next several months, street fighting broke out as far left-wing independent socialists broke off to form the German Communist Party (KPD) in January 1919 behind Rosa Luxemburg and Karl Liebknecht, who attempted to overthrow the provisional government and follow a Soviet-model revolution. Meanwhile, the Social Democrats tried to form defensive coalitions with emerging bourgeois parties who feared revolution, and the new parliamentary democracy struggled to build consensus between the newly empowered working class and the embittered middle class, many of whom refused to accept defeat and instead believed that Germany had been betrayed by Social Democrats and other parties on the left.[13]

Revolutionaries identified psychologically disabled soldiers as symbols of the transition from the authoritarian order to democratic revolution. During the chaotic days of November 9–11, men in the soldiers' and workers' councils stormed hospitals and asylums and liberated war neurotics as working-class political prisoners victimized by capitalism and war. The social democratic-endorsed Association for the Rights and Care of the Mentally Ill (*Bund für Irrenrecht und Irrenfürsorge*) threw its support behind the uprisings taking place in the military hospitals. Paul Elmer, a founder of the association, asked the new government to release the 'imprisoned' mentally ill veterans where, he claimed, they were held against their will by the previous brutal regime:

> By the grace of the people's uprising some of the political prisoners were liberated from the German prisons. But hundreds have still not yet had their prison doors opened. These are the unfortunate ones. They are labeled by the recently unsettled middle class citizens as 'mentally ill whiners' and locked in insane asylums. Their voices and rights that they are entitled to are respected only by the workers and soldiers who must use violence to release them from systematic violence. Many military-run psychiatric field hospitals are meanwhile being cleared out by force applied by workers' and soldiers' councils. In many cases, psychologically disabled soldiers kept against their will break free themselves. Equal rights and equal liberty for all the victims of reactionism![14]

The plight of war neurotics thus served as a symbolic class power struggle between working-class men victimized by war set against middle-class authorities that unjustly criminalized these men. Veterans in these asylums described them as comparable to the front experience. Revolutionaries blamed doctors for the atrocious conditions in the asylums, and called for the asylums' removal and the rebuilding of a more humane hospital system. Social Democrats encouraged traumatized ex-soldiers to demand compensation as victims of both the war and the monarchy. One of the liberated mentally disabled veterans who later applied for health care and pensions to compensate for the material and emotional suffering he incurred in both the war and in prison claimed to be 'forcibly and wrongly kept in the loony-bin (*Idiotenhaus*) until I lost everything'.[15]

The chaos and violence caused by revolution also produced secondary trauma in the form of stressed street fighters. In the tumultuous winter of 1918–19, the new republic had to solve pressing immediate crises, including constant political unrest and economic crisis that threatened to destabilize the new democracy. Psychiatrists found a new form of 'war neurosis' in the republic's newly formed *Reichswehr*, where soldiers distraught by Germany's collapse fell into depression when ordered to fight against their former comrades turned communist in 1919–20. Paul B., for example, fought as a *Reichswehr* officer against the communists in early 1919. His psychiatrist reported that while he was devoted to his duty to repress Germany's 'national enemies', he suffered a nervous breakdown from the guilt caused by killing many former front comrades, resulting in suicidal feelings built on already unresolved stress from combat on the Western front. His psychiatrists judged that these psychological problems were indeed legitimate wounds, and in their testimony to the pension courts Paul B.'s role in fighting against the communists seemed to work in his favor.[16]

The most serious problem, however, was still veterans traumatized by the war in the trenches. Two million soldiers returned home in mass waves beginning in early December 1918. Seemingly overnight, the streets of major cities were clogged with ex-soldiers. Estimates vary on how many men suffered from psychological problems, but one Berlin psychiatrist who defined these wounds broadly believed that nearly half of Germany's two million disabled veterans suffered from some kind of nervous disorder.[17] Psychiatrists disagreed on these statistics, but from the public's point of view, the number of men quivering and shaking in subway stations and sidewalks seemed overwhelming. Police precincts and courts were clogged with cases of recently arrested veterans diagnosed with, or claiming to suffer from, psychological injuries.[18]

State ministers solicited psychiatrists with experience at the front to give testimony on the nature of war neurosis and whether or not these men were authentic war victims or criminals. In March 1919, with strikes and street fighting coinciding with parliamentary debates over the new constitution, the Ministry of Justice and the Interior Ministry authorized state medical representative Dr Kolb, former director of several field hospitals that specialized in war neurosis, to give judges, lawyers and other doctors working for the judicial system guidelines for distinguishing psychologically disabled veterans from men whose mental disorders and sometimes criminal behavior were not directly connected to their wartime experiences.[19] The difference between mentally ill veterans and criminals dominated the state's inquiry. Kolb argued that in order to reintegrate veterans into postwar society, the new republic would have to define 'the narrow gap that existed between war neurotics and chronic psychopaths'. He testified that 'not all genuine war neurotics are chronic psychopaths, but there are some shared traits'. One of the similarities was that they shared characteristics that made them both 'enemies of the nation'.[20] For example, both groups displayed what he called 'immoral behavioral patterns, the inability to control themselves, and exclusive focus on the ego'. If genuine war victims were allowed to display these characteristics without intervention, he warned, they would be beyond repair and become indistinguishable from inborn psychopaths. He noted that it was thus the responsibility of the republic to immediately begin a system of control and discipline to rehabilitate legitimate war victims before they became 'war neurotics who developed a criminal nature'.[21]

Social class played a central role in Kolb's approach to war neurosis. Both middle- and working-class veterans suffered from psychological breakdowns, he concluded, but displayed different types of symptoms. Officers displayed primarily physical symptoms, notably the familiar tremors, tics and shaking that had become a familiar sight – and drew many complaints – on streets and subway stations.[22] In contrast, he argued, enlisted men manifested 'hysterical' symptoms, including criminal behavior such as pension fraud, theft, and 'immoral acts'.[23] Officers thus required treatment techniques to correct their physiological disturbances, whereas enlisted men required discipline, control, and other social correctives. Doctors, Kolb emphasized, had the physical symptoms of middle-class men under control. However, civil society was not doing enough to control working-class veterans. Kolb believed that working-class men who claimed mental injuries would make a career out of pension-hunting and other criminal acts, thus allowing degeneracy to flourish. He recommended a military-style regimen developed during the war, whereby men who experienced genuine psychological trauma in the trenches were quickly disciplined and rehabilitated into functional front soldiers. Kolb feared that because the main disciplinary action available to military psychiatrists, the threat of returning to the trenches, no longer existed, symptoms would remain unchecked, or even worse, men who saw an opportunity for a pension would fake symptoms. He recommended that civil institutions should severely punish war neurotics who were slow to recover through denial of pensions or even imprisonment, otherwise men would not see any reason to let go of their neurotic symptoms.[24]

The new social and political order, in Kolb's estimation, was too weak to rehabilitate psychologically disabled men. Kolb insisted that the postwar world actually worsened rather than healed weak nerves. What he characterized as an overly-permissive new postwar social and cultural environment prolonged the neuroses that emerged in the trenches. 'Immoral' dancing, alcohol, sexual promiscuity, and the cinema only encouraged psychologically fragile veterans to remain 'hysterical'. Kolb appealed to families of healthy returning veterans, particularly those who came from respectable backgrounds and high moral character, to help the state discipline war neurotics. Veterans susceptible to war neurosis could be easily spotted, as they were over-dependent on pensions and health care, and expressed cynicism towards doctors and authority. War neurotics, he argued, were completely fixated on their war experience and their desire to win sympathy and compensation. Pity only worsened the problem because it encouraged men to hold on to their symptoms, gain attention, and gave them an excuse not to integrate into normal postwar life. It was thus best for families, doctors, and social welfare officials to forget about their traumatic experiences and move on with their lives.[25]

Kolb prescribed a structured, moral environment characterized by prewar middle-class codes of social conduct: devotion to family life, hard work, abstinence, and attendance at church were the best paths of recovery. He saw good families come to the assistance of war neurotics by bringing 'mental balance, strength of will and heightened self-trust'.[26] If families let their returning veterans give in to ego-gratification and excess, it would only facilitate their loss of control and the downward spiral to criminal, antisocial behavior. Families, however, were already strained to the brink of collapse. Kolb acknowledged that veterans' dependents suffered from their own set of psychological traumas brought on by the stress of extreme economic sacrifices. While fathers were away at the front, he surmised, women and children left at home experienced psychological breakdowns while working to make ends meet. Many of these families, particularly those with 'weak-minded, psychopathic youth', lost their faith in traditional values and turned to criminal activity to fill their family needs.[27] If families were too dysfunctional to give returning husbands and fathers the moral structure they needed to recover, Kolb prescribed prisons and asylums as a means for disciplinary action.[28]

In addition to a collapsing social environment, Kolb saw the new republic's political order as detrimental to the psychological health of returning veterans. The republic, he argued, catered to the 'weak-willed' and encouraged the spread of immoral, 'hysterical' behavior because it did not validate the values and authority of the middle-class and traditional military institutions. He concluded that 'primitive instincts' towards egotism and social permissiveness would run rampant as faith in authority and responsibility to the nation declined. However, this postwar condition was not the fault of the majority of Germans who dedicated themselves honorably to defending the nation during the war. Bitterness, blame and guilt for Germany's postwar crisis stemmed from the rise of social and political groups that did not represent traditional bourgeois values. Revolutionary groups destroyed the basis for order:

> The revolution, without doubt, triggered the shrinking of traditional authority and blurred the concept of property: with one stroke, the authoritative institutions that until now served as guidelines have been eliminated. New authorities, gaining their position with partly legitimate means, have taken their place. The dominant political party today presents itself as an enemy of all property.[29]

The triumph of social democracy and working-class politics thus lay at the origins of Germany's current crisis. The revolution, according to Kolb, legitimized war neurosis and the 'criminal behavior' that Germany's traditional institutions led by the elite and the military had kept under control.[30] Just as families had been traumatized by a loss of authority in the form of physically and psychologically absent fathers, veterans were further traumatized by the experience of returning to a society where traditional faith in authority had been obliterated.

Kolb's social and political perspective on war neurosis represented a particularly right-wing view of military psychiatrists enlisted to aid the transition from war to recovery. In the months between the end of the war and the creation of the National Pension Law of 1920, the new republic's state ministers also sought advice on war neurosis from psychiatrists who affirmed the legitimacy of the new democratic state, and did not draw connections between war neurotics and the revolution. However, the link between war neurosis and criminal social behavior also dominated investigations made by psychiatrists more sympathetic to the new democracy.

Not all former military psychiatrists believed that the end of the war and the revolution would worsen the war neurosis problem. Berlin neurologist Erwin Loewy-Hattendorf, for example, argued that, with the end of the war, men no longer had to fear the front and thus would not escape that horrifying reality through mental breakdown.[31] A number of psychiatrists, however, worried that, though war neurosis would dissipate with the end of trench warfare, a new set of psychological disorders would evolve to plague the reintegration of men into postwar society. Originally authorized by the Labor Ministry while the war was still going to collect data on war neurosis, the Institute for Applied Psychology at Potsdam, directed by Dr Otto Lipmann, submitted to the new republic's labor ministers in 1920 what they described as the definitive study on war neurosis. *Contributions on the Psychology of War (Beiträge zur Psychologie des Krieges)*, composed of several essays written by state-employed psychiatrists, outlined for the Labor Ministry their findings on the psychological impact of the war on men at the front. Their study focused on the question of whether or not mentally ill veterans would be able to reintegrate into postwar life as healthy, productive members of society.[32]

One of the most interesting aspects of Lipmann's study is that its cornerstone essay, 'The Psychography of Warriors', was written by an ex-non-commissioned officer, Paul Plaut. Lipmann solicited Plaut's expertise as a veteran interested in the psychological effects of the war and problems faced by veterans returning home. Plaut had volunteered for the war and served both on the Eastern Front and in the West at Verdun, where he witnessed the carnage that killed over a million French and German soldiers in 1916. Following a bout of influenza and hospitalization in 1917, he was transferred to police duty at a veterans' hospital in Berlin. Plaut worked for Lipmann's institute and the central registration office of the Labor Ministry until 1933, when the Nazis fired him for being a Jew under the Law for the Restoration of the Professional Civil Service. Similar to many other Jewish veterans, Plaut collected his documents proving his service, including his iron cross second-class, in an unsuccessful bid to keep his job. His friend at the institute, Otto Lipmann, also Jewish, committed suicide the year the Nazis came to power.[33]

Plaut's methodology in his 1920 essay was to investigate the psychological effects of the war by interviewing veterans regarding their responses to combat and the fear it produced. His stated goal was 'to gather observations from the field to determine what soldiers thought at the moment of highest danger in order to conquer the fear of death'.[34] Plaut collected several thousand surveys asking an array of questions on the impact of the war. The bulk of the data came from soldiers interviewed just after they left the front or were on leave. He asked soldiers fresh from the front a series of questions about their attitudes towards danger, stress, and enemy soldiers. Following his question, 'What are the main sources of your so-called excitement for war?' Plaut included options for his subjects to select, ranging from patriotic feelings to individual satisfaction: 'love of fatherland', 'consciousness of duty', 'desire for adventure', 'joy in the craft of war'. Some of the questions asked subjects to offer their own analysis: 'Are you drawn to danger – why?' Plaut also suspected that men were sexually stimulated by war, leading them to become dependent on combat for sexual fulfillment: 'Do your sexual desires increase in the circumstances of war, stress, moodiness, etc'.[35] While Plaut gave veterans considerable opportunity to express their reactions to war, his leading questions can also be taken as revelations of his own assumptions about the psychological effects of combat imposed on his subjects.[36]

Though not a professional psychiatrist, Plaut speculated on the neuropsychological origins of trauma. He argued that war-related psychoses were fundamentally neurological in origin, with secondary emotional effects stemming from the stress caused by initial trauma.[37] The psychological pressure of waiting for days under monotonous artillery bombardments before rushing over the top into machine gun fire resulted in unique nerve damage, in which the electrical streams that passed through the bundles of nerves in the brain were cut off, damaging motor coordination and resulting in debilitating emotional side-effects. While in previous wars 'strong-muscled men' were able to endure the stress of battle, Plaut ventured that even the healthiest individuals broke down psychologically under the unique strains of modern industrial warfare. Though the war caused neurologically based psychological disorders in otherwise healthy men, these physical injuries were not permanent.[38]

Plaut's main concern was the emotional problems that he predicted would persist after men returned from the trenches. 'War neurosis' would disappear. But the 'multifaceted, myriad emotional responses to the war', which appeared in men who did not necessarily experience neurological damage, were more prevalent and longer lasting. Although emotional changes in veterans were manageable enough to allow postwar reintegration, subtle but permanent personality changes could be expected:

> It is false to imagine that the soldier undergoes a complete transformation in his entire emotional life as a result of his experience at the front, to become a completely different person who no longer has anything in common with peacetime events and thinking ... However, though the shocks to which he must always be subjugated are not lasting organic changes, but only temporary psychophysical changes, new peculiarities in individuals may have taken root to produce changes in personality.[39]

The 'new peculiarities' that Plaut described involved a new relationship towards violence, and a dependency on feelings produced by danger.[40] On the one hand, the traumatic scars that produced tics and tremors, nightmares and depression, would eventually heal. But personality disorders would develop in the wake of the front experience.

This disruption of prewar emotional life signaled a trend in the psyches of returning soldiers that potentially threatened the postwar social order: addiction to violence. This addiction was a long-lasting, widespread psychological consequence of the war experience that would not heal.[41] But even more men became so jaded by violence that they had lost the ability to relate to fellow human beings. Most soldiers, Plaut feared, appeared healthy on the surface but harbored an inner crisis. The fact that so many men were able to adjust to the extreme violence that was an everyday part of trench life indicated that a brutal psychological transformation had taken place. This ability to adjust, in Plaut's analysis, was more frightening than men who showed more obvious signs of breakdown. Plaut tried to determine why most men could adapt to pervasive violence by surveying veterans returning from the front, and he hypothesized that for many men, war sapped all feelings of compassion and natural human sensitivity. As recorded by one soldier in Plaut's survey:

> In the trenches lie the stinking corpses one on top of another ... over our group a shrapnel bomb explodes. The first man is dead: shrapnel in the head, he remains there in a sitting position until the next day, when we fetch him. The second, a corporal, dead: bullet in the neck. The third, a non-commissioned officer, shot through with holes like a sieve – head, chest, leg, and hand shots. Life was sucked out of him. The fourth, helmet shot through. The fifth was me. The sixth, shot through the heart, dead. The seventh, shot in the back. The eighth also dead. All from one shrapnel bomb. When one sees all that suffering, both the air and desire certainly drains out of you.[42]

The fatalism and isolation found in the trenches can be found in another veteran's account:

> Death and injury was the daily picture – it came every day and thus one often barely found any time or the opportunity to become acquainted with others by name, let alone get personally close to anyone. So it necessarily followed, that one concentrated on one's own life, as a priority took care of oneself – each person knew they were next.[43]

Speculating as to why men continued to face such horrifying events without rebelling against the military, or trying to escape, Plaut pointed to these men desperately numb to the world around them. So brutalized that they had lost their sense of control over their environment, Plaut argued that men remained relatively passive in the face of slaughter. As their emotions and sense of empathy drained away, they became only hollow shells of their prewar selves.

The psychological destruction inflicted by the war was not confined to only a few weak men. Plaut's conclusions, based on his survey, were that many veterans who were not diagnosed formally as 'war neurotics' nevertheless experienced dramatic psychological changes that potentially threatened the postwar social order. Not all of the soldiers who suffered from psychological problems were 'abnormal', or neurotic. Instead, the environment of the trenches was the abnormal element, producing corresponding mental reactions. While there was no overarching objective conclusion that could be made about the sociopsychological effects of the war from the wide range of answers Plaut received, the brutality of the front had various pernicious effects. 'The minds of soldiers are not fixed, abstract objects', Plaut noted, but rather the products of different social backgrounds that shaped their emotional complexities.[44] For example, prewar sexual experience, marital status, and age, determined soldiers' abilities to cope with the sexual excitement produced by combat. Men from more elite social backgrounds tended to possess more complex emotional lives that provided mechanisms for coping with the brutality and violence of the front. Those from lower class backgrounds were more decisively influenced by a mixture of violence and sexual excitement they experienced in postwar moral and ethical norms. According to Plaut, the war produced a morbid fascination with violence and sexual deviance that tempted the average infantry soldier, particularly men from the emotionally susceptible working class, to become addicted to these unnatural experiences.[45] Plaut feared that veterans would have difficulty readjusting to the postwar routine of work and family life after years of killing smashed the prewar moral universe. From Plaut's perspective, the pension question could be laid to rest, but the long-term psychosocial effects of the war were still problematic. Inner moral conflicts still plagued men who did not necessarily experience what Plaut defined as war neurosis. Returning soldiers who appeared normal, in this scenario, actually concealed a whole range of pscyhopathologies that they transmitted to civil society. This perspective would gain wide currency in both professional and public debates over the effects of the war.

Doctors working on war neurosis independently of state support, particularly psychoanalysts, saw war neurosis as a much less contained and less controllable phenomenon than their counterparts hired by the Labor Ministry. Psychoanalysis was treated with derision by most military psychiatrists, who considered it to be narrowly focused on the psychosexual aetiology of neurosis. During the course of the war, doctors searching for new techniques to deal with symptoms of hysteria seen at the front begrudgingly accepted Freud's interpretations of the interaction between the mind and the body, in particular the influence of traumatic memories in producing physical symptoms.[46] At a September 1918 conference of the International Psychoanalytic Association that brought together leading psychoanalysts from Berlin and Vienna to Budapest, including Sigmund Freud, doctors affirmed plans to build psychoanalytic war hospitals to serve the influx of traumatized veterans. The enlisting of psychoanalysis in the service of the state and military, however, came to an end with the collapse of the central powers only a few short weeks after the conference. Freud, however, felt that the war had 'proven' the validity of his theories, and expected widespread acceptance.[47] At the same time, he feared that war hysteria challenged his fundamental arguments about the origins of neurosis. Even psychotherapists who embraced psychoanalysis pointed out that the theory of psychosexual trauma in childhood as the origin of neurosis seemed to be undermined by the appearance of hysterical symptoms in otherwise healthy men at the front. In his 1920 work *Beyond the Pleasure Principle*, Freud expressed uncertainty about war neurosis, saying that no final conclusions could be made about its origins.[48] Freud conceded that environmental factors, including the enormous stress of combat, had the potential to produce repressed traumatic memories that led to neurosis. The war ultimately drove Freud to reconsider the 'death instinct' (Thanatos) as the central drive in the human psyche over the 'life instinct' (Eros).[49]

Despite Freud's own uncertainties about the origins of war hysteria, his approach to traumatic neurosis was widely influential after the war, especially in circles of professionals and non-professionals critical of military and state psychiatrists. Psychotherapists operating from a Freudian perspective saw the established neuro-psychiatrists who worked in field hospitals during the war and now for the new republic less as objective scientists defining and treating a physical injury, and more as individuals complicit in, and victims of, the whole larger experience of violence and brutality that the war unleashed in both veterans and civilians. To independent psychoanalysts working on psychologically disabled veterans immediately after the war, these war victims were only the most visible victims of mass violence, and scapegoats for a society that suffered from deeper, more widespread neuroses.

War Neurosis and Sexual Crisis

At the Institute for Scientific Sex Research (*Institut der Sexualwissenschaft*) in Berlin, sexologist Magnus Hirschfeld and his colleagues, influenced by psychoanalytic theory, assembled evidence concerning the psychological effects of the war not only on veterans, but also on German society as a whole. With Erich Wulffen, who specialized in serial murders and assisted police as a criminologist, and other specialists at the institute, Hirschfeld published *The Sexual History of the World War* (*Sittengeschichte des Weltkrieges*) and *The Sexual History of the Postwar Period* (*Sittengeschichte der Nachkriegszeit*) for both a popular audience and their professional peers.[50]

Magnus Hirschfeld affirmed Freud's argument that the increased violence of the postwar period was linked to the disruption of psychosexual drives. Hirschfeld argued, however, that the psychoanalysts' theory that the war stimulated preexisting psychosexual neuroses was not their most important contribution to understanding the effects of the war. Instead, Hirschfeld noted in *The Sexual History of the World War* that Freud's link between the violence of the war and the unleashing of sadistic instincts, particularly the death instinct, was more crucial. Further, Hirschfeld emphasized that the war created an overall atmosphere that allowed normally repressed sexual drives to manifest not only in combatants, but also in civilians not directly affected by the war. This 'release of sexual restraints' was fostered by the 'libidinous effects of war enthusiasm' beginning in 1914 and the normalization of violence that unfolded as the war dragged on for years.[51]

Hirschfeld had long been rejected by conservative, mainstream psychiatrists. After the war, Hirschfeld continued to confound neurologists by arguing that war neuroses were a universal experience that transcended class and gender boundaries, suggesting also that these neuroses were a natural, if tragic, outgrowth of the violence unleashed by the war. But one of Hirschfeld's most controversial fields of study was the topic of homosexuality. His contemporaries attacked Hirschfeld for arguing, with a mass of evidence collected at his Sexual Research Institute, that homosexuality was inborn, and thus should be decriminalized.[52] Hirschfeld was denied an academic position by mainstream psychiatrists who denounced him as a 'propagandist for homosexuality' and supporter of the political left. A Social Democrat, Jew and homosexual, Hirschfeld was one of the Nazi regime's first targets, and they destroyed his research institute on May 6, 1933, within weeks after Hitler came to power.[53]

From Hirschfeld's perspective, the war did not create the brutality that seemed endemic to postwar society, as evidenced in the rise of criminality and violence. Rather, the war intensified, accelerated and manifested preexisting unconscious instincts towards violence in society at large, not just among soldiers returning from the front. In this model, the relationship between the trench experience and postwar society was symbiotic, as prewar sublimated instincts towards destruction were unleashed at the front, and these violent urges were brought home where they spread to civilians, aggravating preexisting social and cultural decay and setting in motion a chain of social, psychological and sexual brutalization.[54] For Hirschfeld and his adherents, the war created an atmosphere of violence and lack of respect for humanity that crossed class and gender lines. Hirschfeld and his colleagues at the institute, in contrast to many state and military psychiatrists, emphasized war neurosis as a universal rather than social class specific experience.

The psychological crisis that crossed class and gender lines was the disruption and repression of healthy sexual relationships between men and women, which laid the psychological groundwork for expressions of sadistic behavior. For most veterans, Hirschfeld's colleague Erich Wulffen argued, psychosexual neuroses were uniquely traumatic because they developed in two stages: at the front and during the process of returning home. Hirschfeld and Wulffen studied cases in which soldiers were left sexually dysfunctional by the psychological and physical strain of combat. The intense brutality of the trenches caused men to experience either diminished sexual drive or abnormally powerful, even violent, forms of sexual behavior, thus giving men little chance of returning to a normal life after the war. At the same time, some women at the home front had grown insensitive and distant while their men were in the trenches, and these women were not inclined to comfort depressed and exhausted returning men with intimacy.[55] Other women experienced heightened libido, and were more sexually active than they were before the war. Men turned impotent by the terror of war made excuses to avoid resuming sexual relations, causing a level of nervous strain similar to the stress at the front, leading to nervous breakdowns.[56]

Wulffen's examination of sexual relations after the war focused on the close relationship between brutalization in the trenches and the production of psychosexual pathologies. Embracing the Freudian link between sexual and sadistic instincts, Wulffen and Hirschfeld argued that as wartime conditions of fear and deprivation disturbed normal sexual drives, instincts towards violence rose. Women became secondary psychological victims of the war, as their husbands were unable to return to prewar marital relations. Wulffen detailed cases of wives who displayed 'unbelievable levels of promiscuity' while their husbands were in the trenches, triggering resentment from men. In a number of cases, men retaliated by inflicting the violence they learned at the front on their wives and families.[57]

The case of Frau Annemarie Donner, for example, 'showed the influence of the war on German society'.[58] According to her own testimony, Frau Donner's husband returned from the war a 'more serious, closed-off, harsh and distant' man. But Wulffen did not characterize Herr Donner's condition as 'war neurosis'. What he found was a case typical of the psychological strain experienced in the majority of returning veterans. It was so common, Wulffen noted, that it did not warrant being singled out as a unique medical condition. Postwar economic difficulties further exacerbated Herr Donner's mental condition and, according to Wulffen, Donner became increasingly uninterested in his marriage and work as his thoughts remained fixated on the war. Violent outbursts punctuated his relations with his wife and friends.[59]

Because Herr Donner's condition was not taken seriously as a problem that required medical attention, Wulffen insisted, the situation became catastrophic. Frau Donner told police her husband was 'sexually weak' even before the war, when he had never been a very 'sexually attentive man'. But after the war, violent tendencies replaced all attempts at sexual relations. Frau Donner was unable to get a divorce. In an attempt to escape her traumatic home life she pursued her dream of attending film school, where she fell in love with another man, Otto Krönert. Krönert was also a veteran but, according to Wulffen, he was less brutalized by the war. Frau Donner again confronted her husband with demands for a divorce, a scuffle unfolded, and Krönert unintentionally killed Herr Donner with the old army pistol that the latter carried around with him.[60]

In a sensationalized trial, Annemarie Donner and Otto Krönert were sentenced first to death and then to life in prison for killing Herr Donner. The Dresden court called it a 'crime of passion'. Deferring to a psychiatrist who worked for the Labor Ministry's health care system, the judge concluded that psychological disorders were not a factor in this case. Wulffen argued that the court was wrong, and criticized doctors for ignoring the role played by the war in ultimately destroying the Donners' marriage. Wulffen further argued that the postwar criminal justice system needed to take into account the effects of the war in producing ongoing violence. In the case of Frau Donner, this meant drawing connections between her desperation and the emotionally distant, sexually unresponsive and violent man that emerged from the trenches.[61] Frau Donner's choices and behavior were also a product of the war, Wulffen emphasized. The war destroyed not only her husband and her marriage, but also invigorated her with the notion that she was entitled to radical change and could break free from social persecution. Magnus Hirschfeld also concluded that this sense of independence that sparked greater self-determination was a larger effect of the war for women. For men, however, the war did just the opposite. According to military psychiatrists, the front experience was supposed to harden the nerves of men and counter perceived prewar trends towards decadence and femininity. Instead, men did not develop 'steel nerves' as expected, but psychological deterioration and collapse.

Echoing Freud's thesis in *Civilization and its Discontents*, Hirschfeld interpreted postwar neuroses as a manifestation of already-present and universal drives and instincts towards destruction. In contrast, establishment psychiatrists working for the Labor Ministry and social critics writing for the public were most concerned with how the war disrupted the supposedly stable prewar bourgeois milieu. But there were similarities between Hirschfeld and mainstream psychiatrists. Hirschfeld targeted women as guilty of exacerbating sexual tensions and psychological breakdowns in men. Women were expected to be responsible for understanding what caused their husbands' sexual dysfunction and for nurturing them through their mental anguish. Hirschfeld even apologized for the frustration and anger in returning veterans by arguing that they were too traumatized and exhausted to intimate their psychological problems to their wives.[62] Men's fears about how their wives would react when they learned that they were afraid in combat left them unwilling to initiate the communication necessary to affirm, confront, and heal psychological wounds. In Hirschfeld's picture of postwar social life, women were the agents of healing and recovery, while men were expected to remain passive, too haunted by their traumatic pasts to regenerate themselves and move on.

Women, in Hirschfeld and Wulffen's analysis, were potentially as dangerous as the trench experience. They could inflict secondary trauma if they did not fulfill their prescribed roles. Wulffen portrayed disabled men as helpless objects at the mercy of women:

> At the time the husbands returned home, wives looked at their sick, weakened men, and looked around for new young lovers. Some wives poisoned their husbands in order to live with their lovers ... one woman admitted in front of the judge: 'My dear husband was very sick. I was tired of the long hours of nursing and thought to myself, it would be better for him and for me if he died'.[63]

The desperation women felt to rid themselves of reminders of the war actually drew Wulffen's sympathy. On one hand, Wulffen emphasized the cruel, insensitive character of women in these cases, but he also equivocated on the point of whether women could be blamed for no longer accepting their roles as unconditional care-givers. He portrayed women as ultimately victims of the same uncontrollable, sadistic urges that overtook everyone who witnessed mass violence, whether from the trenches or on the home front.[64]

In this model, anyone who survived the war years was capable of criminal behavior. Veterans from the front were not the only men who transmitted the violence of the war to postwar society. Most of the famous serial killers of the time, sadistic predators whom Hirschfeld and Wulffen characterized as quintessential symbols of Germany's social and cultural crisis, were not veterans and thus not 'war neurotics', in the prevailing definition of the term, which required that their wounds be directly war-related. However, according to Wulffen, they were ultimately psychological victims of the war. 'The war', Wulffen argued, 'mobilized these psychopaths with its violence and its devaluation of human life'.[65] While Wulffen's psychoanalytic model locates the origin of neuroses in psychosexual trauma, the war accelerated and intensified such latent neuroses, and turned men with socially functional, adjustable minor psychopathologies into violent, sadistic monsters. The 'primitive and animal-like atmosphere of the trenches' liberated already present 'perversions' like masochism and sadism from the unconsciousness of those who had been only functional before the war.[66] Fritz Haarmann, one of the Weimar period's most notorious serial killers, was diagnosed before the war as 'mentally weak' (*Schwachsinn*) and unfit for work. His worst crime before 1914 was chronic fighting with his father, landing him, repeatedly, in institutions and prisons. The war, according to Wulffen, transformed Haarmann from a nondescript neurotic into a murderous predator. Though Haarmann himself was never at the front, the nationally ordained mass violence in the trenches created an atmosphere of that released Haarmann's deeper, unconscious drives and stimulated violent behavior. In twenty-six murders committed after the war, characterized by extreme sadism and torture, Haarmann imitated the incomprehensible violence of the trenches in a postwar setting. Another infamous serial killer, Peter Kürten, was also allegedly a product of the war. With neuroses stemming from an abusive father, and a history of hereditary mental illness, Kürten emerged as a sociopath before the war with the murder of an eleven-year-old girl. However, it was not until after the war that he became a fully-fledged serial killer, murdering dozens of young women with a degree of sadism that terrified Düsseldorf for months.[67] Kürten actually provided the real-life model for Peter Lorre's cinematic icon in Fritz Lang's *M*, which brought a new figure to the screen, the 'psycho killer', whose psychological illness and violent urges gave audiences a new glimpse into how the criminal sociopath reflected larger social and cultural disorders. References to the war are imbedded in the film's imagery, reminding audiences of the connections between the trenches and postwar violence.[68] Lang's film mirrors Hirschfeld's thesis that these murderers were merely products of their environment and symptoms of the larger psychoses present in society, where diminished respect for human life infected non-combatants as well as veterans. The murders, Wulffen argued, were outside the state-sanctioned killing zones of the trenches, but they came from the same psychological urges that fed the violence of the Western front.

Hirschfeld and Wulffen aimed at uncovering a larger psychosis that afflicted modern civilization, in which the war was both a symptom, and catalyst, of man's darker instincts. The line between 'criminals' and 'normal' individuals, 'doctors' and 'patients', eroded in this environment. In Hirschfeld's analysis, the state-employed psychiatrists who espoused what Hirschfeld characterized as a limited, neurologically-based definition of war neurosis, were really trying to conceal the widespread psychological consequences of the war. In military psychiatrists' prescriptions of electro-therapy and suggestion therapy, Hirschfeld found evidence of sexual sadism present in the state's treatment of war victims. The electrotherapy known as the Kaufmann method, developed as a cure for war neurosis and used as a way to uncover alleged fakers, was, according to Hirschfeld, really a form of torture that tapped into doctors' sexual perversions and pleasure in causing pain.[69] Hirschfeld pointed to Karl Kraus' war drama, *Die letzten Tage der Menschheit*, in which sadistic doctors enthusiastically carry out the orders of officers looking for shirkers by administering the highest levels of electric current to screaming war neurotics until the patients die. In Kraus' drama, the general even informs the complicit psychiatrist: 'Indeed, it would be best to put all the war neurotics in a barracks and then abandon them to a beautiful artillery barrage. That would help them forget their sufferings and make them useful front soldiers again!'[70] In Hirschfeld's analysis, military psychiatrists held the power to define the boundaries between the 'sane' and the 'insane'. The war ultimately unleashed such a storm of sadism that these boundaries eroded, undermining the notion that war neurosis was a containable, or socially specific illness limited to those from a working-class background who had been in the trenches.

In his list of disorders caused by the war, Hirschfeld added these 'sexual perversions' exhibited by doctors who performed electrotherapy. Such neuroses, according to Hirschfeld, were no less widespread than other forms of mental illness triggered by the war, but they were forms that society made a great effort to cover up by focusing on 'war neurosis' and the particular experiences of those in the trenches. Hirschfeld located a series of sexual neuroses that he believed were directly related to the war, including dependence for sexual stimulation on near death experiences, and a rise in voyeurism, infantilism and other psychosexual neuroses.[71] Here Hirschfeld once again parted company with the state's psychiatrists by deemphasizing social class as a factor determining inclination towards psychological deviance. These neuroses occurred in both enlisted men and officers, he argued, proving that the psychological effects of the war were universally felt.

Even psychiatrists who did not ascribe to the psychoanalytic approach expressed fear that war-related sexual neuroses crossed class lines. Munich psychiatrist Dr P. Lißmann, who served as a military doctor at the front for over three years, wrote in 1919 that sexual pathologies found in front veterans persisted after the war.[72] Like Hirschfeld, Lißmann was convinced that sexual abnormalities were the most widespread psychological consequence of the war, and that these disorders continued to disrupt the postwar social fabric without showing signs of healing. Lißmann, however, did not agree with psychoanalytic interpretations of these neuroses: 'hysterical or severe anxiety neuroses in the Freudian sense did not appear'.[73] Neurosis was not caused by traumatic psychosexual development or mental stress at the front. Instead, Lißmann claimed, these sexual disorders were physical in origin. The 'steel bath of nerves' inflicted such sustained tension that it produced neurological disturbances and hormonal changes that were often permanent.[74] Most men did not manifest the familiar symptoms of war neurosis such as tremors and uncontrollable shaking. Instead, a large number of men – perhaps more than were diagnosed with war neurosis, Lißmann speculated – experienced sexual dysfunctions that were often overshadowed by other psychological and physiological symptoms. These sexual disorders included the inability to achieve erection, sudden involuntary ejaculation without erection, and loss of interest in sexual activity. He linked these symptoms directly to the front experience, where terrifying artillery bombardments shook men so fundamentally that their sexual physiology was permanently altered. Such damage was found in both officers and enlisted men who were otherwise normal before 1914: 'In the field reports I have already explained how many officers and men with otherwise completely normal nervous systems were either totally unable to achieve an erection or suffered from extreme defects'.[75] The psychological tensions found in war, he argued, also led men who had once conformed to accepted Wilhelmian social values to engage in taboo activities in order to relieve stress, including compulsive 'excessive masturbation' and homosexual behavior between what Lißmann described as otherwise 'normal', heterosexual men, including officers.[76]

The social leveling of sexual dysfunction created considerable anxiety. Lißmann was most concerned with the spread of sexual deviance to the middle classes. The war did not create these 'sexual pathologies', as they had already been present in the working class, but the close proximity of men at the front, and widespread stress combined with sexual deprivation resulted in a breakdown of standards of behavior among officers.[77] Lißmann noted that these changes in sexual behavior were particularly dangerous because they occurred in men who appeared outwardly healthy before and after the war, remained in good social standing, but had inwardly become sexually dysfunctional and thus social deviants. He warned that because sexual disorders could be concealed, doctors could not control these psychologically disturbed men. Marriages and moral standards among Germany's social elite were on the verge of collapse, setting into motion a national crisis.[78]

Fears about the moral disintegration of German manhood resonated widely. In the popular press, psychologically disturbed German soldiers were portrayed as sadistic, sexually deviant men who transmitted immorality and brutality learned at the front to German society. In widely disseminated, thinly-veiled sensationalism masquerading as social commentary, psychologically disabled veterans appeared as criminals, sex fiends, and murderous predators. Conservative commentators who penned these tracts warned that 'war neurosis' was only the most obvious example when it came to describing the psychological consequences of the war and Germany's moral condition. Reflecting the studies produced in diverse psychiatric circles, social critics argued that Germany's moral and psychological deterioration was not limited to those highly visible, shaking, mentally disabled soldiers who clogged street corners and subway stations. Instead, they warned, the uncontrollable violence and alleged sexual perversions in the trenches corrupted even, to some degree, the most 'moral' and patriotic veterans, as well as women on the home front.

The taboo-breaking by front soldiers in the trenches allegedly spilled into postwar society because these behaviors seemed so normal. The moral universe of prewar Europe, as many observers noted, had turned upside down.[79] This implosion of the prewar status quo was lamented by a number of groups, in particular conservatives who resented social leveling and the disruption of traditional class and gender roles.[80] Journalist H.A. Preiß, for example, in his 1921 booklet *The Sexual Cruelties of Love-Crazy Men* (*Geschlechtliche Grausamkeiten liebestoller Menschen*), argued that the main 'neurosis' produced by the war was a general deterioration of moral values. The war unleashed 'passions' that could not be contained by pre-1914 middle-class moral structures.[81] The front was an other-worldly place that destroyed 'normal' sexual values and behavior, which he defined as monogamous relations between married partners.[82] Modern industrial warfare was unique, he argued, because it produced such a high level of emotional stress that even 'normal' men, in addition to those who were 'intrinsically degenerate' men, turned to homosexuality, masturbation, fetishism, and other 'abnormal sexual practices' to 'relieve their tense nerves'.[83] Preiß claimed that these sexual practices occurred so frequently that they were not so much the symptom of deeper neuroses, but rather typical reactions of otherwise psychologically healthy men to the extreme conditions at the front. Once men at the front became dependent on such sexual behaviors, Preiß concluded, it became difficult to readjust when they returned home.

Psychological stress at the front was not the only cause of moral deterioration, according to Preiß. The socioeconomic conditions created by total war also contributed to Germany's moral and psychological deterioration. Temporary measures like the Hindenburg program, which brought women from both middle- and working-class backgrounds into the munitions factories, were necessary to run the war economy. But these programs unleashed a pandora's box of social ills. Women with good bourgeois morals who worked on the assembly lines encountered different social standards and succumbed to what Preiß characterized as the sexual behavior of 'the masses'. On the Hindenburg program, Preiß lamented: 'It is no wonder that the present generation grows up without good breeding and morals'.[84] The physical stress of work, Preiß noted, was less dangerous than the psychological independence some women experienced, particularly middle-class women.[85] Because women could now rent their own apartments, and visit movie houses and restaurants unchaperoned, Preiß feared that they would seek to satisfy their sexual desires outside of marriage.

Though very few women actually achieved the independent status Preiß demonized, the image of the 'new woman' was powerful.[86] Preiß predicted that the 'well-bred, loyal German wife' would disappear, to be replaced by the 'sex-crazy girl' who was 'no role model for children'.[87] These women, he believed, would betray their loyal husbands – first by abandoning their good morals, then by abandoning their homes. Exhausted and stressed-out men returning from the trenches, Preiß feared, would find a postwar domestic environment as morally reprehensible as life in the trenches. In these conditions, psychologically strained men would never heal, but actually grow worse. It was thus feared that standards of sexual behavior among the 'well-bred' degenerated until their moral behavior was indistinguishable from those in the lower classes.

Conservative critics perceived a psychological leveling caused by the war, in which boundaries of middle- and working-class values and behavior disappeared. This phenomenon was described by journalist Hans Georg Baumgarth in his sensationalist pamphlet for the public, *Sexual Life in the War*. In Baumgarth's analysis, the war eroded bourgeois morality with 'primitive' instincts.[88] Like Preiß, Baumgarth believed that the war stimulated pathological sexual desires that resulted in a collapse of prescribed sexual characteristics in men and women of good social standing. Morally fit middle-class men were unable to cope with the incredible cruelty and violence of modern industrial warfare, and the result was that these men lost control of themselves and, most alarmingly, their sexual behavior. These veterans then returned home with what Baumgarth called 'primitive sexual instincts' and inflicted violence on women with their 'bestial sexual acts'.[89] Humans, he argued, became like animals, with violence and sexual passion becoming indistinguishable.[90]

For Baumgarth, the only crisis worse than widespread male sexual deviance was the proliferation of sexual passions in women. The war also released 'lust' ('*Wohllust*') in women on the home front, leading to feelings of sexual desire that he believed endangered the existing social structure: 'Of course the war has also unleashed lusts in our women. Men are fewer and fewer, nature and the aroused blood flow forth, especially with young women who, if the sensibility is once awoken, can be much more lustful than men. Are all the divorces thus so odd?'[91] After most wars, he argued, life returned to normal as psychologically traumatized men returned to the arms of nurturing, morally healthy women. However, the sexual degeneration of both sexes in this war, Baumgarth warned, shattered postwar chances for a nurturing environment that would heal the moral and psychological wounds of the nation.[92]

For a number of conservative Germans, the 'primitive instincts' unleashed by the war did more than just corrupt Germans of otherwise good social standing and endanger the postwar social structure. The alleged moral degeneration that ran rampant in the trenches and at home also caused Germany's defeat. These critics placed blame specifically on psychologically disabled men for being morally too weak to make the sacrifices necessary to win the war. Degenerate behavior, civilians argued, distracted front-line troops from the task of defeating Germany's enemies, causing German men to place the survival of the nation second to their own survival.

Parallel to the 'stab-in-the-back' legend that started to take shape in the last weeks of the war, embittered home-front survivors argued that they had been betrayed by soldiers at the front who lacked the necessary self-control to win, leading the nation to disaster. Catholic Church activist Frau Young-Rißmann, in her speech 'The Lost War and the Moral Question', delivered to the White Cross Association for Moral Order (*Der Sittlichkeitsbund vom Weißen Kreuz*) in 1923, argued that civilians remained loyal to the end with a higher level of moral and psychological strength than many men in the trenches. She accused German soldiers of sabotaging the decisive March 1918 offensive by getting bogged down in sexual hedonism and drinking binges when they could have pushed on towards Paris. The common soldier betrayed the nation: 'Though the Germans won the battles, they lost the war through sexual offense and alcohol addiction ... The German giant was not defeated militarily, but it was internally, morally ruined, with God's unbroken sword passed over to the hand of the enemy'.[93] Young-Rißmann bitterly described scenes of soldiers finally breaking through British and French lines in the early summer of 1918, only to waste time with the prostitutes and booze that came with new territorial gains. These men, she noted, then proceeded to ruin the social fabric that held the nation together: the German family. By bringing venereal diseases and alcoholism home with them, veterans were more dangerous at home than in the trenches. These moral transgressions prepared the way for the collapse at home, where easily influenced civilians lost their will when they saw men at the front gratify their own needs rather than make sacrifices for the nation. Most civilians, meanwhile, provided unwavering morale and kept their nerves at home. Young-Rißmann concluded her speech with a general argument that the political and economic collapse of the nation lay in the 'weak inner moral strength' of German soldiers, who were easily taken advantage of psychologically by those on the political left who wanted to end the war and foment revolution.[94]

Battles over Diagnosis: Veterans' Attempts to Define 'War Psychosis'

Psychological wounds played a crucial role in this postwar clash between civilians and soldiers over who lost the war. Who lost their nerves first? Who was most loyal to the nation? In their tracts on the psychological trauma caused by the war, many former front soldiers readily admitted that they were psychologically exhausted by the front experience. However, veterans were also quick to point out that civilians' nerves were no stronger than those of front fighters. According to the far right veterans' organizations like the 'Steel Helmet', civilians were the weakest, and thus the culprits for the defeat.[95] However, many returning veterans embraced the idea that Germany's psychological breakdown was a collective experience, and that both front veterans and civilians suffered from mental trauma, even if they appeared physically whole.

One of the most interesting examples of veterans who admitted that soldiers' nerves were indeed shattered by the war was Eugen Neter, a field surgeon who described himself as first and foremost a front soldier whose aim it was to restore the reputation of the average infantryman. Neter's perspective was exceptional. He was a doctor who expressed such a high level of sympathy for front veterans who broke down under fire. He argued that one needed to strip away the postwar political biases that shaped narratives written by doctors, civilians, and veterans on the psychological trauma caused by the war, and analyze it in the context of the war itself.[96] Neter claimed that as a front doctor he had the unique opportunity to observe the fighting strength of the average soldier, and thus was in a privileged position to know whether or not the army was betrayed at the moment of victory, as many political groups claimed. He argued that the war was not lost because of a 'stab-in-the-back' by the political left, a theory that he described as 'too expressly political in character to be useful'. Instead, the typical front soldier was mentally on the brink of collapse in the summer of 1918, and the war was lost because it became psychologically and physically unbearable. Neter criticized the political right for denying the reality of psychological and physical defeat. At the same time, Neter also chastised the political left, as he insisted that the war was justified, and he idealized what he characterized as the faith of the average front soldier in his nation and victory, which he believed the left did not recognize.[97]

An iconoclast for his social and professional position, Neter was convinced that the average front soldier was the scapegoat of different groups behind the lines who were themselves unwilling to go on making sacrifices and frustrated at the duration of the war. The 'stab-in-the-back' theory, Neter claimed, was actually a conspiracy theory developed by patriotic, conservative civilians who wanted to cover up their own unwillingness to continue making the necessary sacrifices. Unlike civilians, Neter argued, front-line troops 'did their duty' until the end of the war, despite real psychological exhaustion, and revolutionary propaganda had no effect on the fighting strength of the average soldier.[98] Neter accused civilians of losing the will to fight: 'The hunger blockade destroyed the German *Volk* more psychologically than physically [... the blockade] severely shook their belief in victory, indeed even weakened their will to victory'.[99] It was not just groups traditionally labeled disloyal and unpatriotic, Neter observed. Even those who started the war with enthusiasm descended into deep pessimism and eventually defeatism. Instead of empathizing with front soldiers and identifying with them over their shared psychological stress, civilians projected psychological weakness on men in the trenches. This was the origin of 'a deep psychological gulf between the front and home', he added, which 'deepened more and more from 1917 onward. Neither understood the other anymore'.[100] In this vein, Neter was less convinced than many of his colleagues that a betrayal from left-wing revolutionaries was the main problem for soldiers. Instead, he saw a deeper crisis of resentments felt by exhausted civilians who had enthusiastically supported the war, but eventually were unwilling to make the necessary sacrifices, leading them to seek scapegoats for the failure of the home front.

Neter also highlighted what he saw as a betrayal by army commanders who knew that front-line troops were pushed to the limit. The psychological breakdown of the troops, he argued, began long before 1918. It was rooted in the stalemated nature of trench warfare, which caused combat soldiers to sink into a 'fatalistic powerlessness' when they dug in after the battle of the Marne in 1914.[101] The failure of the high command to achieve a breakthrough worsened the morale of the troops. By the spring of 1918, Generals Ludendorff and von Hindenburg knew that the troops were stretched to the limit, but pushed on with the March offensive. Neter claimed that on the eve of the attack, the generals contributed to the fatalism of the average soldier by stating that this was a last-ditch effort to win the war before American troops and resources arrived to tip the balance. This, Neter argued, signaled a lack of confidence in the abilities of front-line troops, leaving these men demoralized and disenfranchised from their leadership.[102] This demoralization, combined with the deep physical and psychological exhaustion that set in by 1918, resulted in Germany's collapse.

The psychological condition of the troops was difficult to verify, and thus a point of heated controversy. Indeed, nobody could prove to what extent front veterans and civilians were psychologically traumatized or intact. Neter argued that the 'stab-in-the-back' legend, most vehemently promoted by veterans and civilians on the political right, was in reality a conscious denial of Germany's psychological collapse, especially in the last days of the war. Historians have noted that in the chaos of September-November 1918 both men and officers, faced with imminent disaster, chose to avoid risk, disobeyed orders, or even fled from duty, and later embraced the 'stab-in-the-back' theory to conceal their own actions and explain defeat.[103] Even General Ludendorff, instrumental in engineering the 'stab-in-the-back' when he tried to deflect responsibility for defeat to the Social Democrats and his political enemies, began his hunt for scapegoats after his own nervous breakdown in late September 1918 when it was impossible to deny the fact that his last offensive had failed.[104] This image of an intact, undefeated army was central to postwar literature written by the political right. It even appeared in the rhetoric of the left, most notably in Friedrich Ebert's speech to returning soldiers in Berlin in December 1918.[105]

Neter rebutted what he believed was the main feature of the 'stab-in-the-back' theory as it was circulated by many veterans and their sympathizers: the average front-line soldier remained undefeated in combat. The image of a physically and psychologically intact army was, Neter argued, easily transparent. In reality, he wrote, the army as a whole had already experienced psychological collapse long before the high command acknowledged the war was over:

When my regiment marched through Mainz on December 2, 1918
– with the unshaken commander, straight from the trenches, at the

head of the troops with his all too familiar pipe in his mouth – they gave the outward impression of being a completely disciplined, able-bodied unit; but in their inner fabric they lacked any strength. They were tired and hopeless, unable to put up any further defense. The soul [Seele – also 'psyche'] had deserted their still strong bodies.[106]

The 'stab-in-the-back' theory was founded on superficial interpretations of German fighting strength, Neter concluded. Veterans who were most vocal about their supposedly 'undefeated' condition repressed their internal weakness and frayed nerves. He warned readers that even if the returning troops marched home in good order and appeared whole, they were internally shattered, changed men.

Neter was also intensely bitter about what he perceived as the unwillingness of civilians to admit that the war was lost. This denial, he warned, had disastrous consequences for the postwar world. Until the majority of Germans acknowledged that the nation in 1918 was in the midst of a widespread collective breakdown, there would be no chance at healing the wounds of war. As long as different social and political groups denied their own responsibility and the role of the war in destroying the mental and physical health of front veterans, they would also deny assistance to these groups and exclude them from the project of postwar recovery. Civilians and front veterans, Neter insisted, had to overcome the shame and stigma associated with psychological breakdown and begin the process of national healing with what he characterized as an objective assessment of the collective mental and physical exhaustion caused by the war.[107] In order to do this, it had to be recognized that the war, and not particular social groups or political organizations, was responsible for Germany's crisis. Only in this context would psychologically disabled veterans be integrated into postwar society, as victims rather than perpetrators of Germany's national catastrophe.

This question of who was most responsible for Germany's breakdown – front soldiers or civilians, middle or working class, political right or left, men or women – dominated postwar debates over the effects of the war. War neurotics were a catalyst for these debates. Different groups fought fiercely over who was responsible for these wounds and whether or not these survivors threatened the postwar order or demanded empathy and support. But an even deeper question within these debates was who, exactly, was 'neurotic'? Veterans categorized as 'insane' challenged the idea of the war neurotic as a construction of the conservative elite who started and enthusiastically supported the war. Those labeled 'war neurotics' were not criminals or deviants, but actually the most 'sane' individuals who protested the slaughter in the trenches. Organizations founded by veterans that declared themselves above party politics, but were pacifist and leftist, sprang up immediately after the war and published tracts on the psychological experience of it. These organizations protested military psychiatrists and conservative social critics who portrayed front veterans as 'psychotic' and responsible for spreading moral degeneracy and disloyalty to the home front. The essential 'psychosis', these veterans argued, lay in the patriotism and war fever that kept the war going long after front soldiers were thoroughly disillusioned. The real criminals of the war years were the perpetrators, not the victims, of the war.

An example of veterans inverting definitions of 'sane' versus 'insane' can be found in the Association of Pacifist War Veterans and Friends of Peace. In 1920, this group published a series of pamphlets that denounced the war enthusiasm that swept Germany in 1914 and they warned against further outbreaks of nationalist sentiment. This excitement for war, association member Hermann Klamfoth argued, was the original 'war psychosis' that infected the German army:

> The lies of diplomats and army leaders and the chatter of professors and journalists hypnotized the *Volk* and aroused a dangerous war psychosis, to which the war literature also gave its stamp of approval. These included murderous, greedy songs of hate and the blood-thirsty, intoxicating calls for heroism and victory.[108]

Klamfoth appropriated the term *Kriegspsychose* to describe the mentality of Germany's military elite and intelligentsia. War psychosis, according to Klamfoth, did not originate in the psyche of the front soldier, or in his alleged weakness in the face of the enemy. Instead, it trickled down from the militarized culture via propaganda and indoctrination.

In order to heal the psychological wounds of war, Klamfoth argued, the home front still had to purge itself of the 'war psychosis' that sent a generation of men to their slaughter. However, this seemed unlikely. The Association of Pacifist War Veterans produced an image of a neurotic, unrepentant home front that awaited returning veterans. Front soldiers, in contrast, were making greater progress in overcoming their traumatic pasts. Veterans had already experienced disillusionment with nationalism, the association asserted, and they characterized this as the first step towards psychological rehabilitation and enlightenment. War neurotics in particular experienced an intense level of 'awakening'. They were so transformed by their experience, Klamfoth claimed, that they were unable to reassimilate into an unreformed world, and thus they were treated as outcasts.[109]

In the world view espoused by the Association of Pacifist War Veterans, psychologically disabled veterans were not the 'deviants'. Rather, they were the most sane individuals, ostracized because the rest of the world had not yet reached their stage of development. This topsy-turvy paradigm was expressed in their first publication, which featured a fictional story by Hans Schlottau on the experiences of a soldier driven insane by the horrors of war. Schlottau describes his narrative as the 'vision' of a mentally disturbed war victim, whom he portrayed as an apocalyptic prophet. The soldier is taken to a field hospital, where he rails at the world that he believes is morally rotten because it enthusiastically embraces the propaganda of hate. The 'robbers, murderers and beasts of the world' have eliminated all traces of love and compassion, he screams at his nurse. The nurse believes that his rants are caused by his feverish dreams, and she tries to shake him out of his delirium, but he screams at her that he is awake, and that it is the world that is feverish and locked in a nightmare of murder and blood.[110]

For Schlottau, the home front remained paralyzed by its own 'delirium' about the war. Front veterans could see through the lies of wartime propaganda. Civilians, however, remained unreformed. This made it impossible for people at home to provide the compassion necessary for disabled veterans to recover. Fearful that their sacrifices were in vain, civilians continued to embrace the 'war psychosis' that had fueled the excitement of 1914 and denied the murderous reality of the trenches. Schlottau created a dichotomy of enlightened veterans versus naive civilians, with the latter living in a dream world. The representatives of care and restoration, embodied in the nurse, refuse to see the world from the soldier's 'awakened' point of view, but rather try to bring him into their own unreality. Long after 1918, psychologically disabled veterans would continue to argue that it was the health care providers who were insane, and that 'war neurosis' was a term that more appropriately described doctors and the state than war victims.

Schlottau's view that mentally disabled veterans held a privileged, more highly developed interpretation of the war rang true for a wide number of men diagnosed as war neurotics. Veterans writing on the psychological effects of the war battled over competing interpretations of the war experience and who possessed the authentic memory of the war. This was a highly politicized debate. As will be explored further in later chapters, organizations on the political left gradually tried to mobilize war neurotics into a pacifist front against right-wing myths of the war experience as a healing, unifying, and strengthening psychological experience. The war literature later adapted by ideologues on the left and the right focused on a central issue of debate: was the war essentially brutalizing and destructive to the psyches of veterans, making them alien to civilians largely sheltered from the horrors of combat? Or did war improve the minds of veterans, sharpening their instincts and elevating them to a plane of existence above that of the fragmented, decaying civilian world?

The question of whether or not the war was ennobling or brutalizing held the key to whether or not men could reintegrate into the postwar order. Men suffering from mental scars, formally diagnosed or not, reflected on this question, and on the issue of whether or not they could ever heal. Some men argued that the horrors of the war equipped them to navigate the rigors of postwar life more effectively. This was a familiar argument from veterans on the political right in particular, as they claimed that they were entitled to lead the nation because they had survived the 'baptism of fire', which had allegedly purified them psychologically.[111] But there were also men who claimed that traumatic memories made them more appreciative of everyday life and less concerned with the hatred and bitterness that seemed to govern postwar politics and society. In his memoirs published in the *Frankfurter Zeitung*, veteran Hans Simons, for example, observed that the end of the war meant something fundamental that was detached from debates over the effects of the war. 'Revolution' simply meant coming home and escaping the trauma of combat:

> With that [armistice] we came home. To us that is what the war meant, when all other meanings had been lost in the decay of time. Thus revolution and republic have one meaning. We call it peace and the unity of nations. *Unsentimental* [italicized in text] – because we have felt things and are able to set aside the sentiments and resentments of others. *Realistic* – we had certainly thrown away illusions with all the other baggage of volunteer soldiers. *Fearless* – because long ago fear was thrust into the world of tranquility[112]

Transitioning home thus brought a state of safety only veterans could appreciate. Debates over the legitimacy of the revolution and the republic seemed inconsequential to Simons who saw these events simply as a new life condition that was free from fear and death. In this context, Simons saw himself transcending the thinking of civilians, whom he characterized as drenched in petty 'sentiment and resentments' and less emotionally or psychologically developed compared to men who survived the trenches. Civilians thus were still traumatized by the war, whereas veterans had broken into another state of existence that made them more rational and calmer.

Simons' interpretation of the war experience as creating a fundamental break between civilians and veterans was widespread in war memoirs and literature. Both the political left and right emphasized that these groups were separated by their memories of the war. Veterans, it was argued, lived in another world through their memories, which formed a psychological barrier between them and those who were not in the trenches. In some cases, this led to civilians imagining veterans as strange beings consumed by the traumatic memories of the war. In a 1920 short novel called *Chains – Victim of the Inner Front*, veteran Rudolf Müller describes his main character as still at war with memories of the trenches, his 'inner front'.[113]

The 'internal tension' (*innere Zerissenheit*) felt by returning soldiers, including those suffering from visible wounds or psychological wounds, could never fully be understood by civilians, he emphasized. Müller's main character feels betrayed that the war left him mentally shattered, when he had been promised that it would strengthen his nerves and make him into a man. At the same time he feels ashamed that his nerves could not stand up to the war experience, and he hates himself as much as he hates insensitive civilians, among whom he feels like a stranger.[114]

Observers argued that those who directly experienced the war saw and thought about the world differently from individuals who had no first-hand knowledge of the trenches. When the film *Westfront 1918* appeared in 1930, Alma Würth, reviewer for the social democratic-leaning war victims' organization, the *Reichsbund*, speculated that it was an entirely different film for men who were actually in the trenches or women who felt the stress on the home front. Audience members who had no direct experience with combat, especially young males, she emphasized, were not able to comprehend the film's graphic depiction of war's horrors. Instead, they distanced themselves from, or even romanticized, the overwhelming terror on screen:

> One would like to be able to look into the psyches of youth [watching *Westfront 1918*], would like to be able to register their feelings, what moves them, if they are fascinated by looking at the film, which shows bomb explosions, going over the top, gas attacks and all the other scenes. The film resuscitates once again the things the deeply traumatized us. Does youth see these things with eyes that are different than ours, which experienced these events. Could perhaps a young man at *Westfront 1918*, if he does not have a voice of enlightenment standing beside him, confuse film and reality with each other and read something romantic out of those places of horror?[115]

In contrast, Würth imagined, it was a whole different film in the minds of people who had been directly traumatized by war. Consistent with other observers in social democratic circles, she described veterans and family members who suffered under wartime shortages and stress as having a shared consciousness when it came to war trauma. In this light, survivors lived with a catalog of traumatic memories triggered by images in the film, which they neither romanticized nor relished:

> Whoever knows war and has learned to hate it sees its cruelty, its terror, its insanity; whoever has not experienced it places their own wishful dreams in that hollow space between representation and reality, the imagination of their unconscious, in short, he sees

something different than us. What is life to us is theater to the next generation.[116]

The *Reichsbund* emphasized that veterans and their families who remembered the war were morally responsible to the younger generation, teaching them the truth of the war and the value of peace against propaganda that mythologized the 'heroic ideal' and sterilized the horrors of modern combat.[117] The social democratic *Reichsbund* designated traumatized veterans and their families as caretakers of the authentic memory of the war. It was these men and women who did not 'confuse representation and reality', but rather preserved the true images of war, and the 'authentic' emotional responses, in their traumatized unconsciousness. On one hand, there was the danger of veterans becoming isolated with their memories, unable to share their traumatic past with a new generation that preferred images of war that resembled prewar myths and ideals. At the same time, the political left tried to mobilize traumatized veterans as educators in what they saw as the authentic memory of the war. A later chapter on the left's approach to war neurosis will explore how the left hoped this role as antiwar activists would give survivors a sense of purpose and chance to overcome the potentially paralyzing effects of nightmares.

The political right also portrayed veterans as living in a different mental world from other individuals. In the literature of the right, however, this was restricted to a masculine experience, with men in the trenches undergoing a unique psychological transformation that made them superior to those at home. The right saw these men as privileged not only because of their 'authentic' experience, but also because that experience allegedly turned them into transcendent individuals. This is explicitly found in the writings of Ernst Jünger, which were cherished by members of the right-wing paramilitary organization, the 'Steel Helmet', and later celebrated by the Nazis who idealized Jünger's glorification of the war experience.[118] Jünger volunteered in the army in 1914 and for his battlefield heroism he won Germany's highest medal, the *Pour le Mérite*. During the brief breakthrough on the Western front in March 1918, Jünger spearheaded newly-invented stormtrooper tactics which he described in spiritual terms in his postwar work. In his most famous writings, published in the 1920s, including *Storm of Steel* and *War as Inner Experience*, Jünger portrayed combat as a transcendent experience that elevated him to status as a Nietzschean 'superman', beyond the trappings of civilized society. In *Storm of Steel*, Jünger described his psyche tormented by the ecstasy and brutality of war, turning him simultaneously into a being where 'the godlike and bestial inextricably mingled ...The tremendous force of destruction that bent over the field of battle was concentrated in our brains. So may men of the Renaissance have been locked in their passions, so may a Cellini have raged or werewolves have howled and hunted through the night on the track of blood'.[119] Though Jünger constantly celebrates how the war experience transformed him into a superhuman, psychologically hardened individual, his representation of war cannot completely shake anxieties that there is a mirror experience in which he is also turned into something inhuman, brutalized and churned into another meaningless unit on the field of modern mechanized warfare.[120]

The war literature extolled by the political right, while celebrating the virtues of combat, often also expressed anxiety about the psychological effects of the war. One of the most popular, and widely published, accounts of the war was Manfred von Richthofen's *The Red Battle Flier* (*Der Rote Kampfflieger*). Probably the most famous German soldier of the war, the popularly known 'Red Baron' wrote, or at least dictated, his memoir of flying at the front while recuperating from a head-shot wound inflicted in July 1917. Von Richthofen's narrative, which appeared shortly before he was killed in April 1918, conveys a sense of enthusiasm for the war and emphasizes the unity, discipline and masculine virtues he discovered while defending the fatherland.[121] In 1925, Berlin came to a standstill when von Richthofen's remains were returned from France for burial in the Cemetery of the Invalids (*Invalidenfriedhof*), with von Hindenburg and numerous military luminaries pronouncing the dead airman a sacred example of Germany's heroic sacrifices.[122] After 1933, the Nazis republished *The Red Battle Flier* in the millions, and they mythologized von Richthofen as an ultimate pillar of German manhood and steel determination in combat, even naming a street after him just outside the Tempelhof airport.

Von Richthofen filled the Kaiser's need for a heroic figure who would take the public's mind off the grinding slaughter on the Western front. But von Richthofen himself gradually broke down under the strains of combat. The head-shot wound von Richthofen received at the height of his career in July 1917 left him a changed man, according to his friends and family. His mother, Baroness von Richthofen, wrote in her January 1918 diary entry that her son's personality drastically altered after a year of combat flying and the head injury that never fully healed:

He was serious – very serious – and quiet. I found Manfred very changed, anyhow. Although he looked healthier and fresher compared to when he was on leave in the fall, so certainly the high spirits – the lightheartedness – the playfulness – were lacking in his character. He was taciturn, aloof, almost unapproachable; every one of his words seemed to come from an unknown distance. Why this change? The thought haunted me, turned over and over, while the wheels beneath me pounded monotonously, as if they had their own language. I think he has seen death too often.[123]

Baroness von Richthofen also recorded an incident in which her son expressed an extreme fatalism, suggesting that there was no point in caring about daily life, as death was imminent.[124]

In his memoir, von Richthofen met the Kaiser's expectations with homages to duty and discipline, but he managed to get past the censors passages that expressed deep pessimism about the war and a warning about its long-term psychological effects. Von Richthofen completed his book while recuperating from the head wound that left him with chronic headaches and, his colleagues noted, deep depression. The book ends with the following passage that is dramatically different in tone compared to what is up until then mostly propagandistic:

> The battle now taking place on all fronts has become awfully serious; there is nothing left of the 'lively, merry war', as our deeds were called in the beginning. Now we must fight off despair and arm ourselves so that the enemy will not penetrate our country. I now have the gravest feeling that people have been exposed to quite another Richthofen than I really am. When I read my book, I smile at the insolence of it. I no longer possess such an insolent spirit ...
>
> I am in wretched spirits after every aerial battle. But that no doubt is an after-effect of my head wound. When I set foot on the ground again at my airfield after a flight, I go to my quarters and do not want to see anyone or hear anything. I think of this war as it really is, not as the people at home imagine, with a Hoorah! and a roar. It is very serious, very grim ...[125]

Von Richthofen's memoir hints at an interesting tension in this genre of right-wing war literature. Embedded in the platitudes for duty and fatherland is the confession that civilians could never comprehend how despicable and brutalizing war really was, and that those who experienced it would never really be the same again. In this vein, the terrors of the front must be sterilized for mass consumption through the language of patriotic rhetoric.

Von Richthofen's account of the war indicates that for veterans returning home, the psychological effects of the war were incredibly complex, even contradictory. By polarizing the debate over the effects of the war as either 'brutalizing' or 'ennobling', the political discourse conceals the psychological reality of the war experience, which was much more nuanced. This problem was identified by Erich Weniger, an essayist and cultural critic with an iconoclastic view on the memory of the war. In a 1929 essay on the war experience, Weniger criticized groups across the political spectrum who sought to distort the psychological realities of the war, taking to task the writings produced by antiwar organizations as well as memoirs by individuals like Ernst Jünger who were extolled by the right. Weniger asked 'whether there is a single overall lesson that comes out of the war, something like "never again war!" as some claim, or "nationalism" as others claim, and yet further, whether there are any overall lessons of war that can be drawn for the work of peace'. The right, he argued, 'concealed moments of weakness, cruelty and despair with the phrases of war glorification'. Meanwhile, he wrote, 'many pacifists hide the heroism, humor, and contentment of the soldier's existence'. Ultimately, Weniger concluded, one had to ask 'whether there was any overall *authentic* memory [emphasis in text] of the war and how one could uncover it'.[126] The 'truth about the war', he speculated, existed only in the form of legend, with truths distorted in the accounts of both survivors and observers seeking to promote their own agendas. Because of this, the real war experience was hidden and complex, most probably locked inside the minds of men who did not express their memories through the polarizing prisms of political groups.

*   *   *

Returning German veterans faced a second trauma that they felt was comparable to the experience of the trenches. Veterans in general were perceived as psychologically different beings, whose invisible wounds were a source of enduring mystery and suspicion for a civilian population embittered by its sacrifices in the war. Psychiatrists conflated war neurotics with criminals, political enemies, and social degenerates. Military psychiatrists and conservative social critics argued that war neurotics were perpetrators of revolutionary activity, criminality, and deviance, and endangered the postwar social and political order, particularly traditional middle-class values. Psychiatrists working outside the circles of former military doctors who now advised the state argued that war neurotics were victims, along with other veterans and civilians who survived the war, of a wider psychological crisis in which the war stimulated latent instincts toward violence in European culture. This perspective was echoed by a public that included veterans groups on the left, who asserted that the war brutalized civilians and doctors, whose cruel treatment of traumatized soldiers concealed their own neuroses.

War victims and psychiatrists feared each other as deviants bent on distorting the memory of the war, and these groups entrenched themselves further into an 'us' versus 'them' mentality that would continue to inhibit recovery and reintegration throughout the Weimar years. Behind these debates over the psychological legacy of the war was a battle over which groups were entitled to control the memory of the war: front veterans, doctors, or civilians. Each of these groups mobilized against those they saw as responsible for the nation's collapse and psychologically not up to the task of defending the fatherland. Even within these groups were intense divisions over whether or not the war had a destructive or regenerative effect on the psyches of combat veterans. For those who celebrated the war experience as a unifying, glorifying event, war neurotics served as a reminder of a counter-experience that had to be contained and denied. However, even the political left expressed ambivalence towards war neurotics. Though Weimar's more progressive forces expressed empathy for war neurotics as ultimate symbols of the horrors of war, deep pessimism existed over whether these individuals could ever be returned to normal postwar life.

The next chapter will focus on the ways in which the public's suspicions about the psychological legacy of the war undermined the new republic's expansive social welfare project for war victims. With postwar society deeply divided over the psychological legacy of the war, the state made it a priority of its war-disabled legislation to heal these invisible wounds. In the construction of a National Pension Law in 1920, the new republic would attempt to heal not only war neurosis, but also deep psychological wounds of society as a whole.

Chapter 3

Neurosis and the Welfare State
The Rise and Fall of the National Pension Law of 1920

'It's my idea that we're sick, Georg. We have the war in our bones still'. Rahe nods. 'Yes, and we'll never get it out again!'
     – Erich Maria Remarque, *The Road Back*[1]

In 1920, the conservative German People's Party (DVP – *Deutsche Volkspartei*) General Secretary Friedrich Galebow from Düsseldorf complained to the *Reichswehrminister* about an incident he witnessed on a train:

> We were barely five minutes out of the station, when a 'war victim' entered our completely occupied car. With the familiar terrible quivering of his head and hands, he laboriously pulled a series of postcards out of his jacket and asked us to buy them. Naturally everybody immediately reached into their pockets! I alone was suspicious ... The train rode further and stopped in Biberfeld at 9:10. Because it was a long wait there, I got off to buy a few newspapers. When I stood at the *Perron*, my 'war victim' passed by without seeing me to approach a second war victim, and I overheard their following conversation:
>
> > The second [war victim]: So how many series [postcards] did
> > you get rid of?
> > The first: 122! When does the next train go back?
> > The second: At 1:20
> > The first: Let's take it![2]

The DVP's General Secretary was convinced that this was conclusive evidence of peddlers faking nervous disorders in order to win sympathy.

'At this rate', he wrote alarmingly, 'Their daily income would be up to 900–1000 Marks. That would give them, with only 308 days of travel, the minimum of 270,000–300,000 Marks in one year!!' Galebow called on the Labor Ministry to take immediate action against these men, naming them 'political enemies' who tarnished the memory of 'our brave warriors who receive deserved paychecks from the fatherland'. He concluded that the state would earn 'the thanks of all clean-living men' and do justice to Germany's veterans by sweeping fakers from the streets.[3]

Weimar's social welfare project was closely intertwined with the healing of Germany's wounds, both physical and psychological. However, as the letter above attests, war victims were perceived with great suspicion. Restoring the health and productivity of the war's victims, including those emerging from the trenches and civilians on the home front, drained one-third of the national budget and required a drastic expansion of the existing welfare system.[4] The implementation of social welfare for disabled veterans, their dependents, and civilian war victims placed a tremendous burden on more than just the national budget and the economic recovery of the Weimar Republic. This expansion of the social welfare system also strained German society's willingness to come to terms with the memory of the lost war and its human costs. Postwar welfare reform culminated in the National Pension Law of 1920 and an expansive bureaucracy needed to administer this enormous social project. The following chapter will examine the creation of the National Pension Law, problems with its implementation, and the significance of war neurotics in the social welfare system.

Shrinking economic resources in the wake of hyper-inflation and the Great Depression formed the backdrop to Weimar's failure to pay for the wounds of war.[5] The establishment of the welfare system, however, required more than just an unprecedented commitment of resources and organization. The successful implementation of the republic's social welfare experiment depended on complex interactions between disabled veterans, health care providers, employers and the general public. The exchanges between these groups attempting to implement, or in many cases obstruct, welfare laws for disabled veterans revealed deep-seated fears over the social and psychological effects of the war on men returning from the front. The battle over the costs of the war played out in doctors' offices, welfare lines, work environments and on the streets.

Psychologically disabled veterans played a central role in the construction of Weimar's social welfare state. Engineers of the National Pension Law saw compensating neurotic veterans and treating them as part of the disabled veterans' community, deserving and capable of reintegration, as a symbolic and practical effort to demonstrate the commitment of the republic to a more progressive social welfare system. Advocates of the new law argued that the war ushered in a breakdown of self-confidence and sense of community that gripped both combatants and civilians, making them hesitant to work at prewar levels of productivity. Healing war neurotics thus came to represent the healing of the nation in general, particularly the loss of faith in work and progress that the new democratic-led government feared was an irreversible consequence of the war.

At the same time, psychologically damaged veterans also played a major role in the breakdown of Weimar's social welfare state. The particular image associated with war neurotics as lazy, undisciplined and over-dependent 'pension neurotics' haunted the Labor Ministry's larger project of convincing employers that disabled veterans on the whole were willing to work. The negative image of the war neurotic and that of disabled veterans became conflated in the public consciousness. In many cases employers and co-workers feared that those who survived the trenches returned as different men, not only physically unsuitable for the scarce jobs available in a shrinking market, but also unpredictable, potentially violent and dangerous, and unwilling to readjust to the social and psychological norms of postwar life. In the National Pension Law of 1920, Social Democrats argued that the public would rally behind disabled veterans and help them reintegrate because the stressed general population could relate to the psychological stresses suffered by survivors from the trenches. However, this shared consciousness did not materialize. Instead, the state had to intervene on behalf of mentally and physically disabled war victims in an attempt to persuade employers and the public that these men were potentially valuable, productive workers.

Conflict between the state's vision for disabled veterans and the public's grew intense. The government's quota-system for putting men with mental and physical injuries into suitable jobs fostered tremendous resentment. In particular, white-collar employers and employees reacted against the state's requirements that men no longer able to perform in their prewar capacities in industrial labor be retrained and assimilated into the middle-class workforce. Private employers were most resistant to the National Pension Law's quotas, seeing it as contributing to low productivity among workers and eroding employers' autonomy in managing the workplace. But most embarrassing for the legislators of Weimar's social welfare system was resistance from state employers. In the postal system, railway administration and banks, managers generally agreed with doctors: war neurotics were intrinsically unwilling to recover their productivity, and lacked the discipline and social skills needed for work. The general public perceived the low productivity and uncooperative behavior they saw in disabled veterans as a consequence of their social background, mixed with fears about the psychologically shattering effects of the war. Thus the key groups needed to reassimilate disabled veterans, employers and the public, looked upon these war victims as intrinsic hazards to the economy and community, not as potential cases for rehabilitation and recovery. By the mid-1920s, the initial goals of the National Pension Law had collapsed, and welfare policy-makers blamed the weak wills of 'pension neurotics' for the failure of disabled veterans to become useful members of society.

The National Pension Law and War Neurosis

The human costs of the war were devastating. The new republic faced nearly two million disabled men returning from the trenches. In addition, the war left approximately 525,000 widows and 1.1 million orphans.[6] The physical and psychological injuries of the war, however, did not end with the armistice. In a series of feature articles for the *Berliner Tageblatt*, journalist and former officer Willy Meyer provided graphic reports on scenes in Berlin hospitals where the 'bitter struggle of the war continued ... inside the walls of hospitals, where real-life tragedies played themselves out behind the barred windows of insane asylums'. Meyer described the deteriorating health of the severely disabled, terribly disfigured men 'whose faces were now only deep holes or folds of scars ... men who lost limbs and succumbed to deepest despair'[7] The horrifying physical wounds produced by the war were used by antiwar groups to shock audiences into political mobilization. The most famous is the antiwar museum founded in Berlin by Ernst Friedrich, a self-described pacifist-anarchist who juxtaposed terrifying photographs of the human costs of war with nationalist propaganda.[8]

Civilians also continued to suffer long after the last shots were fired. The Interior Ministry enlisted doctors in 1921 to assess the effects of the Allies' hunger blockade on German society, and reported to the British and French governments that 'the physical and mental development of a whole generation of young Germans would be ruined by under-nourishment, disease, and neglect'.[9] Finance ministers assessing the war victims' benefits budget predicted that claims for compensation would continue to grow as war victims and health care providers assessed the long-term effects of the war on the nation's health. The Finance Ministry initially set aside 1.2 billion Marks for war victims care, and predicted that this would need to be expanded to over four billion Marks, eventually costing the new republic one-third of its annual budget. The budget for war victims continued to grow beyond this into the 1920s, exceeding initial estimates in 1919–20. As the long-term physical and psychological effects of the war and blockade became apparent, the Labor Ministry began to define 'war victims' in ever broader terms.[10]

Reorganization of the welfare system preceded the National Pension Law of 1920. The democratic coalition in parliament, responding to mass street demonstrations staged in December 1918 by war victims and organized in the Social Democratic and the Communist parties, promised to completely overhaul the imperial government's health care and pension system for disabled veterans and their dependents.[11] The first major changes came with the transformation of war victims' care from military to civil administration. During the war, disabled veterans were processed through a bureaucracy that included regionally administered army pension offices, army pension review courts and social welfare offices. With nearly two million disabled veterans overwhelming these locally-run administrations, the army had to rely on the National Insurance System, administered by the Labor Ministry, and the medical facilities that existed for civilian pensioners. In October 1919, the new Weimar Republic switched the entire war victims' care bureaucracy from the military to the Labor Ministry, thus completing a process already started by wartime necessity. For the sake of expediency, former military administrators retained their positions in the local social welfare offices that provided job training, placement, living arrangements, child care, and health services. These local networks were then brought under the control of a centralized system directed by the Labor Ministry. Anton Kirschensteiner, the labor minister in charge of pensions for war victims, developed three main administrative systems for war victims' care: the Labor Ministry's pension offices, which administered pensions, the National Insurance System, which facilitated medical care, and the pension courts, where panels heard cases and complaints by individuals seeking pensions.[12]

Thus the Weimar Republic did not create an independent system for disabled veterans, but instead subsumed them into the expanded social welfare and insurance institutions. War victims' organizations across the political spectrum recommended that a separate administration be created for war-disabled affairs. However, the parliamentarians working on the new pension system, primarily from the Social Democratic Party and the German Democratic Party (DDP), complained that financial and political pressure to quickly establish a new system shaped their efforts to centralize welfare bureaucracy.[13] This conflation of war-disabled and civilian welfare recipients would later foster resentment and weaken veterans' support for the system and the republic as a whole.

At the same time, the National Pension Law finally enacted in April 1920 did provide new legislation that revealed it was a substantial departure from the imperial government's social welfare system, both in spirit and in nature. Under Article 163 of the Weimar constitution, all citizens were, for the first time, guaranteed the right to work, with the state being responsible for providing employment. The National Pension Law carried this over as a central feature of war-disabled policy:

Every German has the moral obligation, his personal freedom notwithstanding, to exercise his mental and physical powers in a manner required by the welfare for all. Every German shall be given the opportunity to earn his living through productive work – if no suitable opportunity for work can be found, the means will be provided.[14]

Thus the republic aimed to solidify a symbiotic relationship between willing workers dedicated to the common good and the state dedicated to individual welfare. This right to work was extended to disabled veterans, particularly those deemed vulnerable to discrimination due to serious injuries, in the Ordinance Concerning the Employment of Severely Disabled. The ordinance asserted that all public and private factories, bureaus and agencies were required to hire at least one severely disabled veteran for every hundred persons employed.[15] In order to effectively implement this law, war victims' organizations were for the first time permitted to work with social welfare administrators by mediating between war victims, employers, and the Labor Ministry.

In addition to administrative and legislative changes in social welfare for veterans, the republic also overhauled the procedures by which pensions were distributed. According to the National Pension Law, disabled veterans were required to fill out applications at a local office along with other social welfare recipients, including accident victims, women, and other civilians in need of assistance. In practice, this is where war-disabled organizations played an integral role in providing advice, legal counseling, and typewriters for applicants. At the pension and health care office, doctors examined applicants and determined whether their wounds were 'DB' (*Dienstbeschädigungen* – 'war-related injury'). Doctors were then authorized to assess the percentage of the patient's disability. That is, doctors evaluated the patient's reduced capacity to earn a living. In a complex formula over which doctors held ultimate power, individuals were evaluated according to the severity of wounds and how they affected that patient's particular work ability, to determine whether performance capacity was reduced by 30%, 40%, etc. Each of these categories then had a recommendation for pension income to be received. Those evaluated as 'severely disabled' automatically received a 50% higher rating and special allowances. Under the laws of the imperial government, military rank had dictated the amount of the pension – an officer with 40% status thus received more than a soldier with 40% status. Weimar's National Pension Law departed from this system of rating according to military rank. Nevertheless, the Labor Ministry authorized doctors to judge the patient's entitlement based on social class, prewar occupation and level of education.[16]

The pension system became more labyrinthine after the doctor's initial evaluation. Once a rating was assigned by doctors, the patient's pension evaluation was placed in the hands of civil servants. Administrators assigned a 'base pension' to the percentage given for the patient's reduced ability to earn a living. Where necessary, special allowances for severely disabled and allowances for men whose jobs required unusual training or skills were then given as supplements. This was added up to form what was called a 'full pension'. Full pensions were further supplemented to meet higher costs of living brought on by inflation, special occupational training and medical costs, and other needs that were met with 'care allowances' and emergency relief.[17] To qualify for these supplements, disabled veterans often found themselves in a cycle of constantly applying for assistance, undergoing medical evaluations, and waiting for decisions from local pension offices that tried to keep up with directions from the central pension office in Berlin under the Labor Ministry.

War neurotics proved to be the most difficult cases to evaluate and administer. According to the new pension law, war neurotics were entitled to the same rights as other disabled veterans provided that doctors categorized their wounds as directly war-related (DB). Those evaluated as suffering from war-related mental wounds were immediately categorized as severely disabled (50% or more unable to earn a living). The question of what constituted a 'war-related' injury proved a challenge in the case of mentally ill veterans, and it was in this segment of the pension evaluation process that doctors wielded such important power. The instructions given left considerable leeway, as doctors had only to establish that the injury was probably directly war related: 'It suffices when it is shown to be sufficiently probable. On the other hand the mere possibility of a causal connection is generally not sufficient for the medical judge to assume a war disability'.[18] Psychiatrists employed by the Labor Ministry did not agree upon the diagnostic standards that differentiated between war-related neuroses and other forms of mental illness. Thus defining symptoms as 'probably' war-related was not straightforward. The causes of wide forms of mental illnesses displayed by returning soldiers, and the best paths of treatment, were never effectively resolved by doctors at this critical moment when the state was trying to standardize pension evaluation criteria and develop occupational therapy to find suitable work for traumatized veterans.

Immediately after the establishment of the National Pension Law, politicians on the left actively intervened in favor of war neurotics, arguing that their wounds were legitimate and symbolic of Germany's deeper crisis. Social Democrats who helped design the National Pension Law insisted that the nation widely supported compensation for mentally disabled veterans because civilians could relate to their condition. Hermann Beyer, a military doctor who treated war neurotics up to 1918, concluded that mentally traumatized men were being unfairly treated in the front lines and field hospitals by doctors who did not understand the nature of psychological injuries and their connection to the war. An exceptional figure in his profession, he complained that the medical system was class-biased, evidenced by doctors who regularly diagnosed enlisted men as 'neurotic' or 'hysterical' while diagnosing officers with similar symptoms as victims of 'organic nervous disorders', giving the officers an easier path to a pension.[19] Beyer joined the Social Democratic Party and became a representative in the Prussian State Assembly (*Preußische Landesversammlung*). In March 1919 he formed a committee to investigate war neurosis. Beyer argued that doctors who denied war-disabled status to psychologically traumatized veterans acted against what most Germans felt to be true, that these men were indeed war victims whose wounds were sustained as a result of their experiences in the trenches. This ran against the opinion of a number of psychiatrists working for the Labor Ministry. For example, one psychiatrist at the University of Königsberg testified to the Prussian State Assembly that if individuals still displayed nervous disorders after the war, they were no longer the responsibility of the state. Beyer's committee responded:

> The rejection of war-disabled status made by Professor Meyer of Königsberg and other doctors employed by the state is in the majority of cases unfounded and runs against the sentiment of the entire nation (*widerspricht dem Empfinden des ganzen Volkes*). In addition, under no circumstance should purely economic considerations, as quoted by Dr Meyer, be the sole basis for granting pensions to these sick individuals. These individuals should not just be granted further charity, but rather it should be their right to receive pensions ... Society should provide a feeling of justice (*Rechtsgefühl*) for all those whose injuries are the responsibility of the state.[20]

Here the SPD representative claimed that a gap existed between the opinions of doctors and the general public, and that the popular sentiment towards war victims was driven by notions of justice rather than simply economics. Social Democrats like Beyer expected that the public would affirm the new law's treatment of war neurotics and other disabled veterans as individuals entitled to financial compensation and work, which the wider public would enthusiastically provide for wounded veterans. Beyer's thesis would be tested as the republic tried to implement the National Pension Law.

The new law placed the psychological wounds of the war at the center of the social welfare project. Mental trauma was defined in the broadest terms, and included war neurosis, stress caused by economic crisis, and loss of faith in traditional values. Thus mental wounds formed a bridge between combatants and civilians, which, according to advocates of the new law, justified a blanket social welfare system in which disabled veterans, home front survivors, and traditional welfare recipients founds themselves waiting in the same lines.

At the welfare offices, those in line found pamphlets that defined war victimhood and provided an outline of one's rights under the National Pension Law. In *The Rights of War Victims and their Dependents in Accordance with the new National Pension Law*, readers saw on the first page that the law was designed first and foremost to satisfy the wishes of war victims 'in the spirit of modern social legislation'.[21] The new law, labor minister and pension law architect Dr Franz Schweyer argued, provided more than just a more equitable system for distributing financial assistance, it also promised to heal the deeper, 'internal wounds' caused by the war. Schweyer noted that 'the consequences of the lost war and the revolution have caused terrible sufferings not only for actual war victims, but also with few exceptions for all national comrades (*Volksgenossen*)'.[22] According to Schweyer, the National Pension Law was aimed at healing the lost faith in work and progress that struck both soldiers and civilians:

> In spite of the crisis today, these victims among the seriously tested German people will be included [in the National Pension Law], because it is a matter of honor that a debt be paid to the defenders of house and home, of family and fatherland. Above all, this is a matter of restoring a new joy of life [*Lebensfreude*] and productivity to broad layers of our people who desire to be liberated from their tormenting worries. The National Pension Law thus should serve as a rich source of blessing for our war victims and our entire nation.[23]

Thus according to Schweyer, both home front and combat front war victims suffered from a collective trauma characterized by a shattered joy for life that was essential to faith in work, the future, and, subsequently, productivity.

Engineers behind the pension law believed that these mental scars could be healed through state intervention. However, the creators of the law were concerned with the public's cooperation with state programs to reemploy war victims, including those with mental injuries. Schweyer argued that disabled veterans and the entire nation could heal their collective wounds with a unified effort to translate the spirit of the National Pension Law into practice. Social welfare offices and authorities, he noted, were already burdened with the arduous task of evaluating individuals and assigning pensions to disabled veterans and their families. The public now had to help reassimilate war victims into the fabric of society. Schweyer prescribed a positive relationship between the pension bureaucracy and cooperative employers to pull it off:

> The entire national program for war victims is based on more than just financial support provided by the National Pension Law.

> In addition to pension insurance, war victims are to be given free
> medical treatment and occupational training ... in accordance with
> the 6 April 1920 law on the employment of severely disabled veterans,
> the law expressly states that all public and private employers are
> equally bound to give preference to the severely disabled by placing
> them in suitable jobs.[24]

Thus the state could only provide one layer of recovery, the material needs
of war victims. Their long-term recovery depended on the cooperation of
employers who could provide work, and a nurturing environment where
war victims could eventually reach their maximum level of productivity,
which would ultimately benefit employers, the economy and society.[25]

Employers thus played a crucial role in the state's attempts to heal
veterans and psychological wounds. Welfare policymakers argued that in
order for the nation to recover its social and economic strength, there had
to be a national effort to provide encouragement to returning veterans and
their dependents. Psychological health care was defined as the restoration
of war victims' sense of self-worth, and the will to be productive, which
social policy-makers feared was lost in the war. Health care administrator
Karl Ernst Hartmann, who specialized in the social and psychological
recovery of disabled veterans, published the basic instruction manual
for welfare administrators on the general care of war victims and their
families. Hartmann outlined the purposes of war victims' care and its
implications for national recovery:

> War wounded and their dependents have suffered exceptionally
> under the nerve-shattering effects of the world war: their speech,
> their movements, their ability to feel, their inner being has been
> fundamentally changed by today's murderous torments to the body
> and the spirit ... The psychological health care of war victims is of
> the highest significance, not just for the welfare of the individual, but
> also for the collective civil and economic life. It is crucial to convince
> the individual war wounded and war widows to trust themselves
> again, to awake in them the will to act, the desire to live and the
> self-confidence that they are useful limbs of the national community
> and important pieces of the larger economic comradeship.[26]

Hartmann conflated the mentally and physically disabled, ex-soldiers and
their families, as deeply alienated from the basic idea that their work
had meaning and that they were connected to the national community.
Germany's productivity, he observed, depended on the nation's ability to
assist war victims in rediscovering their self-esteem and roles as productive
citizens. Hartmann compared psychological rehabilitation to the fitting of
prosthetic limbs on amputees, noting that the will to be productive had

to be refitted into the psyche of war victims who lost their faith in work, progress, and the future.[27] Social welfare for veterans included much more than what he called 'external and economic rehabilitation', but also the restoration of 'an inner-dwelling goodness that supplements the realm of economic care'.[28]

The activity of work was the therapeutic device for the psychological regeneration of war victims. Work, according to Hartmann, provided a sense of industriousness (*Arbeitsamkeit*) and strength (*Arbeitskraft*) that restored one's inner sense of value to the community. Individuals who lingered on the traumatic memories of the war and the effects of their physical wounds risked adverse health effects in the form of chronic depression and the tendency to become 'work-shy' (*Arbeitscheu*).[29] Hartmann insistently argued that war victims intrinsically wanted to work, and that any indication otherwise was the fault of the war, not the individual. He admitted that 'pension hysteria' appeared in many veterans who chose to depend on state assistance rather than rediscover their full potential for work. However, Hartmann asserted, 'pension hysteria' was symptomatic of a fear of work, not a chronic unwillingness to earn a living. This fear sprang from diminished self-confidence caused by the war, rather than innate flaws in character or misguided social welfare policy.[30]

The problem was civilians, according to Hartmann, not war victims. Hartmann was pessimistic about the civilian population's commitment to assisting war victims with social and psychological reintegration. He anticipated that the war eroded the home front's commitment to the community, leading civilians to focus only on self-preservation and individual gain in a way that mirrored the selfishness of alleged 'pension hysterics'. Hard-working, honest, but psychologically fragile returning disabled veterans, Hartmann feared, would fall easy prey to a self-confident civilian population well-versed in what he characterized as a new postwar moral and economic order, also a legacy of war-induced trauma, in which self-gain trampled any sense of common good. Hartmann warned: 'It is definitely possible that shady riff-raff will try to cross the path of our poor war disabled and their dependents in order to take advantage of them in their time of crisis or even corrupt them'. Lurking in wait for what he characterized as naive, innocent disabled veterans were 'swindlers' at many levels, including untrustworthy employers out to extort pensions from war victims, sham-artists who claimed they had quick cures for injuries and ailments, 'shyster lawyers' (*Winkeladvokaten*) looking to take money from disgruntled veterans, and other individuals who saw pensioned disabled veterans as fragile, easily exploited prey'.[31]

The stage was now set for two camps, disabled veterans and employers, who both had to fulfill mutual responsibilities in this time of crisis. On one hand, engineers of the National Pension Law painted a picture of Germany afflicted by collective psychological trauma, mainly the disruption of faith in work and the future. At the same time, welfare advocates also feared that despite their supposedly shared psychological experiences, war victims and employers were deeply divided in their interests. For the democratic forces behind the law, those on the home front were a potential threat to the law if they did not accept disabled veterans as eager to work and fully capable of reassimilating into normal postwar life.

Public Resistance to the National Pension Law

Mentally disabled veterans played an integral role in eroding popular support for the state's reemployment and welfare programs. Contrary to claims made by social democratic welfare reformers, public sentiment tended to support doctors' conclusions that psychologically disabled men were unwilling to work, unable to recover, 'hysterical', dependent on welfare, and even possibly violent and dangerous. These particular perceptions of war neurotics in work environments, caused employers to revolt against the National Pension Law.

The image of the malingerer was also conflated with an image of potential danger, as mentally disabled veterans provoked fear on the streets of major cities. Just before the end of the war, Major Hans Kropf reported an incident to his superiors regarding a confrontation with a soldier in the *Englischer Garten*, a popular park in the heart of Munich:

> On Saturday, Aug. 31 [1918] a soldier sitting on a bench in the English garden refused to show me the proper respect [salute]. When I gave him some words, he jumped up and pulled out of his coat, which was unbuttoned, a <u>red slip of paper</u> [underlined in original text] – it was about the size of a leave permit – and he stuck this under my eyes, pointing out the clearly underlined word in the top right: 'war neurotic'. He acted really agitated and threatened me, etc., so that I had to move away from him … In what kind of hospital do people like this belong? In my view, such sick people don't belong on the street. Their behavior could have immense consequences.[32]

To Major Kropf and his officer colleague, the soldier in the park represented insubordination, lax discipline, and violent, unpredictable behavior. Major Kropf was shaken by what he saw as a potential threat to the public if war neurotics were not properly controlled by the authorities. The Nervous Disorders Wing (*Nerven-Abteilung*) of Munich's hospital administration quickly replied that local hospitals were not actually distributing red slips of papers marked 'war neurotic' to their patients. They did note, however, that a rise in reported cases of unauthorized leaves and fraudulent papers, in particular men with 'war neurotic' stamped on their identification papers, was currently being investigated.[33]

Quivering hands and shaking bodies vividly described in eyewitness accounts of war neurotics on the streets generated widespread suspicion. The public perceived an epidemic of fakers and dangerous vagrants taking advantage of the public's sympathy for disabled veterans. The imagined boundaries between genuine war victims and frauds eroded. The Weimar government had a difficult time controlling what was becoming a national embarrassment, as labor ministers desperately tried to control the number of destitute war disabled – real or otherwise – clogging Berlin's subway stations and crowded commercial districts. The problem was so widespread that businessmen, politicians, and civil authorities formed a coalition to make a public announcement through the police president: 'While countless war victims summon all their energy to continue working, abusive, fraudulent elements put on the medals of the war wounded, although they were never in the war and bore no injuries'. The announcement was posted in the streets to assure readers that the government was in control. If anyone encountered a disabled veteran on the streets, they were to direct them to the nearest health care or work retraining facility. If they refused, they would face arrest as a swindler.[34]

Doctors warned that the growing 'pension neurosis' and welfare fraud originated with war neurotics. Just as they had poisoned the will of soldiers to fight in the trenches, they now contaminated the will of disabled veterans to work. While amputees and 'war cripples' gradually disappeared from daily news coverage of the crisis of returning veterans, war neurotics continued to make the front page as being part of, or at least inspiring, a 'mass epidemic' of beggars wearing field-grey.[35] The *Deutsche Tageszeitung* sympathized with veterans who experienced 'being buried alive under an artillery explosion whose violence had shattered their nerves to the point of being unhealable'.[36] However, they warned readers that the number of 'beggars with quivering limbs' (*Gliederschüttler*) was spreading, and that only a police crackdown would determine who was shirking work and who was really wounded.[37]

War neurotics, whether fakers or genuine, drew fire from health care officials, welfare administrators and employers as the most difficult war victims to reassimilate into the labor force. The first protests against the National Pension Law's prescription for returning men to work came from doctors. Several days after its ratification, doctors working for regional health care offices aimed criticism against the centralized National Pension Law and its goals for giving war victims the full range of opportunities they enjoyed before the war. At the disabled veterans' health care office in Westfalen, doctors complained that the new laws gave war neurotics too many choices in determining their postwar job prospects, when they should consider first 'in what ways they would be most useful'. One doctor reported that the new welfare law displaced successful wartime occupational training programs and gave disabled veterans unrealistic expectations that they could expand their horizons beyond their prewar conditions:

> It is the occupational therapy specialists as well as the employers who are most qualified to determine where workers can best be used. Nevertheless, a large number of war disabled express the wish or the intention to give up their earlier [prewar] jobs for sometimes general, sometimes specific reasons. Already in time of peace we see many restless workers who wander from one occupation to another. This lack of happiness in their jobs is mainly caused by insufficient training. If someone is an amateur at his job, he will of course not find any satisfaction in it.[38]

Doctors thus saw themselves and employers as most qualified to determine how to reintegrate disabled veterans into the work force. War victims were, according to medical authorities, a potentially unreliable element in the labor force if they were given a sense that they had equal opportunities. It was not society, as the National Pension Law contended, that needed to adjust to new conditions, but war victims. The greatest psychological challenge, according to doctors, was not the shattering effects of the war, but the expectations of war victims who were not content with their place in society

Doctors wanted to maintain their authority over job retraining, but found themselves at odds with advocates of the National Pension Law that sought new solutions, especially in rehabilitation for war neurotics. Social Democrats claimed that their approach to healing psychologically damaged veterans was more progressive as they promised to integrate these individuals fully into the general war victims' community, rather than ostracize war neurotics as social and economic pariahs. However, this proved impractical. The particular problems experienced by war neurotics often fell second to the goal of integration. For example, the Labor Ministry sometimes placed war neurotics and men with head-shot wounds in the same job retraining programs, because their symptoms, like tics, tremors, mild paralysis, were similar. Work therapy for 'brain cripples' (Gehirnkrüppel) since 1914 included intensive occupational reeducation that focused on basic motor and cognitive-intellectual skills needed for work and family life.[39] At a Hamburg program developed by doctors Draeseke and Herms, therapy was described as 'orthopaedic', aimed at controlling quivering limbs with prosthetics and rebuilding speech skills through repetitive oral exercises. In their clinic, Draeseke and Herms treated men who had been buried alive and who displayed symptoms of traumatic neurosis that they admitted were psychological in origin. However, the path to recovery was the same, they argued, and consisted of primarily physical therapy, focusing on correcting defective motor and speech abilities. The common denominator was rebuilding will power.[40]

Medical authorities believed it was a mistake to give war victims the sense that they were entitled to enter into any job they pleased. In programs developed during the war, and in job retraining programs designed by the same doctors after 1918, men were retrained for jobs according to their prewar socioeconomic background, if possible their original occupations. However, occupational therapists complained that not all disabled men were equally enthusiastic about returning to their jobs. At the Gelsenkirchen war-disabled health care office in Westfalen, occupational counselor Becker claimed that veterans suffering from nervous disorders, compared to other disabled veterans, demonstrated less will power when it came to returning to prewar jobs or any other suitable occupations. Unlike amputees, the blind, men suffering from head injuries and other disabled veterans, war neurotics allegedly did not respond well to occupational therapy programs designed to place them in the competitive postwar labor market. Becker judged his patients by their cooperativeness with authorities. Blind veterans, for example, behaved with 'docility and confidence' when trained by occupational therapists for suitable jobs working either on an industrial line as packers, or in positions as handcraftsmen (*Handwerker*) making wicker-basket chairs.[41] In contrast, according to Becker, war neurotics were unmanageable and resistant to work, despite the efforts of 'patient health care workers and cooperative employers'. Instead, and here Becker used the same term as the pension law's advocate, Hartmann, but with different connotations, war neurotics were 'work-shy'. This 'shyness' in Becker's analysis was more an 'aversion', rooted in the innate laziness of war neurotics, also evidenced by their shameful wartime behavior, rather than in their alleged war-shattered self-confidence alluded to by Social Democrats behind the law.[42]

The war, Becker claimed, demonstrated that hysterical men could not be reassimilated into work and postwar society without strong discipline. These men needed to be separated from the physically disabled and placed in special hospital occupational therapy stations, rather than social welfare offices, in order to contain their resistance to work and assess the legitimacy of their symptoms. Becker characterized the fear of returning to work as a national crisis that had to be firmly controlled:

The fight against the aversion to work (*Arbeisscheu*) is a question of conscience of the first order. The occupational counselor must act as the nation's guardian and educator (*Volkserzieher*) in enforcing his program and, like a father, simultaneously use sternness and discipline as well as love and patience … and thus restore the mutual

> love and trust as well as strictness and seriousness that were once
> present in close family circles as well is in the family life of the
> community and households.[43]

The role of the counselor was thus to provide the discipline and nurturing
that no longer existed in traditional family and community structures. In
order to achieve this, Becker prescribed a strict regimen of agricultural
labor for war neurotics, a technique used under the *Kaiserreich*, which he
believed instilled a sense of discipline and the value of being productive.
Unlike other war victims eager to move on with their lives, Becker argued,
war neurotics needed to remain tied to the same programs used during
wartime until they decided that it was in their best interest to join other
disabled veterans and cooperate with occupational programs assigned to
them.[44]

Employers also vigorously opposed the new pension law on a number
of levels. The National Pension Law of 1920 emerged in the midst
of widespread panic among employers about workers' enthusiasm and
returning to prewar levels of productivity. In addition, employers resented
the electoral victories of the Social Democrats and the legitimization of
unions and welfare reform.[45] In 1919–21, as the law was being developed
and implemented, state authorities received widespread complaints from
employers that, after the war, workers in general displayed little desire to
work. The head of the Demobilization Office, Joseph Koeth, concluded
in early 1919 that the government had a national crisis on its hands:
'[T]hroughout the Reich, the labor force is showing no enthusiasm for
work and as a result work performance has diminished significantly in all
areas, now at the very moment when everything depends on doing one's
utmost'.[46]

In this postwar setting of anxiety about returning workers to prewar
levels of productivity, severely disabled veterans came under scrutiny for
their physical capabilities and their willingness to work at full potential.
Health care administrators in Stettin reported that employers lumped
together veterans with chronic internal injuries like lung disorders, right-
arm amputees and men with nervous disorders as those who consistently
could not be reemployed due to lack of jobs that were flexible enough
to accommodate their physical needs.[47] The Munich Invalid Trade
Administration (*Invaliden-Handwerker-Abteilung*) singled out men with
nervous disorders as exceptionally unreliable workers who, despite all
efforts at training, could not be reemployed. Reserve Major Püppl, in
charge of occupational training there for workers on machines used
in clothing and shoe-making trades, argued that in response to budget
problems and a cramped labor market, war neurotics should be removed
from occupational therapy for industrial labor. Püppl noted: 'In this
program we find in particular different workers suffering from nervous

tremors who often times stop work for hours at a time as a consequence of their repeated attacks'. As they were prone to complete breakdowns that could be neither controlled nor predicted, Püppl concluded that neurotic men were totally unreliable, if not dangerous, on an assembly-line, and he sympathized with factory managers' requests to remove war neurotics from this type of work.[48]

With the release of the National Pension Law, labor ministers made a critical decision that further jeopardized relations with employers and local welfare administrators. State officials directed local welfare offices to match severely disabled veterans, including war neurotics, to jobs most suitable to their disability, regardless of their prewar socioeconomic status. The Labor Ministry instructed occupational therapists to retrain former industrial workers for traditionally white-collar jobs, where they believed that more flexible, less physically demanding work environments could be found. In these settings, state authorities insisted that men would recover their self-confidence and reach their maximum levels of work productivity. Employers, however, complained that mentally disabled veterans were unsuitable for white-collar jobs. Managers considered office work too complicated and demanding for mentally traumatized veterans. This was the case for both men who suffered under both head wounds that caused brain damage as well as men who suffered from traumatic neurosis. Ulrich J., for example, a clerk for a coal business before suffering a head-shot wound that resulted in lasting psychological problems, received training to become a note-taker at the Hannover Finance Office (*Finanzamt*). He lost his job after only three months of employment because, as his employers reported, J.'s performance 'simply did not suffice', and he was replaced.[49] Elias E., a technical assistant in a Lauenberg municipal construction office suffered from a 75% reduction in his ability to earn a living due to 'high-grade nervous disposition'. He also lost his job. The reason given was that his tics and tremors broke out too frequently, requiring numerous returns to psychiatric institutions, making him too unreliable.[50] Local welfare administrators reviewing reemployment programs often agreed with employers and reported to the Labor Ministry that no matter how much individualized training the state provided, there were limitations to finding mentally disabled men jobs suited to their particular problems.

Despite conflicts with employers, Labor Ministry officials persisted in surveying different industries to determine which jobs were most appropriate for severely disabled veterans. Closely supervised office assistant jobs, they decided, suited these men well because they presented the least physical strain and offered flexibility in the pace of the job, especially if employers cooperated in developing individually structured work environments. The first employer authorized to assimilate severely disabled veterans was the Berlin railway administration, which offered an extensive network of jobs for both former officers and enlisted men.

Ex-officers, particularly those trained in white-collar industries before the war, were recommended for positions as low-level managers and supervisors. These men, labor ministers recommended, could use their experience to look after other severely disabled veterans who were specially trained as office staff, service clerks, and general assistants (*Hilfsarbeiter*), where they performed according to their level of ability. Labor ministers were more hard-pressed to find jobs for men from working-class backgrounds. They noted crossing-guard positions as possibilities, but also recommended that employers train these men as assistants to office clerks if no other positions that suited their physical needs made themselves available.[51]

Pushing working-class men into traditionally lower-middle-class jobs created a storm of employer resistance. Only a few months after the release of the National Pension Law, employers swamped the Labor Ministry with requests to break the terms of the Employment of Severely Disabled Veterans Law, which required employers to meet quotas, risking 10,000 Mark fines.[52] Physical suitability proved to be only one concern among employers pressured to hire severely disabled men. Personnel managers also complained that men sent from the health care and occupational training centers were not only physically inadequate for lower-level office job environments, but also deficient in character and enthusiasm. Political backers of the National Pension Law came to war victims' aid. Friedrich Weinhausen, a member of the German Democratic Party (DDP), asserted that disabled veterans were virtually beyond reproach, as evidenced by their extraordinary sacrifices for the fatherland. Their status as veterans demonstrated a level of discipline and trustworthiness that compensated for any other shortcomings.[53]

Employers often favored hiring women into white-collar jobs over severely disabled veterans. Paid less, and perceived as naturally submissive and thus suited to lower-level office jobs, women filled this job market, even though a cultural war raged over the emergence of the 'new woman' in white-collar industries.[54] By late 1920, open conflict erupted between disabled veterans, personnel managers, and Labor Ministry officials over the employment of women while veterans were still out of work. In their instructions to employers enlisted in reemploying war disabled, Labor Ministry officials explicitly stated that employers were not permitted to hire women while severely disabled men remained out of work. According to the Labor Ministry: 'They [war disabled] should be used in all positions where the ability to perform is not absolutely necessary. As long as there are jobs for which they are qualified that are occupied by women, disabled veterans should in no way be rejected'.[55] Labor ministers also expressed concern that women in the workplace further strained disabled veterans' fragile self-confidence, especially if women out-performed veterans in jobs men were trained for at occupational therapy clinics. The Labor Ministry only made exceptions for women whose husbands died in combat. The rest had to be stoic examples of the traditional housewife in order not to upset their nervous husbands.[56]

The Labor Ministry worked vigorously on at least one of the goals set by disabled men – to remove women from white-collar jobs. Their reasoning went beyond the question of just opening jobs for the severely disabled. If defects existed in disabled veterans' will to work and moral character, it was the fault of women in the workplace, welfare representatives claimed. When disabled men showed signs of 'uncooperative behavior' on the job, one official claimed, they were understandably demoralized and stressed by having to compete unfairly with women for the same jobs, which made these men feel inadequate. The regional inspector (*Landeshauptmann*) in Saxony, however, chastised the Reichsbank for not exploiting the superior 'joy of work' (*Arbeitsfreude*) of disabled men: 'It is our experience that because their injuries have forced them to change careers, they compensate by bringing an ever-increasing enthusiasm and joy of work ... which keeps them competitive with female work strength'.[57] State officials did not wait for this struggle between enthusiasm and physical disability to play itself out. On the advice of disabled veterans, the Labor Ministry took immediate action to control employers by prohibiting them from dismissing men without first consulting welfare offices. State representatives reminded employers that justice for war victims held greater importance than physical ability, and they called on employers to fire female workers as a gesture of confidence, which would allegedly help disabled veterans to overcome their problems with self-esteem and become productive workers.[58]

War-disabled organizations across the political spectrum placed constant pressure on the Labor Ministry to intervene more decisively. Only a month after the release of the National Pension Law, labor ministers ordered pension offices to punish employers who neglected to hire disabled veterans, especially when men were fired after costly state-run training and replaced by women.[59] Sarcastic letters poured in from war-disabled organizations criticizing 'The Thanks of the Fatherland', including one that detailed the suicide of a severely disabled office employee despondent over being replaced by women, even though he was promised a job by the state after the war. According to the United Association of War Disabled (*Einheitsverband der Kriegsbeschädigten*) the employment of women 'while war cripples and family fathers are thrown in the gutter' suggested that the state lacked real respect for the needs of war victims.[60] Hamburg's Association of German War Disabled (*Bund deutscher Kriegsbeschädigten*) requested that the Labor Ministry enforce its reemployment laws for disabled veterans more strictly, namely by prohibiting employers, no matter how economically hard-pressed, from firing disabled veterans 'until the last healthy employee is dismissed'.[61]

War victims had different ideas about how to handle the situation than the pension law's architects, in particular Social Democrats. In fact, disabled veterans blamed state officials for making unrealistic, unpersuasive arguments regarding their abilities to work. War victims did not want the state to insist that they could compete with healthy workers, including women, in terms of physical performance. Instead, they believed that reasonable compromises had to be made with employers. At the state-run war-disabled occupational training school in Allenstein, which was under the direction of the veterans' health care office at Königsberg, thirty-eight severely disabled veterans who had been unable to secure work organized a petition outlining their demands for welfare reform. In their letter to the Labor Ministry, they argued that the National Pension Law was too idealistic, and that its lofty goals undermined their attempts to be honest with potential employers about the tasks they could or could not reasonably perform. These men agreed that society was obligated to 'show compassion and sympathy that is consistent with progressive social thought', as outlined in the National Pension Law. At the same time, they argued that the state's first duty was to reemploy disabled veterans in any way possible.[62] The war-disabled petitioners harshly blamed the Social Democrats for losing sight of the concrete problems they faced: 'Today the social democratic government seeks to feed severely disabled war victims with empty words ... the Reemployment of War Victims Law sounds great in theory, but in practice it is of little use to disabled veterans'.[63] The state should concentrate on more immediate issues facing disabled veterans in the workplace. Their demands included the following: provide support for men who admitted they could only perform limited tasks, rather than claim that all should be given full opportunities; act as more direct intermediaries between employers and welfare officials to prevent unjust firings; and require employers without exception to immediately dismiss women from jobs that men could potentially fill. 'These demands', they insisted, 'are not unfulfillable or unreachable fantasies, and they must be the state's highest priority'.[64] Disabled veterans at Allenstein thus criticized what they saw as the lofty goals of the National Pension Law, and the state's weak management of relations between veterans and employers.

According to the architects behind the pension law, enthusiasm outweighed ability when it came to employment suitability. However, a series of cases reveal that the state's representatives failed to convince employers that severely disabled veterans could compete with women in terms of social and psychological suitability. Prolonged battles erupted between the Labor Ministry and personnel managers in some of the biggest firms enlisted by the state, including the Reichsbahn (National Railway) administration, the Reichsbank (National Bank), and the postal administration. As welfare representatives pressured these employers to fire women and replace them with disabled men, employers detailed their anxieties over the psychological condition of their disabled employees, which they deemed unfit for white-collar jobs. In the course of these conflicts, the image of psychologically disabled veterans as emotionally unstable, lacking work ethic, and deficient in social skills became conflated with the general image of severely disabled veterans in the work environment.

In the case of the Deutsche Reichsbahn in Frankfurt, one personnel director complained that severely disabled men were socially incapable of performing work as clerks and telephone operators. The director reported that women who had taken over these jobs during the war were more naturally suited for the required social interactions with co-workers and customers.[65] Women from bourgeois backgrounds, many employers claimed, were ideal in clerical jobs because they were trained in girls' schools that socialized them for middle-class codes of behavior. Disabled veterans from working-class backgrounds, in contrast, could not effectively adjust. The Reichsbahn personnel director asserted that the subtle character traits needed in office environments could not be instilled by managers, health care authorities and occupational therapists.[66]

In response to ongoing economic problems immediately after the war, and in particular after the 1923 inflation crisis, Reichsbahn directors ordered management to reassess their hiring practices and eliminate personnel, especially in administrative positions.[67] Men with nervous disorders were fired first, followed by severely physically disabled men. In the Berlin Street Car Administration, the personnel director assigned to creating jobs for severely disabled veterans claimed he could find office jobs for some men who were disfigured, but not for men whose appearance was exceptionally shocking. War neurotics, he insisted, simply could not be employed in service-oriented jobs: 'In my opinion, severely disabled men missing left eyes, exhibiting stiffened or lame left arms or even internal injuries can be employed as service personnel, but men with nervous disorders are not employable'.[68] He did not elaborate on why war neurotics were so uniquely unsuitable, but left it for welfare officials as self-evident that it was impossible to place mentally disabled men in an office environment.

Bank managers fought hiring quotas even more aggressively. They also explained in much more explicit terms why mentally and physically disabled veterans were so unsuitable for work. First of all, the Reichsbank complained that disabled veterans were physically unable to perform necessary tasks. At a branch of the Reichsbank in Landshut, managers reported that in order to fill state-mandated quotas, they were forced to hire disabled veterans 'who were so completely useless that they just hung about with nothing to do'.[69] Many disabled veterans had to take leave to return to invalid care and occupational training for several months at a time. At the Reichsbank in Berlin, personnel managers eagerly replaced them with women, claiming that female secretaries were not only more reliable, but also more skillful.[70] The Reichsbank informed the Labor Ministry that women had natural qualities that made them better than men: 'In the counting of paper money the female hand is indispensable ... in our experience, she performs up to 40% more than the male hand'.[71] Tensions reached a peak when the Labor Ministry tried to send the men on sick leave back into their jobs. Reichsbank managers tried to make their case by playing welfare administrators at their own game, citing the National Pension Law itself. The law, as one manager noted, stressed that men had to be hired into positions in which they were 'suitable', but 'because severely disabled veterans are not suited for these jobs as bank tellers and assistants', the bank acted within the boundaries of the law when they did not hire them.[72]

Social and psychological concerns cropped up frequently in Reichsbank reports. When the Labor Ministry pressed bank managers to describe why, exactly, they deemed disabled men 'unsuitable' for clerical jobs, the character and backgrounds of veterans came to the forefront. Reichsbank managers claimed that severely disabled veterans sent by the welfare offices often hid criminal pasts that made them untrustworthy in white-collar industry jobs:

> We are, by the way, as stated above, happy to hire severely disabled veterans in accordance with our duty and the order of 17 May 1920. But with this in mind we must consider the crucial point, which with respect to Reichsbank teller service is the most pressing point, and that is to hire employees with completely impeccable personalities. We will not hire such people who cannot provide evidence of a completely flawless past, or, as has recently happened, hire people who had been locked up ... not long ago because of theft.[73]

In addition, the Reichsbank complained that these men with questionable moral backgrounds did not possess the necessary work ethic for positions as bank workers and office assistants.[74]

Social welfare authorities responded by reiterating that the moral character of disabled veterans was beyond dispute by virtue of their sacrifices for the nation. The Reichsbank's fears, welfare officials asserted, were based on prejudices and suspicions rather than any proven facts, and that unless the Reichsbank had proof that any of their war disabled had a shady past, employers should withdraw their slanderous claims.[75] Welfare administrators also noted carefully that if the Reichsbank uncovered any individuals with a criminal past, these men were exceptional, and did not represent the morals or character of war victims as a whole. Local welfare offices reported to the Labor Ministry that a few 'trouble-makers' had been found in occupational training programs, but steps were being taken to root them out. These 'bad apples' were being used by bank managers who did not want to meet quotas to smear all disabled veterans as malingerers and criminals.[76]

The Berlin health care office sent a liaison officer to spend a day at the Reichsbank and report on whether or not employers there complied with the spirit of the Reemployment of Disabled Veterans Law. The official concluded that contrary to the Reichsbank's complaints, disabled veterans indeed had the character needed to work effectively as bank tellers. However, he did admit that severely disabled veterans were not physically suitable for a number of required tasks.[77] Arm amputees were not up to the job of counting bank notes every morning at opening time. Men with lung disorders ingested the dust on bundles of paper money, worsening their already fragile condition. Veterans who suffered from brain damage, the official noted, were 'questionable' in their ability to carry out the basic tasks required of clerks and office assistants. The official also found that with their violent, uncontrollable shakes and mental unreliability, war neurotics were incapable of performing work in an office environment, and unable to interact effectively with the public.[78] Nevertheless, he concluded that the Reichsbank was legally required to cooperate with the state and find suitable tasks for these men. If they could not perform tasks as bank tellers, for example, then the Reichsbank had to find disabled veterans other jobs in less high-pressure conditions and, more importantly, out of the view of customers.[79] In reports such as this, the Labor Ministry committed itself to keeping mentally disabled veterans integrated with the general war-disabled population. The Berlin welfare office promised to fund specialized training for building hand-eye coordination in physically disabled veterans, including both purely psychological and head wound cases, so they could maintain white-collar jobs. The Labor Ministry sponsored studies at the psycho-technical institute in Berlin-Charlottenburg to improve occupational training techniques that prepared mentally disabled veterans for the special skills needed in an office environment.[80]

Employers did not accept the argument that success boiled down to finding disabled veterans more suitable work environments or providing adequate training. No matter how much physical training the state promised to provide, employers protested that severely disabled veterans lacked the personalities needed to qualify for white-collar industry jobs. Employers indicated that war victims lacked that same work ethic as long-standing white-collar staff, including women. Even worse, many employers feared, disabled veterans hid psychopathological traits, including violent tendencies. War neurotics dominated the discourse in reports on unruly, uncontrollable disabled veterans. Despite the state's efforts to include mentally disabled men with other war victims in rehabilitation programs, employers portrayed war neurotics as morally different and exceptionally difficult to handle. Though only a small minority of disabled veterans were diagnosed with psychological disorders, the image of the war neurotic, and anxiety about the psychological effects of the war on returning veterans, loomed large in employers' imaginations.

This problem can be seen in the case of disabled veterans in jobs at the postal administration. By 1923, after years of exchanges, the postal administration defiantly informed the Labor Ministry that it would fire its war-disabled employees without consulting welfare offices. The Berlin main welfare office sent in representatives to investigate the firings. The postal director (*Oberpostdirektor*) barred investigators from observing disabled veterans on the job, and instead limited state representatives to an interview with personnel director Dr Neumann. Neumann took a conciliatory line and informed officials that the post office was doing all it could to meet the Labor Ministry's quotas, but complained that the state tried to exert too much control over hiring policies and interfered in the postal administration's domain.[81]

In a report to state officials, Neumann used four cases of war victims fired by the postal administration to illustrate their problems. Two of these men were physically disabled, one was a diagnosed war neurotic, and the last suffered from unspecified problems. Neumann described the first physically disabled veteran as a 'good stenographer and typist' who had to be let go because there was no position open for him, as all the suitable posts were already filled with severely disabled men. The only available job for him, Neumann pointed out, was hauling boxes in the back, but this was deemed too physically difficult. For the other physically disabled veteran, Paul S., Neumann recommended a less strenuous task, such as emptying mailboxes. However, other war victims and women workers already occupied these jobs, Neumann noted, and they performed up to the necessary standards.[82]

Neumann described the other two disabled veterans in his report as psychologically and socially unfit to work in an office environment and interact with other people. The first, Ernst K., was a diagnosed war neurotic. K. asked that he be given a different position in the post office, as his fragile nerves made it difficult to handle the stress of selling stamps and interacting with customers all day at the front window.[83] According to Neumann, K. was a chronic whiner and shirker. An investigator from the welfare office named Zanirum reported on his interview with Dr Neumann:

> Postal representative Dr N[eumann] is of the opinion that K. wants a job that puts less strain on his nerves so that in his free time he will have enough energy to study for his *Abitur* exam. Thus in the opinion of the O.P.D. (*Oberpostdirektor* – postal director) he <u>can</u> do the work, but <u>will</u> not do it. [emphasis in the original text].[84]

Dr Neumann further emphasized his point that K. was not willing to work by describing other job possibilities offered to K. to accommodate his nervous disorder. These jobs, including working in the back and moving boxes of mail, entailed a decrease in status that Neumann claimed K. was unwilling to accept. Further, Neumann portrayed K. as selfishly pursuing his own priorities of studying for his school exam despite the postal administration's flexible and understanding policy of special adjustments made for disabled veterans.[85]

Neumann portrayed the fourth disabled veteran in his report as a psychologically unbalanced, dangerous troublemaker. He did not specify Otto P.'s wounds. Further, the problems described by Neumann did not involve any question of physical ability to perform tasks. Instead, he was solely focused on P.'s behavior and character. P. had already been demoted to manual labor due to uncooperative behavior, but was still unable to meet his managers' expectations: 'P., a large, strong man, is a difficult person to handle who works as a shop steward. In the opinion of the O.P.D [*Oberpostdirektor*], as a box-emptier at SO36 [a particular postal location], P. has become a disturbing nuisance during his short time at work. The O.P.D. has rejected P.'s requests to take his case into consideration'. Neumann also compared K. to P., and noted that such men were not uncommon, even typical of the men sent by welfare authorities to work in the post office.[86]

In subsequent reports, personnel managers in the postal administration omitted the ever-present references to types of wounds and ailments suffered by their disabled workers. The postal administration drew up lists of disabled veterans deemed 'unsuitable as civil servants [here the term *Beamte* is used], despite their civil servant identification cards issued by welfare authorities'. The transgressions included stealing, harassing co-workers, and 'making passes at young girls'.[87] The postal administration insisted that it would not consider further applications of any disabled veterans as long as men sent by the welfare offices continued to display such behavior.[88] The characteristics that were once attributed specifically to men with nervous disorders – unwillingness to work, socially deviant behavior – were now being linked to the general population of disabled veterans in white-collar jobs.

Though employers expressed general resistance to hiring disabled veterans, men diagnosed with war neurosis complained to the Labor Ministry that they were particularly vulnerable to discrimination. Psychologically disabled veterans expressed fears that without direct protection from the Labor Ministry, they would have a uniquely difficult time finding a job. In their letters to the Labor Ministry, men diagnosed with mental trauma, including both neurotic men and men with organic nervous disorders and primarily physical symptoms like tics and tremors, argued that compared to their physically disabled comrades, their chances of finding new jobs were slim.

In Magdeburg, civil service employers fired Willy N. because, they concluded, his nervous disorders and heart ailment made him unsuitable for office work. N. protested that other disabled veterans let go would have a good chance at finding another job in the civil service, especially once the economy and job market started to improve, while his psychological and nervous disorders made potential employers reluctant to accommodate him, placing his family in jeopardy. N. also feared slipping in social status, and worried that his worsening nervous disorder would eventually exclude him from finding any kind of work, salaried or wage-earning. N. insisted that he possessed the same work ethic and commitment as his colleagues, and that with only minor accommodations for his health he could do his job as well as any other man. He asked the Labor Ministry to give his case full consideration in accordance with the laws protecting severely disabled veterans, to reverse his termination notice at his job at the health insurance office, or make arrangements to secure him another civil service position.[89] N.'s expressed fears indicate that war neurotics, even those not labeled as psychologically dangerous or difficult to work with, were aware that employers perceived them as particularly socially and psychologically unfit.

By the time inflation reached its worst levels in 1923, employers refused outright to implement reemployment laws for disabled veterans. The problem was so acute that the Interior Ministry, which in 1920–21 had been held up as a positive example for employing disabled veterans in white-collar jobs, circulated a memo that said the Labor Ministry would have to compromise on its claim that all disabled veterans could be made suitable workers if only given the opportunity and training. Interior minister Freund, after reviewing the performance of severely disabled veterans at the police administration, wrote:

> In accordance with the Disabled Veterans' Reemployment Law, I would gladly make room for these men in the police force. But because the nature and tasks involved in the execution of police service in this branch of administration require that only completely physically and mentally intact persons can be used, the main health insurance office cannot be permitted any opportunity to try and fill such positions with <u>suitable</u> war disabled [emphasis in original text].[90]

The interior minister thus indicated that even 'suitable' disabled veterans were not adequate for certain jobs. These men, according to Freund, did not measure up to other workers either physically or psychologically, suggesting that employers were only tolerating their presence rather than generating productive, or even reliable, levels of work. No longer willing to carry disabled veterans along just to placate the Labor Ministry, Interior Ministry officials rebelled against the welfare system by pressing for autonomy in determining who was suitable for work. Even in the local welfare offices themselves, where many severely disabled men were placed in lower-level office jobs in 1920–21 when nobody else would take them, severely disabled veterans were being let go. Administrators complained that the state bureaucracies set a negative example by not retaining disabled veterans.[91]

By 1924, with even the state's employers unwilling to meet requirements, the Reemployment Law was in shambles. Further, the crisis of inflation changed the shape of the war victim problem significantly. In the exchanges between disgruntled employers and frustrated labor ministers, the latter showed signs of caving in to arguments made by employers and doctors that the National Pension Law was impractical, and that no matter how much the state, employers, and severely disabled veterans committed themselves to full economic rehabilitation, severely disabled veterans were ultimately unable to recover their prewar economic levels of productivity and society's confidence. Employers, however, illegally bypassed the quota law. In Hamburg, the Labor Ministry found employers manipulating the books on how many severely disabled veterans they retained. Labor ministers complained that employers only went through the motions even if they did bother to hire veterans: 'If it were not for the forced imposition of hiring laws and protection from dismissal, the unemployment of severely disabled veterans would undoubtedly be substantially higher than it is among the population of healthy workers'.[92] The engineers of the National Pension Law recognized that the employment of disabled veterans was achieved only through coercion, rather than through the grass roots enthusiasm that they had hoped would follow the spirit of the law.

With the Labor Ministry ineffective, the experiment to assimilate war neurotics into the social fabric collapsed. Looking to win at least some cooperation, the Labor Ministry granted employers greater authority to define work 'suitability' according to their own criteria, labor ministers also permitted regional districts to modify elements of the Reemployment Law. Granting this autonomy to local authorities and employers signaled the end of the Social Democrats' efforts to integrate men with nervous disorders into the general population of disabled veterans. Once given greater control, employers urged state officials to withdraw support for war neurotics. Labor ministers acquiesced, and in January 1927, state representative Dr Heinrich Dietz announced an amendment to the National Pension Law passed through the health insurance courts and the Bavarian Landtag that effectively ended state protection for psychologically disabled veterans. The amendment stated:

Severe hysteria that results in fits alone does not make war victims unfit or unsuitable for civil servant job (Paragraph 33, Section 2, National Pension Law). However, if they display particular irritability, excitability and such tendencies, then the interests of the individual employer are the most important question.[93]

Bavaria thus set a precedent in amending the National Pension Law by handing authority to employers in determining whether or not disabled veterans were psychologically and emotionally fit to hold a job. The leeway given to employers in making these decisions was broad. A coalition of employers and local officials in Bavaria even circumvented medical and diagnostic questions over psychological disorders. They put the diagnosis in broader, popular terms, outlining criteria such as 'level of irritability ... and other tendencies'.[94] Employers thus gained authority to fire men based on their personalities and behavior, and they no longer had to argue with the Labor Ministry and central health insurance offices over the suitability of different categories of war victims to particular jobs.

Bavarian pension courts also determined that employers were not responsible for providing a favorable, nondiscriminatory working environment. This argument had long been articulated by conservatives, who argued that employment of disabled veterans ultimately depended on the men themselves. The frequent firings of disabled men drew steady attention from veterans groups on the political right. Carlo von Kügelgen, a member of the conservative *Kyffhäuser Bund*, insisted that it was time for war victims to finally take reemployment into their own hands. Von Kügelgen, who lost an arm before the war but claimed he understood how disabled veterans felt, wrote that the main obstacles facing men almost ten years after the war were primarily psychological, and that those who were still unemployed were in that situation because they did not want to work. If only wounded men were treated as returning heroes rather than welfare recipients, von Kügelgen argued in his article 'Not Cripples – Victors!', they 'could concentrate on the goal of reaching their own inner strength to make the most out of life'. Without state interference war victims would become psychologically fit enough to work, as they could reclaim a sense of independence and personal responsibility taken away by the republic.[95]

This notion that 'welfare' prevented men from overcoming their psychological wounds would become state-sanctioned after Hitler came to power. In 1935, psychiatrist Alfred Hoche, who would later support the T–4 'Euthanasia' program, argued that neuroses really did exist among disabled veterans, but that it was the pension law rather than the war that prevented men from recovering: 'The individuals are in fact sick, but they would be well, strangely enough, if the law did not exist'.[96] As long as the pension law existed, conservative veterans' organizations and the state's psychiatrists worked to isolate and root hysterics out of the social welfare system before they could contaminate legitimate war victims.

The Physically Disabled Revolt against War Neurotics

A segment of the disabled veterans' population, primarily ex-officers, criticized the Weimar Republic for encouraging what they believed were undisciplined, disloyal and unmanly war neurotics to become 'pension neurotics' dependent on the welfare system. These former officers sought to distance themselves from psychologically disabled veterans and the 'hysterical' symptoms that they believed tarnished the image of the front veteran in the public eye. Officers also resented being lumped together with enlisted men in social welfare programs for war victims. These veterans from middle-class backgrounds equated war neurotics with working-class veterans, both of whom they saw as guilty of shirking their duty in the trenches and malingering at home. This antipathy toward war neurotics as shirkers may be interpreted as a case of projection in light of evidence that in the last weeks of the war officers were eager to cover up their avoidance of duty in the chaos of retreat, leading them to blame others and develop legends like the 'stab-in-the-back'.[97]

Former officers revolted against the inclusion of war neurotics in war victims' care. Labor ministers, desperate to repair the image of the social welfare system that the conservative press portrayed as over-burdened with veterans unwilling to work, cooperated with disgruntled, ex-officers to eliminate war neurotics from rehabilitation and occupational training programs for disabled veterans. War neurotics were a useful scapegoat for middle-class veterans who sought to blame the loss of the war on working-class soldiers' allegedly inferior sense of national duty and masculine character. State representatives picked up these prejudices, isolated war neurotics as illegitimate war victims, and blamed them for the failure of work programs for disabled veterans.

Stretched to the limit, convalescent and nursing homes (*Kriegs-Invalidenheime*) for severely disabled veterans became a battleground for veterans of different class backgrounds, and an embarrassment to labor ministers who sought to portray severely disabled men as on the verge of social and economic reintegration. Shortly after the ratification of the National Pension Law in 1920, the Labor Ministry made a concerted effort to place severely disabled veterans who required more care than families could provide into disabled veterans' homes, many of which were already established under private funding during the *Kaiserreich*. The difficulty experienced by families taking care of a psychologically traumatized returning soldier is reflected in the distribution of disabled veterans at the Johanna-Belenen invalid home run in Volmarkstein. Twenty percent of those applying for full-time care there were war neurotics. At least one-third of those applicants were refused on the grounds that families could provide daily needs while these men periodically visited health care officials and underwent counseling or occupational therapy.[98] Still, mentally ill veterans often composed the second largest group of war victims in permanent homes for disabled veterans, far higher than their proportion in the larger war-disabled population, where they comprised fewer than ten per cent of the overall war-disabled community. Of the 84 severely disabled veterans living in the Johanna-Belenen home in June 1920, 36 suffered from amputations and serious external injuries, 28 were 'neurotic and psychologically ill', 12 suffered from consumption, eight were blind, and one was stricken by chronic 'internal injuries'.[99] These homes were thus a security net for psychologically disabled veterans who were having difficulty assimilating into jobs and whose families could not carry the burden of home care.

The function of these homes for disabled veterans was two-fold: to provide occupational therapy and to give veterans an environment of mutual support. Reflecting the attitude of many doctors, Dr Gau warned that the politically divided veterans' associations were antagonistic towards the state's health care system, and failed to provide for the economic and social rehabilitation of disabled veterans.[100] The Johanna-Belenen invalid home provided disabled veterans with a controlled psychological, social, and economic routine designed to help them readjust to postwar society. Male medical specialists and female nurses, supervised under Dr Gau, offered veterans the calm of recreation rooms with music, a variety of hobbies and work therapy, including basket-weaving, clock-making and wood-working, and a variety of medical treatments that included baths, massages and physical therapy. Dr Gau characterized this setting as individually tailored to veterans' needs, reflecting a new peacetime goal of returning men to a sense of personal happiness that laid the groundwork for work rehabilitation. 'Work care' (*Arbeitspflege*) was adjusted to the individual's abilities: 'Above all, war invalids should be able to give back their good-will and fulfillment through work, as much as their physical and psychological condition permits'. The invalid home specialized in on-site training in clerical work, including typing and secretarial skills.[101]

The inclusion of mentally ill veterans in these disabled veterans' homes was a complete failure. Conservative veterans' groups spearheaded a movement to restrict disabled veterans' homes to the physically disabled. Writing to the Labor Ministry in 1922, the director of the National Association of German Officers (*Nationalverband Deutscher Offiziere*) complained about the democratization of the invalid homes, and noted that 'in earlier times' the homes were reserved for career soldiers, and only 'authentic' war victims such as amputees and blind or deaf veterans who were making their gradual transition back to employment.[102] Organized officers had support from military authorities to return the invalid homes back to the good old days. The National Defense Ministry (*Reichswehrministerium*) complained to the Labor Ministry that the National Pension Law of 1920 transformed veterans' homes from recovery centers for career officers to health care facilities for disabled veterans of mixed social backgrounds.[103] Social leveling, rubbing shoulders with war neurotics, and relinquishing control of veterans' homes to Labor Ministry bureaucrats proved too traumatic for former officers.

The Labor Ministry submitted to officers' complaints and placed restrictions on applications to the invalid homes. In order to be accepted into a disabled veterans' home, men had to demonstrate that they were in control of any mental trauma they still experienced. One disabled veteran named F., documented as suffering from war-related psychological trauma, was not permitted to reapply for residency at a Nuremberg disabled veterans' home when doctors determined he was a 'psychopath' who had no potential for future employment.[104] In their applications, psychologically traumatized veterans learned that they had to emphasize certain values and character traits in order to be admitted. Ernst S. described at length how he was a hard worker who was developing his skills as a stenographer. He noted that the 'psychological depression' he experienced did not impair his 'strength of will' and resolve to work in any way, and he only needed support from similarly troubled veterans in the veterans' invalid homes to help him maintain the routine of work and avoid becoming a permanent burden to the state.[105] Ernst S. included a doctors' medical report that mentioned only knee and foot injuries, which the doctor argued required considerable medical care while S. made the transition to work. His doctor concluded that S. exhibited 'extraordinary mental mobility' that enabled him to reintegrate into normal life.[106] The Labor Ministry was impressed by S.'s case and his exceptional work ethic, and made room for him at the Carlshafen invalid home near Cassel.[107]

Traumatized veterans who did not meet this standard of self-control ran into problems. Complaints from veterans about publicly disruptive comrades in invalid homes flooded the Labor Ministry and reached the press. Upon investigation, health care administrators reported that most of these disruptive individuals were psychologically disabled veterans who could not be kept in war invalid homes for various reasons, or who were upset because their applications to live in the invalid homes had been rejected. In August 1924, doctors at the Berlin veterans' health clinic cut 'war hysteric' Richard W.'s pension, and refused his application to live in a veterans' home, after they decided that his unemployment was due more to his 'weakness of will, inner disposition and hunt for a pension' than psychological wounds, though these were officially recognized as war-related. 'Because W. is a well-known whiner', health care administrators wrote, 'giving him quarters in the invalids' home is not desirable'.[108] Labor Ministry officials concluded that W'.s chronic poverty also reflected his weak character. One official wrote that W. simply refused to work, giving only the appearance of living in poverty in Berlin's working-class district of Treptow, and thus he did not deserve social care benefits. This official cited W.'s propensity to pick fights with everyone he knew, and reported that 'W. spends his time taking short and long tours through the city on his three-wheeled bicycle, even as far as Potsdam, where he seeks to disturb the peaceful routine of the public'. There W. allegedly hid behind bushes in parks at Frederick the Great's Sanssouci palace and frightened pedestrians. The Labor Ministry official concluded that W. would also threaten the 'peace and order' (*Ruhe und Ordnung*) of the invalid home.[109]

The Berlin invalid home system boiled over with the violent outbursts of frustrated disabled veterans. The health care office at Berlin-Schöneberg successfully asked the Labor Ministry to turn down war victim Fritz G'.s application to continue residing at his disabled veterans' home. G. had been originally admitted to the veterans' home for a leg injury and tuberculosis. He worked running errands for a paper manufacturer, but could barely support himself and his wife. At a special concert performance in Potsdam for disabled veterans, G. brought festivities to a halt with violent shrieking and wild behavior. Doctors examined him shortly after and found a tendency towards 'general nervous irritability and conflict'. The health care office also reported that G. was a well-known 'agitator' who went from one clinic to another inciting fights and 'disturbing the peaceful adminis-tration of veterans' homes'.[110] Doctors later concluded that G.'s aggressive behavior stemmed from 'inborn temperament' and not, as G. claimed, from the emotional trauma of the front and the stressful experience of a botched operation on his wounded knee in 1917.[111]

Fritz G.'s friends came to his aid and protested the Labor Ministry's characterization of him as a chronic trouble-maker prone to violence. A friend writing on his behalf, Frau Dr Genthe, described G. as a 'hard-working, dependable, unpretentious family man' who did not deserve to be excluded from the invalids' home. Any 'irritability', she added, was nothing abnormal for anyone living in these stressful times, and it would diminish once his economic situation improved.[112] Another friend, Katherine Otto, informed the Labor Ministry that G.'s 'crude nature' emerged only after he returned from the war psychologically changed, and he was terribly stressed by working to take care of his wife and son.[113] Health care officials responded by saying that even if G. were a calm, responsible person, his living habits were filthy and he was too 'unhygienic' to be allowed to live in a home for disabled veterans.[114] Learning of the case through the social democratic National Association of War Disabled (*Reichsbund der Kriegsbeschädigten*), Reichstag war-disabled committee representative and Social Democratic Party leader Erich Roßmann wrote on G.'s behalf, and got the Labor Ministry to promise to at least reconsider G.'s case.[115]

In war neurotics like Fritz G. and Richard W., state officials found a group of men who allegedly infected the morale of recovering veterans with their defective work ethic and personal character. Further, frustrated policy-makers saw in war neurotics a uniquely dissident group of war victims. Labor ministers construed war neurotics as the most ungrateful and dissident of all disabled veterans, and a potential threat to veterans', and the public's, confidence in the state's welfare programs. State officials did not accept Frau Genthe's diagnosis of Fritz G. as a victim of the mental stress that the times placed on all Germans. Judging them as unwilling to work, and undisciplined burdens on the social welfare system, labor ministers placed the blame on psychologically disabled war victims for failing to recover and reintegrate into postwar society. War neurotics were accused of being the leading 'whiners' and 'grumblers', terms circulated frequently by doctors. Just as the *Kaiserreich*'s doctors convinced the wartime government that war neurotics had to be isolated and removed from healthy soldiers in order to maintain willingness to go over the top, these same doctors convinced Weimar's social policy-makers that these men were a threat to morale, and damaged public confidence, in war victims.

Whiners and Rebels: The War Neurotics Fight Back

Doctors and state administrators were not entirely inaccurate in defining war neurotics as the most dissident group of disabled veterans. Some psychologically disabled veterans were conscious of their special status in the eyes of authorities, and they claimed to represent wider dissatisfaction among war victims. War victim Karl U., diagnosed as a war neurotic since 1917, experienced full paralysis of his lower body by 1923. He was given a psychiatric evaluation at the University of Heidelberg. According to his letter to the Karlsruhe branch of the Association of War Victims (*Bund der Kriegsbeschädigten*), the paralyzed U. was left alone for two days in a hospital bed. When he asked the resident Dr Gessler how much longer he had to stay at the clinic, the doctor replied: 'Until Friday or Saturday, and you certainly don't need a pension, because you could work if you wanted, but you don't want to!' When U. replied that he could not even walk, not to mention work, the doctor reportedly answered sarcastically, 'We know that already!' On the third day of this battle of wills, U. wrote that he attempted to escape, but was ambushed by Dr Gessler who taunted him, saying 'perhaps you'll want to jump quicker than that!' while beating him to the ground.[116]

Karl U. also claimed that he was the only patient at the hospital who had the courage to protest the perceived mistreatment of disabled veterans. In U'.s account, the other patients were weakened by the hospital routine and made submissive by Dr Gessler. When hospital administrators cracked down and searched for culprits in the short-lived riot, U. said his fellow veterans scurried off, fearing retribution in the form of unfavorable pension evaluations.[117] After spending the next year struggling to make his case in the pension courts, U. was finally upgraded from 20 to 50 per cent war-disabled status, acknowledging the legitimacy of his psychological wounds and status as a severely disabled veteran. However, this status was contingent on the approval of doctors, who did not share the pension court's findings. Furious, U. wrote directly to President von Hindenburg, noting that the old field marshal would surely see the injustice perpetrated by state's doctors on a veteran 'who was in the field from the day of mobilization to the end of the war ... who gave my entire savings to war loans and sacrificed my health and happiness for the fatherland'. U. described the 'mockery of the medical evaluation' he experienced at Heidelberg, and reported that the doctors there had to shut down his protests with shots of morphine. He portrayed himself as a heroic fighter defending his disabled comrades, reluctant to cause problems but with his back against the wall.[118]

Karl U. was desperately aware of how war neurotics were perceived as baseless grumblers rather than legitimate advocates of war victims' interests. In the opening of his letter to von Hindenburg, U. asked to be pardoned for sounding like just another complainer in a time when everyone was facing crisis. 'Your Excellency', U. wrote to the former field marshal, 'will not take offense at his loyal subject in receiving yet another complaint in these difficult times. But this dire emergency and unjust treatment of this pension case forces me to take these steps'.[119] War neurotics like U. were seen by doctors as more than just the harmless 'whiners' they were so often labeled. According to the Labor Ministry's doctors, 'whining' about pensions, the most recognizable symptom of 'pension neurosis', was not just a character flaw, but a cancer within the welfare system. The Labor Ministry replied to U. and scolded him for misrepresenting doctors as antagonistic. They concluded that U.'s complaint about brutality in the Heidelberg clinic was unfounded, and that nothing in his medical documents would support further attempts to change his pension status.[120]

War neurotics, even more so than other disabled veterans, complained about much more than just their pension status. Common to all war victims dissatisfied with Weimar's pension system was a sense of betrayal. The 'Thanks of the Fatherland', veterans complained, amounted to a pension that barely met the needs of daily existence, and reflected the republic's lack of respect for the sacrifices of millions of ex-front soldiers.[121] But war neurotics saw their own experiences as uniquely traumatic, and even argued that they were still being traumatized long after the guns went silent. In the stream of complaints that poured into the Labor Ministry, war neurotics characterized their interaction with doctors as an experience that reproduced the psychological terror of the trenches. Psychiatrists brutalized their patients, the latter testified, when they claimed that psychological wounds were not genuine and that 'hysterical' men faked their wounds in order to get a pension. Diagnosed war neurotic August F., for example, drew parallels between the horror of the trenches and the experience of being evaluated by Dr Schulz at the Hannover disabled veterans' nerve clinic. F. recounted that Dr Schulz made him undress, paraded him through the hospital, and then accused him of simulating his mental injuries. F. wrote that he felt as if he had been 'raped':

> Against this type of treatment I submit this firm protest and I will not fail to speak out against this above-described rape of a disabled veteran ... if this gentleman [Dr Schulz] were to have come back sick from the front, or if he had spilled his blood for the fatherland, he would certainly not treat a disabled war veteran like a repulsive dog or deny him a means to exist ... There can be no doubt that after this critique of the state doctor's medical evaluation, my observation will be so embarrassing to the state that it will be rejected, the doctor's examination will be considered justified, reason will be denied and Terror will govern.[122]

F. imagined himself as a heroic whistle-blower on a corrupt health care system led by renegade doctors determined to undermine the National Pension Law. Using the rhetoric of an embattled front soldier, F. portrayed himself as a representative of the interests of fellow war disabled still fighting: 'I seek justice for myself, but also justice for my comrades'.[123] F. believed that doctors systematically scapegoated war neurotics as enemies of the nation. If only the public knew how doctors treated war victims, F. asserted, the state would no longer be able to impose its system of 'Terror', a term that invoked both authoritarian government control and psychological trauma.

War neurotics also believed that discrimination was politically motivated. According to Alex E., diagnosed a war neurotic before 1918, doctors demonstrated prejudices that proved their thinking had not changed since the *Kaiserreich*. E. complained that he was being portrayed as a 'degenerate psychopath' by politically motivated doctors who hid behind a veil of medical objectivity that made them untouchable.[124] Though E.'s letter displayed mangled reasoning and a stream of convoluted evidence that must have made sense to himself, his most repeated theme was that doctors shut down his request for a pension because they opposed his politics. He was a former member of the SPD and a self-described anarchist, and, he claimed, they wished to silence his attacks on the state. E. railed at doctors for calling him a 'whiner' while health care administrators 'considered their doctors nothing less than angels'. He claimed that in reality doctors 'were crows who picked out the eyes of their patients'.[125]

The testimony of war neurotics like Alex E. came from tortured minds with a tenuous grasp on reality. Nevertheless, they were right in accusing doctors of singling out war neurotics as vociferous critics of the pension system and the authority of doctors and the state. At the disabled veterans' health care clinic in Wiesbaden, state medical representative Dr Moll began a systematic purge of war neurotics from the pension rolls, arguing that their criticisms against the state welfare system represented a level of pension neurosis that poisoned the morale of other war victims.[126] Dr Moll recommended that these individuals be removed from the pension system and placed in mental hospitals. In one case, he reported:

> With many tears, [Wilhelm R.] unleashes his loud complaints and wretched whining, saying that the state has destroyed his entire existence. He is not capable of making a reasonable statement about the alleged deterioration of his situation. In addition, he loudly curses the entire National Pension Law, etc. This case involves an especially severe form of pension hysteria. An investigation and evaluation at the health care clinic does not appear possible due to the severity of this case.
>
> In order to conclusively deal with this case, and specifically to stop giving further justification for the rejection of present and future expected applications for pensions, it is recommended that he be placed in the mental ward of a hospital for a short period of observation and evaluation.[127]

Chronic complaints against the welfare system, cursing the pension laws, and criticism of the state earned Wilhelm R. and other veterans the label 'hysteric'.[128] With this label, doctors tried to nullify war neurotics' criticisms of veterans' health care and government policy, and at the same time curry favor with labor ministers by condemning their patients' criticisms of the National Pension Law.

Not all state officials agreed with doctors that war neurotics were whiners, deviants and criminals. When Dr Moll made repeated accusations against war neurotics, as well as other war victims, as fakers and malingerers, this brought intense scrutiny from investigators of problems in the welfare system who felt that Dr Moll crossed the line. Regional inspector Watzenberg, himself a reserve lieutenant and disabled veteran, came to the defense of Wilhelm R. after reviewing Dr Moll. Watzenberg encouraged the Labor Ministry and the main health care office in Cassel, which supervised Dr Moll's office in Wiesbaden, to reprimand Dr Moll for 'besmirching' the good character of so many disabled veterans with 'biased' diagnoses. Watzenberg argued that Dr Moll was wrong in judging R. a hysterical 'swindler', as this implied that he was unpatriotic, when in reality his sacrifice for the fatherland proved otherwise.[129] Watzenberg considered it his 'moral and civic duty' to defend 'good German-minded war victims' against insensitive doctors. 'It has gone so far in our dear German fatherland that war wounded men who defend their rights and have filth thrown at them are being pursued as criminals – oh how depressing it is!'

The complaints made by disabled veterans, whether psychologically or physically injured, he argued, were legitimate frustrations stemming from what he described as the 'psychological torments' caused by the war and postwar era that only other veterans could understand. In Watzenberg's opinion, criticism against the pension system was not treasonous criticism of the state as Dr Moll had implied.[130]

Support from sympathetic fellow veterans, especially reserve officers like Watzenberg, was rare, and it did not sway the Labor Ministry. Instead, the Labor Ministry supported Dr Moll's attempts to systematically remove mentally disabled veterans from the pension system. In August 1925, 100 per cent disabled veteran Ludwig L., a diagnosed war neurotic accompanied by his mother, Mathilde, visited the Wiesbaden veterans' health clinic. According to L.'s father, Dr Moll threatened L. with a trip to an asylum and police involvement if he did not snap out of his mental illness. The doctor repeated these threats to L.'s mother, shouting at her that he would write an evaluation that would cancel her son's pension. With Ludwig in tow, Frau L. pushed her way out of the doctor's office as he taunted her with further threats. Herr L. demanded an apology that would 'rehabilitate the honor of my wife and my son'.[131] The Labor Ministry promptly came to Dr Moll's defense. They argued that Herr L.'s version of events was false and that Dr Moll never acted out of line.[132]

Herr L. assembled a team of lawyers and contacted his relatives and friends in the civil service. He was most aggravated by the implication that his family had lied to protect a son who shirked work.[133] The stress of the Labor Ministry's attack on the L. family honor was apparently fatal. Herr L. reported that as a result of her altercation with the doctor and the ensuing stress from the scandal of being so insulted, Frau L. had died of a heart attack. Herr L.'s lawyers reported the case to the justice system, and he contacted his relative, Dr L., the president of the world court (*Weltgerichtshof*) at the Hague. Herr L. expressed that his goal was to get his mentally ill son, Ludwig, reinstated into the health care system for disabled veterans, where he would be treated with the respect that he deserved.[134]

Further investigations into Dr Moll took place in 1925. The Labor Ministry asked other doctors for their opinions of Dr Moll and his interaction with patients. State medical representative Dr Krummacher, the head of the veterans' health administration in Cassel, confirmed Dr Moll's finding that Wilhelm R., for example, was a 'known psychopath' who 'took Dr Moll's comments out of context'. In his own response to complaints leveled against him, Dr Moll reported:

> I certainly want every disabled veteran to get everything that the National Pension Law allows. There will, however, always be someone else to blame for defects in their [disabled veterans'] will to

become healthy, as long as the public supports the pretension that the law can motivate each individual patient to want to be healthy.[135]

War neurotics themselves were thus not the only culprits. The public, Dr Moll argued, discouraged psychologically disabled veterans from becoming healthy by naively assuming that benevolent laws could motivate these men to work.

Now, five years after the appearance of the National Pension Law, the engineers of the welfare state came around to the medical establishment's point of view. Dr Scholtze, who headed the original committee that designed the National Pension Law, determined that none of the complaints made by disabled veterans against Dr Moll had any foundation. He informed the National Committee of War Disabled that any further appeals were without justification.[136] Repudiating the main argument of the National Pension Law, state officials and doctors coalesced to argue that it was the will of veterans, not their wounds or society's capacity to assist them that determined their path to recovery.

As war neurotics became official pariahs of the state, physically disabled veterans organized against them more aggressively. Veterans suffering from head-shot wounds feared that with their uncontrollable shaking, broken speech, mild paralysis, behavioral disorders and other symptoms that they shared with the psychologically traumatized, they would also be pinned as 'hysterics' and 'whiners'. In 1927, in an attempt to advocate their own particular rights and distinguish themselves from war neurotics, these men established the Association of War Disabled with Brain Injuries (*Bund der hirnverletzte Krieger*) At their first annual meeting in 1927, the committee chairman of the Munich branch B. Böhm, a reserve officer, teacher, and himself the survivor of a head-shot wound, submitted his recently published pamphlet on the needs required by men suffering from brain injuries. In this 23-page pamphlet, Böhm outlined the types of occupational and physical therapy required by men with brain damage, repeatedly reiterating that these were physical wounds that produced a variety of symptoms including blindness, hearing problems and the disruption of motor skills. The latter, Böhm noted, often confused the public, as men on the streets with speech disabilities, paralysis in limbs, and tremors were often mistaken for war neurotics. Men with head wounds had many complaints about health care, Böhm noted, but he went to great pains to reassure his readers that men with brain injuries were entirely different from men who suffered from war neurosis:

To put it briefly, the complaints made by veterans with brain injuries stem from actual alterations in the brain itself. They are to be seen as completely different from the perhaps similar-sounding words produced by neurotics and hysterics. Their [war neurotics'] complaints are often so harsh, that in making them they will never be able to overcome their difficulties.[137]

War neurotics, Böhm thus contends, offered only unconstructive criticism. Further, he suggests that men with head-shot wounds could be excused for their rants because they suffered from actual brain damage and, through no fault of their own, could not control themselves. His tract contains lengthy descriptions on how physically disabled war victims made great strides, even if it took them years to do it, learning new occupations and finding ways to become full members of society. To prove that his fellow wounded veterans made only constructive suggestions about the pension system, rather than grandiose complaints, he offered a solution to the problems faced by the pension courts in trying to assign different pension rates to the wide range of neurological wounds. Böhm favored a flat pension for what the National Pension Law should specify as 'head wounds', rather than 'nerve injuries', putting all cases whose symptoms originated in organic war-related injuries under one category. These, he pointed out, should be distinguished from the neurotic cases because there was no doubt as to whether or not they were caused by an injury at the front.[138]

Eager to avoid being labeled a whiner who criticized the state's health care system, Böhm praised the many nurses and 'efficient health care civil servants'. He expressed loyalty to nurses and extolled their patriotic qualities: 'Yes, they are true heroines and they deserve the sincere thanks of the general public for the sacrifices that they give to us, because they courageously pay off the thanks of the fatherland that is due to us'.[139] According to Böhm, the state could trust that physically disabled war victims wanted to work with labor ministers and doctors to improve the pension system. In contrast, the motives of psychologically disabled veterans were suspect, their reasoning doubtful, their complaints unrealistic, and their attitude ungrateful. No matter what problems existed in the pension system, Böhm assured the Labor Ministry that men with actual head wounds believed that health care administrators and doctors worked sincerely to provide veterans with their deserved thanks of the fatherland.

Böhm's declaration of support for the civil servants and health care officials was part of a determined effort to distance himself and other physically disabled veterans from war neurotics. The demands of men suffering from head-shot wounds were based on legitimate social and economic interests, not the useless 'whining' typical of undisciplined, weak-willed neurotic veterans who failed to adhere to a middle-class work ethic. Former officers like Böhm, and those who organized against psychologically traumatized men in veterans' homes, tried to prove that they had remained disciplined, mentally fit, loyal in the trenches and useful members of society.

*   *   *

The enormous costs and over-bureaucratization, and the resentments felt by disabled veterans, only partly explain the failure of Weimar's social welfare system for returning soldiers. Tensions between civilians and returning veterans prevented social welfare legislation from getting off the ground. In order to explain the failure of the National Pension Law of 1920, one must closely examine the public's resentments towards these men, not only as painful reminders of the lost war, but also as burdens to social and economic recovery. In the National Pension Law, social welfare legislators argued that all war victims deserved to be guaranteed the right to work because they were fundamentally willing to work. Though the war temporarily shattered the faith of war victims in their own productivity and sense of self-worth, social democratic architects of the welfare system argued, this could be remedied through encouragement and efforts to find suitable environments for disabled workers.

Popular perceptions about war neurotics, however, reflected doctors' long-standing arguments that individuals, particularly working-class veterans with their weak characters, not the war, were responsible for what was widely seen as a breakdown in work ethic and productivity. Few disabled veterans accused of disruptive behavior were diagnosed war neurotics. Yet employers saw their severely disabled employees in ways traditionally reserved for men with nervous disorders – as shirkers, whiners and troublemakers. Attributes ascribed to neurotic men conflated with war victims in general. Further, the postal administration and the Reichsbank portrayed war neurotics who had been retrained at the welfare facilities as imposters out of their professional and social spheres, who lacked the character, commitment and discipline to work in traditionally middle-class jobs. Anxieties over psychological stability, social suitability and potentially violent behavior shaped employers' general mutinies against the state's efforts to reassimilate 'hysterical' men.

The Social Democrats and political parties loyal to the new republic constructed the National Pension Law on the basis of a sweeping diagnosis of the nation's psychological condition. They believed that because the nation shared the shattering psychological effects of the war – a collective trauma – the public would enthusiastically identify with and support all war victims in their efforts to recover the self-confidence and will to be productive members of society. Problems with reintegrating disabled veterans into work proved that this was not the case. Conservative doctors, employers and veterans held up mentally disabled veterans as 'confirmation' of their long-standing view on social welfare, that no matter what programs the state designed, certain groups of people were inherently unwilling to work. Thus the war was not to blame for undermining the will to work, and society was not obligated to pay for an expanded social welfare system. War victims, not the public, employers argued alongside doctors, had to carry the burden of social and economic readjustment. Social Democrats' tenacious arguments that men with nervous disorders deserved to be fully integrated into the general war-disabled population drew enormous resentment from employers, forcing welfare officials to pull support for war neurotics in order to salvage their shattered relations with employers and reemployment programs for at least the physically disabled.

The voices of psychologically disabled veterans highlight the continuities between the *Kaiserreich* and the Weimar Republic. Subjected to what they believed were similar forms of violence in the trenches and in the health clinics, war neurotics claimed that the state continued to brutalize the mentally disabled by excluding them from the same rights as other war victims. As war neurotics became more isolated, they also retaliated with greater aggression. The next chapter examines how political organizations on the left appropriated these voices and attempted to defend them as legitimate war victims.

Chapter 4

'The Class Struggle Psychosis'
Working-Class Politics and Psychological Trauma

> The theory of pension psychosis is rooted in the social structure of
> a class-based society.
> — Emil Vogeley, member of the Communist Party (KPD)[1]

Mentally traumatized veterans developed their own theories concerning the origins and significance of traumatic neurosis. Conservative doctors and political groups claimed that 'war neurosis' was faked by intrinsically sick and disloyal working-class veterans to escape the front and, after the war, gain pensions from the coddling new democratic state and its welfare system, which contributed to an epidemic of 'pension psychosis'. Working-class veterans criticized what they saw as the systematic repression of the traumatic war experience by middle-class psychiatrists and political groups, who they believed invented terms like 'pension psychosis' in order to deny responsibility for the human costs of the war or, even worse, prepare Germany for another world conflict. In welfare lines, doctors' offices, and the streets a battle raged over the act of forgetting, as mentally ill veterans mobilized against what they saw as a social and political system in denial of the horrifying effects of modern war.

Working-class victims of psychological trauma used the debate over war neurosis to theorize on the psychological effects of the war on different social classes in Weimar Germany. The two largest parties on Weimar's political left, the Social Democratic Party (SPD) and the Communist Party (KPD) argued vehemently that psychological trauma was a legitimate wound, and that the working classes were the most traumatized survivors of the war. According to these groups, the unified 'national psyche' (*Volksseele)* constructed by conservatives was a myth. Instead, the nation's psyche was fragmented along class lines. A new neurosis, they argued, emerged to replace war neurosis as the greatest threat to the nation. This neurosis was exhibited by the middle class, in particular those who did not serve in the war, and was manifested in the refusal to come to terms with the traumatic effects of the war by paying for the enormous physical and psychological damage inflicted on survivors.

The political left's interpretations of the origins of war neurosis became more developed, and more radical, as pension cuts deepened. The social democratic-oriented war victims organization, the *Reichsbund der Kriegsbeschädigten, Kriegsteilnehmer und Hinterbliebenen* (National Association of War Disabled, Veterans, and their Dependents) claimed shortly after 1918 that war neurosis was a universal experience that unified different groups – combatants and civilians, men and women – who experienced stress under the conditions of total war. According to Social Democrats, the problem of 'pension neurosis' was rooted in a widespread loss of self-confidence and faith in work and the future that originated in the war, and the very real neuroses created by trench warfare and economic crisis at home, not in the deficient character of the working class, as alleged by psychiatrists and conservative critics. After losing parliamentary battles for pensions, however, Social Democrats developed a narrower definition of war-induced psychological illness. SPD officials theorized that the middle class, in their zeal to cut pensions and save the budget, was more neurotic than war victims and less willing than traumatized working-class men and women to heal the social and psychological consequences of the war.

Communist representatives of war victims took this criticism of the 'capitalist classes' a step further. War victims and political activists in the *Internationaler Bund der Opfer des Krieges und der Arbeit* (International Association of Victims of War and Work) argued that psychiatrists were a tool of middle-class conservative interest groups who deliberately repressed the traumatic memory of the war in order to soothe the national memory and prepare Germany for another world conflict. According to communist war victims' representatives, it was the doctors and other members of the social elite, not veterans, who were the real hysterics. The 'pension psychosis' epidemic that doctors believed infected the social welfare system with over-dependent men and frauds was thus really a construction of the bourgeoisie, activists claimed, who sought to cover-up their pathological, neurotic failure to pay for the human costs of the war.

The Social Democrats (SPD) and the Communist Party (KPD) failed to win better pensions and health care for war neurotics. Social democratic representatives did not convince the Labor Ministry and doctors that war neurotics were just the same as other disabled veterans in their moral character and essential willingness to work. In the case of the communist war victims' organization, war neurotics were useful as martyrs in the war on capitalism, but communist leaders were ambivalent about the image of 'hysterical' men in the militant proletarian revolution. By the onset of the Great Depression, the KPD and SPD had proved largely ineffective in staving off budget cuts for war victims' pensions.

Before examining the history of war neurosis through arguments made by social democratic and communist veterans, the controversial release of the film and book *All Quiet on the Western Front* provides a useful framework for analyzing how the image of the 'neurotic' veteran was a lightning rod for different political groups battling over the memory of the war and responsibility for its costs.

All Quiet on the Western Front – The Battle over the 'Neurotic' Front Soldier

Erich Maria Remarque's *All Quiet on the Western Front* set off a storm of controversy in Germany. The immensely popular, American-produced film version appeared in Berlin cinemas on 4 December 1930, opening to tremendous enthusiasm generated by the success of the book and by considerable advertising.[2] The book, which had appeared the previous year, had triggered diverse reactions from veterans over its portrayal of the realities of trench warfare. As historian Modris Ekstein argues, the novel was more a reflection on postwar memory of the trenches than a literal document of life at the front.[3] However, the image of life in the trenches sparked the most controversy, as *All Quiet's* representation of the German soldier became the source of heated debates in publications produced by veterans' groups, as well as the mainstream press. Within days of the film's debut, Nazi propaganda chief Josef Goebbels led demonstrations in Berlin's Nollendorfplatz that drew 6–8,000 people. Center Party member and Reich Interior Minister Josef Wirth, under pressure from the right-wing veterans' organization 'Steel Helmet' (*Der Stahlhelm*), the League of German Officers, the right-wing German National People's Party (DNVP) leader Hugenberg, and the National Socialist Party, encouraged the board of film censors to ban the film only a week after its release. In the Ministry of the Interior's report on why it was being banned, psychiatrist Alfred Hoche also expressed fear that the film would trigger widespread 'psychological depression' with scenes of soldiers traumatized by the brutality of the war.[4]

Both left- and right-wing veterans saw the portrayal of trench warfare, and the hysterical soldiers depicted in the book and film, as a central issue. Veterans debated the film's representation of psychological stress more than any other aspect of trench life. The film showed scenes from the book in which terrified new recruits break down during their first long bombardment and rush out of their shelter or scream uncontrollably until beaten unconscious by their comrades. Right-wing organizations, including the Steel Helmet and the Nazis, spearheaded the call for banning the film and organized demonstrations outside movie theaters. They argued that the depiction of hysterical men was an embarrassment to the memory of the front veteran and it threatened their goal of reconstructing the national character, and a new state, through the image of the steel-nerved front soldier. The Steel Helmet ran a number of articles in its periodical attacking the image of the 'hysterical' soldier. In one banner-headline story, Steel Helmet member Wilhelm Keinau criticized the film's portrayal of men under stress:

> [The film's release] must infuriate every nationalist, every front soldier. This phenomenal distortion of people and events is supposed to be a picture of the German struggle and crisis. These are supposed to have been the German front soldiers, these gallows-faced men who eat like animals, the German volunteers who must first be persuaded by the pompous tirades of their teacher to take action for the fatherland, who at the first shellfire soil their own pants and in the buried dug-out know of nothing better to do than howl hysterically![5]

In this vein, the Steel Helmet protested the alleged disrespect for veterans presented by images of hysterical soldiers, but Keinau also suggested that the behavior of the film's soldiers was a pure fiction, or at least over-exaggerated. Real men, and real Germans, did not 'howl hysterically' under fire, and any who did were not legitimate members of the front community.

The Steel Helmet constructed the debate over *All Quiet* as a battle between pacifists and authentic front soldiers. They also saw it as a debate over whether or not Germany had, as Steel Helmet cofounder Franz Seldte put it, 'strong nerves'. Seldte insisted that 'with strong nerves and strong hearts' Steel Helmet members could recapture the spirit of the front, fulfill their roles as leaders of the German nation, and reconquer the territories lost under the Versailles treaty.[6] The liberal newspaper *Vossische Zeitung* addressed the status of the nation's nerves with an article by literary critic and front veteran Fritz von Unruh, who gave *All Quiet* an enthusiastic review: 'Immediately after the collapse [the end of the war] people's nerves were worn down. In the ten years after the war they have relaxed again and today allow an objective review of the widespread trauma caused by the war'.[7] Steel Helmet member Hans Grote attacked von Unruh's suggestion that all Germans suffered from shattered nerves after the defeat. Grote argued that in reality 'the nerves of front soldiers remained like steel'.[8] Von Unruh's perspective, Grote claimed, was 'too subjective' and did not reflect the universal feelings of veterans. The 'widespread nervous breakdown of the German people' was, according to Grote, a figment of the pacifist literary imagination, and Remarque's work was 'the war experience of the weak'.[9] Grote asked von Unruh whether or not even a pacifist soldier like himself could ignore the 'feeling of comradeship born in the cruelty of war', which Grote said unified the German people and served as the cornerstone of Germany's 'resurrection as a nation'. Grote wrote that Remarque concentrated only on the grotesque aspects of war, 'but he passes over the many, up until death, unforgettable happy hours of the war at the front'. Grote recommended that readers look to Ernst Jünger for more accurate, 'heroic' account of the front experience.[10]

In contrast to the political right, the left claimed that the recognition of psychological damage as legitimate and widespread laid the groundwork for social and political progress. Among veterans and war victims' organizations, the Social Democratic Party (SPD) was the most fervent supporter of *All Quiet on the Western Front's* representation of the war experience. In nearly every edition of their newspaper that appeared in 1930, the social democratic-oriented *Reichsbund* (National Association of War Disabled) featured articles on Remarque's bestseller and the scandal surrounding the film. *Reichsbund* columnists insisted that *All Quiet* accurately depicted the physical and psychological effects of the war in a way that served as an antidote to what they described as the younger generation's dangerous tendency to romanticize violence. In an article aimed at youth, one *Reichsbund* columnist asserted that 'the film [*All Quiet*] shows the true face of war and the physical suffering and psychological shock of the front soldier'.[11] The SPD endorsed *All Quiet* as the most realistic depiction of the war's brutality yet to appear, which was consistent with the antiwar stance that was the basis for a social democratic state.

Opposition to *All Quiet*, Social Democrats argued, was led by men who were not actual front veterans and thus did not really grasp the true front experience. The *Reichsbund* claimed that only genuine front veterans, in particular those within the SPD, understood the subtleties of the trench experience, only they could distinguish between fear, a normal psychological response to combat, and cowardliness. *Reichsbund* chairman and veteran Christoph Pfändner wrote that protesters who attacked the film for its supposed portrayal of German soldiers as 'screaming, wretched cowards', were not capable of such a judgment: 'The film shows the face of the war and the soldiers as they really were. One had to have fought in the war in order to have judged the film'.[12] Pfändner claimed that he had particular insight into the film because of his own trench experience and injuries, and he criticized Joseph Goebbels, who organized the protests against the film, for not knowing what he was talking about and having never served in the war. The natural reaction to the front's terror, according to Pfändner, was instinctual self-preservation, which civilians did not understand:

Who was shown to be a coward in the film? Nobody! ... Did not all of us, when we arrived fresh at the front, instinctively dive into the earth when we heard the first bombs and shrapnel hiss through the air? Officers and noncommissioned, not just those types like Himmelstoss [the overbearing drill sergeant], did exactly that. Did we not later learn how to act in such situations, as those newly arrived young soldiers learned from the old 'front hog' ['Frontschwein'] Katczinski?[13]

Pfändner believed that the screaming of young recruits depicted in the film was an expression of the natural psychological terror that affected everyone who was at the front. These 'trembling individuals' were loyal and normal men with whom all ex-soldiers could identify.[14] To hit home his critique of the right-wing protests, Pfändner also argued that the outcry against *All Quiet* was a form of a betrayal, as civilians invented lies about the front experience to push their own political agenda.[15]

Pfändner proposed that psychological terror transcended the boundaries of social class and nationality. But other *Reichsbund* members, like Max Mühlberger, argued that men had fundamentally different psychological reactions to the war depending on their occupation and educational background:

> Many different age groups experienced terror on the separate fronts and thus had fundamentally different psychological experiences. What accounted for these differences? What conditions? – On the spiritual journey of the individual, his occupation, his political upbringing, his ideological attitude, the war scene, etc. It is natural that an enthusiastic theologian who volunteered on the Eastern front felt different than a politically mature worker on the battlefield of the Somme.[16]

In Mühlberger's view, sociopolitical factors shaped veterans' psychological experiences in the war. This was not limited to class. Religion, political orientation, the particular 'war scene' and other conditions also played a role.

Throughout the Weimar period, tensions existed between social democratic activists over whether or not war neurosis was a universal, shared experience, or one whose origins and nature reflected social and political division in postwar society. Social Democrats, however, did agree that Germans could heal their divisions and unify around the project of coming to terms with the 'true face of war's physical suffering and psychological trauma', as depicted in novels and films like *All Quiet on the Western Front*. One front veteran in the *Reichsbund* wrote:

> The terrors of the war fresh in our memory have given the German people the democratic-republican frame of mind and constitution

which, in order 'to serve the internal and external peace', as it says itself, requires the upbringing of youth 'in the spirit of German character and the reconciliation of the people', which it is the duty of all schools to do.

... Not out of cowardice, but out of love for peace, out of love for country and our people and from the realization that war does not create cultural and moral values, but destroys them, we front veterans are opponents of war. Help German youth to this realization. Therefore: bring out the film *All Quiet on the Western Front*.[17]

Reichsbund members thus proposed that a graphic depiction of war's psychological horrors had great political value in reinforcing social democratic values and reconciling diverse groups through the shared memory of trauma. If only Germans could recognize the 'true face' of war, the *Reichsbund* claimed, they would cease to idealize and romanticize violence, and instead rally around the antiwar politics of social democracy and support psychological victims of war as legitimate war disabled.

Unlike the social democratic-oriented *Reichsbund*, the communist veterans' organization *Internationaler Bund der Opfer des Krieges und der Arbeit* (International Association of Victims of War and Work) did not run extensive feature articles on Remarque's work or the subsequent film scandal. The far left referred to *All Quiet* as sentimental pacifism which distracted constituents from the militant war of the proletariat against imperialism and fascism. In *Die Rote Fahne* ('*The Red Flag*'), Karl August Wittfogel admitted that Remarque described the 'horror of the war of attrition' with 'extraordinary suspense', but the book did not decisively illustrate the class struggle that was essential to understanding the meaning of the war. Remarque, Wittfogel claimed, was actually a stooge who ultimately worked for the same powers that were responsible for the war: 'Remarque is with all justice the favorite poet of the imperialistic bourgeoisie and has become their lower middle class *Mitläufer* [one who runs-with-the-program]'. Communist organizations saw few parallels between *All Quiet* and their own political agenda. In the thinking of communist ideologues, Remarque's own lower-middle-class background tainted him as being in league with conservative interest groups who worked to conceal the economic and political structures that created the horror of the trenches in the first place.[18]

The diverse reactions to *All Quiet on the Western Front* from various political groups reflected their responses to the war neurosis debate and their portrayals of mentally disabled veterans. The scandal surrounding *All Quiet* indicated that psychologically traumatized soldiers, more than any other groups of war wounded, stirred tremendous debate among the defenders and enemies of the Weimar Republic over the memory of the war and the image of the front veteran. War neurotics were also unique because they crossed the lines between soldiers and civilians, women and men, middle and working classes, and were seen by both the left and the right as symbols of a national condition – a 'psychological crisis'. For Social Democrats and communists, this condition played a significant role in explaining the plight of all the war disabled in the labyrinth of social welfare, family and work. Though they took different approaches to the war neurosis debate, the social democratic and communist war-disabled organizations both claimed to rally around the traumatized veteran as a unique symbol of the deeply psychological, unredeemable cruelties of war that only the working class truly recognized. These organizations were, however, unable to convince the state, doctors, and welfare administration that psychologically disabled veterans deserved equal respect.

The Social Democrats in Defense of War Neurotics

The *Reichsbund der Kriegsbeschädigten, Kriegsteilnehmer und Hinter-bliebenen* (The National Association of War Disabled, Veterans and their Dependents was Weimar's largest war victims organization with over 600,000 members in 1921.[19] The *Reichsbund* advocated war neurotics' rights to the same financial assistance and health care as that awarded to physically disabled veterans. With assistance from the *Reichsbund*, men who claimed to suffer from persistent psychological wounds caused by the war argued that their injuries were indeed genuine, and that they could become constructive members of society if they were granted the same access to occupational therapy and financial assistance as other veterans.

Shortly after the war, the Social Democratic Party endorsed the *Reichsbund* and adopted the cause of war neurosis as a means of promoting its social and political interests. Social democratic leaders asserted that psychological trauma was a wound that bridged the experiences of men and women on the combat and home fronts across class lines. The public, *Reichsbund* officials claimed, regardless of gender and class background, would identify with psychologically stressed veterans in ways they could not relate to amputees and gas victims, thus building a shared consciousness between combat veterans, factory workers, and other groups traumatized by the war.

In addition to demanding greater medical and financial provisions for war neurotics, *Reichsbund* officials defended the character of this group of war victims. *Reichsbund* leaders used the testimony of war neurotics to illustrate the prejudices behind diagnoses of the working-class war disabled. According to the *Reichsbund*, doctors discriminated against social democratic patients in particular. Psychiatrists had long accused war neurotics of lacking masculine characteristics because they allegedly relied on social welfare and social democratic organizations to get out of work. *Reichsbund* officials insisted that neither war neurosis, nor social democracy, was unmanly. Their letters to the state on behalf of men, and women, suffering from nervous disorders indicate the degree to which politics, masculinity and the question of willingness to work were intertwined.

Throughout the 1920s, *Reichsbund* officials came to the aid of psychologically damaged veterans struggling with the arduous path back into postwar life. These men entering the public space of civilian life were a visible reminder of the horrifying wounds inflicted by modern war. Social Democrats warned that these men now clogging the streets would provoke fear that could lead to ridicule and persecution. The police posted warnings about the '*Schüttler*' ('shakers') and '*Zitterer*' ('quiverers') on Berlin street corners and subway stations, describing them as 'notorious beggars' faking the tremors and tics that plagued authentic war neurotics.[20] These quivering men on street corners were singled out as suspicious because many believed their tics, tremors and nervous behaviors were easily faked, and public opinion turned against them as probable frauds who should be prohibited from clogging the streets and subways. *Reichsbund* representatives insisted that the state was unjustly conflating authentic war neurotics and chronic malingerers, and they pushed the Labor Ministry to punish the fraudulent beggars who simulated traumatic injuries, rather than stir fear and resentment towards genuine war victims.[21] *Reichsbund* officials further blamed the press for creating an image of war neurotics as swindlers who did not want to work: 'We cannot permit the press to enlighten the public with the idea that the majority of beggars are not war wounded, but people who only disguise themselves as war wounded by putting on a uniform in order to get a nice source of income'.[22]

The Social Democrats were fighting an uphill battle. The popular press frequently published articles by doctors who warned that war neurotics, both real and frauds, were potential 'pension neurotics', chronic 'psychopaths', and social deviants who did anything to avoid work.[23] *Reichsbund* representatives complained to the Labor Ministry that a state doctor named Wolfskehl at Frankfurt am Main's main welfare office was showing disrespect to all psychologically disabled veterans when he described one as a 'psychopath who does not value work'.[24] Columnists for the *Reichsbund* labeled these doctors 'pension squeezers' who fabricated 'pension neurosis' in order to pursue their first priority – budget cutting. Rather than objectively evaluate the condition of mentally ill veterans, Social Democrats argued, doctors regularly exaggerated the abilities of these men to work and recover their health in order to save the state money and curry favor with labor ministers in the hope gaining promotions.[25]

Doctors, war neurotics in the *Reichsbund* insisted, willfully neglected the subtle, lingering psychological trauma caused by the war. In one case, a doctor denied health care and a pension to Mathias S., who was previously diagnosed as having war-induced nervous disorders and an irregular heartbeat that left him completely unable to earn a living. According to S.'s brother, the doctor conducting the check-up found S.'s pulse to be normal, and suggested he was faking his symptoms. One month later, S. died. The 'criminal' doctors, as S.'s brother called them, deserved to be punished for their incompetence. *Reichsbund* officials complained to the Labor Ministry that the doctor actually caused him to die by shocking him with the elimination of his pension, which worsened his already precarious condition. Recommending the 'strongest repudiation' of the doctor and a public inquiry, *Reichsbund* officials asserted that S.'s death was caused by the stress of inadequate health care inflicted by doctors who were insensitive to the prolonged and complex ailments that veterans still endured years after the war.[26]

War neurotics claimed that doctors were doubly prejudiced against them if they were allied with the Social Democratic Party. State-employed psychiatrists did argue that the SPD sapped men of their independence and the will to recover from the war. The widow of war victim Wilhelm Kröger, for example, wrote to the *Reichsbund* about her physician's response when she told him that her son died in the war and her husband died in 1921:

> This man [Dr Burckhardt] wrote that I was completely healthy and explained himself in the following way: 'You are completely healthy and should be happy that your son died for the fatherland. At least he did something. Do not let yourself be won over by the Social Democrats. It hurts your health'. I give this information to the organization and am ready to take testimony under oath.[27]

State medical representative Dr Burckhardt singled out so many social democratic patients as malingerers that *Reichsbund* representatives from his district in Barmen investigated him in 1924. Burkhardt allegedly refused to implement orders from the insurance courts to provide occupational therapy for psychologically disabled patients, and he denied therapy for those with ties to the Social Democratic Party. He reportedly claimed that all persons in the courts and war-disabled organizations were blind to war neurotics' faked symptoms. For example, Burckhardt informed war victim Hartmann S., who suffered from psychological disorders, lung illnesses, and a leg wound, that his wounds were not as bad as he, the *Reichsbund*, and health insurance clerks claimed. S. recounted his encounter with Burckhardt:

> As I stepped into the examination room, I was received by the physician Dr Burckhardt with the following words: 'So how old are you?' 40 years I answered. With that I received the reply: 'What do you, a man of 40 years, still want to be examined for?' He asked

further: 'Do you belong to any association, perhaps the *Reichsbund*? I replied that I was a member of the *Reichsbund*. Then the doctor retorted: 'Why are you in the *Reichsbund*? Surely you are a man and can represent yourself'.[28]

A representative from the *Reichsbund* named Hölter submitted his own report of Burckhardt, describing the doctor as 'unscientific', difficult to comprehend, and prone to making conclusions based on assumptions rather than evidence. According to Hölter, the doctor reported to the Labor Ministry that patients brought under his care with medical certificates stating that they suffered from wartime psychological injuries were actually 'great swindlers'. In one instance, Hölter stood in the room with the doctor as he interacted with a patient previously diagnosed as a war neurotic. Hölter evaluated Dr Burckhardt's confusing assessment of the unusually clad patient with the following:

> Yesterday someone here was diagnosed with a 100% nervous disorder. Now just because this man wears sandals and flowered stockings does not make him neurotic. When I asked Dr Burckhardt whether one could judge the man's character based on his footwear, he said: 'This man got married after the war and he has two children – thus he can't really be neurotic. There is no woman who would marry a man who is so sick'.[29]

Burkhardt's diagnosis – alternately calling the patient 'neurotic' for wearing flowered stockings and 'not really sick' based on evidence that he has a family – is self-contradictory as told through *Reichsbund* representative Hölter. Hölter's report is most important for the perceptions expressed. For example, he added that Dr Burckhardt prejudged Social Democrats like the flower-stockinged patient as unmanly. He further asserted that the state had no authority in administering health care as long as labor ministers employed such prejudiced doctors, and he demanded that Burckhardt be dismissed. With advice from the main veterans' health insurance and pension office at Coblenz, however, the Labor Ministry decided that evidence gathered by *Reichsbund* officials pertained to individual complaints that had to do with personality conflicts, not with professional competence or the systematic oppression of mentally disabled patients connected to the Social Democrats' war victims association.[30]

The Social Democratic Party made a great effort to defend war neurotics because this group was an essential part of their social and political agenda. The SPD aimed to build a shared consciousness between front veterans and civilians, the combat front and the home front, as part of their attempt to construct a welfare state that would meet the needs of wide groups of individuals needing insurance. The *Reichsbund* helped support the Social Democrats' message that 'war victim' should be defined in the broadest terms to include former front soldiers and victims of economic crisis. In this vein, 'war neurosis' was the wound common to the combat and home fronts that also linked men and women and bolstered the SPD's argument that war brutalized all of these groups in similar ways.

Women in the SPD were instrumental in defining the nature of traumatic neurosis experienced at home. Women argued that their sex faced particular difficulty in shedding the haunting memories of the war, and their failure to overcome these memories resulted in symptoms of neurosis comparable to their counterparts who were in the trenches.[31] Traumatic memories of lost family members and shortages, women argued, were intensified by the unbearable stress of surviving postwar economic crisis and, in some cases, providing for severely disabled, dependent husbands. When the popular press reported on a woman who killed herself and her four children in 1926, *Reichsbund* columnists blamed her act on psychological stress caused by caring for her mutilated, invalid husband and children while acting as the sole bread winner.[32] In national debates over the creation of a National Day of Mourning, which was never agreed upon during the Weimar Republic, *Reichsbund* leaders advocated the incorporation of mentally traumatized civilians, especially women, into the memory of the war. In her editorial for the *Reichsbund*'s newspaper, Alma Hißfeld argued that in the national memory of the war, the republic should recognize 'the many physical and psychological sufferings of dependents, whose privations and stress lead to daily crisis and anxiety'.[33]

In 1926, *Reichsbund* leaders used evidence gathered by their women activists to argue in the National Pension Court that veterans' families who claimed to suffer lasting psychological disabilities deserved compensation.[34] Social Democrats pushed legislation through the Reichstag that amended the 1920 National Pension Law and granted pensions to orphans over 18 who were still unable to care for themselves due to mental or physical illness.[35] Thus trauma injuries that came under the responsibility of the state were expanded to include both war and postwar-inflicted trauma, and it included dependents who were secondary psychological victims.

Activists pushed for women to be specifically qualified to receive state assistance for mental trauma that continued after the war. *Reichsbund* member Martha Harnoß noted that men and women experienced the war differently, but estimated that the resulting psychological scars were virtually the same. Similar to disabled veterans, Harnoß argued, women were denied adequate social assistance from those unwilling to recognize the deeper consequences of the war for women:

> For dependents, the psychological agitation and economic conditions
> of the war and postwar period lead to heart ailments and tuberculosis.
> Even today nobody admits, either in the government or among

affluent citizens, that most women sacrificed the best of their health for the fatherland in their stressful work to earn a living. As many of us women have just learned, those under the burden of becoming workers and at the same time having to do housework, collapse. How often have we seen children become complete orphans because their mothers were over-stressed? How often do we still find today that we can barely mention wartime and the psychological suffering with the loss of breadwinners and the economic consequences of the postwar period, without one of the survivors suffering a nervous breakdown? This is the sad picture of the effects of the war on women.[36]

In this diagnosis of mental trauma for women, Harnoß constructs a picture of psychological stress originating in the double-shift of work and home, with care for dependents in the midst of economic crisis leading to continued mental stress into the postwar period. On one hand, she criticizes 'affluent' citizens for denying the stress caused by the war for working women. Yet Harnoß's portrait of trauma also suggests a universal stress that crosses class lines, as both middle- and working-class women had to work during the war. The breakdown of norms for middle-class women gave them a glimpse into the psychological strains experienced by most women under normal conditions, intensified by wartime circumstances.

Reichsbund feature articles on psychological illness emphasized shared trauma and the similarities between front veterans and people on the home front who suffered mental breakdowns across gender and class lines. *Reichsbund* leader H. Hoffmann, who wrote extensive articles on war neurosis, professed admiration for the psychoanalytic theories of Freud and Adler, which he believed accurately identified the lasting effects of psychological violence. War neuroses, Hoffmann claimed, were universally felt and shared common origins. Hoffmann pointed out that German men and women suffered neuroses that grew out of 'repressed sexual instincts' that intensified as the anxiety of war and economic stress disrupted healthy sexual behavior.[37] All war victims, he claimed, also suffered in some degree from a 'feeling of inferiority' ('*Minderwertigkeitsgefühl*') that caused a great sense of mistrust of other individuals and society. This sense of inferiority led to a sense of victimhood that caused the 'mutilated and the mourning' to lash out against the community:

The psychology of war victimhood [*Kriegsopfershaft*] in its entirety has received a special character through the war and postwar period ... The existence of widows and wounded who are not nearly as securely pensioned as they should be causes a strong state of agitation and bitterness from this sense of victimhood. Psychological reactions are manifested in demonstrations, public displays of one's own suffering ... The mutilated throw themselves in front of street cars, mourning widows march in Bamberg against the armoured cars of the state police ... Mistrust of promises and bitterness against the state and society leave the mutilated and mourning withdrawn.[38]

This sense of widespread 'victimhood', which linked war victims from different backgrounds, was caused by the war and the failure of the state to acknowledge or compensate society's deeper wounds. The victimhood was not a condition, as some doctors alleged, of working-class character and lack of will to work, but rather a symptom of the war. Behind Germany's postwar crisis, including the atmosphere of political tension and confrontation, Hoffmann theorized, was a general psychological condition in which survivors lost faith in the future and the traditional values of work.

Hoffmann concluded that the widespread hostility and suffering felt by most Germans could be controlled and overcome through participation in the social democratic movement. Social Democracy reinvigorated one's sense of productivity and meaning in the postwar world, he argued, allowing war victims to recover their 'inner strength' and heal 'feelings of inferiority'. The party, Hoffmann asserted, affirmed war victims' feelings of self-worth by legitimizing the complex psychological stresses inflicted by the war and its aftermath and by providing work that had social value. He observed: 'In the service of the organization one awakens consciousness of one's own productivity again'.[39] Hoffmann ascribed to women a particular role in his prescription for postwar recovery. He claimed that women benefited most from the sense of community provided by social democratic politics, and that women were particularly well-suited to leading veterans and civilians out of the psychological crisis caused by the war.[40] Women discovered early on that the social democratic community provided a basis for overcoming despair, as they had been generally excluded from the state's definitions of psychological trauma and were defined as war victims primarily if they were widows. Hoffmann noted:

> The *Reichsbund* has in the course of its existence returned to many of its members the self-trust lost in shell-holes and in economic crisis. Our mourning women comrades found diversion and psychological resurgence in the activities of the organization ... which has given each member the chance to heal their feelings of inferiority ... by renewing their sense of the joy of life.[41]

Reichsbund officials thus argued that social democracy did not encourage welfare dependency, as doctors claimed, but was rather a catalyst for motivating war victims to work by rebuilding self-esteem and giving them a sense of social inclusion.

In the wake of the 1923 inflation, however, the recovery of one's self esteem proved to be of little consequence in the eyes of the state officials who controlled the pension question. Finance ministers looked to cut war victims who did not show quantifiable progress in their ability to hold a job. With the encouragement of conservative Reichstag representatives from nationalist parties seeking to trim the social welfare budget in 1924, finance ministers complained that, of the 3.4 billion Marks in the national budget, 31.2 per cent went to war-disabled pensions.[42] In 1926 Reichstag hearings on overhauling the pension system, finance ministers concluded that it was doubtful that psychologically disabled veterans who had not yet healed almost ten years after the war actually suffered from directly war-related wounds, the basis for a veterans' disability pension, and thus they should be cut from state support and put into family care. Social Democrats announced that they would propose an amendment to the National Pension Law that would bring state support to these families:

> Treatment (invalid care) is to be guaranteed even if an improvement of the condition is no longer to be expected. Mentally ill and invalids, who require lasting care, are to have their costs brought under the state; to the family members of such persons care is to be guaranteed under the measure of regulations for dependents (paragraph 36–49 of the National Pension Law).[43]

Finance ministers opposed this legislation. When Social Democrats asked for one billion Marks for pensions, finance ministers testified in front of the Reichstag that only 220 million Marks could be spent. The Labor Ministry and conservative Reichstag representatives, shocked by these figures, called on the National Committee on War Victims (*Reichsauschuss der Kriegsbeschädigten*), an advisory committee to the Reichstag, to overhaul the pension system.[44] Labor Ministry officials, including Anton Kirschensteiner who headed the committee, advised Reichstag representatives serving on the committee that mentally ill veterans should be reexamined case by case to determine which families should take some of the costs by providing private care.[45]

The National Committee on War Victims began hearings in December 1926 to determine guidelines for reevaluating pensions for psychologically disabled veterans. Ministry representative and psychiatrist Dr Scholtze was called in to resolve a conflict over whether or not delayed, postwar outbreaks of dementia, schizophrenia, epilepsy and paralysis were really linked to war experiences. Scholtze characterized these different disorders as essentially organic in origin, and only rarely caused by trauma at the front. The basic formula for approaching trauma in war, Scholze testified, had not radically changed since it was set up by military doctors in 1917. 'A mental illness is not a war-related injury', he insisted, 'simply because it breaks out or becomes worse during the time of war service'.[46] Scholtze told the National Committee on War Victims that now, several years after the war, family members who were ashamed of their mentally ill loved ones only wanted to ease the social stigma of their hereditary illness by calling the outbreak of schizophrenia or epilepsy a war wound. Families needed this vindication: 'More often today it is an issue for the family of a relation with the beginnings of mental illness. One still feels shame from the most far-reaching social circles ... and the sick ones themselves feel, even when the symptoms of the illness go away, economically (career!) and socially (marriage!) disabled'. Scholtze further argued that war neurotics were on a path to 'economic and *bürgerlich* elimination' from the moment their symptoms appeared.[47] Men who were diagnosed with war-related psychological trauma during or just after the war but had still not recovered were thus targeted as either hereditarily ill or 'pension neurotics' and placed first on the list for pension cuts.

Social Democrats in the Reichstag started to relent. Where they had once defended war neurotics, including those whose psychological wounds persisted or appeared late after the war, SPD leaders acquiesced to the Labor Ministry's psychiatrists. SPD representative Erich Roßmann admitted that not all psychological problems among veterans could be directly war-related. At the 4 February 1927 Reichstag hearings, he concluded that there were numerous 'cases in doubt' (*Zweifelsfälle*) breaking out now years after the war, and he formed a sub-committee to determine how to evaluate them. Trying to illustrate that psychiatrists themselves were still not certain about these cases, Roßmann recommended to the committee that in cases in which 'the original connection between the injury and military service is not adequately proven' by psychiatrists, disabled veterans and their dependents should be given the benefit of the doubt, and a pension.[48]

The chairman of the National Committee on War Victims, Labor Ministry head Anton Kirschensteiner, accepted Roßmann's general formula, indicating that only in situations in which it was certain that mental illness was not war-related should cases be rejected. This issue of certainty was critical. Roßmann conceded: 'It is fundamentally in the hands of state administrative authorities as to what counts for a doubtful case and what does not'.[49] Roßmann thus grudgingly acknowledged the state's doctors as the ultimate authority in defining war neurosis. Illustrating the limited authority of war-disabled interest groups like the *Reichsbund*, Roßmann remarked: 'The further one distances himself from the war and the more complicated and difficult the sufferings in question become, the more they push themselves into the judgment of doctors, namely particular specialists, which administrators themselves cannot simply ignore'.[50] Immediately after the committee meeting, SPD representatives instructed the *Reichsbund* to reassure disabled veterans who were about to lose their pensions that the SPD-sponsored Unemployment Insurance Law was on the verge of passing through parliament, and that this would fill the gap left by lost pension income.[51]

Losing the battle for pensions, the SPD focused its energies on portraying doctors and the Labor Ministry as the brutal enemies of war neurotics. Social Democrats gave particular attention to cases that victimized dependents. In one such case, Emil S., still suffering in 1928 from wartime diagnosed neurosis, became violent during a medical examination at a psychiatric clinic in Heidelberg, where doctors assessed whether or not he still deserved his pension. When S.'s wife returned to the clinic to pick him up, she found him placed against his will in a ward for the severely mentally ill and given shots. There all hell broke loose as he attacked orderlies and engaged in a fist-fight with doctors, after which he alleged that doctors had stolen his wedding ring as they restrained him. Frau S. claimed that when she asked permission to bring her husband home, a doctor threatened to confine her to a room in the psychiatric ward as well.[52] Her letter to the *Reichsbund* prompted a formal complaint to the Labor Ministry, leading to an inquiry, stories printed in the wider press, and welfare officials in Karlsruhe denying to the Labor Ministry that Frau S. was ever threatened or that the hospital held her husband against his will.[53]

Though they could not win pensions for their constituents, the *Reichsbund* set out to show that the state's psychiatric experts were morally and professionally unfit, or at least cause doctors serious embarrassment. Because of letters from the *Reichsbund*, health care providers found themselves repeatedly explaining to the Labor Ministry and the press their allegedly cruel treatment of psychologically disabled veterans and their families. *Reichsbund* activists published one article on a son whose mother suffered years of poverty because he was put in a prison rather than a hospital for the mentally ill, where the *Reichsbund* columnist said he obviously belonged. The article informed readers that the Labor Ministry gave the mother a hardship pension only after relentless pressure from the war-disabled organization, and that everybody should be outraged that 'an authority in the area of nerve medicine' turned down the claim that the son's insanity was war related.[54] The *Reichsbund* concluded: 'The war was undoubtedly the perpetrator of the limitless misfortune here, which affected not only the sick individual, but also his aged mother, who was unfairly abandoned to shame and disgrace for years after the war'.[55] *Reichsbund* activists thus continued to harangue psychiatrists working for the Labor Ministry, accusing them of narrow-minded, inhumane diagnoses that, even in the eyes of non-professionals, were obviously flawed and driven by their interests in squeezing pensions.

The Social Democrats' attempts to save their reputations as defenders of war victims did not alleviate the backlash that came from loyal constituents. Letters from psychologically disabled veterans flooded the *Reichsbund* and the Labor Ministry shortly after cuts took effect in 1928, and they reached a crescendo in the wake of the Great Depression by 1930. War neurotics who described themselves as dedicated fighters for the republic and social democratic ideals railed against the SPD for betraying veterans by cutting social welfare. One interesting case alluded to eariler involves Konrad D., a former bank clerk who was diagnosed a war neurotic at the end of the war. He characterized himself as a loyal Social Democrat since 1919, when he felt the SPD offered the most support for mentally traumatized veterans with concrete financial assistance. D. received a pension for his mental injuries and after job training through the Labor Ministry and state health care system he found work as a taxi driver. In 1929, however, he was fired for 'mental instability' after he collided into another car, causing a passenger's death. When he attempted to renew his war victims' pension, the Labor Ministry rejected his application on the basis that his wartime and early 1920s diagnosis was no longer accepted. The Labor Ministry ordered a psychiatric evaluation in 1929 that determined his mental problems were no longer war-related and he was now able to earn a living. However, the Labor Ministry reported, it was recommended that he not drive a taxi.[56]

Even more traumatic for many of these men was the fact that while they were losing their pensions for war-related mental illness, women were granted state compensation for nervous ailments caused by economic stress. Konrad D.'s own wife, for example, received support for 'hysteria' after the state cut her husband's welfare. Early on in his pension application, D. used his wife's psychiatric treatment and illness, allegedly caused by economic stress after the Great Depression, to bolster his argument that his family was unable to earn a living. According to D., psychiatrists reported that he possessed a 'psychopathic constitution' that manifested itself in 'severe irritability, delusional whininess, and depression'.[57] Referring to his wife's visit to a psychiatrist, the Labor Ministry eventually granted D.'s family a 100 Marks emergency relief payment, which covered rent and food for two months. The state expected that this would last until D.'s wife recuperated and returned to work as the family's primary wage-earner. The Labor Ministry assessed that D. was entitled to these Depression-era emergency measures because his wife's illness now left the family with no income.[58]

The *Reichsbund* took credit for winning long-standing arguments that women traumatized by wartime stress and postwar crisis were legitimate war victims who deserved compensation. However, women received support in these cases of psychological breakdown because doctors did not doubt the authenticity of 'hysterical' women, not because psychiatrists acknowledged women as equivalent to war neurotics. In one example, Johanna B., widow of a soldier who suffered from war-related psychological problems that resulted in his death in 1924, applied for assistance with support from the *Reichsbund* when she experienced a 'nervous breakdown' and symptoms of 'hysteria' from the stress of work and the depression she suffered after her husband's death.[59] The *Reichsbund* built her case on a December 1924 amendment to the National Pension Law that provided emergency payments for dependents and widows. Since she did not have to prove that her illness was directly war-related, and medical authorities did not accuse her of faking her injuries, B. received a single payment of 200 Marks in 1926.[60]

The SPD failed to prevent psychiatrists and finance ministers from trying to slash the pensions of male war 'neurotics'. But Social Democrats could at least claim partial victory, as women traumatized by postwar social and economic crisis found compensation for their psychological ailments. The state did not recognize these outbreaks of hysteria in women as comparable to war hysteria in front veterans, but labor ministers relied on doctors who were easily persuaded that these women still suffered from real hysteria so many years after the war. Ultimately, the SPD's effort to unite women and men as common victims of a larger psychological crisis was a failure.

Social Democrats also failed at uniting the different social classes around the shared psychological trauma of the war. From the beginning of the Great Depression until the collapse of the republic, the Labor Ministry continuously cut war victims' relief in general, until the entire pension budget was reduced by one-third. In 1930, SPD leader Erich Roßmann declared that the war was being refought over pensions, with conservative forces attacking the left: 'Social reactionary forces have launched a total offensive against the pension system. In parliament, we are engaged at present in a kind of pension trench war'.[61] Social Democrats developed an increasingly militarized language to describe this ongoing 'trench war', and they specifically employed a popularized psychiatric discourse to explain the psychological origins of this postwar battle. The medical profession, state bureaucracy and popular media, *Reichsbund* activists claimed, were all dominated by middle-class conservative interest groups who repressed their own war neuroses. One *Reichsbund* member attacked the 'weak-nerved bourgeois public' that could not stomach the 'many individual tragedies buried beneath stories of finance reform and Reichstag debates'. He wrote further: 'Such reports that befall wounded men cause anxiety and disturbance; but the normal middle class citizen does not want to be disturbed and shocked. He just wants to 'take a break' ('*Feierabend*') when he reads the newspaper. Calm, calm and more calm. His nerves are indeed so weak'.[62]

The party assured their readers that this denial of the psychological consequences of the war was a particularly middle-class neurosis. The nerves of the working class were allegedly strong enough to confront the deep psychological effects of the war. *Reichsbund* theorists defined this middle-class mental disorder as 'savings psychosis'. 'Savings psychosis' could be detected in Labor Ministry officials who were 'obsessive' and 'neurotic' in their zeal to cut the budget for war victims' pensions and evade responsibility for the human costs of the war.[63] Thus in the extremely polarized politics of the depression years, the SPD abandoned their official line just after the war that Germans shared a collective trauma. They now characterized the nerves of the middle class as weaker, evidenced by years of pension cuts that were a manifestation of hidden anxieties and a desire to forget the war.

The SPD now had its own theory of what was wrong with the pension system to counter doctors' long-standing case for 'pension psychosis'. 'Savings psychosis', more than 'pension psychosis', Social Democrats argued, crippled the chances of war victims to recover. In order for working-class war victims to heal, the middle class first had to be rehabilitated by working to overcome their obsession with saving money, and finally come to terms with the human costs of the war. The SPD's rival for working-class votes, the Communist Party (KPD) took these theories concerning social-class neuroses to a different level. Communists argued that the psychosis of the middle class was ultimately untreatable, and that working- and middle-class Germans had fundamentally different psychologies, and their own psychoses, which were endemic to a capitalist society.[64]

The Communist Party's War against Psychiatrists

The communist *Internationaler Bund der Opfer des Krieges und der Arbeit* (International Association of the Victims of War and Labor), which claimed 100,000 members at its peak, had a different focus than their counterparts in the Social Democratic Party. Unlike the SPD, the Communist Party did not make war neurosis a central feature of its strategies for winning support from working-class war victims, though the KPD also saw the interests of disabled veterans and victims of social and economic exploitation as interrelated. Only after the 1926–27 cuts in war-disabled pensions did the issue of war neurosis draw serious attention from Internationaler Bund leaders. After these cuts, Bund activists treated war neurosis as primary evidence of systematic material and psychological oppression of disabled veterans and workers.

For leaders in the Internationaler Bund, the denial of pensions to psychologically traumatized veterans proved that the class war and the revolutionary struggle had a fundamentally psychological dimension. Communist officials portrayed the debate over war neurosis as compelling evidence that the middle class sought to erase the traumatic memory of the war in order to ensure the nation's psychological readiness for another conflict that exploited the proletariat for capitalist gain. Though they argued sympathetically for the pension rights of 'hysterics', as columnists repeatedly referred to them, Bund ideologues were more interested in psychiatrists and their roles as agents of reaction against the working-class revolution. The image of the 'war hysteric' was important in making a case against the cruelties of the capitalist health care system. But the representation of the psychologically disabled veteran in communist editorials also subtly reinforced the medical establishment's claim that these men were probable shirkers.

The communist Internationaler Bund was, in contrast to their SPD counterparts, more ambivalent about integrating mentally disabled veterans into their movement. Similar to their enemies on the political right, the communists argued that the welfare system turned these men into over-dependent, unmanly 'pension hysterics'. It was the capitalist system, however, and not the weak will of these men that made them dependent. As opponents of the republic, the communist Internationaler Bund had the privilege of being against anything that emanated from 'the system'. Thus the KPD, unlike the prorepublic Social Democrats, could remain aloof from debates over pension cuts that eventually implicated the SPD.[65] As political outsiders, the communists thus followed a strategy of sustained, general protest against the treatment of war neurotics, without committing to specific interpretations of war neurosis that might force them to admit that doctors had ultimate authority in defining war neurosis and allocating pensions.

According to the communists, psychiatrists systematically worked to eliminate the psychological trauma caused by the war from the national consciousness in order to make possible a new imperialist war against the proletariat. This project of dispensing collective amnesia lay behind mental medicine and the state health care system. Communist party member Klauber wrote in a 1927 article that one particular psychiatrist, Prof. Neuhaus, was a fraud who denied the real traumatic legacy of the trenches:

> It is this Prof. Neuhaus in Berlin who concluded that a war victim who has several bullets in his skull was healthy and able to work. To him, all others are hysterics. In explaining war hysteria, it is the new method to say that these illnesses already existed in their youth and thus have nothing to do with the war, or that they occurred after the war and are symptoms of age. The war and its consequences are thus supposed to be struck from the consciousness of the people, so that they will agree to new imperialist goals of the German bourgeoisie against Soviet Russia.[66]

Psychiatrists allegedly concealed the horrors of the trenches by falsely labeling war victims, especially those from working-class backgrounds, as 'hysterics'. Bund officials claimed that these doctors insulted the war's working-class victims by promoting war as a strengthening experience that separated the strong-willed officers from the supposedly weak, hysterical proletariat.[67] The Bund defended its constituents as more psychologically fit than the middle classes. Specifically, Bund leaders argued, their men showed more manly character than doctors alleged.[68]

On one hand, the communists portrayed themselves as the most militant defenders of psychologically disabled war victims. At the same time, the party was rather ambivalent about 'hysterical' men in their ranks, and they subtly lay the blame on war victims for failing to recover. For example, KPD representatives admitted that some of their working-class comrades were indeed unable to withstand the stress of trench warfare. This was understandable considering the dual violence caused by class exploitation and modern industrial killing. It was not in the context of capitalist-sanctioned warfare that men proved themselves, KPD leaders argued. Instead, men became real men, or in the case of war victims recovered their manhood, by joining the communist war victims' association. Ironically, the KPD also blamed Weimar's welfare system for fostering unmanly dependence on the state, mimicking assertions made by conservative doctors. One Bund columnist wrote that by joining the KPD, war victims could 'assert their strength as men, which had been stripped away by a state that turned them into dependent beggars'.[69] Thus rebuilding one's self-control and will to work was an expressed priority of the KPD, with the militant revolutionary movement as the primary agent for regenerating those traits that the state's psychiatrists said were missing in traumatized veterans. One KPD leader accused war hysterics of lethargy and lack of will, admonishing them for not joining the revolution sooner: 'You war victims must take control of health care with greater energy, and you must learn through this control that only one world power is capable of healing the wounds of the capitalist war of exploitation: the revolutionary proletariat'.[70] If men did not try to take control of their mental health by joining the class struggle, it was implied, they were indeed as unmanly and dependent as their 'hysterical' label suggested. In this fashion, communist officials did not fundamentally refute psychiatrists' criticisms that an epidemic of 'hysterical men' plagued German society.

While the KPD lambasted psychologically disabled men who did not 'take control' of their recovery, the party reserved its harshest attacks for the doctors and the social class they represented. Party officials argued that war victims were weak if they surrendered their self-control to the capitalist state's psychiatrists. But the psychiatrists themselves were the most dangerous neurotics, turning war victims into passive, helpless welfare dependents unable to overcome the stigma of 'hysteria' they were given. Terms like 'war hysteric' and 'pension neurotic', communist representatives noted, could only be applied by doctors and professors who had no idea what it was like to lose one's mental health in war or in the postwar struggle to find work.[71] Bund leaders insisted that the state's doctors, not the working-class veterans who bore the brunt of the war, were the genuine hysterics and psychopaths. In the most caustic terms, Bund representatives encouraged constituents to accuse doctors of projecting their own disorders on their patients: 'Do not tolerate the proctologists who belittle you and your hard-earned rights. Assert that there is no judgment handed to you that is really not the sickness of your doctor himself'.[72] Sarcastic puns and innuendos frequently appeared in the newspaper, with one allusion to the 'Kaufmann method' of electrotherapy, widely known after the doctor who advocated this technique, as appropriately named (Kaufmann literally means 'businessman'). Doctors were really just 'businessmen in disguise' one columnist claimed, using the term '*Kaufmann*' ('businessmen') to play on the term '*Kaufmann-methode*', the term used to describe electrotherapy administered to war neurotics. In order to take control of their own health care, war victims should find a 'neutral, trustworthy doctor', who was not attached to the state health care system and therefore corrupted by capitalist interests.[73]

The Bund's inflammatory rhetoric drew sharp attacks. Berlin's health care authorities saw themselves as victims of a KPD smear campaign. The medical director at Berlin's main welfare office complained to the Labor Ministry that the Bund's news articles 'incited and influenced disabled veterans', and contributed to worsening, tense relations between patients and doctors, who were 'only trying to carry out the law'.[74] This complaint came in the wake of an October 1928 issue of the *Internationaler Bund*, which the KPD mailed to the Berlin office. The banner headline on this issue was 'Psychiatry and Neurology in the Service of the Capitalist Class'. Bund member Emil Vogeley argued in this article that 'pension psychosis' and 'hysteria' did indeed exist, but originated in the middle-class psyche that was under siege in the class war. Vogeley theorized that 'pension psychosis' was invented by the middle class to justify their status and pin the working class as lazy and irresponsible. He concluded: 'The theory of pension psychosis is rooted in the social structure of a class-based society'.[75] Behind pension psychosis, Vogeley wrote, affluent Germans tried to hide 'a much more dangerous psychosis – the class struggle psychosis (*Klassenkampfpsychose*)'. Vogeley developed this theory in his analysis of a Dr Rosenfeld, who was accused of indiscriminate pension cutting:

Like all other class struggle organizations, [the Bund] suffers from the 'delusional psychosis' that the class-based society is collapsing, and they want to end once and for all the exploitation of one class by another. What a terrible delusion! It provokes all powers of resistance in Dr Rosenfeld. He can do nothing against this delusion but fight, because he himself suffers from a psychosis, the class struggle psychosis of the middle classes, from which he originates and which he must protect.[76]

Thus Vogeley characterizes the middle class as in the last stage of mental degeneration. Their last gasp was to accuse communist revolutionaries of delusional behavior, when in Vogeley's view the 'psychotic' behavior displayed by zealous, cost-cutting doctors was a clear manifestation of class warfare. Interestingly, Vogeley portrays Dr Rosenfeld and his class as victims as well as perpetrators, cast under the 'psychosis' that afflicts everyone in a class-based society.

The whole science of psychiatry, according to the communists, was thus no objective science at all, but just another weapon in the class struggle. In making this argument, the communists concentrated on the social status of psychiatrists rather than their theories, letting the class question take precedence over the origin and significance of wounds. Vogeley argued that for Dr Rosenfeld, who lived securely on a substantial income, it was 'ridiculous to pontificate on the "health," "will to work," and supposed "reasonable economic situation of pension neurotics"'.[77] Vogeley also claimed that psychiatrists, in their effort to cover up their own degeneration, projected their neuroses on the proletariat. The science of psychiatry was thus a manifestation of this desperate, middle-class psychosis:

> We live in the age of decay, corrosion and degeneration of capitalism. Under the pressure of the historically rising class, the proletariat, the middle classes rear their instincts towards self-preservation, and their life-instinct falls into desperation. The feverish delirium with which the middle class tries to preserve themselves truly reflects their psychological life. This delirium is expressed in the specialized bourgeois sciences ... and in the unprecedented cynicism with which their representatives in the sciences more or less conspicuously place themselves in the services of the capitalist class with their requirements, deductions, conclusions and application of scientific ideas.[78]

Using terms like 'instincts', 'self-preservation', and 'delirium' to diagnose the psychotic defense of capitalism by the middle class, Bund representatives appropriated existing psychiatric discourse and turned it against doctors. Using this framework, they argued that the psychologically disabled bourgeoisie was Germany's most dangerous social and political group, as they held the power to repress their neurotic tendencies while at the same time preserve the socioeconomic system that produced their sickness.

In labeling the middle class as the deepest neurotics, communist leaders questioned the boundaries that separated mentally ill war victims from their health care providers. Long before war victims' representatives picked up this argument, however, veterans from various points on the political left had already been criticizing doctors as more neurotic than their patients. Before the communists started to invert the doctor-patient relationship, there were already a number of instances in welfare offices where war victims actively blurred the lines between themselves and their psychiatrists. In 1921, several riots in Berlin's welfare clinics triggered debates in the city council over how to handle chaotic conditions for war victims and welfare recipients. Witnesses testified that a psychologically ill war victim used the pseudonym 'Dr Franzke-Rudolph', false papers and a disguise to impersonate a doctor and infiltrate Berlin's main welfare center. Once inside the administration area of the office, according to police, 'Dr Franzke Rudolph' began to 'incite rebellion ... and set up a communist headquarters' for the revolution. Local papers reported that in his clash with police just before he was hauled off to an asylum, the 'doctor' declared that health care administrators, insurance court clerks, and doctors were all 'mentally ill', and he called for a new system led by war victims themselves.[79]

In their tracts on war neurosis, communist leaders urged constituents diagnosed with war neurosis to take control of their recovery from doctors and, like the enthusiastic revolutionary mentioned above, join the KPD in revolution. Until the success of the planned revolution, however, Bund leaders seemed to have little use for war neurotics in roles other than martyr and victim. Particularly after the onslaught of the Great Depression and the deepest pension cuts, mentally ill veterans appeared in the Bund's sensationalistic articles only as anonymous, helpless figures to be pitied. In a 1932 feature story, 'The Thanks of the Fatherland – the Martyrdom of a 100% Disabled War Victim', a KPD columnist detailed the tragic story of a nameless family in which the 'severely traumatized father' is completely unable to earn a living while his wife and daughter care for his various nervous disorders until they are unable to pay the rent. Doctors allegedly ordered the neurotic father to be placed in a strait-jacket and forcibly removed from his family, who were then compelled to live in poor houses and barns.[80] Another story tells of a nameless mentally ill veteran who shoots himself, leaving a note: 'I shoot myself on my mother's grave, I am a poor, sick man. I can no longer live because I have lost my pension'.[81] In these articles that appeared during the Depression era's deepest pension cuts, there was no longer the earlier prescription for regeneration through active participation in the revolution. While the communist party expressed sympathy for these men, they also confined mentally disabled veterans to the role of pathetic martyrs, unable to rehabilitate themselves or reassimilate into the community. Until the end of the capitalist health care system, it was implied, traumatized men were doomed to remain mentally ill, unable to provide for their families, unable to adjust to the demands of work or overcome their traumatic memories of the war.

* * *

In psychologically disabled veterans the KPD found useful proof that neuroses drove the tortured middle-class psyche to exploit war victims. Meanwhile, the KPD leadership had little use for war neurotics themselves. In communist newspapers, war neurotics appeared as two dimensional victims, with no real voice of their own. Communist portrayals of mentally disabled veterans as martyrs and victims of the capitalist state ironically came to resemble images of the 'pension neurotics' and 'hysterics' generated by the state's psychiatrists. Men who ten years after the war still displayed the tics, tremors and nightmares caused by mental trauma had lost their will to heal and their abilities to become productive members of society. Further, they tarnished the image of the militant, radical arm of the proletarian movement. These 'hysterical' men thus had few options for declaring equal rights until the awaited moment when the existing power structure was transformed by revolution.

In contrast, social democratic leaders assured their constituents that by working from within democratic institutions, war victims could recover from their psychological wounds, whether caused by the trenches or economic crisis. Hysterical men and women could achieve restoration and productivity through faith in the SPD and shared consciousness as victims of war and capitalist exploitation. However, the SPD failed to convince its constituents that they shared a collective trauma. Neurotic men resented the economic compensation easily granted 'hysterical' women, while they languished in a quagmire of pension cuts and intransigent bureaucracies. At the same time, women protested their perceived treatment as second-class war victims, and even argued that they carried the greater burden of secondary trauma inflicted on them through economic stress and functioning as primary breadwinners in the fractured postwar socioeconomic environment. Despite their aims, the SPD failed to build real bridges between shattered soldiers and women at home.

Fatally, Social Democrats had failed to convince medical authorities of their theories concerning traumatic neurosis. With deepening cuts in the pension budget reaching a crescendo with the Great Depression, Social Democrats became more radical in their outlook and revised their perspectives on the nature of the national trauma. SPD leaders and war victims grew more convinced that the interests of different groups could not be bridged, particularly in terms of social class divisions. By 1930–33, the SPD had abandoned its argument for 'collective trauma' in favor of the argument that class tensions dominated the pension war. The war neurosis debate thus gave it a new discourse to explain the psychological undercurrents of the pension crisis and class conflict in general. Social Democrats concluded that, while the working class directly confronted Germany's traumatic past and healed their neuroses through the community built on social democratic politics, the nation's middle classes repressed their memories of the war. The SPD inverted the rhetoric of psychiatrists and conservative state ministers to argue that middle-class Germans lacked the will to confront their traumatic past, and that cutting pensions was just another form of malingering when it came to the memory of 1914–18.

Disagreement over the origins of Germany's trauma lay at the heart of this debate over which social groups experienced the deepest neuroses. War victims and their representatives on the political left insisted that until the nation recognized the war, and not defeat and revolution, as the source of Germany's crisis, there would be no chance at healing. The great 'psychosis' of the middle class was their denial of the psychological damage caused by modern industrial warfare. The collapse of the Weimar Republic, however, signaled the widespread belief that Germany's most devastating trauma occurred between 1918 and 1923. Middle-class groups traumatized by inflation, social leveling, and the disruption of traditional values and hierarchies led them to identify with National Socialism. The Nazis' interpretation of Germany's psychological condition, and their treatment of those traumatized by war, defeat and revolution, would lead to further denials of the war's lingering psychological effects.

Chapter 5

National Socialism
and its Discontents

War Neurosis and Memory
under Hitler

In October 1918, corporal Adolf Hitler was sent to a military hospital in Pasewalk, Germany, following a gas attack. He suffered from a range of symptoms, including blindness. He was treated by Dr Edmund Forster, a psychiatrist who attributed Hitler's symptoms to 'psychopathic hysteria', as noted in his report. Like many of his contemporary psychiatrists, Forster believed that 'war neurosis' was not a real wound, but only a cover for men trying to shirk their duty at the front.[1]

In the years after the war, Hitler did not allude to these injuries except to say, in *Mein Kampf*, that he suffered from a severe shock when doctors told him Germany had lost the war. In fact, after he came to power in 1933, Hitler's medical records were concealed by the SS because of Dr Forster's reference to the wounds as 'hysterical' in origin.[2] Nevertheless, images of psychological breakdown dominated Hitler's rhetoric on the war experience. At the September 1935 Nuremberg Party rally, Hitler outlined his theory of the cause of Germany's 1918 defeat:

> Eight days' drumfire demanded more sacrifices from the battalions and regiments of our old army than does a whole year's peacetime service. But that drumfire did not break the German people in arms. The German people broke only because it lost its inner freedom, its inner faith in the right of the cause. Today that faith has returned[3]

For Hitler, men at the front did not break under fire. The 'stab-in-the-back' legend hinged on the image of mentally fit front soldiers betrayed by civilians who lost their nerve. The right-wing paramilitary organization, the 'Steel Helmet' (*Der Stahlhelm*), emphatically preserved this myth and assured readers that German soldiers 'had nerves like tightly-bound ropes ... The front veteran of 1918, though hard-pressed, was betrayed by those on the home front who lost their nerve'. Instead of breaking down, the front soldier achieved a state of 'mental calm' and purification in the face of combat.[4] This image permeated the right's political discourse throughout the Weimar years, and it became part of the official memory of the war experience after 1933.[5] The language on 'nerves' played a vital role in the National Socialist construction of a memory of World War I, which excluded psychologically disabled veterans and negated their experiences. Only men strong enough to withstand the stress of combat could be part of the Nazi front community (*Frontgemeinschaft*) that would lead the national community (*Volksgemeinschaft*) to avenge the betrayal of the front soldier by the so-called 'November Criminals', including socialists, Jews, and other groups targeted by the Nazis.

Historians have noted the central importance of the 'myth of the war experience' in Nazi ideology. The war neurosis debate gave National Socialists a framework to form a particular interpretation of Germany's traumatic past. Employing a popularized psychiatric discourse to explain the memory of 1918, the Nazis argued that the nerves of the home front collapsed first. The nerves of veterans who made up the 'front community' became hardened, not traumatized, by the combat experience. According to National Socialist leaders, only mentally weak, unpatriotic soldiers succumbed to the 'stab-in-the-back' inflicted by Germany's internal enemies. However, many men who were psychologically traumatized by the war imagined themselves to be legitimate members of the front community, not 'hysterics' and 'November criminals' as they were portrayed by Nazi leaders. This paradox became apparent as the Nazis overhauled Weimar's social welfare system on the grounds that it catered to 'pension hysterics' and malingerers who faked psychological wounds. The Nazis had to confront the fact that many of these veterans excluded from the official memory of the war experience were actually long-time party members who believed they deserved pensions for their real sacrifices for the fatherland. In debates between the regime's Labor Ministry – which still ran the pension system; doctors – who diagnosed veterans and recommended pension status to the state; and Nazi party ideologues – who looked to defend their old comrades loyal to the Nazi movement, the regime's leaders were forced to examine and define their conception of psychological trauma in relation to the war, defeat and revolution.

As with many other social issues, the Nazis were inconsistent in coordinating theory and practice. At the same time, there was essential ideological consistency in the regime's conception of war neurosis, and their allocation of pensions and management of problems in the system reveals a core element in the National Socialist memory of the past and its definition of traumatic injury. In the Third Reich, ideology dictated that the traditional welfare system created cycles of dependency and coddled unproductive citizens who were parasites on the racial health of the nation. These 'unproductive mouths' were labeled 'asocials'. Along with the hereditarily ill, 'asocials' found themselves attacked in sterilization programs before the Second World War, which evolved into programs for mass murder, including the T–4 'euthanasia' program after 1939.[6] 'War hysterics' became a central image in Nazi welfare policy for veterans, as they were held up as a primary example of asocial, deviant, 'national enemies' who symbolized the degenerate Weimar democracy.

Yet in practice, Nazi officials had difficulty dealing with mentally disabled veterans, and actually awarded pensions to particular cases of men who were diagnosed as war neurotics. This inconsistency was driven by ideological rationale that illustrates the Nazi regime's core definition of traumatic neurosis as a real injury, albeit one inflicted after the war, and not in the trenches. Men who could document that they were 'traumatized' during the 'years of struggle' (Kampfzeit) between 1918 and 1933 consistently received pensions. According to Nazi welfare officials, nationalist-minded men, preferably Nazi party members, who broke down fighting against the 'Marxist' Weimar government, Jews and other 'enemies', were seen as legitimate victims of the nation's ongoing struggle. The most successful applicants for psychological disability pensions included Stormtroopers who were allegedly traumatized by chronic street fighting against communists before 1933, veterans of the 1923 Beer Hall Putsch, and civil servants or lower-level bureaucrats who claimed to suffer stress fighting against the Weimar democracy from behind their desks. For these individuals, Nazi leaders and sympathetic doctors eased the stigma of 'hysteria' and 'neurosis' by diagnosing SA-men and other victims of struggle against democracy as 'exhausted' or 'stressed'. Pensions given by the Nazi state reflected their argument that democracy, rather than war, was the source of Germany's trauma. The real 'victims' were those who suffered damage as a result of Germany's defeat and revolution. Thus Germany's essential trauma, according to Nazi leaders, was revolution and democracy, not the war, which they continued to extol as an ennobling experience to be idealized and replicated.

National Socialist Welfare Policy for War Neurotics

The years just before Weimar's collapse were devastating for disabled veterans, who felt the brunt of government spending cuts. Between 1930 and 1932, the Brüning government cut the budget for war victims by about one-third. Over 30,000 of the 839,396 were cut completely from the welfare rolls, and the pensions of those remaining were largely reduced. The numbers of mentally disabled veterans granted pensions had grown from 5,410 in 1924 to just over 20,000 by 1930. During the depression, 5,000 of these were completely cut from the rolls.[7] The growing number of destitute men and women who lost their pensions were increasingly alienated by a stalemated political system unable to solve a worsening economic crisis and found themselves the target of the Nazi movement's search for voters. The National Socialists stepped up their propaganda in an effort to win support from war victims and their families. The Nazis jumped from a fringe party in 1928 with only 2.6% of the vote, to 18% in 1930 and over 30% in 1932, becoming the largest political party. The Nazi party thrived on the economic fears of middle-class Germans long resentful of the Weimar Republic. Pensioners, particularly those from the lower middle classes, turned towards the Nazis in droves when they felt threatened and increasingly desperate in the wake of the Great Depression.[8]

Nazi leaders exploited the plight of war victims to great effect. Hanns Oberlindober, one of Hitler's long-time 'old fighters' going back to the early days of the movement, established the National Socialist War Victims Association (NSKOV – *National-Sozialistische Kriegsopferversorgung*) in 1930, just as pension cuts accelerated in the wake of the Great Depression. Oberlindober argued that pension cuts proved the party's long-standing argument that the 'November Criminals' behind the 'Marxist' Weimar government that betrayed the army in 1918 did not respect the plight of veterans. For Oberlindober, the Weimar Republic was guilty no matter what, whether by turning disabled veterans into 'pension neurotics' with social welfare, or by initiating cuts in that welfare and leaving veterans destitute.[9] Under a National Socialist regime, war victims would be declared 'first citizens of the nation', and party officials promised to give them the just respect and financial compensation allegedly never granted under the Weimar Republic. The nature of this financial compensation was never specifically outlined in NSKOV newspapers, but it was repeatedly promised that a Nazi regime would cherish disabled veterans as the 'nation's core', entitled to all privileges for their service and sacrifice. Oberlindober claimed this new status for disabled veterans would restore their 'spirit' to the days of August 1914, when he said men felt a sense of duty and purpose that gave them the will to fight in the trenches, and would now give them the impetus to work.[10]

After the Nazis seized power in the spring of 1933, however, they did not substantially change the existing pension and health care system for disabled veterans. Many of the problems early on hinged on classic examples of competing organizations within the Nazi government that often led to contradictory social and economic policies.[11] In 1933, Hitler appointed Franz Seldte, former founder of the Steel Helmet and himself a veteran with a disabled arm, to the head of the Labor Ministry. Oberlindober and the NSKOV made proposals for a new pension law that would grant emergency payments to disabled veterans in the wake of the economic crisis. Seldte's Labor Ministry, with support from the Finance Ministry, protested that these measures were too costly. Behind the scenes, Seldte struggled with Oberlindober over who would have greater control over pension decisions for war victims.[12]

In early 1934, Oberlindober announced that the regime would produce a new National Pension Law that would give both financial support and respect to disabled veterans. Again, struggles between competing agencies formed the backdrop to policy-making, and by the time the law went into effect in July 1934, it was clear that the Labor Ministry would retain control over welfare for wounded veterans. Though the Nazi party through the NSKOV claimed it would now take authority in determining pensions, doctors and the Labor Ministry maintained their authority.[13] The Nazi war disability pension system was very similar to the one established under the *Kaiserreich*. Eventually, with the coordination of the Wehrmacht and the *Oberkommando der Wehrmacht* (OKW) takeover of the pension system in 1938, the Nazi regime established the Military Benefits and Pensions Law, which marked a return to the imperial government's emphasis on military rank, type of wound, social status and ability to earn a living in civilian life as determining factors in the allocation of a pension. In contrast to the 1920 law, the 1934 version and subsequent revisions stated that pensions would be allocated only to men wounded in combat, without mention of physical and psychological disorders that might develop in postwar life. On the whole, the Nazi treatment of disabled veterans now reflected the regime's more militarized approach to the welfare system. The only tangible change under the 1934 law would be the supplementary pension (*Frontzulage*) for qualified wounded front veterans. This came out to a mere 60 Marks per year and a campaign medal for those who could document their status as front veterans. Oberlindober declared the new 1934 pension law a 'complete success' in the 'fight for the honor of the German soldier', which he claimed was actually more important than financial reform. Thus the Nazi government represented no radical change in legislation or pensions for disabled veterans, but they heralded a change in attitude as even more important.[14]

The majority of disabled veterans lost economically under the new 1934 pension law. Despite the supplementary 60 Marks single payment, pensions continued to be cut at the same levels as the 1930–33 period.[15] In addition to its economic shortcomings, the new law created a whole new bureaucratic quagmire for veterans to negotiate. Disabled veterans had to prove to the NSKOV that they had never belonged to 'Marxist' organizations in order to qualify for the *Frontzulage*, or even to successfully apply for their basic disability pensions. The NSKOV thus retained a role in these battles over pensions, as it acted as a political arm that worked for or against war victims. Doctors held tight to their autonomy in deciding whether or not wounds were directly war-related. At the same time, NSKOV officials put concerted pressure on doctors and the Labor Ministry to emphasize the political orientation of patients over medical evidence in a number of cases, making one's status as an 'old fighter' for the regime as crucial as one's status as a diagnosed war victim.

The NSKOV was unable to alter structural economic realities that surrounded pensions, but they did succeed in creating a system that was more overtly political. This is most apparent in the way the regime dealt with war neurotics. War neurotics were seen as not just hysterical malingerers, but also threats to the ideology of National Socialism. Doctors enthusiastically collaborated with the NSKOV to root 'hysterical men' out of the pension and health care system completely. Over 16,000 veterans were immediately cut entirely from the pension system in August 1933, and this included all of the remaining war neurotics. The failure to separate genuine disabled veterans from shirkers and cowards, Nazi officials argued, was the core failure of the 1920 National Pension Law. The basic problem was that legitimately disabled men – those with physical injuries – were required to share welfare and health care resources with so-called 'hysterics', who were enemies of the official memory of the war.[16]

The definition of war neurosis, from a psychiatric standpoint, did not substantially change under the Nazi regime. Similar to debates in imperial and Weimar Germany, the definition of war neurosis was complicated by ideological, military and medicotheoretical concerns. Doctors still described men suffering from the psychological effects of war as hysterics, psychopaths, and weak-willed malingerers, reflecting the profession's ongoing suspicions about the legitimacy and causes of these wounds.[17] Even before Hitler's seizure of power in 1933, mainstream psychiatrists were already advocating sterilization of mentally ill individuals, including veterans, on the basis of racial health and eugenics. Under National Socialism, doctors asserted their widespread rejection of social welfare for mentally disabled veterans more confidently.[18]

When the NSKOV enlisted psychiatrists to work with them, they had little difficulty finding support from doctors friendly to Nazi policy. Mentally disabled veterans only imagined their wounds, according to doctors writing for the NSKOV's monthly newsletter, and they were motivated by their aim to gain a pension and war victim status. Dr Haberland at the University of Köln argued that Weimar-era doctors had been far too lenient in granting 'war neurosis' diagnoses to veterans who had become adept at duping psychiatrists into believing that their various symptoms, including irritability, mental stress, anxiety and stomach pains, were caused by sudden traumatic shock experienced in the trenches.[19] Haberland insisted that these men were 'hysterical' and 'weak-nerved' before the war, and thus predisposed either to 'abnormal reactions' to bomb explosions and stress, or to a tendency to fake their symptoms altogether. These male hysterics were driven by 'egotism' and failed to understand the meaning of sacrifice, 'thus placing themselves in sharpest opposition to our National Socialist world view'. Hysterics tried selfishly to draw attention and empathy to their particular injuries, Haberland noted, and 'in a theatrical manner' they staged crying fits and suicide attempts that burdened the nation as they refused to fill their masculine roles as heads of families and productive workers. Haberland called upon 'National Socialist-minded doctors' to take action on behalf of the state and society to identify and expel these social enemies from the pension system and the community of honorable war victims.[20]

Hysterical men were created by Weimar's expanded welfare state and the influences of Marxism, according to Nazi psychiatrists. Dr H. Koetzle, a military physician in Stuttgart, argued that the 'pacifistic' and 'Marxist' attitudes of the postwar period weakened the will of disabled veterans to return to work and family.[21] The Nazis claimed that democracy and a defeatist civilian population produced an epidemic of welfare cheats and mental decay. The entire Weimar welfare system, Koetzle claimed, was made to serve psychopaths, asocials and whiners.[22] Labor Ministry doctor Paul Fraatz criticized the 'Marxist Republic' for conflating disabled veterans and civilians on welfare, which he believed weakened the self-confidence of Germany's heroes. The Weimar pension law brought returning soldiers into contact with 'work shy civilians', already experienced at manipulating the welfare system, and gave veterans the idea of shirking work. In order to distinguish veterans tainted by civilian malingerers and veterans who remained 'pure', Fraatz advised that when disabled veterans who wanted to be productive members of the nation visited doctors they be accompanied by an NSKOV representative 'who represented the voice of the Führer'.[23] This way the NSKOV could mediate between doctors and the Labor Ministry on the political orientation and social values of war victims.

The bridge between the world view of Nazi leaders and psychiatrists proved easy to cross. Nazi ideologues prescribed a return to the spirit of 1914, and a new war could resuscitate German society after 15 years of peace and democracy had weakened the nation's nerves. The front soldier, they believed, would lead the nation's resurrection from mental degeneration. Ernst Röhm, the leader of the SA, wrote on the topic of psychological strength and the front experience for war-disabled newspapers. He portrayed the front experience as the 'spiritual father' of the National Socialist movement, which anointed men with exceptional 'mental powers' that gave them the ability to reinvigorate German society. Their leadership, according to Röhm, had been usurped by 'Jewish-Bolshevist lies' in 1918, which fed on the 'broken mental strength' of civilians who did not have the psychological armor to resist.[24] The war experience of true front soldiers, Röhm asserted, made them immune to the 'complete breakdown in the mental structure' seen in the civilian population, and thus entitled them to rescue the nation at its moment of crisis. Röhm regarded men who claimed to be mentally traumatized by the war as infected by civilian weakness and the 'psychosis' brought on by the postwar welfare system and 'the existing [democratic] social and political order'.[25]

Psychiatrists chimed in on this celebration of war as a psychological fix. Dr Alfred Dick wrote for the NSKOV newspaper that war 'produced a mentally and morally healthier person', and he and other doctors indicated that any veteran who claimed to be psychologically injured should have their service history reviewed to determine how long they were really at the front.[26] Similar to doctors in 1914, Nazi leaders represented war as an ennobling, psychologically healthy event in a stream of films and books. *Attack Troop 1917* (*Stosstrupp 1917*), a film developed as a National Socialist response to the popular *All Quiet on the Western Front*, epitomized this view of war as an agent for revitalizing Germany's mental health. One columnist for the NSKOV wrote that this was the 'best film of the war', because it portrayed the 'unshaken faith of the simple soldier' in spite of the incredible violence experienced at the front, and 'reawakened the great front experience' as a reminder that 'all events of our time emerge from the violent psychological effects of the most profound experience of the century: the world war'.[27] The surviving front soldiers, Nazi leaders believed, would spearhead the national task of educating civilians about the meaning of the front experience and thus counteract the degenerative mental effects of social democracy. Thus the Nazis believed they could purify both the nation and the front community, restoring the image front fighters so they could take their rightful place as Germany's new leaders.

Traumatized by Weimar: The Nazis Redefine War Neurosis

The regime's attempt to root 'hysterical' men out of the welfare system and the 'front community' was vehemently challenged by veterans with psychological problems. By the late summer of 1934–35, streams of letters poured into the Labor Ministry and the NSKOV from veterans diagnosed with, or claiming to suffer from, mental disabilities. These men tried to persuade the regime that though they suffered from mental illness, they were indeed loyal National Socialists and productive members of the national community. Though the regime labeled these men as 'asocials', or individuals who were outsiders to the national community, some of these individuals succeeded in convincing the state that their wounds were both real and deserving of compensation.

Even before the July 1934 law went into effect, mentally disabled Stormtroopers and pre-1933 members of the Nazi movement had been petitioning for benefits once Hitler became chancellor. Shortly after the March 1933 seizure of power, there was a widespread attempt on the part of Hitler's long-term supporters to get what they felt they were entitled to after years of suffering as 'victims' of the Weimar Republic and the 'November Criminals'. One of the more interesting cases in Labor Ministry files is that of Franz F., a Stormtrooper. F. was an early member of the Nazi movement

– known as an 'old fighter' – who joined the SA in 1921. The next year he was promoted to an 'attack unit' (*Stosstrupp*). He participated in the 1923 Munich Beer Hall Putsch alongside Hitler, and he was imprisoned with forty other NSDAP members including the Nazi leader at Landsberg prison.[28] He later reported that he suffered physical and psychological brutality inflicted by police during his 1923 arrest and imprisonment. After his 1924 release, he claimed his health had deteriorated because he never received proper medical treatment while in custody.

Franz F. did not hold status as a war victim under the Weimar Republic, and he did not claim any disability for injuries inflicted between 1914 and 1918. However, the wounds he incurred in the Beer Hall Putsch suddenly gained significance after Hitler came to power. In May 1934, F. hired a local NSDAP representative named Martin in his Hamburg district to appeal on his behalf for assistance with his chronic illness, which he described as a myriad of 'internal injuries'.[29] Martin wrote to a lawyer and staff liaison officer for the Nazi party named Heim that F.'s injuries left him completely unable to earn a living and eligible for a pension from the new regime. Martin concluded his letter detailing F.'s distinguished career as a veteran of the Nazi 'years of struggle' in the 1920s, when he was well regarded by his old comrades, who nicknamed him 'the Frog' (a word-play on his last name).[30]

'The Frog's' self-described 'internal injuries' drew attention from the Labor Ministry, which requested that Franz F. send in a detailed report on the nature of these wounds, and supporting documentation. F.'s party representative, Martin, assured the Labor Ministry that documents would be forthcoming as soon as the doctor who inspected him at Landsberg could be located. Meanwhile, F.'s party lawyer, Heim, pressed Martin for details about the nature of F.'s 'internal injuries'. Martin did not go into specifics. Nevertheless, Heim made the case that since F. suffered mistreatment under police custody while engaged in the Nazi movement, he was eligible for a pension in accordance with the 27 February 1934 Care for the Fighters of the National Uprising Law (*Gesetz über die Versorgung der Kämpfer für die nationale Erhebung*). Heim wrote that as soon as F. presented documentation regarding his treatment and injuries, he would be granted a 900 Marks pension. Heim also affirmed that the Führer's deputies and Hitler himself remembered F. from the old days.[31]

Franz F.'s wounds and documentation proved to be elusive. Six months of correspondence between Heim and Martin elapsed and proof of F.'s injuries were still not made available. Hitler's personal aide, Wilhelm Brückner, an SA-*Obergruppenführer*, intervened in January 1935 and informed the Hamburg health care office that the Führer wished this matter to be brought to a quick conclusion, that F. receive a full pension, and that further reports on his case be sent directly to his office.[32] Doctors, however, opposed this attempt to bypass the Labor Ministry welfare office line of authority. Dr Knüppel at the Hamburg health care office replied to Brückner that F.'s application could not be processed yet because, in accordance with the July 1934 pension law, F. still needed to be examined and his pension approved by a state health official. At this point, Franz F.'s condition as an individual with psychological problems was finally revealed. Dr Knüppel indicated that F. refused to be examined by psychiatrists assigned to him by the health care system. F. demanded that he instead be examined by a 'National Socialist doctor', and he went to a health clinic in Hannover for treatment by a doctor of his own choice. Dr Knüppel, however, insisted that F.'s condition required a state psychiatrist's attention to evaluate the legitimacy of his injuries. Dr Holzmann, a psychiatrist who worked in mental hospitals during the war, was brought in by the Labor Ministry to examine the old Stormtrooper. In a letter to Obergruppenführer Brückner, Dr Knüppel conceded that until the evaluation by Dr Holzmann, F. could receive a minimal 100 Marks per month pension.[33]

Dr Holzmann proved to be sympathetic to Franz F.'s case, and National Socialist-minded in his outlook. Holzmann reported that F. suffered from years of 'extraordinary strain, privations, and agitation' suffered while in the Nazi movement, and that he had been rendered completely unable to earn a living due to a 'state of exhaustion and over-irritation'. Dr Knüppel commented on this judgment and confirmed that F. was indeed disabled by his sacrifices for the Nazi movement and deserved a pension.[34] The Hamburg health care office subsequently sent word that F. was granted a full pension in accordance with the 1934 law, as well as 1,743 Marks in back payments from the time F. had originally applied.[35]

Franz F.'s case illustrates a number of interesting developments for psychologically disabled men under the Third Reich. Eligibility for a pension was no longer exclusively a question of whether or not one's wounds were war-related. The political orientation and background of the individual was now at least as important as the cause, or nature, of psychological problems. Further, euphemisms helped channel men through the system. To avoid the labels that had stigmatized men in the imperial and Weimar years as 'psychotic' or 'hysterical', Nazi doctors collaborated with the regime and patients with the right politics to provide more mild diagnoses like 'over-exhausted' and 'strained'. Thus a 'steel-nerved' SA-man like Franz F. could avoid embarrassment. His history as an 'old fighter' persuaded doctors that he was indeed a 'victim', and not just a malingerer out to avoid work. Though doctors still clung to their authority in determining the origins of wounds, men with the right connections and National Socialist credentials could easily manipulate the system.

The overtly political nature of the Nazi pension system also led to an interesting development. Postwar fighters for National Socialism, even those without war experience, found greater success than diagnosed

1914–18 war victims in winning pensions for mental disabilities. Many of these men were relatively new to the pension war, and did not have files full of medical reports from the 1920s testifying that they were swindlers and chronic psychopaths. Further, Nazi propaganda encouraged individuals who never even saw the Western front to apply for pensions as victims in the postwar struggle against Germany's 'enemies' at home.

The war against Marxists, Jews, and democracy apparently placed a greater strain on nerves than the trench experience, judging from the Nazi welfare system. This phenomenon can be seen in the flood of applications that poured into the Labor Ministry from first-time pension applicants. White-collar workers in particular, many of whom were devastated in the 1923 hyperinflation, took the opportunity after 1933 to gain compensation for their psychological stress inflicted during the 'years of struggle'. Emil H., a bureaucrat and later civil servant is an interesting example of this phenomenon. H. pleaded his case in a series of letters written to the Labor Ministry from 1933–41, where he pushed his ongoing argument that his record fighting against the 'November Criminals' after 1918 qualified him for a pension. Under the Weimar Republic, H. actually applied for a pension as an exceptional case. He had suffered a 'severe shock to the nerves' in a 1915 explosion in a fireworks laboratory where he worked as army clerk. Subsequent epileptic seizures, which doctors linked to the effects of the explosion on H.'s nervous system, gradually worsened after the war.[36] In 1932, he found assistance from the Spandau branch of the National Association of Former Employees of Army and Navy Administration (*Reichsbund ehemaligen Angehöriger der Heeres- und Marine- Verwaltungen*), which asked the Labor Ministry to grant H. financial support as a special case, in recognition of his injuries incurred while working for the army civil service.[37] Health care officials stepped in, however, and rejected H.'s application on a technicality, citing his ineligibility under the conditions of his voluntary discharge from the army.[38]

With Hitler's rise to power in 1933, Emil H. saw an opportunity to cut through the bureaucratic quagmire. Nazi officials in his home town of Siegburg also took this chance to reshape the war victim debate and give status to H., who they perceived as a National Socialist-minded victim of the Weimar 'system'. Within two weeks of Hitler's January 1933 appointment to the chancellorship, they picked up H.'s case and recast it as a political issue. H.'s Nazi party sponsors exerted pressure on the Labor Ministry to make their pension decision from a 'National Socialist perspective'.[39] In a February 1933 report to labor ministers, the NSDAP announced that now that they were in power, they could assist 'victims' of the 1918 revolution. Despite his nervous breakdowns and epileptic seizures, they claimed H. was dedicated to the nationalist cause and fought bravely against the army bureaucrats who collaborated with the 'November Criminals' and betrayed front soldiers in 1918.[40] Bowing to NSDAP pressure to award H. a 'favorable decision', welfare officials now recommended to the Labor Ministry that since it was medically proven that he could not work, H. was indeed entitled to at least a 150 Marks single payment and perhaps continued support.[41]

Nazi party leaders were not satisfied with the compromise made by welfare officials. They characterized the pension administrators as lacking commitment to Germany's heroes who resisted social democracy in the hour of Germany's national crisis after 1918. The Siegburg local branch of the NSDAP brought Emil H.'s predicament to the attention of interior minister Hermann Goering, requesting that he decisively solve the case. In this May 1933 letter, Nazi officials portrayed H. as a heroic civil servant who fought against 'Marxist influences' from within the Weimar bureaucracy with such exceptional dedication that he deserved substantial financial support from the National Socialist state.[42] In a follow-up letter to Goering, they argued further that H.'s case was not unique and that he symbolized the commitment of '400 to 600' civil servants and bureaucrats who deserved the thanks of the National Socialist movement for attempting to sabotage leftist influences in the government during the November revolution.[43] In cases like Emil H.'s, argued his local NSDAP representatives, it was not merely a question of whether or not pension applicants were really ill, or even whether they could work. Instead, it was a matter of rewarding those who had proven themselves as unwilling to run with the program when the Weimar Republic was established.[44] H.'s sponsors pressured the Labor Ministry to retroactively 'give the thanks of the fatherland' and award him status as a 'front fighter', including 36.54 Marks per month on top of his 150 Marks special payment for 'fulfilling his duty as a German civil servant in 1918 for our Führer'. Nazi officials thus portrayed H. as a 'war veteran' and 'victim' because he waged a stressful war on the enemies of National Socialism, albeit from behind a desk.[45]

Emil H., however, believed that his heroism was worth more than a paltry 36.54 Marks per month. In 1935, he appealed directly to Hitler, portraying himself as one of the last defenders of German national pride among his fellow bureaucrats when 'the muddy tide of the Marxist November revolution also swarmed over our army work administration ... and I could not pay my allegiance to them'.[46] In his letter, H. described himself as a sick man in those days in 1918, battling headaches and nervous breakdowns, which he carefully documented with medical reports. Nevertheless, he proudly fulfilled his duty for the fatherland. Mistrusted by his fellow clerks because he 'rejected internationalist thinking', H. said he carried on his war against the enemies of the nation in virtual isolation.[47] H. explained that by 1919 he sought to leave his intolerable work environment and live off a pension. Weimar authorities in 1919 told him that he had not yet worked long enough to be eligible. His 1935 letter to Hitler explains why he left his job:

> At the end of 1918 there were only a few men who considered themselves German and stood at attention for their fatherland. I could not act like everything was all right and run along with the program. I am not a little yes-man. I can only sing the German [anthem], not the International [communist anthem]. It is my natural disposition not to be guilty of or contribute to the breakdown [*Zusammenbruch*] of the fatherland.[48]

Emil H. claimed he still wanted to work, but simply could not because of the political situation. Thus leftist politics were the cause of his nervous disorders. The national 'breakdown' that he witnessed, not his own nervous breakdown, destroyed his will to work.

Emil H. attempted to define himself as a war victim disabled by Germany's political revolution, namely the rise of democratic politics. He ended his letter to Hitler by stating that the fact that he had to endure the 1918 revolution was clear evidence for his mental illness, as it would drive any truly patriotic German to collapse, and he requested a permanent pension for disabled veterans. H. added that if he could he would still fight Germany's 'enemies' despite his poor health: 'I will gladly work as an honest clerk again for my fatherland in its hours of danger, as long as my physical health permits'.[49] Welfare administrators and bureaucracy, however, impeded H.'s drive for a pension. Health insurance officials at Koblenz took over his case and took the next three years gathering all his medical files and pension records. In 1938 they eventually granted a 100 Marks single payment and assured H. that he would receive, in addition to his 36.54 Marks per month, another 57.20 Marks employee insurance pension.[50] At the time of his death in 1941, his monthly payment had increased another 42 Marks per month, and his wife was left a widow's pension.[51]

Emil H.'s case illustrates the National Socialist memory of defeat and revolution and how it influenced pensions for war victims. H., though never in the trenches, was able to blame the enemies of National Socialism, rather than his own psychological problems, for his failure to continue work. The 'wounds' themselves were less important than the pension applicant's political orientation and character. If one could document long-term support for National Socialism, it was assumed that the individual must have been willing to work, but stressed to the point of disability by the feeling of being an 'outsider' in the Weimar democracy. During the Weimar years, pension applicants who supported parties on the left learned that these political issues were always in the background of their struggle with Labor Ministry bureaucrats, and they often had to conceal their political views from unsympathetic doctors. But under Nazism, the opportunity presented itself for 'old fighters' within the far right to recast their case histories and argue that the postwar environment caused their nervous breakdowns.

Nazi party officials looked for ways to help their own. Those who could not document National Socialist support before 1933 were left stranded and their nervous disorders were defined as symptoms of malingering, rather than political oppression. This fine line can be seen in cases of bureaucrats who were given special privileges within the Weimar Republic's civil service because of their social connections, but under Nazism found themselves labeled as 'hysterical' parasites on the nation's welfare system. Max von B., for example, a thirty-one year old who suffered a severe nervous breakdown while working as a court clerk and studying to become a lawyer, won special consideration for a pension under Weimar's Labor Ministry. Von B.'s father was a *Rittmeister* (cavalry captain) and civil servant captured and executed by Bolsheviks during fighting in Poland in 1919.[52] Though von B. himself was not a war veteran, his social status and his father's war record gave weight to his pension application. The Labor Ministry thus considered him for a one-time payment in 1928. Deciding that von B. was unable to earn a living because of his psychological problems, the health insurance office in Giessen recommended that he be given a 100 Marks payment to hold him over until his relatives could secure assistance. Insurance officials justified this exceptional case with a technical point – they noted that von B. had never received an orphan's pension because he had already reached the age of 18 at his father's death.[53]

The privileged status granted von B. by Weimar bureaucrats carried less weight when he applied for further assistance in 1938. At first, von B. had considerable help from doctors and health insurance officials. Dr Haas, director of the Ludwigs-Universität medical clinic, wrote sympathetically on von B.'s behalf, describing his 'severe depression', and recommending social assistance to fund a cure in a sanitarium.[54] The director of the central health and welfare office in Kassel wrote to the Labor Ministry reminding them that von B.'s father had been a martyr against Bolshevism in 1919. Though the director acknowledged the state's official rejection of financial assistance for mentally disabled men, saying that pensions only encouraged the 'weak-nerved' to avoid work, he asked that out of respect to General-Feldmarschall von Mackeson, an old friend of the patient's father, von B. should receive some sort of assistance from a special fund.[55] Only two months later, however, both Dr Haas and the director of the Kassel welfare office reversed their support. Dr Haas reported to the Labor Ministry that von B. was really a 'useless neurotic' who could not be persuaded to work, and was 'unsuitable' for military service.[56] With Dr Haas' new report was a letter from state medical representative Dr Wilhelm Trautmann, who concluded that all medical efforts on behalf of the 'psychopathic' and 'hypochondriac' von B. were futile.[57] The welfare director at Kassel responded by informing the Labor Ministry that a medical program or financial assistance would only encourage von B.'s 'unwillingness to work'.[58] The reasons for this rapid change of opinion on the part of doctors and welfare officials were not overtly stated in their letters to the Labor Ministry. However, it is clear that von B.'s clout within the government networks did not extend past 1933. The new regime had established criteria that von B. no longer met: he was neither a documented front veteran nor a long-time supporter of National Socialism.

Dr Haas's reversal of opinion on von B.'s moral character – changing his conclusion from legitimate mental illness to malingerer – recalled long-held assumptions regarding working-class 'pension neurotics'. Interestingly, in this case the label was applied to an aristocrat. Under the Nazis, social class carried less weight than political orientation in determining the boundaries between malingerer and genuine 'victim'. Those who did not have National Socialist connections, whether a member of the aristocratic elite or from a lower social status, found themselves in danger of being labeled 'hysterical pension neurotics'. Political background also trumped medical evidence. It was not enough to have documented wounds, one also had to document that one was a 'victim' of the Weimar Republic. Political connections played the primary role in determining pension status.

Coordinating Welfare, Doctors, and War Neurosis, 1934–1938

Following the cuts in all pensions to war neurotics after 1934, men with documented status as front veterans suffering from psychological wounds flooded the Labor Ministry with letters protesting what they saw as the betrayal of Hitler's promise to veterans. At first, the Labor Ministry relied on medical documentation as central to determining pensions. But as the Labor Ministry became more thoroughly coordinated under National Socialism after the 1934 law, it reduced these often complex cases to the political background of the individual. Battles between Labor Ministers and Nazi party leaders over who would control the diagnosis of 'war neurosis' was tortuous, but by the time Germany was on the brink of the Second World War, the diagnosis of war neurosis had been coordinated completely by the Nazi party.

Desperate mentally ill individuals often used the new political atmosphere to try to exploit the pension system. In these cases of obvious fraud, the Labor Ministry found it easy to draw the line. One example of this was the case of Klaus W., identified by Weimar's welfare administrators as a long-term fraud who said anything to get a pension. During the 1920s, W. threw a list of incredible stories at the Labor Ministry, including claims that he worked for Vice Admiral of the Navy Graf von Spee, and a story about the sinking of the Lusitania in 1915 leading to the dissolution of his furniture store business in Brooklyn, New York. He provided no documentation for these stories, but in every letter he asked for financial compensation for the enormous material losses and psychological stress allegedly caused by the war, in one case requesting '46,799 gold dollars' to settle his claims.[59]

The republic dismissed Klaus W. as a 'pathological swindler' and 'psychopath' each time he sent the usual letter, the last rejection coming in 1932.[60] But after 1933, W. wrote essentially the same letter to the Labor Ministry, but with one additional story. This time he mentioned that he served as one of the first Stormtroopers in Würzburg, fighting for his 'nation's honor'. He also claimed to have once had a pension, but said that it was 'robbed by Chancellor Brüning's economic policies'. He concluded by challenging labor ministers to prove they really had purged all the 'November Criminals' from their ranks by giving him a pension.[61] W. provided no evidence for his SA background, and had no support from the NSKOV or any Nazi party officials. Labor Ministry files contain no replies to his request.

Labor Ministry records are also filled with letters from men who could document close connections to the Nazi party, but not authentic psychological wounds. These Nazi 'old fighters' hunting for pensions exacerbated existing power struggles between welfare administrators, doctors, and party leaders. Nazi party officials often provided support for their old friends who claimed mental injuries inflicted in 1914–18, and used them to attack the welfare bureaucracy and force compliance with National Socialism, though they were not always successful. An interesting example of this is the case of Friedrich S., a long-time fervent Nazi dating back to the 'years of struggle' in the 1920s. S. bombarded the Labor Ministry with letters after 1933. He referred to the NSKOV's new promises to disabled veterans and called on the regime to reward him for being an 'energetic' member of the Nazi movement since 1928. S. further detailed his vigorous antisemitic views, which he claimed dated back to the 'Stöcker movement', a reference to one of Germany's pre-World War I ultraconservative, antisemitic Christian-nationalist political parties. S. became an artillery officer during the war, where he claimed to suffer 'long months of mental stress', a 'nervous breakdown', and continuous 'shocks' to his nerves that sent him to field hospitals and sanatariums. Like many on the far right, S. believed that the war continued after 1918 as he turned to Germany's 'enemies' at home: Jews, socialists, and those he targeted as responsible for Germany's defeat. He claimed that he was 'punished by Jewish judges' throughout the 1920s when he was robbed of a pension and endured false testimony for crimes he did not specify. Finally, his lingering wounds became unbearable in 1932, and he was unable to earn a living.[62] S. asked welfare administrators to immediately grant him 300 Marks out of respect for his war record as an officer who had given above average dedication to the fatherland that 'ruined both body and mind'.[63]

Friedrich S.'s war experience was the total antithesis of the official National Socialist memory of the war. He unabashedly admitted that his nerves broke down in combat, and he considered these to be legitimate wounds that did not contradict his enthusiasm for the fatherland or the Nazi movement. But though the Nazis officially labeled such a war experience as unmanly and un-German in their propaganda, they gave S. wholehearted support in his battle against the welfare system. S. received letters of recommendation from his local Berlin NSDAP office in April 1934, which emphasized his exploits as a street fighter against the enemies of National Socialism throughout the 1920s. He tried to circumvent the medical examinations needed to gain war victim status, and complained that his case should remain in the hands of Nazi party officials rather than the Labor Ministry's welfare bureaucrats.[64] In fact, S. provided no medical documentation to prove his claims. When his welfare office turned down his request, they described him as a potential criminal, alcoholic, and 'well-known psychopath' who was now hunting for financial assistance that he did not even need. They also noted that he had once been accepted into a treatment program, but did not seriously follow the doctors' advice.[65] Several months later, doctors detailed a long history of S.'s fraudulent activities, including forging stamps and signatures on welfare documents. Further, they concluded that he was never actually treated for any wounds during the war, and never diagnosed as a war neurotic. He only received treatment for an injury to his index finger, and even that was questionable as a war-related wound.[66]

Friedrich S. was outraged and insisted that his psychological problems were real and related to wartime and postwar injuries. He appealed directly to the head of the Labor Ministry, by this time the former 'Steel Helmet' (*Der Stahlhelm*) founder Franz Seldte, and vehemently denied doctors' accusations that he was a delusional alcoholic and fraudulent war victim.[67] After another round of rejection letters, S. played his best political card, soliciting a letter of support from SS-*Obergruppenführer* Dietrich, in command of Hitler's elite SS bodyguard unit (SS-*Leibstandarte Adolf Hitler*), whom he hoped would pressure the Labor Ministry to give in. Dietrich offered his help and asked that the case be reopened in the light of the fact that S.'s son was a member of Hitler's elite SS bodyguard unit, and he vouched for S.'s moral character and commitment to National Socialism.[68] This did not impress the Labor Ministry enough. They responded that it was not possible to grant S. a pension, not even emergency relief, because his health problems were non-war related. Labor ministers acknowledged the political pressure, including the fact that Hitler himself expressed interest in the case when informed by Dietrich, but nevertheless concluded that the criteria for awarding a pension did not exist.[69]

When these political strategies failed, Friedrich S. resorted to reinventing the nature of his war wounds. Suddenly he realized his problems were not psychological, but rather physical. He revealed for the first time that he was suffering from a terrible pain in his left foot caused by bomb shrapnel. He ranted at the Labor Ministry for letting a war victim suffer, asking if this was 'the thanks of the fatherland'. Perhaps anticipating that health care providers might find his late-breaking story dubious, he provided a report by his former commanding officer who claimed to have witnessed the foot injury. S. sarcastically asked if the Labor Ministry could now deny that the shrapnel wound to his foot was war-related.[70] He also revealed that he suffered pains in his spinal chord since 1914. He claimed he never mentioned it because he so badly wanted to be accepted in the army in the early days of the war. Supporting evidence, he wrote, could not be provided because it was destroyed by 'the parties of opposition'.[71] After an investigation, doctors concluded that S.'s shrapnel wound, finger injury and other problems were contrived, stating: 'It is improbable that a war veteran could not document the place and time in which a wound was received'.[72] The NSKOV sent another letter of support insisting S. was not a liar, and in a letter where he promised to clear up problems in his medical records, S. also mentioned a war wound to his jaw.[73] The Labor Ministry was unimpressed and did not reply despite S.'s support from the Nazi war victims' organization.

In this early 1933–35 period of the Nazi regime, the Labor Ministry and its doctors insisted that at least some medical documentation for the war-related nature of psychological and physical wounds needed to exist if they were to justify political favors to Nazi leaders who intervened on behalf of their traumatized constituents. Demonstrating a record of loyalty to the Nazi movement did not entirely suffice. Men still had to show good faith that their wounds, and their willingness to work, were real – Friedrich S.'s Nazi party connections did not dissolve skepticism that he was a crank hunting for a pension, and his reputation as a swindler was sealed within the welfare bureaucracy. By 1936, however, the NSKOV, the Labor Ministry's welfare administrators and doctors began to find significant common ground. Nazi officials and doctors both saw the patient's war record as central to his character and will to work, and it was in this area that political and medical interests merged. When a patient's condition seemed ambiguous, doctors relied on Nazi officials to determine whether patients qualified as authentic war victims. For the Nazis, this status could be acquired if one were the right kind of 'front fighter', that is, both a war veteran and a documented loyalist to National Socialist ideals.

Thus veterans had to scramble to prove themselves as healthy, patriotic men in 1914–18 who were also 'victims' of defeat, revolution, and the Weimar Republic. It was difficult to document both front service and dedication to the Nazi movement in the 1920s, and many veterans found themselves stranded without the right military or political credentials. Johann E., a long-standing pariah of welfare offices during the Weimar years, found himself struggling again after 1933. E. spent over a decade fighting with Weimar's Labor Ministry over the medical causes of his psychological problems. In 1927, one welfare official labeled E. a 'hysterical character', for whom there was no medical proof for war-related injuries.[74] The following year, E. hired a lawyer to collect medical evidence from various doctors to prove that his client was perfectly healthy and able to work until his service in 1915, the year he was first hospitalized with numerous 'nervous disorders' and physical problems including stomach ailments and a heart condition.[75] In 1931, the Labor Ministry's doctors compiled their own case to refute E.'s lawyer and deny state assistance, citing the lack of convincing medical evidence to prove that E. was healthy before entering the service.[76] Doctors pointed to his hysterical behavior and malingering as evidence that war trauma was out of the question. In 1936, E. submitted a new application to his welfare office with a different focus, this time emphasizing his war service as justification for a pension. His welfare officials in Bavaria were unimpressed, and they noted, 'Your war service was only ten days of garrison duty'. E. spent more time in the hospital than at the front, they emphasized, indicating this was 'an illness that existed before service'.[77] Thus doctors asserted their authority, as they had before 1933, in determining whether or not mental problems actually originated in front service.

Men suffering from nervous disorders often had a much more impressive record as authentic front fighters than E., but nevertheless found themselves stranded if they did not have matching National Socialist credentials. Men had to be more than documented 'heroes'. They also had to be proven Nazis. When the July 1934 law summarily cut war neurotics from the pension rolls, regardless of their history at the front, the Labor Ministry was flooded with men who had amassed piles of documents highlighting their history of exploits at the front, willingness to work, and loyalty to their nation. However, without a history of pre-1933 fighting for National Socialism, the regime was unwilling to support men with traumatic injuries.

Nazi officials were willing to rationalize mental wounds caused by fighting against the Weimar Republic, but not fighting on the Western front. This is exemplified in the case of Eugen R. When Hitler came to power, R., like many other veterans, saw a new opportunity to get a pension as a 'first citizen' of the Reich. R. suffered from multiple sclerosis, epilepsy, migraines, and alleged traumatic neurosis, all of which he described as legitimate war-related injuries. The welfare office in Berlin turned down his application for a pension, as they had during the Weimar years, citing his wounds as not war related.[78] Frustrated with the welfare system, R. went to his NSKOV office. They supported him as an authentic front veteran and counseled him on seeking a medical evaluation from a private doctor who could substantiate that at least some of his wounds were legitimate. On this issue they were very particular, and stressed that he should claim his injuries were physical, that is, actual organic damage to his nervous system, rather than psychological in nature.[79]

From this point R. would place less emphasis on his psychological problems and instead push for recognition of his physical disorders. This was crucial, as patients with multiple sclerosis and epilepsy were officially targeted under the Law for the Prevention of Progeny with Hereditary Diseases that called for forced sterilization.[80] Private doctors suggested that his multiple sclerosis and chronic headaches were most likely linked to combat trauma. In addition, the NSKOV backed him up by reminding the Labor Ministry that R. was a decorated lieutenant who had stormed Fort Douaumont at Verdun in 1916. For this he had been recommended for, though he never received, the *Pour le Merité*, Germany's highest medal awarded to soldiers up until 1918.[81] One doctor at the Berlin welfare office eventually concluded that R.'s war experiences, including an episode in which he reportedly lay for hours in the mud and snow, indicated that his nervous system may indeed have suffered permanent injury. He cited R.'s 'personal profile' and his irrefutable record as a war hero and promised a thorough review of the case. In this 1935 report, however, the doctor specified that, though the physical damage to R.'s neurological system was probable, psychological damage was out of the question. 'Traumatic neurosis', the doctor asserted, was defined differently in 1916 than in 1935. Though he did not explain the nature of this difference, it was clear that welfare offices were willing to cooperate with the NSKOV only if psychological injuries were taken out of the picture.[82]

Proof of war hero status tipped the balance for war victims, at least in regards to their physical injuries. Eugen R. was finally granted a pension and full status as a disabled war victim. But this was not enough. He demanded further assistance to pay for a myriad of physical and psychological illnesses he claimed to suffer from, including exhaustion and depression that left him unable to earn a living. This total inability to earn a living, he argued, required a higher level of compensation. Years of battles with an inadequate health care and the welfare system, R. complained, exacerbated his physical and psychological stress. In 1936, R. lamented that on state support he could only afford a cure at a health resort that was inadequate and actually made his condition worse. Instead, he wanted enough money to afford a cure at Bad Dürkheim, the premiere, most expensive resort. R. reminded the Labor Ministry that under the regime's new definition of veterans as 'first citizens' of the Reich, he was entitled to no less.[83] Four years later, during the Second World War, he wrote to his welfare office that he needed an extra 60 Marks per month to buy a car, otherwise he would be unable to get to work. R. expertly appealed to the regime's rhetoric of what constituted a valuable individual when he highlighted his unflagging will to be productive in spite of his health problems: 'I would like to make use of my strength to work (*Arbeitskraft*), especially in the present-day time of war … because despite my severe disabilities I am completely able to work (*arbeitsfähig*)'.[84] Here R. challenged the image of disabled veterans as potentially unproductive malingerers and portrayed himself as struggling with ongoing illnesses while at the same time remaining a valuable asset to society.

Labor ministers drew the line on further assistance, and Eugen R. was forced to replay his war hero card. He wrote to the head of the Labor Ministry and old front comrade Franz Seldte, to whom he was personally introduced as an honorary participant in a ceremony marking the Battle of Tannenberg anniversery.[85] R. reminded Seldte that he had been considered for the *Pour le Merité* medal in 1916, Germany's highest award for gallantry in combat, and he mentioned that the extra money for a car would be the greatest expression of the Nazi regime's respect for his loyal devotion to his country. The OKW (*Oberkommando der Wehrmacht*) – which by this time in 1941 was in charge of pensions – agreed to make a one-time payment of 400 Marks, which the Berlin office cut down to 300 Marks.[86] Furious, R. submitted an essay he had written on 'The Attack on Douaumont', glorifying his exploits for his country. The OKW was through trying to make concessions. They acknowledged that R. 'displayed the highest devotion to duty' in 1914–18, but asserted that he no longer qualified for any further financial assistance beyond his initial base pension.[87]

R. is a classic example of war victims in Nazi Germany trying to take advantage of Nazi leaders' propaganda on veterans, while facing the frustrating reality of limited economic support behind the regime's rhetoric. At the same time, R. exemplifies the circumstances that many men with complex mental and physical wounds found themselves in: their irrefutable status as war heroes got them grudging recognition from doctors and labor ministers who had to bow down to this new focus on war experience over medical evidence. But on the question of psychological disorders, the regime was reluctant to acknowledge that these could be war-related. Thus by 1935–36, the Nazis coordinated a functional relationship with old welfare bureaucracy. The Labor Ministry and its doctors were willing to give pensions to documented war heroes in questionable cases, as long as they continued to back the party's complete repudiation of war neurosis as a legitimate wound.

'What would the Führer say?' – Hysterical Men Battle for the Regime's Respect

As the coordination of the veterans' care system took place, many war neurotics held on to the false reality that by documenting their status as war heroes, they could cut through all bureaucratic and medical obstacles and gain support from the Nazi state. Mentally disabled veterans cherished an image of Hitler as the sympathetic everyman veteran and war victim who himself knew of the real terror involved with combat. Many rationalized that if he only knew of their plight, Hitler would clear up problems with doctors and 'the system' that they blamed on stubborn bureaucrats with no personal knowledge of the horrors of trench warfare. In the imagination of war victims, the National Socialist leadership was a body separate from the Labor Ministry and its doctors. However, even with a long-standing history of devotion to the National Socialist movement, connections to local party officials, and proof of extensive war experience, numerous mentally ill veterans discovered that none of these criteria overruled the fact that they had broken down mentally in war. This ultimate sin was an affront to the official memory of 1914–18, and left these men permanently stigmatized as outsiders in the national community.

Interestingly, mentally disabled soldiers desperately fought against this stigmatization and considered Hitler their loyal ally in the struggle for a pension. Max K. is a fascinating case of how the 'Hitler Myth', where the idea of Hitler and the reality were totally opposite, dominated the perceptions of psychologically traumatized veterans.[88] During the last years of the Weimar Republic, K. fought with his welfare office in Breslau over whether or not his health problems were caused by the war. In 1928, Max K.'s doctors diagnosed his severe psychological disorders and attacks that paralyzed the left side of his body as war-related, and they granted him a pension that assessed his inability to earn a living at 30%. In 1929, after a medical check-up, doctors reversed themselves and determined that K.'s health problems were not war-related after all, and they rescinded his pension.[89] Max K. was unable to make a living as the Great Depression worsened. He went to the Association of German War Victims, one of the smaller, more politically moderate war victims' groups, in 1932 with medical documents that stretched all the way back to 1915 to support his case, but failed to convince the Labor Ministry and his welfare office that doctors had made a mistake.[90]

With the Nazi takeover, Max K. applied again. But his pension office in Breslau reaffirmed its earlier decision, finding 'no new facts' to support his case. They emphasized that the medical basis for war-related wounds was lacking, and hinted that K. simply lacked the will to work: 'It is thoroughly improbable that a sudden collapse in one's ability to work is connected to a war-related injury'.[91] K. responded with a barrage of letters to the Labor Ministry protesting this suggestion that he was a malingerer. Further, he was on his own, as the only war victims' association, the NSKOV, no longer endorsed his case.

Max K.'s first strategy was to present the medical evidence for his case. He argued that the Labor Ministry's doctors must have been unaware of his case files, which he believed proved the war-related nature of his mental problems. K. did his own research and dug into the federal archives, submitting *Reichsarchiv* file 19K 119/28. In July 1936, he claimed to have found both a psychiatrist's report proving that he suffered from war-related deterioration of nerves, and the results of a 1928 blood test – the basis for his original pension – proving that he did not suffer from hereditary diseases. K.'s letters reveal his desperation to prove he was an authentic war victim, mixed with an anxiety that had apocalyptic overtones: 'As it said in the report [by psychiatrist Dr Weiler], I reacted to the emotional stress of the war as a rational and sane man. Since the war I noticed that the population at home fell apart. A divine power did not and would not intervene for them, even if they had been knocked down to the last man'.[92] K. saw no shame in breaking down in war, and he emphatically denied that he was a whiner or grumbler (*Querulant*) with hereditary psychological disorders, as doctors had suggested since 1929.[93] The Labor Ministry once again turned down his request, reiterated that his nervous disorders were not the consequence of wartime injuries, said the case was closed and they would answer no further inquiries.[94] Over the next three years, K. researched psychiatric medicine and documented cases in which doctors noted that psychiatrists were 'only human' and could err in their judgment. He also read a monograph written by his psychiatrist, Dr Weiler, *Nervous and Psychological Disturbances in Participants from the World War*, which he claimed supported his argument that his psychological problems were indeed war-related, not manifestations of hereditary disorders.[95] The Labor Ministry offered no response to K.'s letters.

Failing to convince the regime with medical evidence for his psychological wounds, Max K. turned to a political approach. He complained bitterly that psychiatrists held more respect for the state than for veterans. In his letters from 1939–40, K. challenged the Nazi leadership to make good on its rhetorical commitment to veterans by firing what he called incompetent doctors and welfare administrators, and he stated directly that the regime was hypocritical if it did not admit that the Labor Ministry's doctors could be wrong. K. quoted Nazi propaganda back to the regime, in one instance selecting a speech by Goebbels: 'Should relevant legal paragraphs and orders not be sufficient, it remains an irrevocable intention of the government, a moral duty of the state, to help the national comrade [*Volksgenossen*], and support him in order that he not become destitute'.[96] Max K. firmly believed that if Hitler and the Nazi leadership knew of his case, they would recognize his war victim status and clear his pension. Nevertheless, he received no replies from the state until his daughter, Margarete, wrote to the Labor Ministry in November 1941 to complain that it was impossible to live under wartime conditions on the 62 Marks per month in welfare insurance that the family received, which barely paid for the medication needed to relieve her father's pain. Margarete sarcastically criticized the Labor Ministry for leaving her 'obviously war-disabled' father, who had proof of military service and, she claimed, eyewitness accounts attesting to the psychological stress he experienced in the war. She asked bitterly: 'Do all war victims go through such a grueling struggle to get health care? ... With horror I must think about what lies ahead in my life. Indeed I'm afraid to get married, in case the same fate awaits my future husband as that which has struck my father'. Only two weeks later the Labor Ministry replied, assuring Margarete that they would send a request to the welfare office in Breslau to review her father's case – a minor victory considering that the Labor Ministry had declared the case closed since 1936.[97]

Despite the boost from his daughter's letter, the OKW notified Max K. in December 1941 that they would take no further action in his case. By this time, K. had abandoned hope of actually receiving a war victim's pension, and he focused on defending his character against the state's implicit accusations that he was a liar and a swindler. K. wrote in March 1942, quoting Hitler: 'in every struggle there is a victory.' He proceeded to list his 'victories': eyewitness accounts of his front service, further research into the nature of his psychological wounds, documenting contradictions and errors in psychiatric reports. He declared that despite the verdict, he knew he was right, and he was convinced to the end that he would be vindicated if only Hitler heard his case. Max K. signed his last correspondence with 'Heil Hitler', and blamed labor ministers, doctors and welfare bureaucrats for conspiring to conceal the truth from his beloved Führer.[98]

Max K.'s case reveals interesting patterns in how mentally ill veterans imagined themselves in the national community. While these men often perceived the Labor Ministry and its doctors as a separate entity from party interests, this was not at all the case by the mid-1930s. Labor Ministry officials enacted the NSKOV's policy of excluding psychologically traumatized men who claimed to be victims of front-line combat. Medical documents and proof of war service alone did not shake the regime's line that individuals like K. were malingerers, faking their wounds to escape work. Max K. was on his own as he attempted to break this image, and he pleaded that he held up under fire as any 'normal' man could be expected ('I reacted to the emotional stress of the war as a rational and sane man'). Like many other men who enthusiastically supported Hitler, K. believed that there was nothing for a German soldier to be ashamed about if his nerves collapsed in combat. However, without credentials in the Nazi party, and the more acceptable argument that defeat, revolution, and social democracy inflicted his mental wounds, psychologically disabled men were stigmatized as permanent social outsiders.

Faith in Hitler as savior of war victims was a powerful narcotic for mentally ill veterans who found themselves completely ostracized. Many refused to believe that Hitler would allow fellow front soldiers to be so humiliated. Paul J., for example, hoped to meet with Hitler personally to discuss his case. He had received pensions for psychological wounds in

1920 and 1924, but in 1932 doctors decided his psychological disorders were no longer war-related. He was again rejected in 1937, with doctors citing the same reasons as his 1932 rejection.[99] At this point he requested his medical files, but received no word from the Labor Ministry or the welfare system. In frustration, J. wrote to the Chancellery of the Führer and asked to meet with Hitler immediately. In his letter, he related his experiences trying to prove to pension and welfare clerks that his medical files validated his claim to war victimhood. He emphasized sarcastically that his rejection letter had been stamped by the same bureaucrats who had approved his application in 1920 and 1924. According to his own testimony, Paul J. stomped furiously out of the Berlin welfare office and shouted at bystanders on Unter den Linden, a main boulevard through the city's center, about his plight as a war victim denied his rights. When a crowd gathered during his lively lecture, the police arrested him and hauled him away. In his letter, J. asked: 'What would the Führer say if he knew about my case?'[100]

Despite having his pension, and voice, shut down by the regime, Paul J. fervently defended Hitler, and saw his plight through the lens of Nazi ideology. He defended himself by saying that he was only following Hitler's advice, quoting the Führer: 'Whoever believes he has been cheated out of his rights, should fight for his rights'. J. claimed disbelief that his 'National Socialist doctors' could deny him, since they must have been appointed by Hitler who had first-hand knowledge of the stress of the front.[101] Antisemitism appealed to him as he sought blame for his situation, and J. described the treachery of 'Jewish doctors' who oppressed him at the end of the Weimar Republic. His hatred of Jews, and what he saw as a pension bureaucracy still influenced by a Jewish conspiracy to denigrate veterans, began to permeate his letters after 1938:

> In the service of the state I lost my strength to work and the ability to nourish myself. This is the central point, which justifies my claim to compensation. I am fighting for my rights, for my wife and child, against Jews and their supporters. *Der Stürmer* [Nazi propaganda newspaper] writes: 'Whoever takes Jewish qualities is a also a Jew'. It is not my intention to insult honest people or civil servants who don't have anything to do with such intrigues. Honest people will take no offense from this letter.[102]

Believing that a Jewish conspiracy lurked in the pension system, and that it thrived on the complicity of welfare bureaucrats who succumbed to 'Jewish qualities', J. challenged Nazi leaders to take a stand with war victims: 'In my opinion, you are the representative of the people, not the defender of civil servants'.[103] J. maintained the image of Hitler as the pure defender of war victims and protecting Hitler from insidious forces within the government. He imagined that the Nazi leadership perceived war neurotics as no different from other veterans who sacrificed for their nation, willing to work and become useful members of the community if it were not for Jewish 'intrigue' within the welfare system.

A strange paradox emerged in battles between war victims and the Nazi state. By blaming the pension bureaucracy for their plight, psychologically disabled war victims reinforced the assumption, long held by doctors, which was now cemented by the regime: 'war neurosis' did not exist, rather the welfare system was the cause of 'pension hysteria'. Doctors after 1933 even conceded that the horrors of the war may have contributed to the symptoms of traumatic neurosis, but they argued that 'real men' should have been able to forget these memories twenty years later. Thus men could blame the welfare system, but if they suggested the war caused mental breakdown, they found themselves stranded. Hermann J., for example, appealed to members of the Nazi hierarchy, including Hermann Goering and Rudolf Hess, with an elaborate history of his experiences in the trenches, and he carefully outlined the connections between being buried alive and enduring constant shellfire and his current psychological problems. His welfare office in Darmstadt, however, was more interested in his postwar history:

> Even if [Hermann J.] was aggravated by terrifying events, being buried alive, grenade explosions that wore him down and agitated and frayed his reliable activity in war service, the symptoms of nervous illness should have gradually faded away in passage of time over the course of years. But these still exist now with Jacoby, as they are kept alive by his sickly tendencies, by the effects of the environment, and by the need and struggle for pensions. But they are in no way a return back to any kind of wounds from war-service.[104]

Though his doctors acknowledged that Hermann J. may have once suffered from authentic war neurosis, they now blamed him for failing to overcome these traumatic memories. The Labor Ministry refused to restore Hermann J.'s status as a war neurotic – he had received a war victim pension since 1924 – but they did grant him a 100 Marks per month emergency relief package to care for his children.[105]

Thus with cooperation from doctors, the Nazi regime consolidated its official memory of the war as ennobling rather than brutalizing, and welfare as the real cause of neurosis lasting twenty years after the war. However, the fact remained that psychologically disabled veterans did not simply disappear. Whether they were war victims or pension neurotics, reintegrating them proved no less difficult after 1933 than it had been in the Weimar years. Neither the NSKOV nor the Labor Ministry developed any new occupational programs for traumatized veterans. It was expected that once the regime did away with pensions and granted new 'respect' for veterans, men would regain their manliness, will to work and usefulness as productive members of the national community. Those who did not recover were completely marginalized as burdens on the newly constructed 'racial state', and enemies of the official memory of the war. 'Asocial' characteristics such as being 'work-shy' were marked as hereditary traits. Those diagnosed as hereditarily ill eventually became targets of the Nazi state's sterilization and 'euthanasia' programs, which resulted in the murder of over 150,000 mentally and physically disabled people.[106]

The elimination of mentally disabled veterans from the pension system produced considerable stress for local governments who now had to deal with the burden of costs. In February 1937, the German Council of Municipalities (*Deutscher Gemeindetag*) sent a request to all welfare offices to report on their compliance with the 1934 law's expulsion of mentally disabled veterans. Their letter suggests alarm at the failure of all municipalities to make the necessary cuts, and the council reminded local leaders that mental disabilities allegedly stemming from war service were no longer to be defined as authentic war wounds, but rather as inherent, hereditary mental illness.[107] A number of complaints from mayors poured into the council, illustrating the grass roots problems generated by across the board pension cuts. The mayor of Herlohn complained that his city's welfare was unable to cope with the state cuts. In particular, he asked who would pay for an individual who had been unemployed and receiving a war victim's pension for nearly twenty years and who was completely dependent on medical care for his survival. He painted a vivid picture of mentally ill men unwilling to move from welfare office waiting rooms, with no means of self-sufficiency.[108] The mayor of Frankfurt am Main pushed this further by arguing that there were indeed men who suffered from authentic psychological wounds, and he asked that the state at least offer some economic assistance as local welfare offices tried to provide economic security for the families of these men.[109] The finance secretary in Hannover also complained that whether or not these men were legitimate war victims, the economic question of how to pay for their security remained.[110] In these instances, local welfare offices leveled no protests against the rationality of cutting war victims' pensions from war neurotics, but they complained that such cuts placed an economic burden on their resources because the families of these men still needed support.[111]

In some instances, local officials reacted to the state's inquiries testily, and they indicated that the July 1934 law had become unwieldy on a practical level and unjust for a few cases of authentic war victims caught in the sweeping net of cuts. The mayor of Munich sent a detailed report on the consequences of the July 1934 law, which he complained created an economic and bureaucratic quagmire. Over 300 mentally disabled war victims in his district were cut from the pension rolls, leaving an impossible burden on welfare resources to pay food and housing for these unemployed men. Further, they supported cases of two men who suffered from psychological problems diagnosed in 1916 as war-related, who had been receiving over 500 Marks in pensions for full medical care.[112] The welfare office in Braunschweig asked if one individual, Gustav R., who had been recognized as a legitimate psychologically disabled veteran since 1916 and possessed decades of medical reports attesting to his condition, was really to be cut from welfare support without at least a review of his case.[113] Heidelberg also gave a detailed report on how the cuts affected their welfare system. They listed cases of men who they believed were hereditarily ill and thus justifiably eliminated from the pension rolls, but they also asserted that there were a minority of instances where bomb explosions had caused psychological trauma, or at least intensified already existing problems.[114] Whether war victims or mentally ill, city leaders reminded the Council of Municipalities that patients newly released onto city streets posed a crisis that someone would have to pay for. When the council appealed to the Labor Ministry for advice, they received word that an emergency payment would be provided to local welfare offices. However, the Labor Ministry also asserted that these emergency payments should not go to single men whose mental illness had been proven to be not war-related. Labor Ministry officials explicitly stated that after the distribution of emergency payments, these men were no longer within the responsibility of the welfare system.[115] The problem of war neurosis was thus dropped on local authorities. At a grass roots level, this meant an increasing nightmare for cities that had to face the fact that mentally ill veterans – whether frauds, chronic psychopaths, or authentic war neurotics – were now set loose onto the streets, or to their families who had to scrape together a way to care for them.

In addition to the protests coming from local officials, veterans continued to protest in the one forum left to them – the pension courts. However, Labor Ministry files suggest that no psychologically disabled veterans who claimed there was a link between war experiences and mental injuries won their cases in the pension courts after the July 1934 law. Many of these men continued to characterize themselves as true believers in National Socialism, loyal to Hitler and the nation, and they responded in shock and disbelief that they could be ostracized from the front community and the national community. Emil L., whose wounds and capacity for work had been an ongoing matter of debate for the pension and welfare bureaucracies of imperial Germany, the Weimar Republic, and now the Third Reich, bombarded the Labor Ministry with letters in 1937. Back in 1917 he received a pension for an 'organic brain disorder causing depression and agitation', which doctors confirmed was connected with the war. In 1924, a psychiatrist granted him 70%-unable to earn a living wage. This was cancelled in 1927 following the wave of pension cuts for mentally disabled veterans, leaving L. fighting to prove that his psychological disorders stemmed from the brain injuries. L.'s ambiguous status – on one hand a victim of actual physical wounds but also suffering from a host of mental problems – is reflected in the Nazi regime's confusion about his case. He was initially given the *Frontzulage* special one-time award in 1934, but then this privilege was repealed in 1936. This rejection was based on doctors' findings that 'an organic disorder of the brain never existed. What was recognized in 1917 as a war-related wound has since faded away. The present psychopathic disturbances, which reduce his ability to earn a living by less than 25%, are not the consequences of a war wound'.[116] Though he did once suffer physical war damage, Nazi doctors argued, he also possessed a 'psychopathic constitution' that made him unwilling to recover and work.[117] Emil L. protested that he was indeed a genuine war victim: 'I call on the labor minister to restore my rights. I am indeed sick and my sufferings are a consequence of war service'.[118]

The problem, according to Emil L., was that the medical establishment had not yet been thoroughly Nazified. L. shot off letters to both Hitler and Goering, expressing his disbelief. 'That war victims are so unjustly handled', he wrote, 'is not in accordance with the Führer's wishes'.[119] L. argued that his willingness to work was drained by doctors' conclusions that his condition was not war-related, exacerbating his depression. He pleaded with Hitler that he would like to work but the disrespect he received from doctors and the removal of his pension weakened him. Doctors, he believed, were not faithfully adhering to Nazi ideals: 'How can a doctor in the National Socialist Reich practice with such a lack of conscience, and take from me, a recognized war victim, every possibility of making a living'. Hinting that doctors joined the party only to further their careers, rather than out of conviction, L. requested a 'non-party affiliated' (*unparteiisch*) doctor who specialized in brain disorders. He received no reply to this request.[120]

Emil L. had become a local embarrassment in his home town of Hackelspring by 1938, where doctors and even the mayor tried to stifle his trouble-making letters to the Nazi hierarchy. The Berlin central welfare office pressed L.'s local welfare office at Frankfurt an der Oder on why he had not yet been put to work. Frankfurt informed the Labor Ministry that they had done all they could to find L. a suitable job. Unfortunately, they claimed, L.'s doctor could not convince him that he was now an able-bodied man who should be able to earn a paycheck. The mayor of Hackelspring intervened to help him get a job, but alleged that L. did not really want work and did not take on responsibility for his family.[121] The Frankfurt welfare office did grant reduced emergency assistance to keep L.'s two children afloat, but emphasized that he would never receive his war victim's pension back.[122] This pension, they concluded, was the root cause of his failure to recover and find a job, its removal was the best thing that could happen to L., and he would 'once again find the strength to work'.[123] Thus his local welfare office assured their supervisors that L. was under control.

When the Second World War broke out, L. continued to bypass the welfare and Labor Ministry officials with direct letters to the Nazi elite. He first wrote to Goering on 12 September 1939, begging him to bring his case to the personal attention of the Führer. Emil L. maintained: 'I have always fulfilled my duty and certainly belong to the national community (*Volksgemeinschaft*)'.[124] He did not receive a reply to this letter, but it did stir up problems in the NSKOV, which corresponded with the *Reichspropaganda* ministry representative Dieckmann regarding whether or not L. was a legitimate war victim who had slipped through the cracks.[125] In 1941, the *Oberkommando der Wehrmacht* (OKW) took over L.'s case and after a review of records informed him that there was no possibility of changing his status from malingerer to disabled veteran. The OKW reprimanded L. for blaming the Nazi state for his depression and outlined his duties as a member of the national community: 'It must be expected from you as from every national comrade [*Volksgenossen*], that you find your keep through work, for which there is no shortage and which you are capable of doing, rather than become a burden to the general good'.[126] L. responded indignantly in May 1942, insisting that he had never been a 'burden' to society, and he mentioned bitterly that while he was being condemned as an outsider to the national community, his two sons were fighting on the Eastern front with the Waffen SS. L. maintained that he had always fulfilled his duty to National Socialism, and that the Führer would bring him justice if only he knew the facts of the case.[127] Now completely isolated, Emil L. desperately clung to the hope that a sympathetic Hitler would come to his aid.

The regime was successful in deflecting blame on bureaucrats and doctors, long hated by war victims. Whether they were sincere or opportunistic, the vast majority of mentally ill veterans defended Hitler to the end. But no matter how much they expressed devotion to Nazi ideals, psychologically disabled veterans could not convince the state that their wounds were legitimate. It is interesting to observe that most of these men writing to the government did not attempt to conceal their psychological condition and refused to accept the regime's formula linking mental breakdown in war to 'asocial' behavior. Some of these individuals held substantial rank in the expanding Nazi party bureaucracy when they found themselves condemned as hysterical enemies of the nation. Otto M., for example, was a former lieutenant working as a government inspector in 1940. While in this job he applied for a pension for war-related injuries from his First World War service, stating that his epileptic seizures and psychological problems stemmed from his war experience. The welfare office in Hannover accused him of trying to deceive the government and described his condition as hysterical and psychopathic.[128] M. challenged doctors' reports, which he called contradictory, pointing out that his epileptic seizures stemming from neurological damage in the war were also responsible for ongoing stress and depression. The government, he claimed, was blatantly denying the impact of the war on his psychological health in order to save on a pension. He gave up on trying to win compensation, but focused his letters instead with an indictment of National Socialism's treatment of war veterans. He wrote that while he had 'done his duty for Führer and *Volk*' by fighting at the front, he was being treated like a 'non-wounded syphilitic Jew, punished as a deserter'. He demanded that he once again be counted as a wounded member of the 'front community', with all the respect accorded him as a reserve lieutenant.[129]

Otto M. is a typical example of a psychologically damaged veteran who saw no discrepancy between his mental wounds and his dedication to 'Führer and Volk'. M. appropriated Nazi antisemitic rhetoric in his case for winning a pension, constructing 'the Jew' as a group that escaped the trauma of the war. From here, however, his interpretation of the front experience diverged from Nazi ideology, as he placed mentally disabled men in the category of legitimate victims loyal to the nation. Though attracted to Nazi ideas and explanation for defeat, these men were not ashamed to admit that the war, and not the pension system, caused the traumas that the enemies of National Socialism allegedly avoided. Thus mental illness was seen as a proof of sacrifice, not a badge of malingering. Traumatized veterans who believed in Hitler sought to revise the regime's definition of authentic war wounds as exclusively physical, and change the image of psychologically disabled veterans as degenerate swindlers who lacked the manly will to recover and work.

*   *   *

National Socialist leaders constructed the 1918 defeat, revolution, and democracy, not the war, as the nation's original trauma. The National Socialist War Victims' organization advocated rewarding psychologically disabled Stormtroopers and 'heroic' civil servants – both 'victims' of the Weimar Republic rather than the war – more fervently than they did front veterans. NSKOV officials believed that the trauma of defeat and revolution understandably caused enormous psychological stress in nationalist-minded Germans. On one hand, Nazi officials blamed the Weimar Republic's pension system for turning otherwise healthy men into neurotic pension-seekers. At the same time, they legitimized psychological trauma inflicted while fighting against 'the system'. Meanwhile, those who depended on social welfare during the Weimar years were constructed as weak-willed collaborators with democracy and defeat. Like many other Nazi social policies, this was fraught with contradictions, rationalizing help for 'old fighters', and the confusion of competing bureaucratic agencies. However, there was consistency in the regime's official myth that real soldiers did not collapse in the test of combat.

For men who claimed their psychological health deteriorated in the war against the 'Marxists' and 'November Criminals', the regime removed the stigma of hysteria and legitimized their constituents' nervous disorders. This was done with the active cooperation of doctors, who were not fundamentally opposed to redefining war neurosis as a political, rather than medical, phenomenon. In this way, Nazi leaders successfully and smoothly led doctors into following the regime's official line that 'war neurosis' did not exist at all. Before 1933, doctors regularly used medical evidence to conceal their ultimate aim in cutting 'pension neurotics' from the welfare rolls, particularly if patients belonged to left-wing organizations. With the new emphasis on the patient's willingness to work, war record and politics, doctors no longer needed to hide their long-standing prejudices towards war neurotics that they believed were out to cheat the system. The Nazi state gave these doctors license to wage open war on hysterical men as 'asocials' who threatened the nation's health.

Despite coordination at the level of Nazi officials and doctors, the regime was unable to coordinate war victims. 'Traumatic neurosis' in Nazi Germany was not a monolithic concept, and it continued to be contested at the level of veterans themselves. Thus the 'first citizens' of the Reich constructed by Nazi leaders expressed divergent views on trauma and war that often countered the regime's official memory of 1914–18. War neurotics expressed support for Hitler as many did in a broad revolt against 'the system' shared by segments of the German population, in particular those in the lower-middle classes whose incomes were decimated by hyperinflation and felt threatened by the Great Depression. These men imagined the Nazi movement as one that would support traumatized veterans. They also assumed that the front soldier Hitler would share their common experience and knowledge of the traumatic effects of trench warfare. Hitler was 'one of them', while doctors and welfare administrators were run by 'national enemies'. Most traumatized men did not want to accept that the Nazi myth of the war experience did not include them.

A battle over the memory of the war lay just beneath the surface of the pension war. The regime's rejection of mentally disabled veterans as illegitimate members of the 'front community' and the 'national community' mobilized these men to criticize the cherished myth of the front experience. Despite Nazi leaders' claims to defending the authentic memory of the war, memory divided even those within Nazi ranks. War veterans suffering from mental wounds– including those who considered themselves dedicated Nazis – insisted there was no shame, or contradiction in being a psychologically traumatized German. The next chapter explores the voices of war neurotics who criticized not just doctors and the welfare system, but also the Nazi party leaders.

Chapter 6

Nazi Germany's Hidden 'Psychopaths'

Case Studies of Mentally Disabled Veterans in the Third Reich

In 1935, frustrated with the Nazi regime's attack on war neurotics and the cancellation of his pension, veteran Konrad D. submitted an essay on war-disabled rights to the Labor Ministry. Konrad D. described himself as 'the nation's leading grumbler', and in this essay he appointed himself authority on the memory of the war and its psychological consequences. Real men, Konrad D. explained, had an obligation to tap into the comradeship of the trenches and assist the vulnerable:

> [O]nly a strong man provides for the nation's victims; with complete devotion he places his total spirit in the service of the common good ... and he maintains the spirit of battle in this still unhealthy world against the aggressive, primitive men who represent violence ... Bring honor to the concept of welfare again. Practice comradeship like we had in 'No Man's Land' and recognize the love of your neighbor as common sense for self-preservation.[1]

By focusing on the perspectives of war neurotics, it is possible to reconstruct a history of trauma, memory and masculinity 'from the margins'.[2] The Nazi regime's self-proclaimed embodiment of veterans' interests and the memory of the front experience had little resonance for men actually brutalized in the trenches. Despite attempts by Nazi leaders to marginalize war neurotics, their voices of dissent remained disturbing reminders of the deep destruction inflicted by modern warfare just as Germany prepared for another war.

Though they cannot be characterized as a coherent 'movement', or an example of substantial resistance against the regime, these individuals

189

reveal an interesting layer of protest against the Nazis' official version of the war experience. Psychologically disabled men often constructed themselves as defenders of the authentic memory of the war and the conscience of veterans, and they rejected Nazi propaganda and policies that demonized traumatized men. Though isolated and few, the voices of these men give us a glimpse into a hidden layer of dissent against militarism and the celebration of violence in Nazi Germany. With no hope of regaining pensions, mentally disabled veterans reinvented themselves as critics of the regime, and even reveled in their status as ignored war victims. The marginalization of mentally disabled veterans as economic and social pariahs suggest that there existed considerable fear of these men as burdens on the health of the nation. But in addition to being perceived as economic burdens on the national community, war neurotics also presented a threat to the official narrative of the war experience as healthy for the individual and the nation.

After the July 1934 pension law, the Labor Ministry systematically shut down correspondence with mentally disabled veterans. Nevertheless, the ministry collected folders labeled 'individual problems' (*einzelne Probleme*) filled with letters from indignant mentally ill individuals. Several of these men wrote letters that were up to fifteen pages in length every month after 1933 and into the war years. These were often crammed with the same repetitious stories of their case histories. Within their accounts, however, we also catch a glimpse into the resentments and world view of traumatized men, many of them barely holding on to reality. Their perspectives on politics, the social welfare system and the meaning of the war offer a glimpse into the thinking of some of Nazi Germany's most embittered outcasts. Most repulsive to these men was what they saw as the regime's efforts to conceal the traumatic realities of warfare under an image of the war experience as psychologically rejuvenating and healthy for the nation. While the Nazis celebrated brutality and violence, these veterans warned against brutalization and its long-term effects on individuals and society. No longer able to claim entitlement as war victims or 'first citizens' of the Reich, war neurotics pointed to their pariah status as evidence that they held an important secret feared by the regime.

The voices of war neurotics also present the most vivid example of how the language of 'nerves', 'hysteria' and 'neurosis' became part of the popular discourse and battles over the memory of World War I. With nothing to gain in terms of pensions and status, traumatized veterans appropriated, often in ironic and colorful language, a whole discourse on 'psychosis' that they used to criticize the Nazi regime's welfare policies and propaganda. Ignored by the Labor Ministry, neurotic men intensified their attacks on what they saw as a neurotic regime. The state's persecution of its most vulnerable citizens, war neurotics warned, was a symptom of a deeper sickness in society. Mentally disabled veterans embraced their wounds as evidence of their unique status as prophets who would educate the nation in the traumatic effects of modern war and debunk what they perceived as hollow nostalgia for the spiritual value of the trenches. Though easily hidden away in filing cabinets, these voices reveal the degree to which the official memory of the war was contested in everyday life.

'The Nation's Leading Grumbler': The Case of Konrad D.

The pension cuts that followed the Great Depression left mentally disabled veterans without support, and unleashed them from the lobbies of welfare offices and into everyday life. Labor Ministry files are filled with letters from these men, who turned their attention from welfare office lines to their typewriters and pens, where they gave up on social assistance and turned to write their personal histories and political testimonies. One of the most interesting examples is Konrad D., who reflects some of the complex and often contradictory social and political perspectives of traumatized men in Weimar and Nazi Germany.

With a sense of ironic pride, Konrad D. embraced his status as a self-styled mad prophet on the streets whose new 'job' it was to torment the many enemies he blamed for his plight. He cultivated this image in the tumult of 1932, following the severance of his pension and while witnessing the electoral successes of the Nazi party. Konrad D. described himself as a lone madman who 'howled at the moon' though no one would listen.[3] He was a real changeling in terms of his politics and world view. A bank clerk from a lower-middle-class background and a reserve lieutenant in World War I, he later expressed disdain for capitalism and agreed with Marxist theories but attacked the Communist Party. He vilified Hitler as Weimar came apart, then he expressed admiration for Hitler after 1933 before once again lambasting him. He alternated between deep cynicism and religious grandiosity. Expressing hatred for militarism, he prided himself on being a loyal defender of the fatherland with an honorable war record. Whether he was an opportunist or iconoclast, Konrad D. at some point saw himself as a victim of every ideology and political group. He reveled in his label as an outsider, and used this status to analyze the meaning of his traumatic wounds and construct his own memory of the war.

Konrad D.'s problems began to develop in the late 1920s when, according to his account, mental illness forced him to give up his career as a bank clerk. His letters to the Labor Ministry illustrate his interpretations of his own psychological problems. He described himself as able and willing to work, but also depressed and still haunted by traumatic images of the trenches into the 1920s. Though willing to work, he claimed that his mental breakdowns made it impossible to interact with others and maintain the routine of a job. He wrote to the Labor Ministry: 'I am at my wits' end. My restless nerves and their depressing effects that I brought home from the war and the revolution leave me unable to hold a job'.[4] He shared his traumatic memories in graphic terms to point out that his wounds were real: 'The collapse of my nerves was singularly caused by the war and its terrifying stresses, its deprivations ... the crashing artillery fire that gave me a glance into death'.[5] As early as 1916 he was diagnosed by doctors as having a 'psychopathic constitution with psychogenic-nervous damage, in particular irritability, tendency towards grumbling, and bouts of depression', all of which worsened in the postwar years. Medical reports collected by his doctor in 1930–31 indicate that the war exacerbated these problems, and that he was rated as 50% unable to earn a living, but his mental illness was not confirmed as war-related.[6]

Konrad D. was discharged in 1920 from the *Reichswehr*, as the army was called under the Weimar Republic, because of 'high-level nervousness', according to his letters. He went through a series of examinations at his health care clinic throughout the 1920s, unsuccessfully trying to prove that his wounds were indeed war-related. Meanwhile, he prided himself on being able to work, and he did not draw welfare support while in his job as a bank clerk.[7] However, the job became too stressful in 1928. According to his own account, he could barely control his aggressive behavior, moodiness, and 'quarrelsome personality', which he attributed to his wartime stress.[8] When the bank let him go after an incident with customers, he applied for an officer's pension, to which he was entitled, and a war victim's pension for his alleged psychological wounds. The pension courts turned him down for the latter, stating that his mental problems had up to this time never been recognized as war-related.[9] He drew from his officer's pension, but this did not cover his monthly expenses.[10] To make ends meet during the period he was applying for pensions, he worked for as a taxi driver in Berlin for several months, when he collided with another car and killed a passenger. A doctor at his welfare and health clinic examined him and concluded that he was too 'mentally unstable' to operate a car.[11] When he reapplied for a full pension, the welfare office informed him that despite his mental illness, he was indeed able to earn a living, as long as it did not involve driving taxis.[12]

Similar to many front veterans, Konrad D. felt betrayed by the Weimar Republic. But what made him exceptional among disabled veterans between 1930 and 1933 was that while bitter with the Weimar government, he remained a staunch advocate of democracy. He claimed to have fought in 1919–20 to preserve the new social democratic-led republic against the Kapp Putsch, an attempted right-wing coup that failed. He concluded a July 1929 letter to the Labor Ministry by reminding them he was 'an old front soldier and fighter for the republic'.[13] Konrad D. believed that he was owed not only the 'thanks of the fatherland' but also the thanks of the democracy:

The war, which I volunteered for as an 18-year old, disabled me so I could not maintain my secure *bürgerlich* (middle-class) career. It is also worth mentioning that I continued to serve after 1919 and volunteered to take up weapons during the Kapp Putsch in order to save the young republic! That doesn't count at all any more – I've been abandoned: the thanks of the republic is a clear reflection of 'The Thanks of the Fatherland', which is as known to us as the 'Amen' in church! A front fighter might as well hang himself – it is as they say: All Quiet on the Western Front [here he writes 'Im Westen Nichts Neues' – literally 'Nothing new on the Western Front', the German title of Remarque's famous work.][14]

Portraying himself as a savior of the new democratic state, Konrad D. was unusual as a former officer who defended the republic and identified with it. Unlike many in the middle class, he blamed the war rather than the republic for his slip in social status. The republic, he believed, owed him for his loyalty as a staunch defender of democracy when it was threatened by the radical right.

With the severance of his pension and the onslaught of the Great Depression, his slip from the middle class accelerated, and so did his disillusionment with the republic. He cited article 163 of the constitution, which guaranteed economic security to all citizens, noting again that he had risked his life to defend it. Unemployment insurance, he complained, simply did not cover food and rent. The alleged insensitivity of the welfare system left him feeling dehumanized: 'Not only does the welfare office treat me like filth [*Dreck*], but they also trample all over my basic rights'.[15] In 1930, he paid 25 Marks to a private doctor for a diagnosis of his psychological health. This did not work decisively in his favor, as the doctor reported to the Labor Ministry that Konrad D. possessed a 'psychopathic constitution', with symptoms that included 'severe irritability, whininess and depression'. The doctor conceded that these psychological problems had begun in 1916 and worsened through the postwar years, but he did not clarify whether the war had caused these disorders. Further, his doctor confirmed that Konrad D.'s ability to work was reduced, but only at 50%, not the full disability.[16]

Outraged at being called a whiner, Konrad D. blamed the pension cuts for turning him into a chronic complainer: 'That I am fundamentally embittered, nobody can hold against me! Nobody will look at this embitterment exclusively as whining delusions, but instead they will wonder how I came into this whining streak, and how it could be related to my illness'. After denouncing the war for 'immorally taking away my life's hopes', he listed nineteen 'breaches of rights inflicted by the pension and health care system under the Weimar Republic'.[17] These included accusations against the Labor Ministry and the *Reichswehr* for cheating him out of both his officer's pension and his war-disabled pension. His disillusionment ultimately went deeper than with the republic's health care and welfare system. He connected his loss of faith with all traditional institutions and authority to the devastating psychological violence he experienced in the war. 'I was an excited volunteer and idealist', he recounted in 1931, 'who went to war, ready to die for fatherland and *Volk*, who believed in the Kaiser, Empire, state, officers, superiors, authority, civil servants – all of whom I identified with justice and truth!' But the war awakened him to the idea that these 'god-like authorities' were responsible first for producing the disastrous war and then denying the connection between the trench experience and psychological wounds.[18]

Doctors aggravated this pervasive disillusionment. It was understandable for wartime doctors to be compromised, Konrad D. admitted, but to be rejected by doctors under the republic's military (the *Reichswehr*) and bureaucracy in 1920 was unfathomable, considering his dedication to defending them and the guarantees written in the constitution. He aimed the full weight of his anger at the doctors for denying the reality of his wounds. 'If I were missing an arm', he remarked bitterly, '[the doctors] would not have concluded that I was fit for duty … The doctors' investigation in 1920 paid no attention to my anemia, total exhaustion, malnourishment, and nervous disorders that never healed …' In Konrad D.'s mind, the insensitivity of doctors symbolized continuity between the violence of the trenches and his postwar suffering.

'The *Reichswehr* and welfare doctors', he wrote, 'are responsible because their diagnoses are full of contradictions! They are in conflict with themselves and destroy their own believability'. He characterized psychiatrists' rejections of traumatic neurosis as still driven by military and economic interests that concealed the horrifying effects of the war. His doctors made conclusions that were implausible and inconsistent with widely accepted psychiatric theory:

> This doctor declared me 'fit for duty' and said further 'If you get stirred up psychologically from time to time, it will increase your fitness for duty. But if the bombs explode, the machine guns chatter, and the bayonets menace, then naturally I also get psychologically stirred up and it wipes out my fitness for duty.' What a great diagnosis. So illuminating to read further that 'at the time' [in the trenches] nothing took place that caused illness! Most doctors admit that such moments, and others, can trigger these consequences … When one thinks about it, it springs to mind, that this doctor is not free to make his own judgment'.[19]

Doctors, in Konrad D.'s eyes, exemplified the compromises and biases that undermined the democratic welfare system and its social security agenda. Doctors betrayed the ideals of the republic, which he said was no longer a 'people's state', and he blamed them for the erosion of democratic institutions and loss of faith in Weimar.[20]

Unlike many veterans, Konrad D. was not drawn to Hitler as a reaction against the hated 'system'. The onslaught of the Great Depression and the Brüning government's deflationary tactics and spending cuts drove many on fixed salaries, including pensioners, towards the extreme right, resulting in Hitler's jump from 2.6% to 18% electoral support in 1930, and up to 37% in July 1932. Konrad D. predicted that with Hitler, Germany's nerves would fall into ruin.[21] He blamed Hitler's electoral successes on the same welfare bureaucrats who took his pension. 'The bureaucrats', he wrote sardonically, 'perspired blood and sweat in the artillery fire and hail of grenades in the wild paper wars of their offices'. These same bureaucrats, Konrad D. warned, were fueling Hitler's success by dividing the German people, subverting the democracy with emergency powers, and running the nation without popular consent. He characterized Hitler's rise as the responsibility of short-sighted government ministers. With a detached and cynical style, he suggested that those in power exploited Hitler to push their own agenda. Prophetically, he warned that Hitler might be exploiting them:

> You egoists in ministry sofas only mock us and throw us into the most bitter crisis with your 'taking things into consideration', during which time you exert the arbitrary power to make laws! You can only thank Hitler's violent speeches for your place. But think about the day on which a Hitler could perhaps actually be offered a single little chance! The support of the people is always changing – the thanks of the fatherland will certainly be yours![22]

Hope for an uprising of impoverished Germans by any means filled Konrad D.'s letters. He acknowledged that his letters 'would probably end up in the waste basket', but, he reassured himself: 'I'll take it at face value that it will at least be read by the Herr Labor Minister and his colleagues … What does the moon that sits so high have to worry about the howling dog!? But however high he stands, he should see to it that he does not fall'.[23]

Konrad D. himself was an ideological and political chameleon, but his experience gives an interesting glimpse into the pressures exerted on Germans traumatized by the depression. This former officer and bank clerk who aspired to middle-class security was so disillusioned by his loss of a pension that he turned into a fervent anticapitalist. He described Brüning as 'the worst capitalist enemy' and the rest of the cabinet as 'the unconscionable hyenas of the capitalist system', evidenced by their health care and pension policies that left war victims in poverty. On one hand, he reflected the frustrations and resentments of the slipping lower middle class with his celebration of the 'little man' struggling to keep his white-collar status. At the same time he lambasted the 'tyrannical capitalist state' that he had believed abandoned democratic principles in the interests of business and greed.[24] He admitted agreement with Marxist doctrine that property, capital, and economic inequality had corroded German society, but he said he was not actually a communist because he was fundamentally too national-minded. Germany, he believed, would 'go the Russian way' if the government ruled without democratic consent, unless all Germans were immediately 'insured against hunger and despair'.[25] The Hindenburg government would destroy democratic institutions, he predicted, leading frustrated voters to move to the extreme left and right-wing antirepublican forces. If the nation went communist or National Socialist, it was only the fault of those in power: 'The republic has long lost its status as the people's state'.[26]

Konrad D. experimented with his self-created role as an irreverent, tortured prophet who had collapsed along with democracy. His letters took on a feverish intensity and he documented in apocalyptic tones the deterioration of his own sanity and that of the nation. 'Herr Minister!' he wrote, 'Shadows in my awakened mind begin to overtake my mental darkness. My power to resist is broken, my nerves are cracked'.[27] These visions of individual breakdown spilled into his descriptions of the social and political environment. He characterized the Weimar state as sick as long as it was run under Brüning's emergency economic decrees. Calling Brüning's government 'rabid animals' who 'sinned against the German spirit' with their cuts in pensions and tax benefits for the rich, Konrad D. complained that Brüning's deflationary approach to the economic depression annihilated all hope, drained his will to live, and cast Germany into 'the terrors of hunger'.[28] In Konrad D.'s imagination, his own mental breakdown paralleled that of the Weimar Republic, which he saw engaged in a suicidal collapse. He painted welfare officials in the same terms that they portrayed him, as pathological and psychotic in their antipathy towards war veterans.[29] The cuts in pensions became an act of psychological and physical violence that brutalized the population, which caused widespread antipathy between state and the economically vulnerable, and fueled extremist movements like National Socialism.

Konrad D.'s prediction that the democratic institutions would be abandoned by the republic's elected representatives proved true. In January 1933, von Hindenburg, on advice from former chancellor von Papen, appointed Hitler chancellor, and the Nazis set into motion the destruction of Weimar's democratic institutions. Konrad D. marked the occasion with one of his many sarcastic, yet stylistically tortured, poems, this one condemning Weimar for failing to make good on support for disabled veterans, while at the same time lamenting the end of the democracy and with it any hope:

The Thanks of the Fatherland is and certain [sic – 'certainly yours']
And that thanks, along with the republic, was also shit down the
   toilet
The 'Third Reich' will bring it to a close
And pay the bill right away with a hanging rope.[30]

Konrad D.'s fatalism grew as Hitler destroyed the republic. He no longer
expected a pension, but rather cultivated his image as a professional
grumbler. In his March 1933 letter, shortly after the Reichstag fire
decree that gave Hitler the pretense for eliminating opposition parties, he
introduced himself to the Nazi regime by detailing his case history to the
new head of the Labor Ministry, Franz Seldte, the former head of the 'Steel
Helmet' and himself a disabled veteran. Konrad D. began with a sardonic
apology for his existence and for the trouble he would bring to the Nazis:
'Potatoes with Knorr's sauce is the main nourishment of severely disabled
lieutenants ... Excuse me, Herr Minister [Seldte] if I torment you with
these letters, but the state torments me with tortures, including severe
war wounds, decades-long withholding of pensions, the elimination of my
ability to work, emergency decrees ... in addition to my health strength,
youth and life, the state robbed me of 30,000 Marks in withheld officer
pensions and bank clerk insurance'.[31] He also wrote to Hans Lammers,
Hitler's personal legal advisor and a head of the Reich Chancellery, that
he was 'honored to get to know a member of the government personally',
and he asked that the state secretary do all he could so that 'one would
not be severely disabled, unable to work, psychologically ill, and hunted
by the emergency decrees all in vain'.[32] A representative from the Labor
Ministry sent a report to Lammers that essentially apologized for the
nuisance that Konrad D. had become. 'The Labor Ministry has been busy
with reserve lieutenant D. for many years now', they wrote, noting that it
was doubtful Konrad D.'s wounds were war-related, and his accusations
against the state were baseless. They portrayed Konrad D. as just another
miscreant created by Weimar's welfare system, looking to defraud the
government.

One of the more interesting aspects of Konrad D.'s correspondence at
this stage was his appropriation of labels assigned to him by the Weimar
doctors and Labor Ministry. He relished his assigned role as a social
outsider and used it to create an identity to parade in front of the Nazi
regime. He signed his letters from early 1933 onward with variations
of, 'D., severely disabled veteran, pensioner, and grumbler'.[33] Employing
the term that often cropped up in medical and Labor Ministry reports
– 'Querulant' – meaning 'grumbler' or 'whiner', Konrad D. mocked his
own official diagnosis and cast himself in the role of an agitator against
those he believed persecuted him. His role as 'grumbler' allowed him, at
least at this early stage, some space to criticize the regime without drawing

attention to himself as an actual member of any official opposition party targeted by the regime.

The 'grumbler' drew little attention. For the next year the Nazi regime treated Konrad D. with benign neglect, carefully filing his letters away but not responding to them. Meanwhile, he appointed himself as an authority on war victims policy and an advisor for the regime. Konrad D. spent the rest of 1933 studying National Socialist social welfare policy and at the beginning of 1934 wrote a response to the war victims policies of the Nazis. On the whole, he saw Nazi welfare as benefiting the same interest groups as those under the Brüning government, but this time dressed up in Nazi propaganda rhetoric. In a letter signed with apparent irony, 'Heil Hitler', Konrad D. provided his own interpretation of Nazi ideology and the memory of the war from the perspective of a veteran suffering from psychological wounds. The essay was divided into different sections with titles such as 'Der Führer' and 'Volksgemeinschaft' ('national community'), providing his own interpretation of Nazi social and political concepts, and then his critique. He argued that the Nazi memory of the war was severely distorted. In particular, he criticized the regime's portrayal of a front soldier's consciousness while in combat. Nazi propaganda depicted soldiers motivated by 'love of fatherland', 'spirit of sacrifice' and idealized heroic death in battle, he summarized. However, the primary factor that motivated front soldiers was the need to survive. 'A terrible partnership with death', he noted, ultimately outweighed the spirit of 1914, and a soldiers' main concern was to find different ways to cope with their fears and the horrors of combat.[34]

Konrad D. also questioned Nazi propaganda's picture of the soldier's postwar mind. Returning veterans did not dwell on nostalgia for comradeship or seek above all to be part of the 'front community', he argued. Instead, their main struggle was to find adequate care for wounds and return to work and family. Nazi social welfare was filled with ideals but no substance:

> [Hitler] calls us war victims 'heroes': but does one let the 'heroes' become impoverished and depraved when they have sacrificed their last bit of strength? Or should they just fling themselves on their swords and hand over their crisis, poverty and sickness to their children, for whom the state will also show no interest? ... I could not have volunteered for the war, nor could I expect my son to volunteer for another, if I knew I would have returned as a war victim to experience gratitude and defeat.[35]

Konrad D. criticized Hitler's idealization of the front veteran as a surrogate for actual support. The Füherprinzip and the whole structure of the Nazi government, he noted, so far struck him as another form of the 'self-serving state' that had alienated war victims from the Weimar Republic in the depression years.[36]

Justice for war victims was inextricably linked to financial compensation, which Konrad D. argued had to be controlled by veterans rather than bureaucrats and finance ministers. He called for an end to empty rhetoric about war victims being the 'core of the nation', and he asked that each of Germany's 750,000 remaining disabled veterans be given at least a 100 Marks per month increase in welfare payments.[37] The Nazi regime, he claimed, was essentially a tool of capitalist powers, and not the 'people's state' that it claimed to embody. Hitler continued the 'capitalist exploitation' of the German people and did not make good a promise of radical change: 'The "Führer principle" fully realizes the power of the state … It is not the grand presence of a great capitalist who will save the national community, but the masses of the people'.[38] Mimicking communist rhetoric despite claiming not to be a communist, Konrad D. saw the Nazi welfare system serving financial interests more than disabled veterans, who had to survive on the promise of national respect.

The notion of war neurotics taking control of the war neurosis problem and creating what Konrad D. described as a moral revision of the welfare state permeates his second major tract that he wrote and submitted to the regime, 'The Echo – A War Victim's Essay on the new "Honorable Rights of the German War Disabled"'. This essay appeared in May 1935, a year after the 1934 law and its sweeping pension cuts took effect. The playful 'grumbler' of 1933–34 who characterized himself as an advisor willing to sign 'Heil Hitler' at the end of his letters disappeared, replaced by a much more confrontational style that openly criticized the regime's policies. While his rhetoric contained repetitious attacks on private property and the self-serving state, he also developed themes on the moral implications of Nazi policy. He wrote: 'Only in the spirit of love for one's neighbor lies the triumph of eternal life over death. Violence is no longer the prerogative, only love is'. Justice for war victims and the future of the nation rested on 'the eternal law of love for one's neighbor'.[39] A strong pacifist message wove through these musings on love, as Konrad D. criticized the Nazi cult of the front that glorified violence, and he appealed to the regime to embrace pacifism before another war drove the next generation to insanity. This pacifist vision was closely connected to welfare justice, as Konrad D. stressed that a nation at war could never respond to war victims' needs, financially or spiritually, and he concluded that substantial reforms in welfare could only be achieved in an era of global peace.[40]

Konrad D. challenged the Nazis on their pervasive claim that their movement was led by front veterans, which entitled them to govern the nation. Most National Socialist ideologues, he claimed, actually had no first-hand knowledge of combat. Instead, veterans like himself, especially those suffering from psychological trauma, were entitled to define the meaning of the war experience and determine who was a legitimate victim. He attacked images generated by Nazi leaders that portrayed combat as an ennobling experience that hardened the will and spirit of men. These war narratives seemed inherently contradictory to Konrad D. On one hand, they emphasized the extreme violence of the trenches in a way that seemed relatively accurate. At the same time, Nazi propaganda failed to highlight the effects of this violence on normal human beings. 'It is a fact', he noted, 'that the war was a hell of injuries, pain and sacrifice ... why should it not also be a fact that it destroyed human beings, broke their nervous systems and the harmonic cooperation of organs, and weakened the mental, physical and spiritual powers of combatants?'[41] The regime's cherished images of the 'storm of steel' and the 'baptism of fire' seemed to Konrad D. to be a tacit admission that the haunting memories in the minds of German soldiers were not figments of their imagination. He accused the Nazis of denying the psychological trauma of the war, and called for a reawakening of the heroic spirit he found in the war. This spirit motivated war victims to continue fighting against economic and social injustice: 'The most pressing task of the national community is to provide sufficient welfare to war victims. Only the heroic spirit is able to obtain state support and defend against a world of enemies ... only by granting justice can the national psyche avoid becoming sick and the spirit of truth not fall into decay'.[42]

Similar to many psychologically disabled veterans, Konrad D. associated men like himself with the values of the front experience – heroism, sacrifice, comradeship. In contrast, the state represented degeneration, sickness and deviant behavior. This inversion of 'sickness' and 'health' was closely connected to redefining welfare and the memory of the front experience. Welfare had to be redefined as an expression of the spirit of sacrifice and comradeship. It was welfare, not the experience of combat, that he believed should be awarded respect by postwar society. Where the Nazis maligned the whole notion of welfare as the opposite of the image of the hardened front veteran, Konrad D. emphasized welfare as entirely consistent with the image of the front fighter. Not only were disabled veterans entitled to compensation, he also saw the front experience as the foundation for a new spirit for valuing welfare: 'Bring honor to the concept of welfare again. Practice comradeship like we had in "No Man's Land" and recognize the love of your neighbor as common sense for self-preservation'.[43] Konrad D.'s front ideology thus entailed something very different from what he encountered in Nazi propaganda. He portrayed the regime's rhetoric that celebrated combat while abandoning disabled veterans as an act of continued violence that revealed the immorality of the state. The front experience trained him to celebrate the brotherhood of the trenches by combating postwar poverty and despair, rather than celebrating the violence. 'Comradeship' meant 'love of one's neighbor', and could be transposed to postwar civil society by expanded health care and welfare. Thus there was nothing unmanly or deviant about being dependent on the state. Instead, the spirit of welfare was closely linked to the same values celebrated in the trenches.

By marginalizing and destroying those groups deemed unproductive in the national community, Konrad D. argued, the state actually sapped the will of its increasingly demoralized citizens, who worked out of a sense of fear rather than sacrifice for the community. In 'The Echo', Konrad D. redefined 'national community' to signify a society that defended the security of its vulnerable citizens. Those accused of 'grumbling' and 'whining' he characterized as the last vestiges of the 'heroic spirit' fighting against the systematic attempt to forget the human destruction caused by the war.[44] The regime was not reinvigorating the social body, but rather draining its spiritual dimensions – compassion, sacrifice, love – and thus laying the groundwork for its destruction.

For war neurotics now, twenty years after the war, the core of the war neurosis debate was how normal men should realistically respond to the horrors of combat. Konrad D. speculated that most of the Nazi leadership and their constituents, having no first-hand knowledge, were not qualified to interpret the authentic war experience. War neurotics, having experienced the horror of combat most intensely, were uniquely entitled to diagnose psychological wounds, paths of treatment, and compensation. However, Konrad D.'s self-appointed status as caretaker of the authentic memory of the war threatened no one. He had become an irritating character for a regime that did not know what to do with him. Though they amassed a stack of letters from him criticizing the regime's social policy and ideology, labor ministers expressed indifference. Nevertheless, his rants against the Nazi social welfare system in 1935 eventually compelled the director of his Berlin welfare office to offer the main welfare office and Labor Ministry an explanation for Konrad D.'s opinions and frequent letters. The welfare official emphasized that Konrad D. was a 'well-known whiner' and 'grumbler' with an 'especially sensitive and nervous disposition'. The official also apologized that his clinic was unable to control Konrad D.'s outbursts in the letters.[45] The last report in Labor Ministry files on his case suggests that his local welfare office was desperate enough to take the last resort. In September 1935, the Labor Ministry informed him that the main welfare office decided he would be categorized in the 'lowest salary grouping' for emergency relief, which gave him a monthly payment of 48 Marks, not enough to pay for even the basic necessities of food and rent.[46]

Konrad D. could hardly claim victory, as his local welfare office was condemned by upper-level bureaucrats for making concessions to a lunatic. Konrad D.'s outbursts drew wide attention from other welfare adminis-trators who frowned on the Berlin welfare office for placating what they saw as an obvious fraud, even with a paltry sum. The Labor Ministry representative at Brandenburg-Pommern's main welfare office concluded that all of Konrad D.'s complaints were the fantasies of a sick man out to defraud the state.[47]

Despite the Berlin office's concession, the Labor Ministry's last reports on Konrad D. made clear that they considered him a fraud. These conclusions circulating among welfare officials cemented Konrad D.'s status as a social outsider within the Third Reich. Those labeled as 'whiners' and 'grumblers' were officially designated as 'asocials', who included, according to the Ministry of the Interior in 1937, 'persons who demonstrate through behaviour towards the community, which may not in itself be criminal, that they will not adapt themselves to the community'.[48] This broadly defined group of people was targeted by the Criminal Police and sent to concentration camps. Individuals defined as 'asocials', especially those with a background of psychological ailments, were also being conflated with the hereditarily ill and isolated as threats to the 'racial health' of the national community. Konrad D. anticipated the Nazi state's physical destruction of the mentally and physically ill. He observed prophetically: 'A state that simply kills all of its sick annihilates the spirit and preparedness of sacrifice – it digs its own grave!'[49] The hereditarily ill were attacked in sterilization programs, and just before the Second World War they were targeted in the T–4 'euthanasia' program, under which more than 70,000 adult mentally and physically handicapped individuals were murdered.[50] Konrad D.'s file does not leave a trace of his fate.

Hitler's War through the Lens of Great War Trauma: The Case of Erich G.

The vociferous attacks made by psychologically injured veterans against Nazi social welfare policy and the memory of 1914–18 heightened with the outbreak of the Second World War. Within weeks after the invasion of Poland in 1939, the Labor Ministry received letters from disgruntled veterans of 1918 whose traumatic memories were rekindled by the new war. These psychologically disabled veterans saw in the Second World War the ultimate betrayal of their interpretation of the front experience. The new war, they argued, marked a deliberate attempt to bury the unresolved memory of 1914–18. In particular, veterans still haunted by the horrors of the First World War's trenches accused the Nazi regime of concealing the traumatic nature of modern combat in order to harness mass consent. The aging war neurotics of the first modern industrial war prophesized in 1939 that Germany was headed for an even more destructive trauma from which it would not recover.

One of the most interesting examples of a psychologically disabled First World War veteran who agitated against the Nazi regime is Erich G.

During the Great Depression, he began a routine of writing every few months to the Labor Ministry and other government officials. His letters often exceeded twenty pages in length, detailing his social, economic and political problems as a mentally ill veteran. Like many other disabled veterans, Erich G. turned to National Socialism, which he hoped would solve his health care and pension problems that plagued him during the Weimar years. But gradual disillusionment following deepening pension cuts peaked with the outbreak of the Second World War. He argued that Nazis betrayed the victims of the Great War as the *Kaiserreich* and the Weimar Republic had. He accused the regime that had promised to make war victims the 'first citizens' of Germany of condemning his children's generation to an even worse fate than his own.

Erich G. came from a working-class background. Court documents referred to his occupation simply as *'Arbeiter'* (worker), and he served on both the Western and Eastern fronts during the First World War.[51] The flashpoint for G.'s case history began with his experiences in the trenches. He claimed that he suffered physical and mental trauma after a series of combat experiences. In one instance he was buried alive under layers of mud in an artillery barrage, and in another he was pinned under a tree that collapsed in a bombardment.[52] In 1916, he was treated in a field hospital on the Eastern front for 'weakness of nerves' following trench combat. At this stage, his symptoms did not last long and he was released. His captain filed a report on the incident, saying that Erich G. had not been punished, but rather sent on for further treatment, suggesting that his mental breakdown at first drew suspicion that he was trying to shirk his duty.[53] His fellow soldiers and officers attested to his service and key events, but the traumatic effects of these experiences would remain a point of controversy for the rest of his life.

In the years after the war, Erich G. was diagnosed by a series of private doctors who reported that he suffered from epileptic seizures, various nervous ailments, and rheumatism, all of which they linked to neurological and psychological damage caused by experiences in the trenches. He divorced his wife and married again in 1925, but had difficulty finding even temporary work. When economic times reached their worst, he resorted to petty crime. Eventually, the various illnesses he claimed were caused by the war completely overcame him. Between 1925 and 1929, he applied for a war-disabled pension and went through a series of evaluations by Labor Ministry doctors. He submitted medical reports from these private doctors supporting his claims to war-related psychological problems and letters from fellow veterans who witnessed his traumatic injuries and bravery in combat.[54]

The Labor Ministry's official doctors did not agree with the diagnosis made by Erich G.'s private physicians. Dr Max Nonne, one of Germany's premiere experts on war neurosis since the war and director of the Hamburg neurological treatment clinic, turned down G.'s case in 1929 as not related to war service, thus denying him a pension. Erich G. accused Nonne of bias, complaining that the psychiatrist was fixated on his character rather than objective medical facts and his history of war service. According to Erich G., Nonne concentrated on his petty criminal record as evidence of deficient character and a disposition to fake his wounds, compounded by preexisting nervous disorders. Infuriated, Erich G. hired a lawyer through the *Reichsbund der Kriegsbeschädigten* (National Association of War Victims), and brought a lawsuit against the famous doctor. They assembled nine medical reports by doctors outside the Labor Ministry who concluded there was a connection between G.'s problems and his war service. The independent doctors concluded that physical stress and trauma caused by being buried alive and exposure on the Russian front produced his wide range of physical and nervous disorders. G. emphasized in his letters that he suffered from actual neurological damage. But Dr Nonne, he complained, reduced everything to 'hysteria', suggesting that his injuries were simulated or purely psychosomatic. Erich G.'s main goal was to get the Labor Ministry to appoint another doctor for an official diagnosis that would be acknowledged by the courts:

> 'The thanks of the fatherland will certainly be yours'. What a great thanks this is ... A new conclusive evaluation above all other evaluations will bring proof that my sufferings are the result of war service. If this new evaluation denies a connection [to war service], then I can be satisfied. But up to now there has been no precise and sensitive examination. But if the evaluation affirms that my current problems are the result of war service, then it will affirm what I've suspected since 1925.[55]

Erich G. believed that, as an actual veteran, he held greatest authority to interpret the damage caused by the war experience. Doctors, he claimed, focused on his moral character because they had no idea what it was like to be in the trenches. He complained that Dr Nonne and his colleagues gave him a superficial medical exam because they already made up their minds. Because he had no 'external injuries', Erich G. wrote, doctors concluded his problems must be caused by 'nervous illness' unrelated to the war. He characterized this as a blanket term for more complex injuries that doctors could not explain.

Erich G. enlisted the *Reichsbund* to help petition for a pension, and specifically asked that labor ministers grant him a medical review by 'professional doctors' outside the state-run health care system.[56] Private doctors were less biased, he argued, because they were not wrapped up in the debate over pensions.[57] He pointed to the reports from his private doctors and letters from his fellow veterans to substantiate his case, and he appropriated the language used by doctors to accuse Nonne of being a fraud: 'Prof. Nonne has revealed himself to be a swindler and a liar ... one can see that he is afraid he will be brought out into the open and his fame will be tarnished'.[58] In addition, he blamed Nonne for the break-up of his marriage due to the economic strain placed on his family in the wake of the pension rejection.[59]

Erich G.'s experience with Dr Nonne became a second trauma that overshadowed his war experience as the origin of his medical and personal crises. Before the lawyers could go into battle over the testimonies of doctors and veterans, the court determined that Erich G.'s lawsuit could not be pursued because he had missed the deadline for submitting his evidence.[60] This rejection on bureaucratic grounds led him to shower the Labor Ministry and government officials with letters over the next ten years. His wave of letters in 1932, as Weimar was beset with paralyzing political polarization and the depths of the Great Depression, concentrated on what he saw as the medical, political and social prejudices rampant in the state's treatment of veterans. Interestingly, Erich G.'s arguments were more systematically developed and focused than those often encountered in the letters of other mentally ill veterans. State doctors, he claimed, ignored medical diagnoses offered by private doctors because they supported his case that various wounds were war-related. Doctors were further biased against war victims whose wounds were invisible, particularly if they belonged to left-wing political groups. Finally, he complained that his criminal history, bouts with venereal disease, and working-class status unjustly stigmatized him as having a degenerate moral character and thus an inclination to swindle the government.[61]

Suspicion that his criminal past stigmatized him in the eyes of doctors troubled Erich G. the most, judging from the pages he devoted to refuting the doctors' image of him as a low-class swindler. He admitted that he had been imprisoned for three months in 1905 at age 21 for stealing food, explaining that he regretted his act but had no choice because his father was an unemployed alcoholic and his family was starving. He defended his one-month jail term in 1921 for forgery in much the same way, complaining that economic desperation drove him to make a mistake. Erich G. was certain that his letters of recommendation from various employers and friends attested to an otherwise good moral character. In fact, he wrote, this 1921 crime was really committed under the influence of his second wife. He told the Labor Ministry that while he worked hard to preserve a respectable marriage, his wife repeatedly committed adultery and gave him a venereal disease, leading to entanglements with the vice police (*Sittenpolizei*) that further tainted his record and convinced doctors he was a criminal. These blemishes on his record, he insisted, had nothing to do with the psychological and physical damage he experienced in the war, and could not be considered as evidence that he was a degenerate character.[62]

One of Erich G.'s problems included sexual impotence, which his doctors described as a form of neurasthenia stemming from his gonorrhea. He argued that this problem preexisted the infection and was instead linked to war-induced stress.[63] His shady past, he contended, was behind him – his criminal history was an aberration and his postwar bout with gonorrhea had quickly healed. But doctors could not let it go, he complained, and they held his criminal record over his head to rationalize his current health problems and alleged attempts to swindle the state. 'I would have never believed in 1918', he wrote, 'after having won the iron cross that I would be treated this way by my own fatherland ... Prof. Dr Nonne has a bad conscience and is afraid that he will be brought out in public ... for the lies and fraud that my documents prove his medical evaluation to be'.[64] State health officials 'took no consideration of my complicated illnesses', Erich G. wrote. He went to the Brandenburg psychiatric clinic and Dr F. Zimmerman, who, Erich G. sarcastically noted, performed more tests than all the Labor Ministry doctors combined. After taking X-rays of Erich G.'s spinal column in 1929, Zimmerman concluded that physical damage caused by wartime trauma had produced G.'s history of neurological disorders.[65]

When Hitler came to power, Erich G. quickly changed his tactics and politics. He abandoned his activities with the social democratic-oriented *Reichsbund*. Further, he no longer focused on his medical exams and the alleged bias of doctors. Instead, with an eye on Nazi rhetoric regarding veterans as the 'first citizens of the Reich', Erich G. concentrated on his loyalty to the nation and dedicated service at the front. On March 24, 1933, the day after the Enabling Act banned all parties in opposition to the National Socialists, Erich G. saw the writing on the wall and wrote directly to Hitler. He mixed an obsequious tone with a question that must have been on the minds of other frustrated disabled veterans:

Although until a short while ago I belonged to no political party or organization, I am contacting you to express interest in the following writings [produced by the NSDAP]: 1. Essay on economic struggle and the Nazi program, vol. 16. 2. National Socialism and war disabled. These two short essays convince me that Hitler is the best path for war victims. But I would like to place the question to you: As chancellor do you now have control over the welfare authorities?[66]

Like other disabled veterans, Erich G. placed his hopes in Hitler as a figure who would rise above the petty fray to cut through the bureaucracy and grant him justice. His next letter, again directly to Hitler, challenged the Nazi leader even more directly to put substance behind party rhetoric: 'You can show myself and all the war wounded that you and your party will strengthen your commitment to our justice ... Until now war victims have been very hesitant to support your party, but your writings on the war victim question appear to be proof of your commitment'. Erich G. then outlined his history of being buried alive and his treatment for psychological and physical disorders. He mentioned his 1905 and 1921 brushes with the law and doctors' suspicions about his character, but asked how the state could question the integrity of a front veteran, especially when his criminal record 'had nothing to do with the wounds'.[67]

When no response from the Nazis came, Erich G.'s initial optimism about Hitler quickly deteriorated within a few months, and he accused the new regime of betraying disabled veterans. His quick turnaround suggests that he had never put much faith in the Nazis. Erich G. turned to the head of the Labor Ministry, Franz Seldte, to announce that the regime should 'clear up the error, or whatever one wants to call it'. He then wrote testily: 'You yourself have declared in your speeches that "the war wounded and front fighters will soon get their rights". But up to now I have waited in vain for the fulfillment of your plan'.[68] He received no response, and for the next several years he continued to write ceaselessly about his experience of being buried alive under shellfire, the subsequent conflicts over medical treatment, and his various illnesses, with comrades from the front providing further testimony. His writing became more and more sarcastic as he relished quoting Nazi leaders back to them. Referring to the head of the Nazi War Victims' Association, Hanns Oberlindober, and his promise of 'peace, honor and justice to war victims', Erich G. asked, 'Have I not like other German soldiers and war victims done my duty for the fatherland, and given the fatherland my health and ability to earn a living?'[69] He quoted passages from Nazi pension laws that guaranteed funding for war victims, followed with lists of how much his family received in invalid and emergency care pensions, then compared this to the cost of living.[70] Welfare administrators did not reply to Erich G., but in 1937 they did circulate to the Labor Ministry a detailed report on his case history since 1925, emphasizing the long string of pension rejections and his repeated refusal to go away. Frustrated by the lack of response from the Labor Ministry, Erich G. turned back to writing directly to Hitler. He argued that nothing had changed for disabled veterans since Weimar: 'Since 1933 it has been made known: "What was promised you in the time of the system [Weimar] will be fulfilled in the Third Reich" – and where is this fulfillment?'[71]

Despite his written attacks on Nazi rhetoric, the regime left him alone, treating him as an isolated grumbler. After the July 1934 pension cuts, Nazi leaders deflected most criticism as physically and psychologically disabled veterans blamed doctors, bureaucrats, and the oft-cited conspiracy of Jews and the 'November Criminals' for their plight. As so often was the case, the 'Hitler myth' played a strong role in shaping consent, even from frustrated war victims who did worse under Hitler than under

Weimar. Erich G., however, was rather exceptional in that he focused his resentment on Nazi leaders within months after the seizure of power. Taking the Nazis at face value for their propaganda, and challenging them on their claims to have coordinated control over the bureaucracy and welfare system, Erich G. held party leaders responsible for failing to fulfill their image as crusaders for the rights and honor of veterans. Left unchallenged, his personal war against the Nazis from behind his typewriter desk continued to escalate.

The outbreak of the Second World War in 1939 led Erich G. to criticize Hitler directly. The war marked the end of any lingering myth of Hitler as beyond party politics. It confirmed to G. his suspicion that Hitler was the great betrayer of the memory of 1914–18 and the experience of authentic front veterans like himself. With the invasion of Poland, Erich G. prophesized that a new generation would be traumatized by the stress of the war. Only the aging victims of 1914–18, he argued, particularly the forgotten psychological victims, could genuinely understand their experiences. Erich G. provides a rare glimpse into how a brutalized survivor of the First World War interpreted the Second.

On one level, Erich G.'s view of the Second World War was consumed by jealousy over how the Nazi regime treated the new generation of soldiers. Within weeks after the invasion against Poland, he was furious that Wehrmacht soldiers were treated like victorious heroes while front veterans from his war remained neglected: 'Didn't we, the front veterans of the world war, suffer more from hunger, stress, etc? Didn't we suffer in Russia from the monstrous cold ... didn't our war last four years?'[72] A sense of insecurity ran through Erich G.'s attacks. Propaganda that portrayed the new generation of soldiers as exceptional pillars of German manhood was a slap in the face to the generation of 1914, he complained. He read such propaganda as a subtle critique of his own generation as psychologically unprepared, or less determined, than Hitler's soldiers. The men of 1939 were no more healthy, or courageous, than his own generation: 'The front fighter of the world war was exactly like the front fighter of 1939, recruited into the army as a healthy man ... the veteran of the world war showed the exact same courage and energy as the front fighter of 1939'. Economic jealousy also boiled over. Erich G. asked why he was living on 58.90 Marks per month drawn from pension funds and emergency pensions for invalids, still not qualifying as a disabled veterans, when his newspaper told of a soldier in Poland who received over 150 Marks per month just for family support, having not even been wounded.[73] While Wehrmacht soldiers in France and Poland 'get everything they need', Erich G. asked Hitler why the Nazi regime acted like a 'wicked stepmother' towards soldiers of the 1914–18 war.[74] 'Hysterical men' of the Great War now saw themselves as doubly traumatized by the Second World War: forgotten as losers and treated as economic burdens.

Erich G. aimed his resentment at the Nazi regime rather than Wehrmacht soldiers. He empathized with the younger generation and saw them as comrades in victimhood. He bitterly asked the government: 'Will the front fighter and war victim of 1939 be so quickly forgotten as the front soldier of the [1914–18] world war who suffered injuries and whose wounds were rejected as non-war related? ... or perhaps front fighters just won't get sick in Poland'.[75] The soldiers of 1939, he predicted, would face psychological and physical depravations similar to his own. He projected his own experience on to them, and warned that doctors would characterize their 'weak nerves, neurasthenia and nervous disorders' as unrelated to the war. Doctors were incompetent and driven only by their zeal to save the state's pension budget. The 'countless different diagnoses' needed to cure complex illnesses brought on by stress, deprivation, and experiences like his own being buried alive, would require a more objective, sensitive and sympathetic medical establishment. Nazi propaganda about fulfilling health care and economic needs of both First and Second World War veterans struck him as hollow.[76]

The invasion of the Soviet Union in 1941 turned Erich G. into an even fiercer critic of the Nazi regime's failure to match theory with practice. In particular, he considered Operation Barbarossa to be a suicidal military blunder that relied on Hitler's false assumption that the modern German soldier was more psychologically and physically fit than any other. In October 1941, Erich G. attacked Hitler for calling German soldiers in Russia 'supermen', while treating veterans of the First World War as weak-willed:

> From Hitler's speeches comes word that the soldiers in the present war have performed deeds like supermen. Now comes the question: Didn't we front fighters of the world war [1914–18] also do our duty? Did we not also have to endure stress, hunger, terrible weather and everything possible? Didn't the world war also bring us wounds and illnesses exactly like the comrades of the current war? ... We front fighters hope that the young fighters won't get the same treatment as the old. Hopefully the welfare claims of the young soldiers won't also be turned down with your words.[77]

Erich G. felt bitter about the attention heaped on Germany's younger generation. But he also empathized with them, and saw through the propaganda that portrayed them as supermen. By describing men in this way, soldiers would be given no leeway to respond to combat in a normal sense. He was certain that National Socialist doctors would be as skeptical of complex physical and psychological injuries as those under the *Kaiserreich* – perhaps even more so now that soldiers had to live up to an impossible racial image. 'Let's all hope', Erich G. wrote sarcastically, 'that today's soldiers all return home healthy and able to earn a living, and they need to make no welfare claims. But hundreds and thousands will bring home exactly the same types of rheumatism-like illnesses that manifest themselves in the first years after the war'.[78]

After the catastrophic defeat at Stalingrad in February 1943, where over half a million German soldiers were killed or captured, marking the turning point of the war in Europe, Erich G. became even more bold in asserting that the regime's superhuman image of the German soldier was a myth. German soldiers could not press on through sheer will power, and those who broke down should not be accused of weakness. Erich G. used the debacle at Stalingrad to vindicate his own generation. Regardless of the propaganda, normal men break down under extreme stress:

> If I went to the front as a healthy man, without an inclination or disposition towards illness, then my problems must certainly have been caused by war service, or at the last, through the terrible weather and stress ... Please take into consideration the two winters on the Eastern front, which our Eastern front fighters must survive, and which we all know about from every newspaper, radio (front reports) and weekly. We also had to survive such terrible climate in 1914–18. We German soldiers are not Russians, who are able to take the stressful climate etc. without getting sick ... let's hope that the comrades of today's war won't have to experience what we world war front fighters did, namely, to be told [years after the war] 'the problems can't be traced back to war service'[79]

He portrayed the winters on the Eastern front as proof that the Nazi memory of the First World War was false. Germany lost in 1918 because the men at the front were ultimately human, not because they were betrayed by the home front. The Wehrmacht soldier's experience in Russia, G. observed, was identical. He could not survive the demands placed on his body and mind. Wars are not won through sheer will. This was the reality that the Nazi leadership tried to repress. Thus the Second World War betrayed, rather than fulfilled, the memory of the first front experience for traumatized survivors.

The last letters from Erich G. preserved by the Labor Ministry were dated mid-1943. There is no explanation for the end of his correspondence. But at this stage, he was being treated in hospital for rheumatism, neurological disorders that produced constant shaking and paralysis, and various other illnesses for which he continued to lobby for state compensation. His final letter collected in Labor Ministry files was a medical diagnosis of himself, even written in the third person style of an official report. In this instance, Erich G. assumed totally the role of an authority on psychological trauma in war and the nature of his wounds.

He outlined detailed connections between events in the war and the symptoms. Entrapment between a fallen tree and the wall of a trench during a bombardment, and the ensuing abandonment in cold and rain, had caused the rheumatism and physical ailments in his joints and limbs. The incident in which he was buried alive, he concluded, had caused his nervous disorders and heart ailment. Thus he turned the tables and positioned himself as in full control of his diagnosis, if not his health or economic condition. After lengthy descriptions of his front experience and symptoms, he concluded with a challenge: 'Now I would like to ask you, what is your own opinion and judgment about the causes of my injuries?'[80] Exasperated with the Nazi regime's treatment of veterans, Erich G. thus ended his diatribe by turning himself into physician, welfare expert, and authentic caretaker of the memory of the war.

Germany's Armageddon and Psychological Collapse

Hitler's war, unlike 1914–18, was characterized by a policy of racial annihilation and genocidal violence that made it exceptional. At the same time, Hitler's war was often conducted in the shadow of his interpretation of why Germany lost in 1918. On one hand, Hitler argued that 'enemies of the nation' had betrayed the army just before the moment of victory, and that the Second World War would signal the mobilization of Germany's will power into a hardened, unflinching weapon, psychologically ready to follow Hitler to the end.[81] However, Hitler's policies on the home front suggested deep-seated fears that enormous economic strain would weaken the will of even the most loyal Germans on the home front, thus undermining the war effort.

In the early phases of the war, that is before the German army met defeats that finally required total war measures, Nazi leaders attempted to shield the nation from strains that might lead to low morale. In order to avoid the shortages and subsequent disillusionment seen at the end of the First World War, the Nazis tried to maintain a 'business as usual' economy that provided consumer goods at an uninterrupted level. This was often done by looting occupied territories to provide for Germans at home, who enjoyed what one historian has described as a 'semi-mobilized economy scarcely different from that of the prewar Nazi state'.[82] In addition to sustaining an illusion of economic normality, the Nazi state also made every effort to shield the public from the gruesome reality of modern warfare. Images of combat in the print and film media, even in the NSKOV's *German War Victims' Care* periodical, depicted bloodless combat, with images of wounded men contented, well-cared for, and neatly bandaged, in hospitals behind the lines.[83]

While the Nazi regime attempted to shelter Germans from the horrors of war in order to avoid another breakdown like that of 1918, allied bombing brought the trauma of war home. By 1942–43, the British and American air campaigns began to routinely reach German cities, taking their toll on Germany's capacity to effectively organize its war machine, and inflicting enormous physical and psychological injuries. In their reports on the effects of Allied bombing on morale, officials began to refer to 'air-raid psychosis' as a widespread effect of constant attacks.[84] The scope and consequences of the air raids grew enormously. In Berlin, for example, air attacks killed a few hundred civilians per month in early 1943. By December 1943, raids had killed 8,000 Berliners and left more than 250,000 homeless. Even before Germany's civilians began to see these enormous losses, doctors had mobilized to cope with the rising psychological injuries sustained on the combat and home fronts. In March 1941, Dr Borchers, the Director of the regional welfare office in Pommern, was flooded with psychiatric casualties. Individuals arriving at his welfare office showed 'illnesses caused by sudden terror (*Shreck*), unforeseen psychological problems and the effects of shock from air attacks, the influences of war (*Kriegseinflüsse*) on soldiers, etc.'[85] Dr Borchers looked for a quick method of treatment to deal with these myriad causes of mental illness. He asked the president of the welfare administration in Stettin for permission to follow the program developed by doctors at a hospital in Ückermünde, where it was reported that electrotherapy was leading to 'quick improvements'. Borchers called on the National Welfare Office to investigate how the electrotherapy was successfully applied and how many had been treated. Specifically, he wanted to know whether or not a one-time treatment was enough, or if repeated shock therapy was needed to achieve a cure. Interesting to note in Borcher's letter was the simple conflation of traumatized soldiers and civilians, and the absence of judgment on their character or the legitimacy of their wounds. Borchers' language suggests a matter-of-fact attempt to deal with new psychological problems created by the war, with his primary focus on finding an efficient model for relieving the burden total war placed on health care resources.[86]

Dr Borchers' relatively neutral approach to mentally ill war victims was exceptional. The explosion of psychiatric casualties sent psychiatrists into a panic that Germany was on course for another 'pension psychosis' epidemic. Doctors resurrected First World War representations of mentally disabled soldiers as deviant men who were at the epicenter of a national psychological crisis that needed to be controlled before it destroyed Germany's ability to wage war. After the defeat at Stalingrad and increased civilian bombings, doctors were already imagining Germany's postwar crisis in the care of war victims. They warned that there would be a repeat of post-1918 patterns in pension dependency, with even higher levels of psychological degeneration among Germany's male population, unless doctors took control. Dr C. Morocutti, chief doctor in charge of invalid welfare in Graz, predicted an enormous rise in war-disabled pension claims, and with it the potential for chronic, widespread dependency:

> Weak and war-weary people pursue this search for care in great numbers in these special cases of pension dependency (*Rentensucht*). Especially physically and psychologically exhausted people, as most returning home from war are, lack the defensive powers and restraint. Instead of turning to an active lifestyle, they allow themselves to slip into being passive recipients of state care and pension dependence.[87]

The state would be responsible for this 'addiction' to pensions if it continued to give 'with open hands'. State care ultimately weakened, Moricutti argued, rather than cured, disabled soldiers.[88]

State health care and financial support, Morocutti noted, posed a two-fold danger. Welfare sapped men of their masculine characteristics, including their sense of will and productivity, and it eroded the National Socialist ideal of a racial state:

> [State assistance] would also contradict the foundations of a National Socialist lifestyle and racially pure behavior if the principle of performance and productivity in work is dissolved by the principle of excessive welfare and through the possible approval of unproductive pensions.[89]

Germany's economic potential and its racial strength were simultaneously threatened by pensions, Moricutti claimed, which drained the nation's capacity for production and undermined its National Socialist principles.

Pensions were in direct opposition to the Nazi conception of masculinity and racial fitness. The psychological and racial survival of the nation was at stake, Morocutti feared, if pension dependency was allowed to spread in the climate of total war. State care posed 'a terrible psychological and racial danger for hundreds of thousands and millions of young German men who will develop an invalid complex and pension complex'. Morocutti provided a detailed regimen for ensuring that disabled men received just enough help to recover their physical strength without crossing what he saw as a fine line that led to 'psychosis' and racial degeneration. Patients were to be told immediately that they are not invalids, but potentially productive racial comrades. Therapy was to emphasize the restoration of the will, and the patient was to be disciplined and not allowed to fixate on his psychological and physical injuries: 'The sinking down of millions of men into the psychological paralysis of invalids and pensioners signifies a very dangerous diminishing of will and a weakness of will in the entire nation (*Volkes*)'. The emergence of an 'inferiority complex' (*Minderheitskomplex*),

Morocutti predicted, was the 'most difficult psychological and social problem for the nation in the wake of a difficult war'. The best tactic, for both the individual and the nation, was for doctors to have complete control over when financial assistance should be distributed to disabled men. Once doctors determined that men were ready to leave the hospital, welfare should be cut off.[90]

Failure to control the 'psychological paralysis' brought on by pensions and welfare spelled nothing less than defeat, Morocutti warned. He predicted that giving handouts to otherwise healthy men would only recreate the conditions of the Weimar period: 'The docile state and complacency of the defeated German people after the 1914–18 World War was in no little way due to the democracy's support for invalids and pensions'. This only fueled the rise of the traditional enemies of the nation, the political left and the 'Marxist-led masses of workers' who easily dominated the 'work-shy' population made submissive by democracy, unions, and social welfare.[91] Thus the war was not the source of trauma in Germans, but rather these illnesses originated in weak-willed individuals who caved into their own defeatism and ultimately brought on the collapse of the nation.

While doctors blamed disabled veterans and civilians for the spread of nervous disorders, the Nazi regime's police system secretly reported, with increasing concern, on the psychological effects of the war and its ramifications for home front morale. Gestapo agents worked to gauge the responses of everyday Germans to various Nazi policies and the war. They recorded their eavesdropping on conversations in restaurants, movie theaters, the street and other forums in SD (*Sicherheitsdienst* – the regime's state security apparatus) reports sent from their offices throughout the Third Reich. These reports, part of the state's investigation of domestic opposition to the regime, provide an often surprisingly candid glimpse into how the regime viewed the public, and the swings between enthusiasm, passivity, and distaste for the Nazi leadership and their policies.[92]

The regime was convinced that any criticism came from organized political groups, in particular underground communist cells. But what they most often recorded was the unease expressed by disparate groups and individuals, sometimes unified in their views on events but fragmented and isolated by the regime.[93] At the same time, while the regime was successful in quashing resistance, the SD reports painted a picture of widespread 'grumbling' that often undermined the government's attempts to create a unified, militarized society that believed in the propaganda machine, especially after 1941, when total war conditions began to affect the population and losses on the Eastern Front and in civilian bombings were taking their toll.[94] Propaganda minister Joseph Goebbels felt increasingly hard-pressed and recorded his concern over reports of a 'very critical and skeptical' population, where 'depression in the broad masses' had taken hold despite propaganda guaranteeing victories and cultural events (films, operas, concerts) staged to distract people from the losses suffered in the war.[95]

The regime's impressions of public discontent were often framed in a popularized psychiatric language through the prism of fears about a repeat of 1918. These fears reached a fever pitch as the military situation worsened. As defeat at Stalingrad loomed in January 1943, the SD reported that the German population was on verge of psychological collapse. The 'psychosis of fear' (*Angstpsychose*) gripped the public as it learned through the networks of soldiers back to their families that the German army faced disaster on the Eastern front.[96] The SD confidently indicated that this psychological breakdown was successfully countered by propaganda, in this case speeches by Nazi leadership, including Göring and Goebbels: 'The developing psychosis of fear in the population has recently been thwarted [by the speeches], and the party comrades' strongly diminished faith in victory caused by the military situation has been strengthened once again'. Thus the regime's security apparatus predicted that the regime could control perceptions, and anxieties, about the war. At the same time, the SD reported that people were complaining about overly bombastic propaganda: 'The general population wishes that the press should remain sparing and concise in expressions of feelings and evaluations [of the situation at the front], because ideas like "heroism", "heroic", "victims", and "martyrdom" are becoming empty as a result of daily repetition'.[97] The SD in Würzburg indicated that there was widespread criticism of Göring and even Hitler as overly fanatical and unrealistic in their assessment of the situation at the front and the capabilities of the Soviet army.[98] Cynicism about the war had deepened, and fewer were willing to believe in the regime's official myths of the war experience.

The catastrophe at Stalingrad that was announced publicly on 3 February 1943, however, led the SD to admit that the home front was losing its nerve. A 4 February SD report noted, 'The announcement at the end of the battle in Stalingrad has deeply shaken the general population yet again'.[99] The SD reported further that propaganda could not conceal the horrifying reality of the war after this decisive defeat, and that there was 'increasing skepticism' about the outcome of the war, especially in 'working class quarters, and among women who are increasingly pressed under the burden of balancing family and the lack of bread-winners'.[100] In an 18 February report, the SD reported on women who complained that they could not hold out while their loved ones fought on the Eastern front.[101] Traditional 'enemies' responsible for 1918 – the working class and defeatist women on the home front – thus found themselves once again targeted for psychological weakness at the nation's decisive hour.

The SD's post-Stalingrad reports on the German population's nerves indicated that if anything positive were to come out of the defeat, it was that Stalingrad would 'shock the general public out of its trance-like state and into the reality of total war'.[102] However, while the SD placed blame on a population for psychological weakness, the security police also detected elements in the populace who saw the escalating war as evidence of mental shortcomings in the Nazi leadership. Even before the invasion of Russia and subsequent military disasters, the regime was concerned that support for the war was precarious. Chain letters circulated surreptitiously through Hitler Youth and League of German Girls meeting halls, and the regime blamed communist organizations for an increase in underground 'agitation flyers'(Hetzzettel) proclaiming 'Down with the robbers and mass murderers of Hitler & Co'. But the SD gave most of its attention to a particular underground pamphlet that outlined ways in which disgruntled individuals could resist the regime in everyday life. Calling on Germans to refuse military service, listen to foreign radio broadcasts, and circulate information about the 'crimes of the Nazis, who incited us into war', the pamphlet writer also borrowed psychiatric terms to denounce the regime's repression of dissent: 'The hysterical struggle against "spies, sabotage, and traitors" is especially funny'.[103] The SD noted that the pamphlet 'sounded like communist rhetoric'. However, the list of resistance tactics, including a call to 'behave towards "enemy" parachutists in a completely friendly way', and the salutation 'with true German greetings from a "zealous national comrade"' suggested that the pamphlet came from a more iconoclastic individual. His use of the term 'hysterical' to describe the regime's control tactics reveals the degree to which a popularized psychiatric discourse was appropriated by those discontented with the militarization of society and the war.

As the Soviet and American armies pressed into German territory, the regime and its opponents continued to fight over who had lost their nerve first. Nazi leaders wrapped themselves in the fantasy that they restored Germany to psychological health, and they accused the home front of weakness and blamed them for the present crisis. In February 1945 Martin Bormann, head of the Party Chancellery and personal secretary to Hitler, released an official pronouncement, with the Red Army at the gates of Berlin, recalling the effects of defeat in the First World War. Hitler, he claimed, saved the nation from its psychological torment, where '50,000 suicides per year and 7 million unemployed were produced by the [1918] defeat'. Victory, Bormann theorized while hiding with the Führer in the bunker, could only be achieved now through extraordinary will and mental resilience:

> Whoever gives up nothing and would rather fall amidst the rubble than yield a single step is unbeatable; and under this inflexible law of nature dissolves all calculated reasoning, every superficially smart weighing of the pros and cons, because as in all times the strong and

not the cowards, the unshakeable and not the waverers, the fighters and not the fearful calculators, come out victorious in the end.[104]

Consistent with Nazi ideology since the 'years of struggle', Bormann constructed the war in terms of an inner battle between strength and weakness. Only through participation in the party could one find this inner strength:

> Party comradeship has itself been an unshakeable rock in the tide of war ... every man who can carry a weapon, in order to defend his homeland, which he loves, for the defense of women and children, must have the will to throw his body against the enemy. Every woman devotes herself to the demands of the hour and remains courageous in the face of adversity, even during separation from home and husband, through the demands on psychological and physical strength, even in the case of danger and the threat of death.[105]

In the last days of the Third Reich, Nazi leaders insulated themselves in a myth of the war experience in which sheer will replaced reason, and victory could only be assured when every man and woman fulfilled their prescribed roles with determination and dedication to the nation. Unified in their struggle against the enemy, Germans would overcome the defeat of 1918, with the party leading them towards psychological and physical restoration.

Despite their construction of Nazi ideology as a bastion of psychological strength, even top Nazi leaders were driven to reflect on the stress produced by five years of war. In his last political testament, dictated to his secretary in the bunker on 29 April 1945, a few hours before his suicide, Hitler began with a reference to his 'modest contribution in the [1914–18] World War'. The thirty years since that time, however, took their toll: 'In these three decades love and loyalty to my people have guided all my thoughts, actions and my life. They gave me the strength to make the most difficult decisions ever to confront mortal man. In these three decades I have spent my strength and my health'.[106]

Hitler's last testament reflected his simultaneous celebration of the redemptive powers of war and his feeling of victimhood and frayed health in the face of struggle against the nation's enemies. Once again repeating his blame for the war on 'international Jewry', with Germany as a victim of aggression, Hitler then blamed the 'scoundrels' who undermined resistance against the enemy, and those who 'surrendered' at the eleventh hour, like Göring and Himmler who attempted independently to negotiate peace terms. He praised '[m]any of our bravest men and women [who] have sworn to bind their lives to mine to the end' and he called on them 'to strengthen the National Socialist spirit of resistance of our soldiers by all possible means, with special emphasis on the fact that I myself, as the founder and creator of this movement, prefer death to cowardly resignation or even to capitulation'. He predicted that 'the glorious rebirth of the National Socialist movement' would emerge 'through the sacrifices of our soldiers and my own fellowship with them unto death'. His choice to stay in Berlin, he claimed, was motivated by the desire to remain resolute to the end:

> I, too, as founder and creator of this movement, have preferred death to cowardly flight or even capitulation ... I wish to share my fate with that which millions of others have also taken upon themselves by remaining in this city. Further, I shall not fall into the hands of the enemy who requires a new spectacle, presented by the Jews, for the diversion of the hysterical masses.[107]

With the end of the Nazi movement and his role as Führer, Hitler predicted Germany would once again be corrupted in the wake of defeat. On one hand predicting the resurrection of National Socialism through the passing of the front experience to the next generation, Hitler also envisioned a postwar society dominated by the 'hysterical masses' allied with Germany's enemies. In the end, Hitler chose to commit suicide in the insulated universe within the bunker rather than in combat. But the myth of the front experience persisted in Hitler's mind to the end, promoting combat as psychologically rejuvenating, and calling for the subordination of individual self-preservation to the will of the nation. Linking himself to the psychologically hardened, pure soldier in the field, Hitler imagined himself to have to have been a victim of the same forces that brought defeat in the First World War. In Hitler's mind, 1945 was a repeat of 1918, with 'the nation's enemies' taking advantage of a traumatized Germany.

*   *   *

Despite their total isolation and loss of the pension war, war neurotics considered themselves victorious in a struggle of wills with the regime, battling against Nazi revisionist history over the memory of the war. Though only lone 'psychopaths' armed with typewriters, they served as hidden reminders that the Nazi myth of the war experience did not reflect the beliefs of all veterans, allegedly the backbone of the Nazi movement. Instead, the most traumatized veterans living in the midst of this highly militarized society became some of the most ardent critics of a memory constructed in their name.

Criticism of the regime focused on one particular element of Nazi ideology – its idealized representation of the war experience as psychologically rejuvenating. War neurotics tried to wrest back control of the war from the Nazis and their myths of the front experience. In their minds, there was nothing unmanly or unpatriotic about breaking down in combat or depending on the state for health care and financial assistance. Though they did not represent organized resistance against the regime, their criticism of Nazi propaganda represented a layer of protest that undermined the regime's claims to representing the world view of veterans.

Long after hope for regaining pensions disappeared, mentally disabled veterans reinvented themselves. No longer passive pension seekers and neglected victims of mass violence, they imagined themselves as agents of change, retaking authority over the pension system and educating the state on the authentic war experience. Neurotic veterans appropriated the language that had made them pariahs since the war and 'asocials' in the Third Reich. Throwing accusations of 'hysteria' and 'sickness' at the regime, these men reveled in their newly acquired status as agitators. Though isolated and unthreatening, their voices increasingly reflected that of the mainstream as Hitler's war inflicted wider trauma throughout society. As the regime's security police uncovered, Nazi leaders were widely seen by 1942 as the real 'hysterics'. Though the leadership insulated itself from its own crimes and violence, the experiences of most Germans brought them closer to the perspective of victims of the original trauma of 1914–18, exactly what the regime hoped to avoid. When total war devastated civilians and soldiers indiscriminately, the decades-long struggle on the part of traumatized veterans to convince people at home that their psychological wounds were real came to a close.

Conclusion

To what degree was Germany's traumatic experience with World War I unique? How does this traumatic past contribute to our understanding of Hitler's rise to power? German soldiers did not experience trauma differently to other populations, but through the lens of defeat and revolution, war neurosis came to have more symbolic resonance for social and political groups scrambling to make sense of the legacy of the war. Germany's experience with war neurosis was exceptional in its intense politicization. This was largely due to the effects of defeat, which magnified the social and political significance of this otherwise medical phenomenon. In the wake of 1918, the war neurotic became a lightning rod for blame and resentment as postwar political groups mobilized to use the war to promote their visions for Germany's future. Depending on politics and experience, war neurotics were seen alternately as empathetic victims of total war's extreme brutality or symptoms of psychological weakness that led to the nation's collapse. These divisions would contribute significantly to German society's inability to come to terms with the war and with defeat. The haunting effects of the war, embodied in the image of mentally traumatized men clogging the streets and waging a never-ending war with the public, doctors, and welfare administrators, would also weaken Germany's first democracy.

The trauma of 1918 did not inevitably lead to the rise of Hitler in 1933. Reductionist attempts to explain Nazism as the symptom of a uniquely traumatized society are problematic, as they assume a hegemonic, heterogeneous traumatic experience that is historically not accurate. Instead, trauma was deeply fragmented along social and political lines. There was no singular 'German trauma'. Interestingly, this fragmentation is what made Germany's postwar experience with trauma exceptional, especially compared to the cases of Britain and France. In those countries, political groups engaged in the pension question and debates over whether shellshocked men were cowards or legitimate war victims. Further, postwar Britain and France saw relative consensus emerge over time in debates on the origins and significance of shell shock.[1] In Germany, it was the opposite case, as debates became more fiercely polarized.

The significance of war neurosis in Germany was exceptional in the degree to which class played such an intense role not only in defining the wound, but also in shaping postwar debates over memory and 'national psychosis'. Social class also affected the ways in which shell-shocked soldiers in neighboring belligerent nations were defined and treated.[2] But in Germany, the fragmentation of trauma and memory along class lines was more seismic, and it continued to intensify long after 1918. The war neurosis debate in Germany was appropriated by competing social and political groups to construct memory, decide welfare responsibilities, and apportion blame for defeat and revolution. In the politics of memory, social class was the primary prism through which the political left and right battled over who had caused the war, and who failed to come to terms with it. Conservatives dominated the wartime discourse on trauma as they accused working-class Germans of being most prone to 'neurosis' in the face of total war. However, after the war, working-class Germans organized a counteroffensive in the war neurosis debate, accusing 'hysterical' middle-class Germans of starting the war, denying its traumatic effects, and failing to heal the war's wounds. Traumatic neurosis was thus constructed as class-specific, with middle and working-class Germans using psychiatric discourse to construct their explanations for the deeper, psychological origins of Germany's experience with war, defeat and revolution.

The image of the war neurotic also problematized assumptions about masculinity in Germany. In contrast to the medical discourse on 'war hysteria', popularized debates over traumatic injuries elevated class over gender politics. Nevertheless, fears about a breakdown in masculinity were always latent. As a result of the First World War, ideas about masculinity became more closely aligned with the image of the soldier – steel nerved, psychologically hardened, and combat-ready.[3] The Nazis would try to capitalize on this image and the celebration of war as the nation's path to salvation. Men suffering from the psychological trauma of war were seen as a serious threat to this shift towards a more militarized concept of masculinity. *Kriegszitterer* ('war quiverers') shaking in the streets were visible, daily reminders that war did horrific damage to the male psyche and body. More widespread were forms of war neurosis that were less publicly visible, but just as debilitating for postwar society. Modern war left men emotional wrecks, sexually impotent, unable to function in postwar family life and work. Though conservative doctors and social critics tried to control and define war neurosis by defining these men as 'deviant', it was impossible to return to prewar constructions of social class, gender norms, and myths of the war experience. Indeed, ideas about masculinity became more closely intertwined with hypermilitarized visions of manhood. Nevertheless, there was widespread suspicion about this militarized paradigm of masculinity. After 1918, war could no longer be seen absolutely as the savior of the male psyche, even the psyche of middle-class, 'moral' and patriotic men.

The dominant narrative of men in war cultivated by the Nazis was only one narrative, and, most interestingly, it was critiqued from within the same groups the Nazis claimed as their main constituents. On one hand, pre-1914 views of 'hysterical men' as dangerous and deviant continued. Among conservatives, prewar perceptions of male hysteria persisted and even worsened, as the right radicalized constructions of these men as degenerate, unmanly pension neurotics partially responsible for defeat. However, this increasingly radical view, culminating in National Socialist conceptions of mentally ill veterans, was not necessarily the dominant perspective on war neurosis. Rather, it was a bitterly contested site where traumatized men and their representatives in left-wing political organizations attacked the Nazi myth of the war experience and its explanations for defeat. The largest disabled veterans' organization, the *Reichsbund*, supported by the Social Democratic Party (SPD), constructed mentally ill men as the ultimate sympathetic survivors of industrialized war. Civilians, the SPD pleaded, should identify with war neurotics as symbols of the psychological stress modern war inflicted on all Germans. Ultimately, the SPD's call for the recognition of war neurosis as a universal wound broke down into class warfare under the weight of pension politics and socioeconomic divisions. However, the political left's attempt to integrate war neurotics into the national community undercuts the notion of a 'master narrative' leading straight to 1933.

The failure of both the left and the right to develop a master narrative was also a symptom of deep divisions between those coming back from the trenches and their families at home. Interwar divisions between combat and home front survivors exacerbated these competing interpretations of trauma. As Karen Hagemann has observed, total war conflated the home and combat fronts, but both spheres were deeply divided and suspicious of each other.[4] Civilians stigmatized veterans, who were themselves deeply divided over this issue of losing their nerve, and their manliness, under fire. Meanwhile, veterans from different backgrounds and across the political spectrum cast blame on the home front, but developed starkly different narratives regarding when the home front broke down. Conservative groups focused on defeat and revolution as the primary trauma and blamed 'unmanly' shirkers and traditional 'enemies of the nation' who were allegedly coddled by democracy and welfare. In contrast, both the moderate and extreme left constructed the war itself and postwar failures to come to terms with its memory, or pay for its costs, as the principle trauma. The new, popularized psychiatric language infected with accusations of 'neurosis' and 'hysteria' reflected a deeper battle over who had authority to diagnose the nation's 'psychosis' – those who survived the trenches or those on the home front who suffered from the strains of economic and political crisis.

Debates over war neurosis raise interesting questions about who wields control over the mental and physical consequences of modern warfare. What psychological behaviors are 'normal', and what is 'abnormal'? The voices that have most often been overlooked in studies of traumatic wounds in Germany are those of the men who suffered these wounds themselves. Deborah Cohen has rightly argued that disabled veterans struggled to define themselves as subjects with a voice in the labyrinthine welfare system.[5] Another way in which veterans tried to exert agency was by trying to diagnose and control the memory of their own wounds. Veterans insisted that war neurosis was the 'normal' response to surviving trench warfare. Psychological 'disorders' were not a manifestation of inborn pathologies, or a lack of masculine character, but rather a natural response to extreme stress and violence. There was no shame in acknowledging the reality of psychological trauma. Just as traumatic as the trenches, veterans complained, was postwar society's failure to recognize these as normal symptoms of stress. The real 'neurosis' lay in civilians' refusal to take responsibility for the costs of the war.

In addition to trying wrest control from doctors over who defines war neurosis, veterans also tried to wrest control from political groups over the memory of the war. The Social Democratic Party was the most strident in defending traumatized veterans and trying to build a bridge between them and civilians, but they ultimately failed to win over either side. Though they claimed to empower mentally disabled veterans and make them active members of a movement to condemn modern industrial war as exploitive, social, political and economic conditions made it impossible to translate theories into reality. The SPD could not salvage pensions in the depths of the Great Depression, nor could they convince wider social and political groups to empathize with these men and reintegrate them into society through job training and social welfare. The Communist Party did not pretend to give 'war hysterics' their own voice. Though eager to use these men as evidence for their theories of class warfare and capitalist exploitation, the far left was ambivalent at best about 'hysterical men' in the militant revolutionary movement. In this environment, mentally disabled veterans, though excluded by right-wing veterans' associations during the Weimar years, were just as susceptible as their comrades to the Nazis' promise that it would make them the 'first citizens' of the nation.

The plight of war neurotics in Weimar's welfare system is a useful starting point for a history of welfare from below, but the voices of disabled veterans are both advantageous and frustrating for historians. On one hand, they are a treasure for anyone seeking grass roots perspectives from some of Germany's most traumatized and marginalized citizens during this age of total war. At the same time, these voices frequently remind us that historians must peel through the layers of perception that often governs historical subjects more than reality. In her comparative work on

Britain and Germany, Deborah Cohen has raised the interesting question concerning why Weimar's progressive welfare system, which actually provided more benefits to disabled veterans than their counterparts in Britain received, was perceived in such a negative light by returning soldiers. Cohen and other historians effectively point to over-bureauc-ratization and the Great Depression in fostering resentment towards Germany's new democracy. This contributed to the dissatisfaction of many disabled veterans, who felt objectified by the Weimar Republic, and helped fuel Hitler's growing support, especially in the wake of the depression.[6] But the war neurosis debate gives us a further glimpse into Weimar's dilemma, as the failure of Weimar's social policies is also a history of public perceptions of those on welfare. German society was unwilling to reintegrate traumatized veterans into the social fabric. Many considered welfare pathogenic and the culprit for 'pension neurosis', as Greg Eghigian has demonstrated.[7] At the same time, welfare recipients themselves were widely seen as a disease, destroying society from within. Disabled veterans brought home not only an economic burden, but also, it was feared, the psychopathologies caused by modern war. Uncontrollable violence, sexual disorders, apathy towards work and family – all of these characteristics associated with war neurotics were projected upon disabled veterans, and the population of welfare recipients as a whole. For those already opposed to welfare, war neurotics magnified what they perceived as a degenerate system exploited by degenerate outsiders. Despite traumatized veterans' claims to be 'normal', and their political mobilization behind groups that promised to defend them, the wider public never really accepted them into the fabric of postwar life. Social anxieties mixed with economic resentment ultimately sabotaged the Social Democrats' attempts to reintegrate these men via a progressive welfare system.

The perspectives of disabled veterans also give us a much more nuanced glimpse into the history of Nazi Germany. War victims, and in particular those defined as social outsiders within this group, are so often a group that is being acted upon and manipulated by political interest groups that it is easy to slip into an approach that neglects their agency. Mentally disabled war victims cannot be constructed as an organized group, and their actions do not suggest concerted resistance against the regime. Nevertheless, their letters to the Nazi party elite reflected a previously hidden layer of opposition within Nazi Germany. How deep this dissent, against the Nazi myth of the war experience, ran is difficult to discern, but the voices of traumatized men indicate that even within the Nazis' allegedly most faithful constituents, there was widespread suspicion against the regime. Though the Nazis were quite successful at coordinating doctors, the Labor Ministry, and the welfare bureaucracy at national and local levels, their success at winning the hearts and minds of war victims themselves was limited.

Studying veterans after 1933 sheds light on why so many survivors of the Great War hated the Weimar 'system'. For veterans, the belief that Hitler would restore respect, and of course pensions, was a longing for what they felt had been neglected by the Weimar government. However, it was not only pensions and respect for sacrifice that these men wanted. They wanted an acknowledgement that their wounds were real, and they believed that Hitler, as a wounded front veteran, would share their conviction that war was a brutalizing experience that inflicted genuine psychological wounds. Though this anticipation went against everything embodied in the Nazi myth of the war experience, the 'Hitler Myth' was a powerful bulwark against the reality of Nazi ideology. Disillusionment grew after the 1934 law made it clear that there would be no substantial change in the pension laws for physically disabled veterans, who went into revolt against what they saw as a welfare system that was actually worse than Weimar's, especially in economic terms. Mentally disabled veterans, completely cut from the pension rolls and denounced as pariahs, reveal that this discontent was not only rooted in economic resentment, but also had a deeper cultural component. Traumatized veterans became the vanguard of a quiet revolt, carried on in barrages of letters railing against doctors, administrators, and eventually party members themselves, and the Nazi myth of the war experience as a whole. Discontent was triggered by economic and political disillusionment, but it was articulated as a revolt against how the memory of the war was being reconstructed after 1933.

War neurotics became isolated yet crucial voices in ongoing debates over the memory of the war. The well-known rhetoric employed by the Nazis about 'comradeship' and 'sacrifice' was fervently contested by veterans who felt these terms had been distorted. Even men who claimed to be drawn to the National Socialist movement criticized the Nazis' vision of the national community as it pertained to memory, trauma and welfare for veterans. The Nazis envisioned 'comradeship' as the basis for a militarized society – with veterans entitled by the experience of combat to lead the nation – which would be organized into a racially-driven national community that excluded 'outsiders', including psychologically disabled men. In contrast, traumatized veterans saw 'comradeship' as the basis for an inclusive society where veterans promoted a spirit of sacrifice fostered in the trenches that they hoped would inspire civilians to come to terms with war's deeper horrors and the need to pay for its costs. In this vein, 'hysterical men' were not 'the other', but rather the core of the nation, as they embodied the authentic memory of Germany's shattering experience with the war. War neurotics saw themselves as integrated, normal members of the national community. They contested the Nazis' conception of masculinity as well as their myth of the war experience. Manliness, traumatized men asserted, was not determined by one's ability to meet the stress of combat with steel nerves. Rather, being 'manly' was rooted in ongoing battles to heal the psychological wounds of war. Traumatized veterans saw the Nazis as cowardly because they denied the reality of life in the trenches and deceived future generations into believing that war would somehow heal the nation. The communists appealed to relatively few disabled veterans, but their critique of the right for conspiring to cover up the reality of psychological trauma in order to prepare for another war held currency among wider groups, especially after 1933.

War neurotics' perspectives can help historians trace the unraveling of the 'Hitler Myth' from a previously overlooked angle. The ever-present propaganda depicting heroic males transcending the psychological and physical stress of war might suggest an anxiety on the part of the regime that this image had to be constantly reinforced, as few Germans actually believed that the front experience was healthy. Veterans felt they did not receive the 'Thanks of the Fatherland' from Weimar, and this contributed to alienation from the republic. But this disillusionment with the system also persisted into the Nazi years, when the regime's promise of respect quickly lost its luster. After 1933 this breakdown in support for the Nazis' memory of the war stemmed from both the continued pension cuts and the Nazis' sterilized memory of the war. War neurotics were at the forefront of growing dissatisfaction with the regime among physically and psychologically disabled veterans. Though the 'Hitler Myth' deteriorated most rapidly after the invasion of the Soviet Union and the civilian bombing in the last stages of the Second World War, the unraveling of this myth had begun much earlier for the so-called 'first citizens of the Reich'. By the mid-1930s, when disabled veterans realized that their welfare expectations were being compromised once again by finance administrators and the economics of militarization, protest against the Nazis reached fever pitch, expressed in an avalanche of letters to the regime. While some veterans continued to cling to the image of Hitler as their loyal comrade who empathized with traumatized victims of the Great War, most accused him of betraying the front soldier by denying any psychological wounds.

Throughout Germany's experience with total war, mentally traumatized men found themselves constructed as enemies of the national community and threats to the memory of the war. Nevertheless, this stigmatized group persisted in reminding German society of the deeply disturbing wounds inflicted by modern warfare. Though often denounced by those who feared them, the voices of traumatized men buried in archival files, often by bureaucracies at a loss as to how to categorize and deal with them, give us a glimpse of a hidden discourse of dissent against militarism and myths of war. The forgotten hysterical men of the Great War frequently relished their self-proclaimed roles as trouble-makers. Konrad D., in his interminable letters stuffed away in Labor Ministry files, characterized those accused of 'whining' as the real 'heroes' who fought against the Nazi regime's sterilized version of the war. He railed against that vision of war as an insidious form of violence against the memory of the front experience.[8] The writings of mentally disabled veterans attest to minds tortured by the trenches, with only tenuous grips on reality. But despite being ignored and suppressed, these victims of mass violence were prophetic in warning Germans of the dangers of worshiping the front experience and celebrating the alleged healing qualities of war.

Notes

Introduction

1 Bundesarchiv Berlin-Lichterfelde (BA Berlin), R3901/Film 37011. Konrad D. to RAM, 13 February 1930; see also his letter to RAM 9 October 1931, and the letter from the HVA Brandenburg-Pommern to the RAM, 31 May 1930.

2 BA Berlin, R3901/Film 37011. Konrad D. to RAM, 10 July 1929.

3 BA Berlin, R3901/Film 37011. Konrad D. to RAM, 21 July 1929.

4 BA Berlin, R3901/Film 37011. Report by Dr Bratz, hired by Konrad D., outlining D.'s case history, 25 July 1931.

5 BA Berlin, R3901/Film 37011. Konrad D. to RAM, 9 October 1931, see also attached doctor's reports.

6 BA Berlin, R3901/Film 37011. Konrad D. to Labor Minister Dr Stegerwald, 9 August 1931.

7 BA Berlin, R3901/Film 37011. Konrad D. to Labor Minister Franz Seldte, 12 March 1935. Attached to his cover letter is D.'s essay 'Das Echo – Kriegsopfer-Denkschrift zu dem neuen Ehrenrecht der deutschen Kriegsopfer'.

8 ibid.

9 Joachim Radkau, *Das Zeitalter der Nervosität – Deutschland zwischen Bismarck und Hitler* (München: Carl Hanser Verlag, 1998), 15.

10 Elaine Showalter, 'Rivers and Sassoon: The Inscription of Male Gender Anxieties', in Margaret Randolph Higonnet, *et al.* (eds), *Behind the Lines: Gender and the Two World Wars* (Yale University Press, 1987), 61–69. See also Jay Winter, 'Shell Shock and the Cultural History of the War', *Journal of Contemporary History* 35:1, January 2000, 7–11.

11 Doris Kaufmann, 'Science as Cultural Practice in the First World War and Weimar Germany', *Journal of Contemporary History* 34:1, January 1999, 125–26.

12 Ernst Röhm, 'Über Frontsoldaten', *Deutsche Kriegsopferversorgung*, Berlin, 2 Jahrg., Folge 4, January 1934, 5.

13 'Der erste und gewaltigste Film der deutschen Frontsoldaten und Kriegsopfer, "Stosstrupp 1917"', *Deutsche Kriegsopferversorgung*, Berlin, 2 Jahrg., Folge 4, January 1934, 5.

14 Erich Maria Remarque, *All Quiet on the Western Front* (New York: Little, Brown & Co., 1929), preface.

15 Wilhelm Keinau, 'Im Westen Skandal! Wir fordern Verbot!' *Der Stahlhelm*, Nr. 50, 14 December 1930.

16 'Protest und Aufruf – Schützt die Jugend vor gewissenlosen Kriegshtzern!'
   in *Reichsbund – Organ des Reichsbundes der Kriegsbeschädigten,*
   Kriegsteilnehmer und Kriegshinterbliebenen, Nr. 24, 24 December 1930,
   222.

17 Thomas Kühne, 'Gender Confusion and Gender Order in the German
   Military, 1918–1945', in Karen Hagemann and Stefanie Schüler-Springorum
   (eds), *Home/Front: The Military, War and Gender in Twentieth-Century*
   Germany (New York: Berg, 2002), 234. On constructions of 'comradeship'
   see Kühne's *Kameradschaft: Die Soldaten des nationalsozialistischen*
   Krieges und das 20. Jahrhundert (Göttingen: Vandenhoeck and Ruprecht,
   2006), 9–14.

18 Kühne, 'Gender Confusion', 233–34.

19 On the Nazis' intertwining of racial and social policy, and the regime's
   attacks on traditional welfare, see Michael Burleigh and Wolfgang
   Wippermann, *The Racial State – Germany 1933–1945* (Cambridge:
   Cambridge University Press, 1991), especially Chs 1 and 6.

20 Radkau, *Das Zeitalter der Nervosität*, 15.

21 Andreas Killen, *Berlin Electropolis – Shock, Nerves, and German*
   Modernity (Berkeley: University of California Press, 2005), 10.

22 Paul Lerner, *Hysterical Men – War, German Psychiatry, and the Politics of*
   Trauma in Germany, 1890–1930 (Ithaca: Cornell University Press, 2003),
   4–7.

23 See for example Detlev Peukert, *The Weimar Republic: The Crisis of*
   Classical Modernity (New York: Hill and Wang, 1989), 6–7 and Ch. 6.

24 Robert W. Whalen, *Bitter Wounds – German Victims of the Great War,*
   1914–1939 (Ithaca: Cornell University Press, 1984), see Chapters 10 and 11
   in particular. See also David F. Crew, *Germans on Welfare – From Weimar*
   to Hitler (New York: Oxford University Press, 1998), Ch. 8.

25 Michael Geyer, 'Ein Verbote des Wohlfahrtstaates – Die
   Kriegsopferversorgung in Frankreich, Deutschland und Grossbritannien
   nach dem Ersten Weltkrieg', *Geschichte und Gesellschaft* 9, 1983, 230–77;
   James M. Diehl, *The Thanks of the Fatherland* (Chapel Hill: University of
   North Carolina Press, 1993), see Ch. 1; Deborah Cohen, *The War Come*
   Home, Disabled Veterans in Britain and Germany, 1914–39 (Berkeley:
   University of California Press, 2000), Ch. 4.

26 David Crew, 'The Ambiguities of Modernity: Welfare and the German State
   from Wilhelm to Hitler', in Geoff Eley (ed.), *Society, Culture and the State*
   in Germany, 1870–1930 (Ann Arbor: University of Michigan Press, 1996),
   345–70.

27 Greg Eghigian, *Making Security Social – Disability, Insurance, and the*
   Birth of the Social Entitlement State in Germany (Ann Arbor: University of
   Michigan Press, 2000), 245–46.

28 Killen, *Berlin Electropolis*, 3.

29 Young-Sun Hong, *Welfare, Modernity, and the Weimar State, 1919–1933*
   (Princeton: Princeton University Press, 1998), 9–15.

30 Paul Lerner, 'An Economy of Memory: Psychiatrists, Veterans, and
   Traumatic Narratives in Weimar Germany', in Alon Confino and Peter
   Fritzsche (eds), *The Work of Memory – New Directions in the Study of*
   German Society and Culture (Urbana and Chicago: University of Illinois
   Press, 2002), 175. For a fascinating study on how shell shock is both a

constructed and experiential reality, see Allan Young's *The Harmony of Illusions: Inventing Post-Traumatic Stress Disorder* (Princeton: Princeton University Press, 1995), especially Chs 1 and 2. For further theories on the construction of traumatic memory, see Ruth Leys, *Trauma: A Genealogy* (Chicago: University of Chicago, 2000), 83–92.

31 Lerner, 'An Economy of Memory', 188.

32 Lerner, *Hysterical Men*, 250; Anton Kaes, *Shell Shock: Trauma and Film in Weimar Germany* (Princeton: Princeton University Press, forthcoming); Maria Tatar, *Lustmord – Sexual Murder in Weimar Germany* (Princeton: Princeton University Press, 1995).

33 James M. Diehl, *Paramilitary Politics in the Weimar Republic* (Bloomington: Indiana University Press, 1977), 22.

34 George L. Mosse, *Fallen Soldiers – Reshaping the Memory of the World Wars* (New York: Oxford UP, 1990), 7.

35 ibid.

36 Lerner, *Hysterical Men*, 18–21, 40–43.

37 Modris Eksteins, 'All Quiet on the Western Front and the Fate of a War', *Journal of Contemporary History* 15:2, April 1980, 345–47.

38 Lerner, *Hysterical Men*, 3. Lerner argues persuasively that we must place imperial and Weimar Germany's psychiatrists in the context of a rationalizing welfare state rather simply on the *Sonderweg* towards the horrendous crimes of the Third Reich against the mentally disabled.

39 Robert Gellately, *Backing Hitler – Consent and Coercion in Nazi Germany* (Oxford: Oxford University Press, 2001), 2.

40 Ian Kershaw, *The 'Hitler Myth'* (Oxford: Oxford University Press, 1987), 1–10.

Chapter 1: Healing the Nation's Nerves: Imperial Germany at War

1 Ernst Toller, *Eine Jugend in Deutschland* (Hamburg: Rowohlt, 1963), 70, quoted from Robert W. Whalen, *Bitter Wounds – German Victims of the Great War, 1914–1939*, 64.

2 Bernd Ulrich and Benjamin Ziemann (eds), *Frontalltag im Ersten Weltkrieg* (Frankfurt am Main: Fischer, 1994), 103.

3 Paul Weindling, *Health, Race and German Politics between National Unification and Nazism, 1870–1945* (Cambridge: Cambridge University Press, 1989), 106–18. On the electoral success of the SPD and its effect in mobilizing conservative groups, see Geoff Eley, *Reshaping the German Right* (New Haven: Yale University Press, 1980), 316–34.

4 See Wolfgang Kruse, 'Die Kriegsbegeisterung im Deutschen Reich zu Beginn des Ersten Weltkrieges: Entstehungszusammenhänge, grenzen und ideologische Strukturen', in Marcel van der Linden and Gottfried Mergner (eds), *Kriegsbegeisterung und mentale Kriegsvorbereitung: Interdisziplinäre Sudien* (Berlin: Dunker & Humblot, 1991); Modris Eksteins, *The Rites of Spring* (Boston: Houghton Mifflin, 1989), 90–94. For a convincing reappraisal of how widespread the 'spirit of 1914' actually was, see Jeffrey Verhey, *The Spirit of 1914: Militarism, Myth and Mobilization in Germany* (Cambridge: Cambridge University Press, 2000), 58–64.

5 See Roger Chickering, *Imperial Germany and the Great War, 1914–1918* (Cambridge: Cambridge University Press, 1998), 192–204.

6 Doris Kaufmann, 'Science as Cultural Practice in the First World War and Weimar Germany', *Journal of Contemporary History* 34:1, January 1999, 125–26; Franz Lemmens, 'Zur Entwicklung der Militärpsychologie in Deutschland zwischen 1870–1918', in Winau and Müller-Dietz (eds), *'Medizin für den Staat – Medizin für den Krieg': Aspekte zwischen 1914 und 1945* (Husum: Matthiesen, 1994), 41–42.

7 On debates over 'pension neurosis' in pre-1914 Germany, see Greg Eghigian, *Making Security Social*, 236–44.

8 Radkau, *Das Zeitalter der Nervosität*, 405.

9 On the conservatism and pro-war sentiment of *Kaiserreich* doctors, see Heinz-Peter Schmiedebach, 'Sozialdarwinismus, Biologismus, Pazifismus. Ärztestimmen zum Ersten Welkrieg', in Blecker and Schmiedebach (eds), *Medizin und Krieg: Von Dilemma der Heilberufe, 1865–1985* (Frankfurt am Main: Fischer, 1987), 93–121.

10 Geoff Eley, *Forging Democracy – The History of the Left in Europe, 1850–2000* (Oxford: Oxford University Press, 2002), see Ch. 7.

11 Weindling, *Health, Race and German Politics*, 80–89.

12 Otto Binswanger, *Die seelischen Wirkungen des Krieges* (Stuttgart und Berlin: Deutsche Verlags-Anstalt, 1914), 7.

13 ibid, 8.

14 ibid, 8–10.

15 Lerner, *Hysterical Men*, 32–45. Lerner provides an excellent overview of the competing psychiatric movements and their theories at the outbreak of the war.

16 See Reinhard Rürup, 'Der Geist von 1914 in Deutschland – Kriegsbegeisterung und Ideolisierung des Krieges im Ersten Weltkrieg', in Bernd Hüppauf (ed.), *Ansichten vom Krieg – Vergleichende Studien zum Ersten Weltkrieg in Literatur und Gesellschaft* (Königstein: Forum Academicum, 1984). On the persistence of these myths, see also Bernd Hüppauf, 'Schlachtenmythen und die Konstruction des "Neuen Menschen"', in G. Hirschfeld, G. Krumeich, and I. Renz (eds), *'Keiner fühlt sich hier mehr als Mensch …' Erlebnis und Wirkung des Ersten Weltkrieg* (Frankfurt am Main: Fischer, 1997), 53–103.

17 Binswanger, *Die seelischen Wirkungen des Krieges*, 13–16.

18 ibid, 21.

19 ibid, 15–23.

20 ibid, 27.

21 ibid, 30–39.

22 ibid, 23.

23 Ernst Schultze, *Die Mobilmachung der Seelen* (Bonn: A. Marcus & E. Webers Verlag, 1915), 12.

24 ibid.

25 ibid, 8. On the stigma attached to men who did not exert 'will' and bravery in combat, see Jose Brunner, 'Will, Desire and Experience: Etiology and Ideology in the German and Austrian Medical Discourse on War Neuroses, 1914–1922', *Transcultural Psychiatry* 37:3, 2000, 295–320.

26 ibid, 18–24.

27 BA Berlin, R8034/2765 (article title and precise date not decipherable in Reichspressearchiv file), *Vossische Zeitung*, March 1918.

28 F. Gonser, *Der Alkohol und der Krieg* (Berlin: Mäßigkeits-Verlag, 1915), 11.

29 ibid, 5–6.

30 ibid, 7.

31 ibid, 8.

32 W. Fuchs, Medizinalrat, '... *Weil wir nicht Kriegsbereit sind!' Eine psychologische Studie, gewidmet den deutschen Eltern, den deutschen Lehrern und der deutschen Jugend* (Berlin: Verlag C.A. Schwetschke und Sohn, 1914), 13.

33 ibid, 13–14.

34 ibid.

35 See Verhey, *The Spirit of 1914*, 173–78.

36 See George L. Mosse, 'Shell-Shock as a Social Disease', *Journal of Contemporary History* 35:1, January 2000, 101–8. On class and war neurosis in Britain, see Joanna Bourke's *Dismembering the Male* (Chicago: University of Chicago, 1996), 111–12.

37 Lerner, *Hysterical Men*, 4–6.

38 ibid, 37–39.

39 Whalen, *Bitter Wounds*, 63.

40 Lemmens, 'Zur Enticklung der Militärpsychologie in Deutschland zwischen 1870–1918', 41–42; Kaufmann, 'Science as Cultural Practice', 45–46.

41 Ulrich and Ziemann, *Frontalltag im Ersten Weltkrieg*, 103–4.

42 ibid.

43 For examples of symptoms in the British and French armies, see Ben Shephard, *A War of Nerves – Soldiers and Psychiatrists in the 20th Century* (Cambridge: Harvard University Press, 2000), 33–52. A classic example of shell-shock symptoms can be found in the cases of British officers Siegfried Sassoon and Wilfred Owen – see Elaine Showalter's 'Rivers and Sassoon: The Inscription of Male Gender Anxieties', 61–69.

44 Philipp Witkop (ed.), *German Students' War Letters*, translated by A.F. Wedd, foreword by Jay Winter (Philadelphia: University of Pennsylvania Press, 2002, originally published 1929). Jay Winter's foreward expands on the anthology's publication history and some of its biases and usefulness, v–xxiv.

45 See Paul Fussell, *The Great War and Modern Memory* (New York: Oxford University Press, 1975).

46 Witkop, *German Students' War Letters*, 300.

47 ibid, 325.

48 ibid, 280.

49 ibid, 281.

50 Bernd Ulrich, *Die Augenzeugen – Deutsche Feldpostbriefe in Kriegs- und Nachkriegszeit* (Essen: Klartext, 1997), 194–97.

51 ibid, 199.

52 Ulrich and Ziemann, *Frontalltag im Ersten Weltkrieg*, 103.

53 See Joanna Bourke, *An Intimate History of Killing – Face to Face Killing in 20th Century Warfare* (New York: Basic Books, 1999), see Chapters 1 and 2 for the competing memories of wartime brutalization.

54 Hermann Oppenheim, 'Der Krieg und die traumatischen Neurosen', *Berliner Klinische Wochenschrift* 52, 1915, 257–61. See also Lerner, *Hysterical Men*, 62–65. On early debates over symptoms of traumatic neurosis and industrial accidents before the war, see Ralph Harrington, 'The Railway Accident: Trains, Trauma, and Technological Crises in

19th Century Britain', in Mark Micale and Paul Lerner (eds), *Traumatic Pasts*, 31–56.

55 Quoted in Whalen, *Bitter Wounds*, 101–5.

56 ibid.

57 Quoted from Lerner, 'Hysterical Men: War, Neurosis, and German Mental Medicine, 1914–21', Dissertation: Columbia University, 1996, 116.

58 Eghigian, *Making Security Social*, 71.

59 See Paul Lerner's article, 'From Traumatic Neurosis to Male Hysteria: The Decline and Fall of Hermann Oppenheim, 1889–1919', in Mark Micale and Paul Lerner (eds), *Traumatic Pasts* (New York: Cambridge University Press, 2001), 140–71. This argument is also central to Lerner's *Hysterical Men*, see Ch. 3.

60 Lerner, 'From Traumatic Neurosis to Male Hysteria', 145.

61 K.J. Neumarker, 'Karl Bonhoeffer and the Concept of Symptomatic Psychoses', *History of Psychiatry* 12:46, 2001, 216–17.

62 Lerner, 'Hysterical Men', Dissertation, 134–39.

63 ibid.

64 Mosse, 'Shell Shock as a Social Disease', 101–8.

65 BA Berlin, R3901/Film 36069. 'Bädischer Heimatdank – Bericht über die Sitzung des Badischen Landesauschusses der Kriegsbeschädigtenfürsorge am Freitag, 26 Oktober 1917 im Ministerium des Innern in Karlsruhe' (Karlsruhe: Braunschen Hofbuchdruckerei, 1917), 40–41.

66 Alfred Hoche, 'Über Wesen und Tragweite der "Dienstbeschädigung" bei nervös und psychisch erkrankten Feldzugsteilnehmern', *Monatschrift für Psychiatrie und Neurologie* 39, 1916, 351–54.

67 BA Berlin, R3901/Film 36069. 'Bädischer Heimatdank', 41.

68 Lerner, *Hysterical Men*, 147. See also Hans-Georg Hofer, 'Nerven-Korrekturen: Ärzte, Soldaten, und die "Kriegsneurosen" im Ersten Weltkrieg,' *Zeitgeschichte* 27, 2000, 249–69.

69 On the history of psychotherapy and hypnosis in *Kaiserreich* Germany, see Hannah Decker's *Freud in Germany: Revolution and Reaction in Science* (New York: International Universities Press, 1977).

70 Lerner traces these debates in depth in *Hysterical Men*, Chapters 3 and 4.

71 ibid.

72 BA Berlin, R3901/Film 36069. 'Bädischer Heimatdank', 42–43.

73 Fritz Kaufmann, 'Die planmässige Heilung komplizierter psychogener Bewegungsstörungen bei Soldaten in einer Sitzung', *Münchener Medizinische Zeitschrift* 63, 30 May 1916, 802–4.

74 ibid, 803.

75 Quoted from Lerner's 'Hysterical Men', Dissertation, 185.

76 K. Weiler, 'Ein Jahr Kriegsneurotikerbehandlung im I. bayer. A.K.', *Münchener Medizinische Wochenschrift* 66, 1919, 402.

77 M. Lewandowsky, 'Über den Tod durch Sinusströme', *Deutsche Medizinische Wochenschrift* 43, 1917, 1169.

78 Kurt Mendel, 'Die Kaufmannsche Methode', *Neurologisches Zentralblatt* 36, 1917, 190.

79 Ulrich and Ziemann, *Frontalltag im Ersten Weltkrieg*, 106–9.

80 Robert Gaupp, *Nervenkranken des Krieges: Ihre Beurteilung und Behandlung* (Stuttgart: Evangelischer Presseverband, 1917), 16–18.

81 Lerner, *Hysterical Men*, 110.

82   BA Berlin. NS 5/239. 'Nervenkranke Kriegsbeschädigte', *Reichsbote Berlin*, 18 October 1918.

83   BA Berlin, R3901/Film 36069. 'Bädischer Heimatdank', 43–44.

84   Different representations of middle versus working class psychological disorders will be further developed in Chapter 2. This division of 'hysterical' working class soldiers versus 'exhausted' middle class officers also emerged in Britain. See Joanna Bourke's *Dismembering the Male – Male Bodies, Britain and the Great War* (Chicago: University of Chicago, 1996), 111–12.

85   BA Berlin, R3901/Film 36070. Reichsauschuss der Kriegsbeschädigten-Fürsorge. Sitzung 16 March 1918.

86   ibid.

87   BA Berlin. R3901/Film 36070. *Verhandlungen der Außerordentlichen Tagung der Deutschen Vereinigung für Krüppelfürsorge, 7. Februar 1916* (Leipzig: Verlag von Leopold Voß, 1916.) From a panel led by Stabsarzt Dr Werner Hartwich vom Reservelazaratt Paderborn, 64.

88   BA Berlin. R3901/Film 36070. *Verhandlungen*, from report made by Professor Kurt Goldstein, 'Über Übungsschulen für Hirnverletzte', 83.

89   ibid.

90   W. Poppelreuter, *Verhandlungen*, 84–88.

91   Professor Gutzmann, *Verhandlungen*, 91–92. Se also 'Die gewerbliche Berufsfürsorge für Kopfschüsse', *Zeitschrift für Krüppelfürsorge*, Nr. 6, June 1916.

92   Friedrich Schneider, 'Die Kölner Nervenstation für Kopfschüsse und ihre Bedeutung für die pädogogische Psychologie und Berufsberatung', *Kölnische Volkszeitung*, 18 August 1918.

93   Karl Wilmanns, 'Die Behandlung der Kranken mit funktionellen Neurosen im Bereich des XIV A.K', *Deutsche Medizinische Wochenschrift* 43, 1917, 427. See also, as quoted in Lerner's 'Hysterical Men', Dissertation, BA Berlin RAM, R3901/Film 36069, Karl Wilmanns, 'Bericht über die Sitzung des bad. Landesausschusses der Kriegsbeschädigtenfürsorge', 26 Oktober 1917.

94   BA Berlin, NS 5 VI/239. 'Ziele der Verwundetenfürsorge – Ein Beitrag zur Psychologie der Arbeit', *Die Hilfe*, 10 August 1916.

95   ibid.

96   Lerner, 'Hysterical Men', Dissertation, 259–69.

97   Whalen, *Bitter Wounds*, 64.

98   See essay by Bernd Ulrich, ' " ...als wenn nichts geschehen ware" – Anmerkungen zur Behandlung der Kriegsopfer während des Ersten Welkriegs', in Gerhard Hirschfeld, Gerd Krumeich and Irina Renz (eds), *'Keiner fühlt sich hier mehr als Mensch ...' – Erlebnis und Wirkung des Ersten Weltkriegs*, 150–53.

99   Quoted from David Clay Large, *Berlin* (New York: Basic Books, 2000), 139.

100 Hans-Ulrich Wehler, *The German Empire, 1871–1918*, translated by Kim Traynor (Leamington Spa: Berg Publishers, 1985), 105–13.

101 Kurt Walter Dix, *Psychologische Beobachtungen über die Eindrücke des Krieges auf Einzelne wie auf die Masse* (Langensalza: Hermann Beyer & Söhne, 1915), 25.

102 ibid, 8–9.

103 ibid, 26–28.
104 Felix Muche, *Wir müssen und werden siegen! Der Einfluß der Suggestion auf unser Nervensystem 2. Die Macht der Suggestion im Weltkriege* (Leipzig: Verlag von Oswald Mutze, 1916), 22.
105 ibid, 24.
106 ibid, 23.
107 Hans Schulze, *Starke Nerven*, predigt am 24 Juni 1917 (Stettin: Fischer & Schmitt, 1917), 1–7.
108 Elsa Hasse, *Der Große Krieg und die deutsche Seele – Bilder aus den Innenleben unseres Volkes* (München: Verlag Jos. Köselische Buchhandlung, 1917), 42–43.
109 ibid.
110 Federmann, *Der Krieg und die deutsche Volksseele* (Berlin: Verlag des Evangelischen Bundes, 1915), 3.
111 Karl Lindenberg, *Der deutschen Kriegers inneres Erlebnis* (Stuttgart: Druck und Verlag von Greiner & Pfeiffer, 1917), 7–8.
112 See Richard Bessel, *Germany after the First World War* (Oxford: Clarendon Press, 1993), 25–26.
113 Paul Haffner, Johannes Janssen, E. Thillen (eds), 'Planmäßiger Kampf gegen Würdelosigkeit im weiblichen Geschlecht', *Frankfurter Zeitgemäße Broschüre*, Band XXXV (Hamm: Breer & Thiemann, 1916), 1.
114 ibid, 3–6.
115 ibid, 6–8.
116 Alfred Hoche, *Krieg und Seelenleben* (Freiburg: Speyer & Laerner, Universit ätsbuchhandlung, 1915), 35.
117 ibid.
118 ibid, 28–29.
119 ibid, 32–33.
120 ibid, 35.
121 ibid, 8–10.
122 ibid, 19–20.
123 ibid, 21.
124 Roger Chickering, *The Great War and Urban Life in Germany* (Cambridge: Cambridge University Press, 2007), 534–35.
125 Hoche, *Krieg und Seelenleben*, 24–25.
126 Weindling, *Health, Race and German Politics*, 395–96.
127 BA Berlin, NS 5/239. 'Gewerkshaftliches-Arbeitgeber-Zeitung und Kriegsinv alidenfürsorge', *Vorwärts*, 15 December 1915.
128 BA Berlin, NS 5/239. 'Nachdenkliches zur Kriegsinvaliden-Fürsorge', *Vorwärts*, 27 July 1917.
129 ibid.
130 ibid.
131 James M. Diehl, 'German: Veterans' Politics under Three Flags', in Stephen Ward (ed.), *The War Generation – Veterans of the First World War* (Port Washington: Kennikat Press, 1975), 143–44.
132 F.L. Carsten, *War against War – British and German Radical Movements in the First World War* (Berkeley: University of California Press, 1982), see Chapters 7 and 8.
133 ibid.
134 Quoted from Lerner, *Hysterical Men*, 199.

135 ibid.
136 BA Berlin, R3901/Film 36069. Carl Schneider, *Das Kriegsbeschädigten-Problem – Zur Frage der Sonderorganisation der Kriegsbeschädigten* (Essen: Kray, 1918), 43–48.
137 Whalen, *Bitter Wounds*, 119–21.
138 Roger Chickering, *Imperial Germany and the Great War, 1914–1918*, see Ch. 5. See also Belinda Davis, *Home Fires Burning – Food, Politics and Everyday Life in Berlin* (Chapel Hill: University of North Carolina Press, 2000), 190–96.
139 Whalen, *Bitter Wounds*, 127.
140 Lerner, 'Hysterical Men', Dissertation, 359.
141 ibid, 365.
142 ibid, 363–64. On doctors' blame for the revolution placed on war neurotics, see also Peter Riedesser and Axel Verderber, *'Maschinengewehre hinter der Front': Zur Geschichte der deutschen Militärpsychiatrie* (Frankfurt: Fischer Taschenbuch Verlag, 1996), 80–90.
143 Eugen Kahn, 'Psychopathen als revolutionäre Führer', *Zeitschrift für die gesamte Neurologie und Psychiatrie* 52, 1919, 90–91. On antisemitic links between hysteria and Jews, see Sander Gilman's *The Jew's Body* (New York: Routledge, 1991).

Chapter 2: The War Neurotics Return Home: Psychologically Disabled Veterans and Postwar Society, 1918–1920

 1 Magnus Hirschfeld, *Sittengeschichte des Weltkrieges, Zweiter Band* (Leipzig: Verlag für Sexualwissenschaft Schneider & Co., 1930), 64.
 2 BA Berlin, R1501/11804. Prof. J.H. Schultz, University of Jena, 'Seelischen Krankenbehandlung', *Berliner Tageblatt*, 5 October 1921.
 3 For a study of the connections between Weimar Cinema and traumatic memory, see Anton Kaes, *Shell Shock: Film, Trauma and Weimar Germany* (Princeton: Princeton University Press, forthcoming).
 4 BA Berlin, R1501/11804. Letter from Dr Bonhoeffer, Direktor der Psychiatr. u. Nervenklinik der Universität Berlin, to Regierungsgesundheitsamtes Geh. Rat. Dr Bumm, 13 March 1922.
 5 BA Berlin, R1501/11804. Niederschrift, Vorsitzender Regierungsrat Dr Seeger, Oberprüfstelle Berlin to RMdI, 1 December 1924.
 6 Albrecht Mendelssohn-Bartholdy, *The War in German Society: The Testament of a Liberal* (New Haven: Yale University Press, 1937).
 7 See Richard Bessel, *Germany after the First World War* (Oxford: Clarendon Press, 1993), 223.
 8 On the 'stab-in-the-back' legend, see Wilhelm Deist, 'Der militärische Zusammenbruch des Kaiserreichs: Zur Realität der 'Dolchstosslegende', in Wilhelm Deist (ed.), *Militär, Staat und Gesellschaft—Studien zur preussisch-deutschen Militärgeschichte* (Munich: R. Oldenbourg, 1991), 211–33.
 9 Contemporary psychiatrists have identified 'secondary trauma' in studies of returning Vietnam veterans, victims of genocide and war, rape, incest and AIDS. Dr Jonathan Shay's study of returning Vietnam veterans, *Odysseus in America – Combat Trauma and the Trauma and the Trials of Homecoming* (New York: Scribner, 2002), makes comparisons across wars

and offers analysis of the different forms of secondary posttraumatic stress disorder. Secondary trauma is also explored in the context of decolonization movements in Marian Mesrobian MacCurdy's 'Truth, Trauma, and Justice in Gillion Slovo's *Every Secret Thing*', *Literature and Medicine* 19:1, Spring 2000, 115–32.

10 The classic work on this subject is Jürgen Kocka's *Klassengesellschaft im Krieg: Deutsche Sozialgeschichte 1914–1918* (Göttingen: University of Göttingen, 1973).

11 See George L. Mosse, 'Shell-shock as a Social Disease', *Journal of Contemporary History* 35:1, January 2000, 101–8.

12 Eberhard Kolb, *The Weimar Republic*, trans. by P.S. Falla (New York: Routledge, 1988), 5.

13 ibid, 5–17.

14 BA Berlin, R1501/14153. Letter from Bund für Irrenrecht und Irrenfürsorge, Berlin, signed by Schriftsteller Paul Elmer, to the Reichsregierung der deutschen Republik/Rat der Volksbeauftragen, Berlin, 18 November 1918. In addition to Elmer, the Bund was represented by W. Winsch, Arzt; Adolf Thiele, Schriftsteller, Dr R. Händel, Rechtsanwalt; Dr Bruno Isaac, Rechtsanwalt. See also *Die Irrenrechtsreform – Zeitschrift des Bundes für Irrenrecht und Irrenfürsorge* (Berlin, 1919).

15 BA Berlin, R1501/14153. Letter from Otto S. to Reichsministerium des Innern, 24 October 1919.

16 BA Berlin, R3901/36139. Report by Regierungsrat Dr Hartrodt at 21 June 1924 meeting of the Reichsversorgungsgericht. See also report here by court psychiatrist Dr Weber.

17 See Paul Lerner's 'Hysterical Men: War, Neurosis and German Mental Medicine, 1914–1921', Dissertation, 378. The actual number of war neurotics who returned home varies according to psychiatrists and their definitions of psychological injuries.

18 Kolb, Meizinalrat, Direktor der Heil- und Pflegeanstalt Erlangen, *Die nervös Kriegsbeschädigten vor Gericht und Strafvollzug – Nach einem Vortrag für Richter, Ärzte, Strafanstaltsbeamte* (München: J. Schweitzer-Verlag, 1919).

19 ibid, 7–8.

20 ibid, 44–46.

21 ibid, 59–63.

22 ibid, 21.

23 ibid, 21–30.

24 ibid, 34.

25 ibid, 35–37.

26 ibid, 35.

27 ibid, 77.

28 ibid, 36–37.

29 ibid, 75–77.

30 ibid, 75.

31 Erwin Loewy-Hattendorf, *Krieg, Revolution und Unfallneurosen* (Berlin: Verlagsbuchhandlung von Richard Schoetz, 1920), 21–22. See also Karl Pönitz, *Die klinische Neuorientierung zum Hysterieproblem unter Einflüsse der Kriegserfahrungen* (Berlin: Verlag von Julius Springer, 1921), 36–37.

32 *Beiträge zur Psychologie des Krieges*, published as a supplement for the

Zeitschrift für angewandte Psychologie (Leipzig: Verlag von Johann Ambrosius Barth, 1920). Includes essays by Paul Plaut, 'Psychographie des Kriegers'; Walter Ludwig, 'Beiträge zur Psychologie der Furcht im Kriege'; E. Schiche, 'Zur Psychologie der Todesahnungen'.

33 Bernd Ulrich, *Die Augenzeugen*, 294–95. Ulrich draws some of the background on Plaut from the latter's *Nachlass*.

34 Paul Plaut, 'Psychographie des Kriegers', *Beiträge zur Psychologie des Krieges* (Leipzig: Verlag von Johann Ambrosius Barth, 1920), 130.

35 Plaut, 'Psychographie des Kriegers', *Beiträge zur Psychologie des Krieges*, 110–18.

36 Ulrich analyzes the problems in Plaut's methodology in *Die Augenzeugen*, 298–301.

37 Plaut, 'Psychographie des Kriegers', *Beiträge zur Psychologie des Krieges*, 3–5.

38 ibid, 34, 46–47.

39 ibid, 18–19.

40 ibid.

41 Recently there has been some interesting scholarship on modern warfare's attraction for men. See, for example, Joanna Bourke's *An Intimate History of Killing – Face to Face Killing in 20th Century Warfare* (New York: Basic Books, 1999); Niall Ferguson, *The Pity of War* (New York: Basic Books, 1999), see Chapter 12. On the psychological underpinnings of fascism and male violence, see Klaus Theweleit's fascinating *Male Fantasies*, vols 1 and 2 (Minneapolis: University of Minnesota Press, 1987).

42 Plaut, 'Psychographie des Kriegers', *Beiträge zur Psychologie des Krieges*, 102–3.

43 ibid, 82.

44 ibid, 110–18.

45 ibid, 54–55. For more on sexual anxieties produced by the war, see Jason Crouthamel, 'Male Sexuality and Psychological Trauma: Soldiers and Sexual "Disorder" in World War I and Weimar Germany', *Journal of History of Sexuality* 17:1, January 2008 (Univ. of Texas Press), 60–84.

46 Lerner, *Hysterical Men*, 186–89.

47 For an in-depth narrative on this conference, see Lerner, *Hysterical Men*, 175–85.

48 Sigmund Freud, *Beyond the Pleasure Principle*, trans. by James Strachey (New York: Norton, 1961).

49 Sigmund Freud, *Civilization and its Discontents*, trans. by James Strachey (New York: Norton, 1961).

50 Wulffen had worked on sexual crimes before the war as well. See Erich Wulffen's *Der Sexualverbrecher: Ein Handbuch für Juristen, Verwaltungsbeamte und Ärzte* (Berlin: Langenscheidt, 1910). During the Weimar years, he published *Kriminalpsycholgie des Täters* (Berlin: Langenscheidt, 1926). On the social and cultural history of serial killers, see Maria Tatar's *Lustmord – Sexual Murder in Weimar Germany* (Princeton: Princeton University Press, 1995), 41–67.

51 Magnus Hirschfeld, *The Sexual History of the World War*, translation of the 1941 edition (Honolulu: University Press of the Pacific, 2006), 30.

52 Weindling, *Health, Race and German Politics*, 108.

53 Erwin J. Haeberle, 'Swastika, Pink Triangle and Yellow Star: The

Destruction of Sexology and the Persecution of Homosexuals in Nazi Germany', in Duberman, Vicinus and Chauncey, *Hidden from History: Reclaiming the Gay & Lesbian Past* (New York: Nal Books, 1989), 365–69.

54 In addition to the psychoanalytical perspectives discussed earlier, the environmental factors that stimulate violence and brutalize humans needs to be considered. Recent works that investigate the cycle of brutalization caused by war include Christopher Browning's classic work on the Holocaust, *Ordinary Men* (New York: Harper Perrenial, 1993). See also Barbara Ehrenreich's *Blood Rites – Origins and History of the Passions of War* (New York: Owl Books, 1997), for a fascinating look at the origins and brutalizing effects of violence and war.

55 Magnus Hirschfeld. *Sittengeschichte des Weltkrieges*, Zweiter Band (Leipzig: Verlag für Sexualwissenschaft, Schneider & Co., 1930), 506. For an interesting comparison, the progressive stages of posttraumatic stress disorder in Vietnam veterans have been expertly delineated by Jonathan Shay in *Achilles in Vietnam – Combat Trauma and the Undoing of Character* (New York, Maxwell Macmillan, 1994), see Chapter 11 in particular.

56 Hirschfeld, *Sittengeschichte*, 506.

57 ibid, 506–7. On the history of domestic violence in Weimar Germany, see Sace Elder, 'Murder, Denunciation and Policing in Weimar Berlin', *Journal of Contemporary History* 41:3, July 2006, 401–19.

58 Hirschfeld, *Sittengeschichte*, 480.

59 ibid, 483.

60 ibid, 483–85.

61 ibid, 485.

62 ibid, 485. Recently, psychiatrists studying posttraumatic stress disorder in US soldiers in the Iraq war have found that less than half of men and women who show signs of mental illness seek health care due to stigmatization and subsequent unwillingness to acknowledge the existence of problems. See Charles W. Hoge, *et al.*, 'Combat Duty in Iraq and Afghanistan, Mental Health Problems and Barriers to Care', *The New England Journal of Medicine* 351:1, 1 July 2004, 13–22.

63 Hirschfeld, *Sittengeschichte*, 485.

64 ibid.

65 ibid, 492. See also Hirschfeld's *Zwischen Zwei Katastrophen* (originally *Sittengeschichte der Nachkriegszeit*, Hanau am Main: Verlag Karl Schustek, 1966), 463–64.

66 Hirschfeld, *Sittengeschichte des Weltkrieges*, 60–61.

67 ibid, 496–503.

68 For an insightful analysis of Fritz Lang's *M* and its links to the traumatic memory of the war, see Anton Kaes, *M* (London: British Film Institute, 2000), esp. 26–53.

69 Hirschfeld, *Sittengeschicht des Weltkrieges*, 71–73.

70 ibid, 72.

71 ibid, 68–71.

72 P. Lißmann, *Die Wirkungen des Krieges auf das männliche Geschlechtsleben* (München: Verlag der Aerztlichen Rundschau Otto Gamelin, 1919), 22.

73 ibid, 8.
74 ibid, 6–7.
75 ibid, 9–11.
76 ibid, 13–22.
77 ibid, 28.
78 ibid.
79 See Bernd Widdig, *Culture and Inflation in Weimar Germany* (Berkeley: University of California Press, 2001), see especially Ch. 8 on gender and inflation.
80 For a study on the breakdown of Wilhelmian values in the wake of the war, see Ute Frevert, *Women in German History* (Oxford: Berg Publishers, 1990), Chs 13 and 14.
81 H.A. Preiß, *Geschlechtliche Grausamkeiten liebestoller Menschen* (Frankfurt a.M: Süddeutsche Verlagsanstalt, 1921), 6.
82 ibid, 8–9.
83 ibid, 33–34.
84 ibid, 41–43.
85 On the effects of shortages on the Berlin home front, see Belinda J. Davis, *Food, Politics and Everyday Life in World War I Berlin* (Chapel Hill: University of North Carolina Press, 2000). For an interesting comparison on the experience of British women at home, see Angela Woollacott's, *On Her Their Lives Depend – Munitions Workers in the Great War* (Berkeley: University of California Press, 1994). For an interesting look at literary representations of trauma on the home front, see Tiffany Joseph's '"Non-Combatant's Shell-Shock": Trauma and Gender in F. Scott Fitzgerald's *Tender is the Night*', *NWSA Journal* 15:3, Fall 2003, 64–81.
86 Frevert points out that the number of women who actually gained economic independence had not radically changed since pre-1914, but the image of the 'new woman' was most powerful as an image that mobilized different sociopolitical groups. See *Women in German History* (Oxford: Berg, 1990), 176–77.
87 Preiß, *Geschlechtliche Grausamkeiten liebestoller Menschen*, 46.
88 Hans-Georg Baumgarth, *Das Geschlechtsleben im Kriege – Eine Rechtfertigung für viele Unglückliche* (Berlin: Rosen-Verlag, 1920).
89 ibid, 47.
90 ibid, 10–11.
91 ibid, 47.
92 ibid, 46–47.
93 Young-Rißmann. 'Der verlorene Krieg und die Sittlichkeitsfrage, Als Vortrag von Frau Young-Rißmann gehalten zu Freiburg i.B. am 30 September 1923 zur Tagung des Weißen Kreuzes' (Dinglingen: St. Johannes Druckerei, 1930), 1–2.
94 ibid.
95 *Der Stahlhelm*, 'Die Pflicht des Frontsoldaten', 1. Beilage, 14 August 1927, 5–8.
96 Eugen Neter, 'Die seelische Zusammenbruch der deutschen Kampffront', *Süddeutsche Monatshefte*. München. Heft 10, 22. Jahrg., July 1925, 45–46.
97 ibid, 1–2.
98 ibid, 39.
99 ibid, 9.

100 ibid, 16.

101 ibid.

102 ibid, 2–6.

103 Wilhelm Deist, 'Verdeckter Militärstreik im Kriegsjahr 1918?' in Wolfram Wette (ed.), *Der Krieg des kleinen Mannes: Eine Militärgeschichte von unten* (Munich: Piper, 1992), 146–66.

104 Roger Chickering, *Imperial Germany and the Great War, 1914–1918* (Cambridge: Cambridge University Press, 1998), 189–90.

105 See Heinrich August Winkler, *Von Revolution zur Stabilisierung: Arbeiter und Arbeiterbewegung in der Weimarer Republik 1918 bis 1924* (Berlin: Verlag J.H. W. Dietz, 1984), 100.

106 Neter, 'Die seelische Zusammenbruch der deutschen Kampffront', 44.

107 ibid, 44–45.

108 Hans Schlottau, 'Kriegsfurioso – Visionen eines Verwundeten', Erste Flugschrift, Friedensbund der Kriegsteilnehmer und Friedensfreund, Vorwort, Hermann Klamfoth (Hamburg: Pionier-Verlag, Carl Thinius, 1920), 3.

109 ibid.

110 ibid, 6–13.

111 The portrayal of the front experience as psychologically purifying runs through the discourse of the far right. See for example Hitler's speech at the September 1935 Nuremberg Party rally, translated by Norman H. Baynes in *The Speeches of Adolf Hitler*, vol. I (Oxford: Oxford University Press, 1942), 560.

112 Hans Simons, 'Kriegsfeier und Friedenskampf', *Frankfurter Zeitung*, Nr. 568, 1 August 1924, excerpted in B. Ulrich and B. Ziemann's *Krieg im Frieden – Die umkämpfte Erinnerung an den Ersten Weltkrieg* (Frankfurt am Main: Fischer, 1997), 170.

113 Rudolf Müller, *Ketten – Opfer der Inneren Front* (Leipzig: Anzengruber-Verlag Brüder Suschitzky, 1920).

114 ibid.

115 Alma Würth, 'Warum ist der Krieg – modern?' *Reichsbund. Organ des Reichsbundes der Kriegsbeschädigten, Kriegsteilnehmer und Kriegerhinterbliebenen*, Jahrgang 13, Nr. 19, 10 October 1930. Excerpted from Ulrich and Ziemann, *Krieg im Frieden*, 151.

116 ibid.

117 ibid.

118 James M. Diehl, *Paramilitary Politics in Weimar Germany*, 219. On *Der Stahlhelm* in particular, see Volker Berghahn's *Der Stahlhelm, Bund der Frontsoldaten, 1918–35* (Düsseldorf: Droste, 1966).

119 Ernst Jünger, *The Storm of Steel – From the Diary of a German Storm-Troop Officer on the Western Front* (New York: Howard Fertig, 1996), 255.

120 See also Jünger's *Der Krieg als innere Erlebnis* (Hamburg: E.S. Mittler & Sohn Verlag, 1922).

121 On constructions of masculinity in flyers' literature, see Stefanie Schüler-Springorum, 'Flying and Killing – Military Masculinity in German Pilot Literature, 1914–1939' in Karen Hagemann and Stefanie Schüler-Springorum (eds), *Home/Front – The Military, War and Gender in Twentieth Century Germany* (Oxford: Berg, 2002), 205–32. See also

Peter Fritzsche's *A Nation of Flyers: German Aviation and the Popular Imagination* (Cambridge: Cambridge University Press, 1992).

122 On the parades and rituals that overtook Berlin with the return of von Richthofen's remains from France in 1925, see Whalen, *Bitter Wounds*, 'The Return of the Red Baron', Ch. 1.

123 Suzanne Hayes Fischer, *Mother of Eagles – The War Diary of Baroness von Richthofen* (Schiffer Military History, 2001), 157.

124 ibid.

125 Manfred von Richthofen, *Der Rote Kampfflieger*, translated as *The Red Baron* by Peter Kilduff (San Diego: Aero Publishers, Inc., 1969), 119–20.

126 E. Weniger, 'Das Bild des Krieges: Erlebnis, Erinnerung, Überlieferung', in *Die Erziehung – Monatschrift für den Zusammenhang von Kultur und Erziehung in Wissenschaft und Leben*, 5, 1929, Heft 1, 1–21. Excerpted from Ulrich and Ziemann, *Krieg im Frieden*, 163. For an interesting study of soldiers' narratives that refreshingly avoids trying to place them in strict pro- or antiwar categories, see Ann P. Linder, *Princes of the Trenches – Narrating the German Experience of the First World War* (Columbia: Camden House, 1996).

Chapter 3: Neurosis and the Welfare State: The Rise and Fall of the National Pension Law of 1920

1 Erich Maria Remarque, *The Road Back*, translated by A.W. Wheen (Boston: Little, Brown and Company, 1931), 213.

2 BA Berlin, R3901/Film 36137. DVP Düsseldorf, Generalsekretär Friedrich Galebow to Reichswehrminister, 3 January 1920.

3 ibid.

4 Detlev Peukert, *The Weimar Republic*, 129.

5 Whalen, *Bitter Wounds*, see especially chapters 10–12.

6 ibid, 131.

7 BA Berlin, R8034 II/2326. 'Eindrücke aus Berliner Lazaretten', by Willy Meyer, *Berliner Tageblatt*. Nr. 458, 29 September 1920.

8 Ernst Friedrich, *Krieg dem Kriege!* Berlin, 1924.

9 BA Berlin, R1501/9403. 'Gesundheitliche Schäden der Kriegs- und Nachkriegszeit', Director Czerny of University Kinderklinik to Interior Ministry, 24 March 1921. Reports on the particularly harmful effects of the blockade, and its creation of a generation of 'geisteschwache Kinder', whose development was curtailed by undernourishment. The *Frankfurter Zeitung* also filled its front pages with similar stories, e.g. 'Berliner Kinder – Ein Kapitel des deutschen Elends', 30 January 1921. Such reports were used across the political spectrum to argue against the Allies' continued blockade during the presentation of the Versailles Treaty.

10 Whalen, *Bitter Wounds*, 132.

11 BA Berlin, R8034 II/2330. For popular press accounts, see 'Straßendemonstration der Kriegsbeschädigten-Rundgebund des Internationalen Bundes der Kriegsbeschädigten', *Tägliche Rundschau*, Nr. 389, 11 August 1919. In *The Road Back*, his sequel to *All Quiet on the Western Front*, Remarque describes 'shivering' war neurotics standing out in the columns of disabled veterans at one of these demonstrations, 269.

12 Whalen, *Bitter Wounds*, 132–33. See also David Crew, 'The Ambiguities

of Modernity: Welfare and the German State from Wilhelm to Hitler', in Geoff Eley (ed.), *Society, Culture and the State in Germany* (Ann Arbor: University of Michigan Press, 1996), 345–70.

13 Peukert, *The Weimar Republic*, 130–32.

14 Peukert, *The Weimar Republic*, 132. See also Young-Sun Hong, 'World War I and the German Welfare State: Gender, Religion and the Paradoxes of Modernity', in Geoff Eley (ed.), *Society and Culture and the State in Germany, 1870–1930*, 345–70.

15 Whalen, *Bitter Wounds*, 134.

16 ibid, 134–36. See also James M. Diehl, *The Thanks of the Fatherland* (Chapel Hill: University of North Carolina Press, 1993), see Ch. 1; also Michael Geyer, 'Ein Verbote des Wohlfahrtstaates – Die Kriegsopferversorgung in Frankreich, Deutschland und Grossbritannien nach dem Ersten Weltkrieg'. *Geschichte und Gesellschaft 9*, 1983, 223–77.

17 Whalen, *Bitter Wounds*, 137–38.

18 Paul Lerner, 'Hysterical Men: War, Neurosis and German Mental Medicine, 1914–1921', Dissertation, 389. The medical guidelines provided by the state that Lerner refers to are found in 'Anhaltspunkte für die militärärztliche Beurteilung der Frage der Dienstbeschädigung oder Kriegsdienstbeschädigung bei den häufigen psychischen und nervösen Erkrankungen der Heeresangehörigen. Auf Grund von Beratungen des Wissenschaftlichen Senats bei der Kaiser Wilhelms-Akademie', 1–2.

19 BA Berlin, R3901/Film 36206. Verfassungsgebende Preußische Landesversammlung, Förmliche Anfrage der Abgeordneten Dr Beyer (Westpreußen) und Genossen, 28 March 1919.

20 ibid.

21 Franz Schweyer, Ministerialdirektor im Reichsarbeitsministerium. *Die Ansprüche der Kriegsbeschädigten und Kriegshinterbliebenen nach dem neuen Reichsversorgungsgesetz* (Berlin: Carl Heymanns Verlag, 1920), 1.

22 ibid, 18.

23 ibid, 18–19.

24 ibid, 3.

25 ibid, 3–4.

26 Karl Ernst Hartmann, *Lehrbuch der Kriegsbeschädigten- und Kriegerhinterbliebenen-Fürsorge mit besonderer Berücksichtigung der neuen sozialpolitischen Maßnahmen der Reichsregierung* (Kreisfürsorgestelle Minden im Westfalen: Selbstverlag des Verfassers, 1919), 32–33.

27 ibid.

28 ibid, 49.

29 ibid, 49–50. A fascinating history of work and German identity is Joan Campbell's *Joy in Work, German Work – The National Debate, 1800–1945* (Princeton: Princeton University Press, 1989), see especially Ch. IX.

30 Hartmann, *Lehrbuch*, 49–50.

31 ibid, 51–52.

32 Bayer. Hauptstaatsarchiv, Abteilung IV, Kriegsarchiv, Stv. Gen. Kdo I. Ak 159. Report by Major Hans Kropf to Kommandatur der Haupt- und Residenzstadt München, Nr. 14132, gez. Schacky, 9 September 1918.

33 Bayer. Hauptstaatsarchiv, Abteilung IV, Kriegsarchiv, Stv. Gen. Kdo I. Ak 159. Report by Sanitätsamt I.A.K. Nr. 62588 to the Kommandatur der Haupt- und Residenzstadt München, 6 September 1918.

34   BA Berlin, R3901/Film 36137. Polizeipräsident Richter to the RMdI and
     RAM, Berlin, 24 July 1922.
35   BA Berlin, R3901/Film 36137. 'Eine Massenepidemie geheilt', *Deutsche
     Tageszeitung*, December 1919 (day of issue not noted in file).
36   ibid.
37   ibid.
38   'Über Berufsberatung und Berufswechsel'. *Wesfälische Kriegsfürsorge
     – Amtliche Mitteilungen der Hauptfürsorgestelle für Kriegsbeschädigte
     und Kriegshinterbliebene der Provinz Westfalen*, 20 April 1920, Nr. 8.
39   J. Draeseke and O. Herms, *Die Hilfschule im Dienste der
     Kopfschussverletzten – Beobachtungen in der vom hamburgischen
     Landesausschuß für Kriegsbeschädigte eingerichteten Schule für
     gehirnverletzte Krieger* (Berlin: Vossische Buchhandlung Verlag, 1917),
     1–3.
40   ibid, 22–29.
41   'Berufsberatung der Kriegsbeschädigten', *Westfälische Kriegsfürsorge
     – Amtliche Mitteilungen der Hauptfürsorgestelle für Kriegsbeschädigte
     und Kriegshinterbliebene der Provinz Westfalen*, by Berufsberater,
     Oberstadtsekretär Becker, Gelsenkirchen, 1 June 1920.
42   ibid.
43   ibid.
44   ibid.
45   Stefan Berger, *Social Democracy and the Working Class in Nineteenth and
     Twentieth Century Germany* (London: Longman, 2000), 127–28.
46   Bessel *Germany After the First World War*, 146–47.
47   BA Berlin, R3901/Film 35419. HVA Stettin to RAM, 15 February 1921.
48   BA Berlin, R3901/Film 36091. Invaliden-Handwerker-Abteilung
     Reichsbekleidungs-Amtes München to Ministerium für soziale Fürsorge,
     signed Püppl, Major a. D und Leider, Zacherl, Betriebsrat, 9 March 1921.
49   BA Berlin, R3901/Film 36090. Finanzamt II Hannover, Zur
     Entlassung kommenden Schwerkriegsbeschädigten to RAM, signed by
     Obersteuerinspektor, 3 February 1921.
50   BA Berlin, R3901/Film 36090. Lauenberg Reichsbauamt to
     Reichsschatzminister, 16 February 1921, sent on to RAM, 1 March 1921.
51   BA Berlin, R3901/36090. Reichsarbeitsministerium Abschrift – Einstellung
     von Kriegsbeschädigten, 19 January 1920. The Labor Ministry categorized
     two types of jobs: 'Im mittleren Dienst', which included 'Kanzlisten,
     technische Büroassistenten', and general service-type jobs, and jobs for
     'war invalid officers', which included Betriebsingenieure, Vorsteher,
     Obersekretär'.
52   BA Berlin, R3901/Film 36091. Der Magistratskommissar für die Kriegsbesc
     hädigtenfürsorge to RAM, 5 October 1920.
53   Friedrich Weinhausen, Mitglied der Nationalversammlung, 'Die
     Kriegsbeschädigten und der Wiederaufbau'. *Weimarische Zeitung*, Nr. 232,
     25 August 1919.
54   On women in white-collar occupations in the Weimar Republic, see Ute
     Frevert's *Women in German History – From Bourgeois Emancipation to
     Sexual Liberation*, translated by Stuart McKinnon-Evans. Oxford: Berg,
     1988, 178–85. On the changing meaning of work for women and its effects
     on social and political identity, see Young-Sun Hong, 'Gender, Citizenship

and the Welfare State: Social Work and the Politics of Femininity in the Weimar Republic', *Central European History* 30:1, 1997, 1–24.

55 BA Berlin, R3901/Film 36090. Reichsarbeitsministerium Abschrift – Einstellung von Kriegsbechädigten, 19 January 1920.

56 ibid.

57 BA Berlin, R3901/Film 36092. Hauptfürsorgestelle der Kriegsbeschädigtefür sorge in der Provinz Sachsen, to RAM, 28 May 1921.

58 ibid.

59 BA Berlin, R3901/Film 36090. Der Reichsminister an die Hauptfürsorgestelle für Kriegsbeschädigten und Kriegerhinterbliebenen Königsberg, 8 May 1920.

60 BA Berlin, R3901/Film 36090. 'Freiheit – Der Dank des Vaterlandes', 11 September 1920. This letter was part of a list of demands sent by the Einheitsverband der Kriegsbeschädigten.

61 BA Berlin, R3901/Film 36090. Bund deutscher Kriegsbeschädigter, Sitz Hamburg to the RAM, 5 May 1920.

62 BA Berlin, R3901/Film 36092. Letter from Hauptwerk-Amt Königsberg, Zweigstelle Allenstein to the Personalberichterstatter für Schwerbeschädigtenfragen beim Reichsarbeitsministerium, 28 January 1922.

63 ibid.

64 ibid.

65 BA Berlin, R3901/Film 36093. Report by Landeshauptmann, Hauptfürsorge für Kriegsbeschädigte und Kriegerhinterbliebene in Regierungsbezirk Kassel to RAM, 11 March 1925.

66 BA Berlin, R3901/Film 36093. Report by Landeshauptmann, Hauptfürsorge für Kriegsbeschädigte und Kriegerhinterbliebene in Regierungsbezirk Kassel to RAM, 11 March 1925.

67 Alfred C. Mierzejewski, *The Most Valuable Asset of the Reich – A History of the German National Railway, vol. 1, 1920–1932* (Chapel Hill: University of North Carolina Press, 1999), 171–72.

68 BA Berlin, R3901/Film 36091. Der Magistratskommisser für den Kriegsbesc hädigtenfürsorge to RAM, 5 October 1920.

69 BA Berlin, R3901/Film 36092. Reichsbanknebenstelle Landshut to RAM, 2 February 1921.

70 BA Berlin, R3901/Film 36092. Reichsbank-Direktorium Berlin to Hauptfürsorgestelle Breslau, 9 February 1921.

71 BA Berlin, R3901/Film 36092. Reichsbank-Direktorium Berlin to Reichsarbeitsminister, 3 May 1921.

72 ibid.

73 ibid.

74 ibid.

75 BA Berlin, R3901/Film 36092. Hauptfürsorgestelle der Kriegsbeschädigtenf ürsorge in der Provinz Sachsen, to RAM, 28 May 1921.

76 ibid.

77 BA Berlin, R3901/Film 36092. Hauptfürsorgestelle der Stadt-Berlin für Kriegsbeschädigte un Kriegshinterbliebenen, 25 October 1921.

78 ibid. See also BA Berlin, R3901/Film 36091, Reichsbankdirektorium to Reichsbankanstalten, 30 June 1921. Here bank administrators argue that the precise, high pressure task of counting money was impossible for war neurotics as well as men with severe physical disabilities.

79 ibid.
80 BA Berlin, R3901/Film 36092. Hauptfürsorgestelle der Stadt-Berlin für Kriegsbeschädigte und Kriegshinterbliebenen, to RAM, 4 June 1921.
81 BA Berlin, R3901/Film 36093. Report on Berlin Postamt War Disabled Re-employment Policy, signed by Zanirum, Berlin Hauptfürsorgestelle representative for disabled veterans, 10 September 1923.
82 ibid. Neumann's comments are included in the Zanirum report.
83 ibid.
84 ibid.
85 ibid.
86 ibid.
87 BA Berlin, R3901/Film 36093. Postal administration report to RAM on disabled workers, 14 December 1923.
88 ibid.
89 BA Berlin, R3901/Film 35414. Vertragsangestellter Willy N. to RAM, 14 December 1923.
90 BA Berlin, R3901/Film 36092. Minister des Innern Freund to RAM, 16 April 1923.
91 State ministries were unenthusiastic about implementing the quota laws in their own work environments. See BA Berlin, R3901/Film 36090. Reichsministerium für Soziale Fürsorge an Staatsministerium des Äußern, 30 August 1920.
92 BA Berlin, R3901/Film 36089. Der Präsident der Reichsarbeitsverwaltung to the RAM, 13 February 1925. According to these statistics, unemployment rates in Hamburg between 1924–25 fluctuated from 5% to 11.8% Disabled war veterans never rose above 3.8% of the unemployment population for that year.
93 'Entscheidungen des Bayerischen Landes-Versorgungsgerichts', *Versorgung-Fürsorge-Zeitung*, Nr. 1, 16 January 1927.
94 ibid.
95 Carlo von Kügelgen, 'Nicht Krüppel – Sieger!' *Versorgung-Fürsorge-Zeitung*, Nr. 1, 16 January 1927.
96 Alfred Hoche, 'Geisteskrankheit und Kultur'. *Aus der Werkstatt*. Münich, 1935, 16, quoted from Paul Lerner, 'Psychiatry and Casualties of War in Germany, 1914–1918', *Journal of Contemporary History* 35:1, January 2000, 15.
97 For an interesting argument on officers creating the 'stab-in-the-back' legend to cover up their own attempts to escape injury in the chaotic last weeks of the war, see Bessel, *Germany after the First World War*, 87–88.
98 Dr Gau, *Kriegs-Invaliden-Heime* (Volmarkstein i.W.: Johanna-Belenen-Heim, 1920). According to Dr Gau, 146 severely disabled veterans applied for care at the home. These included 68 physically disabled (amputees, external wounds), 36 mentally disabled, 3 epileptics, 14 tuberculosis victims, 6 with various internal disorders, 18 blind, and 2 others. Of the 36 mentally disabled applicants, 28 were accepted and seven were listed as 'doubtful' potential patients. Dr Gau also lists another 26 cases reviewed that the clinic did not decide on. Statistics for disabled veterans were similar in proportion of accepted to rejected cases.
99 ibid.
100 ibid.

101 ibid.
102 BA Berlin, R3901/Film 35825. Nationalverband Deutscher Offiziere to RAM, 18 April 1922.
103 BA Berlin, R3901/Film 35825. Reichswehrminister (signature illegible) to RAM 14 April 1920.
104 BA Berlin, R3901/Film 35825. HVA Nürnberg to RAM, 8 September 1922.
105 BA Berlin, R3901/Film 35825. Ernst S. to HVA Berlin, 5 February 1922.
106 BA Berlin, R3901/Film 35825. Ärztliches Zeugnis [signature illegible] regarding Ernst S., 1 March 1922.
107 BA Berlin, R3901/Film 35825. RAM to HVA Berlin, 12 June 1922.
108 BA Berlin, R3901/Film 35826. VA Berlin to RAM, 12 August 1924.
109 BA Berlin, R3901/Film 35826. RAM to VA Berlin, 14 September 1924.
110 BA Berlin, R3901/Film 35826. HVA Berlin to RAM, 20 August 1925. While the veterans' health care administration was ejecting war neurotics from Invalidenhäuser, veterans suffering from organic injuries to the central nervous system were given continued care in special facilities designed for chronically disabled veterans. See also Hauptversorgungsamt Berlin, 16 March 1926 letter, signed Ober Reg. Rat Dr Caesar to RAM, concerning disabled veteran Hoffmann.
111 BA Berlin, R3901/Film 35826. Gerichtsarzt des Versorgungsgerichts Berlin to RAM, 15 December 1924.
112 BA Berlin, R3901/Film 35826. Frau Dr Genthe to HVA Berlin, 18 February 1926.
113 BA Berlin, R3901/Film 35826. Katherine Otto to HVA Berlin, 21 February 1926.
114 BA Berlin, R3901/Film 35826. HVA Berlin to RAM, 24 April 1926.
115 BA Berlin, R3901/Film 35826. RAM to Reichstagsabgeordneten Roßmann, 12 March 1926.
116 BA Berlin, R3901/Film 36028. Karl U. to the Bund der Kriegsbeschädigten und Hinterbliebenen, Ortsgruppe Karlsruhe, 18 October 1924.
117 ibid.
118 BA Berlin, R3901/Film 35826. Karl U. to President von Hindenburg, 22 June 1926.
119 ibid.
120 BA Berlin, R3901/Film 35826. RAM to Karl U., 13 November 1926.
121 See Diehl, The Thanks of the Fatherland, 18–30.
122 BA Berlin, R3901/Film 36027. August F. to RAM, 26 October 1921.
123 ibid.
124 BA Berlin, R3901/Film 36027. Alex E. to RAM, 11 August 1921.
125 ibid.
126 BA Berlin, R3901/Film 36028. Regierungs-Medizinalrat Dr Moll to VA Wiesbaden to RAM, 24 September 1924.
127 ibid.
128 ibid.
129 BA Berlin, R3901/Film 36028. Landes-Inspektor Watzenberg to HVA Cassel, 25 February 1925. See also in same file Watzenberg's letter to RAM, also dated 25 February 1925.
130 ibid.
131 BA Berlin, R3901/Film 36028. Carl L. to RAM, 10 August 1925. See also L.'s 10 October 1925 letter.

132 BA Berlin, R3901/Film 36028. RAM to Carl L., April 1926.
133 BA Berlin, R3901/Film 36028. Carl L. to RAM, 8 April 1926.
134 ibid.
135 BA Berlin, R3901/Film 36028. Hauptversorgungsamt Cassel, Ob. Reg. Med. Rat Dr Krummacher to RAM, 1 January 1926. See Dr Moll's attached report, 19 November 1926.
136 BA Berlin, R3901/Film 36028. RAM Ministerialrat Dr Scholtze to Reichsbund der Kriegsbeschaedigten, 23 February 1923.
137 BA Berlin, R3901/Film 36252. B Böhm, *Die Notwendigkeiten einer besonderen Versorgung und Fürsorge für hirnverletzte Kriegsbeschädigte* (München: Druck von C.W. Rau, Buchdruckerei und Verlag, 1927), 11–12.
138 ibid.
139 ibid, 16–17.

Chapter 4: 'The Class Struggle Psychosis': Working Class Politics and Psychological Trauma

 1 Emil Vogeley, 'Die Psychiatrie und Neurologie im Dienst der kapitalistischen Klasse', *Internationaler Bund – Organ der Kriegsbeschädigten, Kriegsteilnehmer und Kriegerhinterbliebenen*, October 1928.
 2 See Martin Broszat, *Hitler and the Collapse of Weimar Germany* (Leamington Spa: Berg, 1987), 32–37.
 3 See Modris Eksteins, 'All Quiet on the Western Front and the Fate of a War', *Journal of Contemporary History* 15:2, April 1980, 345–66.
 4 BA Berlin, R1501/26080, See Film-Oberprüfstelle report, Vorsitzender: Ministerialrat Dr Seeger, 11 December 1930.
 5 Wilhelm Keinau, 'Im Westen Skandal! Wir fordern Verbot!' *Der Stahlhelm*, Nr. 50, 14 December 1930.
 6 Franz Seldte, 'Der Stahlhelm – Das Bollwerk Deutschlands', *Der Stahlhelm*, 1. Beilage, 'Die Bewegung', 12 October 1930, 5–8.
 7 Fritz von Unruh, 'Im Westen nichts Neues – Erich Maria Remarques Roman', *Vossische Zeitung* (Berlin), in *Das Unterhaltungsblatt*, 5 February 1929, 26.
 8 Hans Hanning Freiherr Grote, '"Im Westen nichts Neues" – Offener Brief an Fritz von Unruh', *Der Stahlhelm*, 1. Beilage, 'Die Bewegung', Nr. 11, 17 March 1929, 5–8.
 9 ibid. On the right-wing's conception of the trench experience, see George L. Mosse's *Fallen Soldiers – Reshaping the Memory of the World Wars* (New York: Oxford University Press, 1990), 182–89.
10 ibid.
11 'Protest und Aufruf – Schützt die Jugend vor gewissenlosen Kriegshetzern!' *Reichsbund – Organ des Reichsbundes der Kriegsbeschädigten, Kriegsteilnehmer und Kriegshinterbliebenen*, Nr. 24, 24 December 1930, 222.
12 Christoph Pfändner, 'Zensurskandal – Der Streit um den Remarqueschen Film, "Im Westen Nichts Neues"', *Reichsbund*, Nr. 24, 24 December 1930, 222.
13 ibid.
14 'Heraus mit dem Remarque-Film' and poem 'Im Westen Nichts Neues',

Reichsbund, Nr. 1, 10 January 1931. See also 10 April 1931 issue for discussion of the film and novel.

15 ibid.

16 Max Mühlberger, 'Bedeutende Kriegsbücher – Vergleichende Betrachtung nach ihrer Weltanschaulichen Stellung', *Reichsbund*, Nr. 23, 10 December 1930, 215–16.

17 'Protest und Aufruf', *Reichsbund*, Nr. 23, 10 December 1930, 222.

18 ibid, 78–79. Karl August Wittfogel, 'Der Fall Remarque', *Die Rote Fahne* (Berlin), 26 July 1930.

19 Whalen, *Bitter Wounds*, 128.

20 BA Berlin, R3901/Film 36137. 'Spenden für Kriegsbeschädigten und Kriegshinterbliebenen, Allgemeines'. Polizeipräsident Richter to the Interior Ministry, Berlin, 24 July 1922. See also newspaper clippings in this file, including 'Eine Massenepidemie geheilt', December 1919 (exact day of issue not given in the file).

21 BA Berlin, R3901/Film 36137. Letter from Reichsbund to Labor Ministry, 3 January 1921.

22 ibid.

23 See George L. Mosse, 'Shell Shock as a Social Disease', *Journal of Contemporary History* 35:1, January 2000, 101–8.

24 BA Berlin, R3901/Film 36027. Letter from Reichsbund to RAM concerning medical examinations at Versorgungsamt Frankfurt a.M, 13 April 1927.

25 BA Berlin, R3901/Film 36027. Letter from Reichsbund to RAM, 7 February 1923.

26 BA Berlin, R3901/Film 36028. Letter from Reichsbund to RAM, 23 June 1927.

27 BA Berlin, R3901/Film 36027. Letter from widow of Wilhelm Kröger to the Reichsbund, 2 March 1921.

28 BA Berlin, R3901/Film 36027. Letter from Hartmann S., included in Reichsbund report, sent to RAM, 21 October 1924.

29 BA Berlin, R3901/Film 36027. Report from Reichsbund member Hölter, Barmen district, delivered to RAM, 26 September 1924.

30 BA Berlin, R3901/Film 36027. Letter from Reichsbund to RAM, 12 November 1924. See also report from HVA Coblenz to RAM, 5 December 1924.

31 On the social and psychological impact of the war on working class women, see Ute Daniel, *The War from Within – German Working-Class Women in the First World War*, translated by Margaret Ries (Oxford University Press, 1997), 231–72; see also Ute Frevert, *Women in German History – From Bourgeois Liberation to Sexual Liberation*, translated by Stuart McKinnon-Evans (Oxford University Press, 1989), 149–204. On the SPD's approach to the woman question, see Stefan Berger, *Social Democracy and the Working-Class in Nineteenth and Twentieth Century Germany* (New York: Longman, 2000), 121–23.

32 'Zwei feindliche Welten', *Reichsbund*, 1 May 1926.

33 Alma Hißfeld, 'Stellungsnahme der Hinterliebenen zum nationalen Trauertag', *Reichsbund*, 1 April 1921.

34 The number of physical and psychological cases processed by the National Pension Courts was enormous. Pension offices dealt with 1,629,000 cases in 1927. In 1928, this rose to 1,663,000. See Whalen's *Bitter Wounds*, 157.

35 'Waisenrente nach dem 18. Lebensjahr', *Reichsbund*, Nr. 7, July 1926.
36 Martha Harnoß, 'Zur Heilbehandlung der Kriegerhinterbliebenen', *Reichsbund*, 1 May 1926.
37 H. Hoffmann, 'Psychologie und Kriegsopfer', *Reichsbund*, 1 July 1926.
38 ibid.
39 'Im Dienst der Organisation erwacht wieder das Bewußtsein eigener Leistungsfähigkeit', *Reichsbund*, 1 July 1926.
40 H. Hoffmann, 'Psychologie und Kriegsopfer', *Reichsbund*, 1 July 1926.
41 'Im Dienst der Organisation erwacht wieder das Bewußtsein eigener Leistungsfähigkeit', *Reichsbund*, 1 July 1926.
42 Whalen, *Bitter Wounds*, 157–58.
43 'Abänderungsanträge zum Reichsversorgungsgesetz', *Reichsbund*, 1 February 1925.
44 Whalen, *Bitter Wounds*, 159. Whalen convincingly argues that the Labor and Finance Ministries had more weight than the Reichstag or war-disabled organizations in shaping pension legislation between 1924–28.
45 'Die Veränderungen im Reichsversorgungsgesetz', *Reichsbund*, 15 August 1926.
46 BA Berlin, R3901/Film 36252. 'Geisteskrankheiten und Dienstbeschädigungen', Dr Scholtze's 2 December 1926 Reichstag testimony transcript. See also 'Geisteskrankheiten und Dienstbeschädigungen', *Reichsbund*, 15 February 1927. In this issue the Reichsbund published the transcript of Dr Scholtze's testimony in front of the Reichstag committee.
47 ibid.
48 'Geisteskrankheiten und Dienstbeschädigungen', *Reichsbund*, 1 March 1927. This article on mental illness, war service, and the Reichstag hearings was part of a series in several 1927 issues.
49 ibid.
50 ibid.
51 See Ludwig Preller's *Sozialpolitik in der Weimarer Republik* (Stuttgart: Franz Mittelbach, 1949), 363–65. Preller demonstrates that unemployment insurance legislation was the Social Democratic Party's priority during the 1925–27 period.
52 BA Berlin, R3901/Film 36029. Letter from Reichsbund to RAM, 10 March 1928.
53 BA Berlin, R3901/36029. Letter from Der Minister des Kultur und Unterrichts, Karlsruhe, to RAM, 16 May 1928.
54 'Kriegspsychose – Trotz Geisteskrankheit jahrelang hinter Kerkermauern', *Reichsbund*, 1 September 1928.
55 ibid.
56 BA Berlin, R3901/Film 37011. HVA Brandenburg-Pommern letter to RAM, 5 March 1930.
57 BA Berlin, R3901/Film 37011. Konrad D. to RAM, 9 October 1931.
58 BA Berlin, R3901/Film 37011. His wife's status as unable to earn a living was summarized by D. in his 8 September 1930 letter, and confirmed by the Berlin pension office. The pension office did not elaborate on her condition except to note that a psychiatric evaluation indicated that she was unable to earn a living.
59 BA Berlin, R3901/Film 36139. Letter from Reichsbund to RAM, 28 January 1926.

60 BA Berlin, R3901/Film 36139. RAM to Frau B., 3 February 1926.
61 Quoted from Whalen, *Bitter Wounds*, 169–170. From 'Die Entwicklung der parlamentarischen Lage für die Kriegsopfer seit dem Hamburger Bundestag', *Reichsbund*, 25 May 1930.
62 'Die Liquidierung der inneren Kriegslasten', *Reichsbund*, 25 January 1930.
63 'Sparpsychose', *Reichsbund*, 25 February 1930.
64 For more on the SPD's struggle with the issue of war neurosis, see Jason Crouthamel, 'War Neurosis versus Savings Psychosis: Working-Class Politics and Psychological Trauma in Weimar Germany', *Journal of Contemporary History* 37:2, April 2002, 163–82.
65 'Geisteskrankheiten und Dienstbeschädigungen' (excerpts from transcript of Reichstag hearings), *Reichsbund*, 15 Feburary 1927.
66 'Kongreß der Werktätigen – Referat des Genossen Dr Klauber', *Internationaler Bund – Organ der Kriegsbeschädigten, Kriegsteilnehmer und Kriegerhinterbliebenen* (later changed to *Organ des Internationalen Bund der Opfer des Kriegs und der Arbeit*), Nr. 3, February 1927.
67 ibid.
68 'Der Wert der ärztlicher Gutachten', *Internationaler Bund*, Nr. 9, September 1926.
69 'Kriegs-Hysterie', *Internationaler Bund*, Nr. 12, December 1925.
70 ibid.
71 'Renten Neurose', *Internationaler Bund*, Nr. 8, August 1928.
72 ibid.
73 'Geschäftsmann oder Arzt!' *Internationaler Bund*, Nr. 3, March 1928.
74 BA Berlin, R3901/Film 36029. Letter from medical director at the Berlin main health care and pension office (signature illegible) to RAM, 19 November 1928.
75 Emil Vogeley, 'Die Psychiatrie und Neurologie im Dienst der kapitalistischen Klasse', *Internationaler Bund*, Nr. 10, October 1928.
76 ibid.
77 ibid.
78 ibid.
79 BA Berlin, R8034/2326. 'Der Fall Franzke-Rudolph vor dem Stadtparlement – Hinter den Kulissen der städtischen Kriegsbeschädigten-Fürsorge', *Berliner Lokale Anzeiger*, Nr. 423, 9 September 1921.
80 'Der Dank des Vaterlandes! – Das Martyrium eines 100% Kriegsbeschädigten', *Internationaler Bund*, Nr. 3, March 1932.
81 'Selbstmord', *Internationaler Bund*, Nr. 2, February 1930.

Chapter 5: National Socialism and its Discontents: War Neurosis and Memory under Hitler

1 Rudolf Binion, *Hitler Among the Germans* (DeKalb: Northern Illinois University Press, 1976), 5–6.
2 Ian Kershaw, *Hitler, 1889–1936: Hubris* (New York: W.W. Norton & Co., 1998), 102–3.
3 Norman H. Baynes (editor and translator) *The Speeches of Adolf Hitler – April 1922–August 1939*, vol. I, (Oxford: Oxford University Press, 1942), 560.

4 'Das Kriegserlebnis – Die Batterie um 4 Uhr früh', *Der Stahlhelm*, 15 February 1924.

5 Just a few examples include Ernst Jünger's *In Stahlgewittern* and *Der Kampf als inneres Erlebnis*. Right-wing publishers were instrumental in cultivating the ideology of the front – see Gary D. Stark, *Entrepreneurs of Ideology: Neoconservative Publishers in Germany, 1890–1933* (Chapel Hill: University of North Carolina, 1981).

6 Burleigh and Wippermann, *The Racial State – Germany 1933–1945*, 167–82.

7 Whalen, *Bitter Wounds*, 178.

8 Thomas Childers, *The Nazi Voter: The Social Foundations of Fascism in Germany, 1919–33* (Chapel Hill: University of North Carolina Press, 1981), 263–69.

9 Hanns Oberlindober, 'Ein Jahr National-Sozialistische Kriegsopferversorgung', *Deutsche Kriegsopferversorgung – National Sozialistische Monatschrift*, 2 Jahrg., Folge 8, May 1934, 13.

10 'Ein Rückblick auf die Enstehungsgeschichte des neuen Versorgungsrechts', *Deutsche Kriegsopferversorgung*, 2 Jahrg., Folge 8, May 1934, 9–10.

11 See Martin Broszat, *The Hitler State* (New York: Longman, 1981), Chapters 8–9.

12 James Diehl, *The Thanks of the Fatherland* (Chapel Hill: University of North Carolina Press, 1993), 37–39.

13 ibid, 40–45.

14 ibid.

15 ibid.

16 ibid.

17 Klaus Blaßneck, *Militärpsychiatrie im Nationalsozialismus – Kriegsneurotiker im Zweiten Weltkrieg* (Baden Baden: Deutscher Wissenschafts-Verlag, 2000), 13. See also Helmut Haselbeck and Gerda Engelbracht, '"Vom Aufbruch in eine andere Zukunft" – Bremer Psychiatrie zwischen 1945 und 1975', in Franz-Werner Kersting (ed.) *Psychiatriereform als Gesellschaftsreform – Die Hypothek des Nationalsozialismus und der Aufbruch der sechziger Jahre* (Paderborn: Ferdinand Schöningh, 2003), 260.

18 Michael Burleigh. *Death and Deliverance—Euthanasia in Germany, c.1900–1945* (Cambridge: Cambridge University Press, 1994), 37–42.

19 Prof. Dr Haberland, 'Hysterie', *Deutsche Kriegsopferversorgung*, 2 Jahrg., Folge 6, March 1934, 16–17.

20 ibid, 17.

21 Dr H. Koetzle, 'Gedanken zur Reform des Reichsversorgungsrechts', *Deutsche Kriegsopferversorgung*, 2 Jahrg., Folge 1, Berlin, October 1933, 10.

22 ibid.

23 Dr Paul Fraatz, 'Die Bedeutung der Neuordnung der Reichsversorgungsrechts', *Deutsche Kriegsopferversorgung*, 2 Jahrg., Folge 12, September 1934, 20–21.

24 Ernst Röhm, 'Über den Frontsoldaten', *Deutsche Kriegsopferversorgung*, 2 Jahrg., February 1934, 2.

25 ibid, 1–2.

26 Dr Alfred Dick, 'Soldatenversorgung vor und nach dem Weltkrieg', *Deutsche Kriegsopferversorgung*, 4 Jahrg., Folge 8, May 1936, 8.

27 'Der erste und gewaltigste Film der deutschen Frontsoldaten und Kriegsopfer "Stosstrupp 1917"', *Deutsche Kriegsopferversorgung*, 2 Jahrg., Folge 4, January 1934, 5.

28 BA Berlin, R3901/Film 37012. Letter from Gesundheitsbehörde und Fürsorgebehörde Hamburg to Verbindungsstab der NSDAP, 9 May 1934. Signed by Regierungsrat Martin and cosigned by Franz F.

29 ibid.

30 BA Berlin, R3901/Film 37012. Letter from Regierungsrat Martin to Rechtsanwalt Heim, Verbindungsstab der NSDAP, 15 June 1934.

31 BA Berlin, R3901/Film 37012. Letter from Rechtsanwalt, Verbindungsstab der NSDAP Heim to Regierungsrat Martin, 26 June 1934.

32 BA Berlin, R3901/Film 37012. Letter from SA-Obergruppenführer Wilhelm Brückner to VA Hamburg (Altona), 31 January 1935.

33 BA Berlin, R3901/Film 37012. Letter from Dr Knüppel at VA Hamburg to SA-Obergruppenführer Wilhelm Brückner, 6 February 1935.

34 BA Berlin, R3901/Film 37012. Letter from Dr Knüppel at VA Hamburg to HVA Niedersachsen-Nordmark, Hannover, 13 March 1935.

35 BA Berlin, R3901/Film 37012. Letter from Regierungsrat at Gesundheits und Fürsorgebehörde Fürsorgewesen Hamburg to RAM, 27 April 1935.

36 BA Berlin, R3901/Film 37014. Letter from Reichsbund ehem. Angehöriger der Heeres- und Marine- Verwaltungen, Sitz Spandau, to RAM, 20 October 1932.

37 ibid.

38 BA Berlin, R3901/Film 37014. Letter from HVA Brandenburg-Pommern to RAM, 12 November 1932.

39 BA Berlin, R3901/Film 37014. Letter from Kreisleitung der NSDAP, Siegburg, to RAM, 11 February 1933.

40 ibid.

41 BA Berlin, R3901/Film 37014. Letter from Hauptversorgungsamt Rheinland to RAM, 26 April 1933.

42 BA Berlin, R3901/Film 37014. Letter from National-Sozialistische Deutscher Arbeiterpartei, Kreishauptabteilung Siegburg through Verbindungsstab der NSDAP to Innenminister Goering, 26 May 1933.

43 BA Berlin, R3901/Film 37014. Letter from NSDAP, Kreishauptabteilung Siegburg to Goering, 30 May 1933.

44 ibid.

45 ibid.

46 BA Berlin, R3901/Film 37014. Letter from Emil H. to 'Kanzlei des Führers und Reichskanzlers zu Händen unseres Führers Adolf Hitler', 25 May 1935.

47 ibid.

48 ibid.

49 ibid.

50 BA Berlin, R3901/Film 37014. Letter from VA Koblenz to HVA Rheinland, 23 November 1938.

51 BA Berlin, R3901/Film 37014. Letter from VA Koblenz to HVA Rheinland, 16 July 1941.

52 BA Berlin, R3901/Film 37011. Letter from VA Giessen to RAM, 8 August 1928.

53 BA Berlin, R3901/Film 37011. Letter from VA Giessen to RAM, 18 June 1929.

54 BA Berlin, R3901/Film 37011. Letter from Prof. Haas, director of the Medizinsiche Poliklinik der Ludwigs-Universität, 2 June 1928.

55 BA Berlin, R 3901/Film 37011. Letter from the director of the HVA Hessen at Kassel to labor minister Sieler, 29 March 1939.

56 BA Berlin, R3901/Film 37011. Letter from Dr Haas to VA Giessen, 19 May 1939.

57 BA Berlin, R3901/Film 37011. Letter from Regierungsmed. Rat (Facharzt für innere Medizin) Dr Wilhelm Trautmann at VA Giessen to HVA Hessen, 20 May 1929.

58 BA Berlin, R3901/Film 37011. Letter from director of HVA Hessen at Kassel to the RAM, 23 May 1939.

59 BA Berlin, R3901/Film 37019. Karl Maria W. to Ministerialrat Hoppe, RAM, 19 October 1932.

60 BA Berlin, R3901/Film 37019. VA Frankfurt a.d. Oder to HVA Brandenburg-Pommern, 26 August 1932. See also RAM letter to W.'s employer Herr Laverrenz, 30 September 1932.

61 BA Berlin, R3901/Film 37019. Klaus W. to RAM, 16 October 1933.

62 BA Berlin, R3901/Film 37017. Letter from Friedrich S. to RAM, 26 April 1934.

63 BA Berlin, R3901/Film 37017. Letter from Friedrich S. to RAM, 25 April 1934.

64 BA Berlin, R3901/Film 37017. Letter from NSDAP Kreisleitung Halensee (Berlin) to RAM, 25 April 1934.

65 BA Berlin, R3901/Film 37017. Letter from HVA Brandenburg-Pommern to RAM, 28 April 1934.

66 BA Berlin, R3901/Film 37017. Letter from HVA Brandenburg-Pommern to RAM, 16 July 1934. See also HVA letter to RAM, 10 November 1934.

67 BA Berlin, R3901/Film 37017. Letter from Friedrich S. to Minister Seldte, 14 August 1934.

68 BA Berlin, 3901/Film 37017. Letter from Leibstandarte Adolf Hitler to RAM, 3 May 1935. Signed by an SS-Hauptsturmführer (name illegible) who reports that he is writing on Friedrich S.'s behalf under the direction of SS Obergruppenführer Dietrich.

69 BA Berlin, R3901/Film 37017. Letter from RAM to Leibstandarte SS Adolf Hitler, 27 May 1935.

70 BA Berlin, R3901/Film 37017. Friedrich S. to RAM, 16 July 1935.

71 BA Berlin, R3901/Film 37017. Friedrich S. to RAM, 22 August 1935.

72 BA Berlin, R3901/Film 37017. RAM to Friedrich S., 3 September 1935.

73 BA Berlin, R3901/Film 37017. Friedrich S. to RAM, 24 February 1936. See also NSKOV letter to RAM, 28 October 1935.

74 BA Berlin, R3901/Film 37012. Letter from Versorgungsamt Landshut to HVA München, signed Meiser, 7 March 1927.

75 BA Berlin, R3901/Film 37012. Letter from Rechtsvertreter Diedrich to Reichsarbeitsminister, 23 August 1928.

76 BA Berlin, R3901/Film 37012. Letter from VA Landshut to Hauptversorgungsamt Bayern, 17 December 1931. See also HVA Bayern report to RAM, 24 December 1931.

77 BA Berlin, R3901/Film 37012. Letter from HVA Bayern to Johann E., signed Reiland, 27 June 1936.

78 BA Berlin, R3901/Film 37017. Report from HVA Brandenburg – Pommern to Labor Ministry, 26 October 1934.
79 BA Berlin, R3901/Film 37017. Letter from NSKOV to RAM, 31 August 1934.
80 Burleigh and Wippermann, *The Racial State*, 136–38.
81 BA Berlin, R3901/Film 37017. Letter from NSKOV to RAM, 31 August 1934.
82 BA Berlin, R3901/Film 37017. Letter from VA Berlin to RAM, 22 July 1935, doctor's signature illegible. See also RAM letter to HVA Brandenburg-Pommern, 26 July 1935.
83 BA Berlin, R3901/Film 37017. Letter from Eugen R. to RAM, 9 July 1936.
84 BA Berlin, R3901/Film 37017. Letter from Eugen R. to RAM, 13 March 1940.
85 BA Berlin, R3901/Film 37017. Letter from Eugen R. to Reichsminister Seldte 25 April 1940. R.'s welfare office in Berlin turned down his request in a 19 April 1940 letter.
86 BA Berlin, R3901/Film 37017. Letter from Oberkommando der Wehrmacht (OKW) to VA Berlin, 7 May 1940. See also letter from VA Berlin to HVA Brandenburg-Pommern, 16 January 1941.
87 BA Berlin, R3901/Film 37017. Letter from NSKOV to OKW Regierungsrat Klückmann, 16 March 1942. See also Letter from OKW to HVA Brandenburg-Pommern, 4 June 1942.
88 On 'The Hitler Myth' and its function in winning support for Hitler, see Ian Kershaw, *The Hitler Myth – Image and Reality in the Third Reich*, 3.
89 BA Berlin, R3901/Film 37015. Letter from HVA Schlesien to RAM, 21 January 1932.
90 BA Berlin, R3901/Film 37015. Letter from Bund der deutschen Kriegsbeschädigten und Kriegerhinterbliebenen-Breslau to RAM, 10 February 1932.
91 BA Berlin, R3901/Film 37015. Letter from HVA Schlesien to RAM, 12 August 1935.
92 BA Berlin, R3901/Film 37015. Letter from Max K. to RAM, 30 July 1936.
93 BA Berlin, R3901/Film 37015. Letter from Max K. to RAM, 15 October 1936.
94 BA Berlin, R3901/Film 37015. RAM to Max K., 11 November 1936.
95 BA Berlin, R3901/Film 37015. Max K. to RAM, 6 May 1940. Max K. refers in this letter to a text by Dr Weiler titled *Nervöse und seelische Störungen bei Teilnehmern am Weltkrieg, ihre ärztliche und rechtliche Beurteilung.* The interpretations of Weiler's book are Max K.'s.
96 BA Berlin, R3901/Film 37015. Letter from Max K. to RAM, 23 October 1940. K. attributes this quote to Goebbels.
97 BA Berlin, R3901/Film 37015. Letter from Margaret K. to RAM, 8 November 1941.
98 BA Berlin, R3901/Film 37015. Letter from Max K. to RAM, 8 March 1942.
99 BA Berlin, R3901/Film 37014. VA Frankfurt a.M. to HVA Hessen, signed by Regierungsrat Caspari, 19 June 1937, See also RAM letter to Paul J., 21 October 1937.
100 BA Berlin, R3901/Film 37014. Paul J. to Die Kanzlei des Führers, 17 August 1938.

101 ibid.

102 ibid.

103 ibid.

104 BA Berlin, R3901/Film 37014. Report from Regierungsmedizinalrat at VA Darmstadt, 21 November 1935.

105 ibid. See Hermann J.'s various letters and RAM letter to VA Darmstadt, 6 June 1939.

106 Burleigh and Wippermann, *The Racial State*, 161–67. See also Michael Burleigh, *Death and Deliverance*.

107 BA Berlin, R36/1781. Betrifft: Versorgungsrente der kriegsbeschädigten Geisteskranken. 3 February 1937, signed Dr Zeitler.

108 BA Berlin, R36/1781. Der Oberbürgermeister der Stadt Herlohn an den Deutscher Gemeindetag, 22 February 1937.

109 BA Berlin, R36/1781. Der Oberbürgermeister Frankfurt and den Deutscher Geimeindetag, 5 March 1937.

110 BA Berlin, R36/1781. Schatzrat Dr Hartmann, Hannover, an den Deutscher Gemeindetag, 2 March 1937.

111 BA Berlin, R36/1781. Lippisches Landeswohlfahrtsamt an den Deutscher Gemeindetag, 20 October 1937; Der Oberbürgermeister der Landeshauptstadt Dresden, Stadtwohlfahrtsamt-Kriegerfürsorge and den Deutscher Gemeindetag, 24 September 1937.

112 BA Berlin, R36/1781. Der Oberbürgermeister der Hauptstadt der Bewegung an den Deutscher Gemeindetag, 17 February 1937.

113 BA Berlin, R36/1781. Landesfürsorgeamt Braunschweig an den Deutscher Geimeindetag, 3 December 1937.

114 BA Berlin, R36/1781. Der Oberbürgermeister der Stadt Heidelberg an den Deutscher Gemeindetag, 22 March 1937.

115 BA Berlin, R36/1781. Der Reichs- und Preussische Arbeitsminister an den Deutscher Gemeindetag, 19 August 1937.

116 BA Berlin, R3901/Film 37015. VA Frankfurt an der Oder letter to HVA Pommern, 9 February 1937. See also RAM letter to Emil L., 28 June 1937. In his 28 May 1937 letter to the Reichsarbeitsminister and his 24 January and 29 January 1938 letters to the Reichskanzler, L. recounted his problems with the pension system since 1917. The initial pension he received in 1917 is confirmed in the Labor Ministry documents. The 1924 findings in his favor and the 1927 pension counts are recounted in his letter, but these are not substantiated by further documents.

117 BA Berlin, R3901/Film 37015. Letter from HVA Brandenburg-Pommern to RAM, signed by Regierungsrat Panse, 30 December 1937.

118 BA Berlin, R3901/Film 37015. Letter from Emil L. to Reichsarbeitsminister, 28 May 1937.

119 BA Berlin, R3901/Film 37015. Letter from Emil L. to Reichskanzler, 29 January 1938.

120 ibid.

121 BA Berlin, R3901/Film 37015. Letter from VA Frankfurt am Oder to HVA Brandenburg-Pommern and RAM, signed Regierungsassessor Karstedt, 18 March 1938.

122 BA Berlin, R3901/Film 37015. Letter from Reichsarbeitsminister to Emil L., 26 May 1939.

123 BA Berlin, R3901/Film 37015. Letter from RAM to HVA Brandenburg-Pommern, 14 April 1938.
124 BA Berlin, R3901/Film 37015. Letter from Emil L. to Generalfeldmarschall Göring, 12 September 1939.
125 BA Berlin, R3901/Film 37015. Letter from Reichspropagandaamt to Reichsministerium für Volksaufklärung und Propaganda, signed by Referent Dieckmann, 4 July 1940.
126 BA Berlin, R3901/Film 37015. Letter from OKW to Emil L., signed by clerk Mühlbah in the name of OKW Chief Christoph, 25 November 1941.
127 BA Berlin, R3901/Film 37015. Letter from Emil L. to Reichsarbeitsminister, 20 May 1942.
128 BA Berlin, R3901/Film 37010. Letter from OKW to Otto M., 14 June 1940.
129 BA Berlin, R3901/Film 37010. Letter from Otto M. to OKW through the HVA Hannover, 6 November 1940.

Chapter 6: Nazi Germany's Hidden 'Psychopaths': Case Studies of Mentally Disabled Veterans in the Third Reich

1 BA Berlin, R3901/Film 37011. Konrad D. to Labor Minister Franz Seldte, includes D.'s essay 'Das Echo', 12 March 1935.
2 The importance of examining the history of marginalized groups as a way of revaluating the master narrative is stressed by Geoff Eley in 'How and Where is German History Centered', in Neil Gregor, Nils Roemer and Mark Roseman (eds), *German History from the Margins* (Bloomington: Indiana University Press, 2006), 274–75.
3 BA Berlin, R3901/Film 37011. Letter from Konrad D. to RAM, 23 March 1932. Documents in these files alternatively spell his name 'Konrad' and 'Conrad'. 'Konrad' will be used here to remain consistent.
4 BA Berlin, R3901/Film 37011. Konrad D. to RAM, 10 July 1929.
5 BA Berlin, R3901/Film 37011. Konrad D. to RAM, 21 July 1929.
6 BA Berlin, R3901/Film 37011. Report by private doctor Bratz, hired by Konrad D., outlined D.'s case history since World War I, to RAM, 25 July 1931.
7 BA Berlin, R3901/Film 37011. Konrad D. to RAM, 13 February 1930.
8 BA Berlin, R3901/Film 37011. Konrad D. to RAM, 9 October 1931.
9 BA Berlin, R3901/Film 37011. HVA Brandenburg-Pommern to RAM, 31 May 1930.
10 BA Berlin, R3901/Film 37011. Konrad D. to RAM, 8 June 1929.
11 BA Berlin, R3901/Film 37011. HVA Berlin to RAM, report made by Oberregierungsrat Detring, 24 January 1929.
12 ibid. See also Konrad D. to RAM, 8 September 1930 – medical confirmation of Frau's condition is contained in HVA Berlin documents attached to this correspondence.
13 BA Berlin, R3901/Film 37011. Konrad D. to RAM, 10 July 1929.
14 BA Berlin, R3901/Film 37011. Konrad D. to RAM, 8 June 1929.
15 BA Berlin, R3901/Film 37011. Konrad D. to RAM, 25 July 1931.
16 BA Berlin, R3901/Film 37011. Konrad D. to RAM, 9 October 1931, see attached doctor's reports.

17 BA Berlin, R3901/Film 37011, Konrad D. [undated] February 1933 letter to RAM.

18 BA Berlin, R3901/Film 37011, Konrad D., undated letter to RAM, appears just before 13 July 1931 letter.

19 ibid.

20 BA Berlin, R3901/Film 37011. Konrad D. to RAM, 22 September 1931.

21 BA Berlin, R3901/Film 37011. Konrad D. to RAM, 9 October 1931.

22 BA Berlin, R3901/Film 37011. Konrad D. to RAM, 23 March 1932.

23 ibid.

24 BA Berlin, R3901/Film 37011. Konrad D. to Labor Minister Dr Stegerwald, 21 July 1931.

25 ibid.

26 BA Berlin, R3901/Film 37011. Konrad D. to RAM, 22 September 1931.

27 BA Berlin, R3901/Film 37011. Konrad D. to Labor Minister Dr Stegerwald, 9 August 1931.

28 BA Berlin, R3901/Film 37011. Konrad D. to RAM, 22 September 1931.

29 BA Berlin, R3901/Film 37011. Konrad D. to RAM, 23 March 1932.

30 BA Berlin, R3901/Film 37011. Konrad D. to VA Gotha, 8 February 1933.

31 BA Berlin, R3901/Film 37011. Konrad D. to head of Labor Ministry Franz Seldte, 19 March 1933.

32 BA Berlin, R3901/Film 37011. Konrad D. to Staatssekretär Dr Lammers, 19 March 1933.

33 ibid.

34 BA Berlin, R3901/Film 37011. Konrad D. to Staatsekretär Dr Lammers, 19 March 1933.

35 ibid. See also letter attached to report from Ministerialrat Sieler to Staatssekretär Dr Lammers, 5 April 1933.

36 ibid.

37 BA Berlin, R3901/Film 37011. Konrad D. to Labor Minister Franz Seldte, 19 April 1934, with enclosed essay by D., 'Die national-sozialistische Kriegsopferversorgung und ihre Finanzierung'.

38 ibid.

39 BA Berlin, R3901/Film 37011. Konrad D. to Labor Minister Franz Seldte, 12 March 1935. Enclosed is D'.s essay 'Das Echo – Kriegsopfer-Denkschrift zu dem neuen "Ehrenrecht der deutschen Kriegsopfer"'.

40 ibid.

41 ibid.

42 ibid.

43 BA Berlin, R3901/Film 37011. Konrad D. to Seldte, 19 April 1934, attached essay 'Das Echo'.

44 ibid.

45 BA Berlin, R3901/Film 37011. Der Leiter Versorgungsamts V Berlin [signature illegible] to Direktor des Hauptversorgungsamts, 13 July 1935.

46 BA Berlin, R3901/Film 37011. RAM to Konrad D., 10 September 1935.

47 BA Berlin, R3901/Film 37011. Der Direktor des HVA Brandenburg-Pommern, Berichterstatter: Oberregierungsrat Schellong, to RAM, 23 July 1935.

48 Burleigh and Wipperman, The Racial State, 173.

49 BA Berlin, R3901/Film 37011. Konrad D. to Seldte, 12 March 1935, essay 'Das Echo'.

50 Michael Burleigh, *Death and Deliverance*, 160. This statistic reflects only the adults killed in the 1939–41 'Aktion T–4' program, the number of people killed was approximately 200,000 when one includes waves of murder programs aimed at disabled children and adults that took place through the end of the war.

51 BA Berlin, R3901/Film 37013. Erich G. to RAM, 16 July 1932, see attached court documents from 6 November 1922.

52 BA Berlin, R3901/Film 37013. Strafgericht report regarding case of Erich G. vs. Prof. Dr Nonne, issued by Strafjustiz administration, 5 September 1931. Reports from Dr Med. F. Zimmerman at Brandenburg, Dr Med. Kronheim, Kriegskameraden Gustav Schunorth, Ernst Lindecke and others are included in these documents.

53 BA Berlin, R3901/Film 37013. See attachments to Erich G.'s 11 December 1931 letter, including report from the captain of his artillery regiment.

54 BA Berlin, R3901/Film 37013. See Strafgericht report, 5 September 1931.

55 BA Berlin, R3901/Film 37013. Erich G. accused his doctors of basing their reports on his character rather than medical history in numerous letters – including his 12 November 1932 letter to the Labor Ministry.

56 BA Berlin, R3901/Film 37013. Erich G. to RAM, 12 November 1932.

57 BA Berlin, R3901/Film 37013. Report by Dr F. Zimmerman, Brandenburg psychiatric clinic, 14 May 1929. This document was included with the RAM's files on Erich G.'s lawsuit.

58 ibid.

59 BA Berlin, R3901/Film 37013. Strafgericht report, 5 September 1931.

60 ibid.

61 ibid.

62 BA Berlin, R3901/Film 37013. Letter from Erich G. to RAM, 30 September 1932.

63 BA Berlin, R3901/Film 37013. Erich G. to RAM, 16 February 1937.

64 BA Berlin, R3901/Film 37013. Erich G. to RAM, 12 November 1932.

65 BA Berlin, R3901/Film 37013. Report by Dr F. Zimmerman, Brandenburg psychiatric clinic, 14 May 1929.

66 BA Berlin, R3901/Film 37013. Erich G. to Adolf Hitler, Führer der NSDAP, 24 March 1933.

67 BA Berlin, R3901/Film 37013. Erich G. to Reichskanzler Adolf Hitler, 25 April 1933.

68 BA Berlin, R3901/Film 37013. Erich G. to Reichsarbeitsminister Franz Seldte, 22 May 1933.

69 BA Berlin, R3901/Film 37013. Erich G. to Reichsarbeitsminister Seldte, 30 November 1936.

70 ibid.

71 BA Berlin, R3901/Film 37013. Erich G. to Reichskanzler Adolf Hitler, 20 January 1938.

72 BA Berlin, R3901/Film 37013. Erich G. to 'die Deutsche Reichsregierung', 6 November 1939.

73 ibid.

74 BA Berlin, R3901/Film 37013. Erich G. to Reichskanzlei, 25 February 1940.

75 BA Berlin, R3901/Film 37013. Erich G. to 'die Deutsche Reichsregierung', 6 November 1939.

76 ibid.

77 BA Berlin, R3901/Film 37013. Erich G. letter to 'die Deutsche Reichsregierung', 5 October 1941.

78 ibid. On the physical and psychological trauma of war on the Eastern front, see Omer Bartov's *The Eastern Front, 1941–45, German Troops and the Barbarisation of Warfare* (Oxford: Palgrave, revised edition, 2001), 21–37. See also Frank Biess' excellent study on how the trauma of the Second World War affected returning veterans and their communities, *Homecomings: Returning POWs and the Legacies of Defeat in Postwar Germany* (Princeton: Princeton University Press, 2006), 70–94.

79 BA Berlin, R3901/Film 37013. Erich G. to RAM, 21 March 1943.

80 BA Berlin, R3901/Film 37013. Erich G.'s 'Bericht über die mutmassliche Ursache des Leidens', appears undated in this file after the 21 March 1943 document.

81 Ian Kershaw, *Hitler, 1936–45: Nemesis* (New York: W.W. Norton & Co., 2000), 277.

82 Gordon Wright, *The Ordeal of Total War, 1939–1945* (New York: Harper & Row, 1968), 46–47.

83 'Dem besten Soldaten die beste Versorgung', *Deutsche Kriegsopferversorgung*, 9 Jahrg., Folge 1 und 2, Oktober/November 1941, 4–5. The NSKOV newspaper rarely depicted disabled veterans, but when it did, they were sterilized photos of bandaged men in hospital care. This is in notable contrast to *Reichsbund* periodicals that described war victims' wounds in graphic detail, usually connected to pacifist-oriented articles.

84 David Welch, *The Third Reich – Politics and Propaganda* (New York: Routledge, 1993), 116.

85 BA Berlin, R89/6904, Der Leiter der Landesversicherungsanstalt Pommern, Dr Borchers, an den Herrn Oberpräsidenten Verwaltung des Provinzialverbandes Stettin, 29 March 1941.

86 ibid.

87 BA Berlin, R89/4922. Landesversicherungsanstalt Graz, Dr C. Morocutti, Der Chefarzt der Invalidenversicherung, April 1943.

88 ibid.

89 ibid.

90 ibid.

91 ibid.

92 Detlev Peukert, *Inside Nazi Germany: Conformity, Opposition and Racism in Everyday Life* (New Haven: Yale University Press, 1987), 62–63.

93 Ian Kershaw, *The Hitler Myth*, 165–66.

94 Peukert, *Inside Nazi Germany*, 165–67.

95 Ian Kershaw, *Hitler, 1936–45: Nemesis*, 632.

96 BA Berlin, R58/180. Meldungen aus dem Reich, Nr. 355, Der Chef des Sicherheitspolizei und des SD, 1 February 1943, 3–4.

97 ibid.

98 Kershaw, *The Hitler Myth*, 186.

99 BA Berlin, R58/180. Meldungen aus dem Reich, Nr. 356, Der Chef des Sicherheitspolizei und des SD, 4 February 1943, 34.

100 ibid, 36.

101 BA Berlin, R58/180. Meldungen aus dem Reich, Nr. 360, Der Chef des Sicherheitspolizei und des SD, 18 February 1943.

102 BA Berlin, R58/180. Meldungen aus dem Reich, Nr. 358, Der Chef der Sicherheitspolizei und der SD, 11 February 1943, 97.

103 BA Berlin, R58/151. Meldungen aus dem Reich, Nr. 96, Der Reichsführer SS und Chef der Deutschen Polizei, der Chef der Sicherheitspolizei und des SD, 13 June 1940, Nr. 96, 25.

104 BA Berlin, NS6/353, 13019, Der Leiter der Partei-Kanzlei, Martin Bormann, 24 February 1945, 66.

105 ibid.

106 Werner Maser (ed.), *Hitler's Letters and Notes* (New York: Bantam, 1974). The translated political testament appears on pages 342–57.

107 ibid.

Conclusion

1 See for example Peter Leese, *Shell Shock: Traumatic Neurosis and the British Soldiers of the First World War* (London: Palgrave, 2002), 57–64; Marc Roudebush, 'A Battle of Nerves: Hysteria and its Treatments in France during World War I', in *Traumatic Pasts*, 253–79.

2 Leese, *Shell Shock*, 107–9; Showalter, 'Rivers and Sassoon: The Inscription of Male Gender Anxieties', 61–70.

3 Mosse, *Nationalism and Sexuality – Respectability and Abnormal Sexuality in Modern Europe* (New York: Howard Fertig, 1985), 153–55 and *The Image of Man—The Creation of Modern Masculinity* (New York: Oxford University Press, 1998), esp. Chs 6 and 8; Karen Hagemann, 'The Military, Violence and Gender Relations in the Age of the World Wars', in Hagemann and Schüler-Springorum, *Home/Front*, 1–42. See also Birthe Kundrus, 'Gender Wars – The First World War and the Construction of Gender Relations in the Weimar Republic', in Hagemann and Schüler-Springorum, *Home/Front*, 159–80.

4 Karen Hagemann, 'The Military, Violence and Gender Relations in the Age of the World Wars', in Hagemann and Schüler-Springorum, *Home/Front*, 1.

5 Cohen, *The War Come Home*, 170.

6 ibid, 168–70.

7 Eghigian, *Making Security Social*, 234–35.

8 BA Berlin, R3901/Film 37011. Konrad D. to Seldte, 19 April 1934, in his enclosed essay 'Das Echo'.

Bibliography

Glossary of Terms

DB	Dienstbeschädigung (war-related injury)
DVP	Deutsche Volkspartei (German People's Party)
DNVP	Deutsch-Nationale Volkspartei (German National People's Party)
HVA	Haupversorgungsamt (main pension/welfare office)
KPD	Kommunistische Partei Deutschlands (Communist Party of Germany)
NSDAP	Nationalsozialistische Deutsche Arbeiterpartei (National Socialist German Workers' Party, or Nazi Party)
NSKOV	Nationalsozialistische Kriegsopferversorgung (National Socialist War Victims' Care)
OKW	Oberkommando der Wehrmacht (High Command of the Armed Forces)
RAM	Reichsarbeitsministerium (Labor Ministry)
RMdI	Reichsministerium des Innern (Ministry of the Interior)
RVA	Reichsversicherungsamt (National Pension/Welfare Office)
SD	Sicherheitsdienst (Security Service)
SPD	Sozialdemokratische Partei Deutschlands (Social Democratic Party of Germany)
VA	Versorgungsamt (Pension/welfare office)

Archival Sources

Bundesarchiv Berlin-Lichterfelde (BA Berlin)

R3901 Reichsarbeitsministerium (RAM) files
    Bd. 4 Versorgungsangelegenheiten
        Film 35824–35826 Invalidenhäuser
            36027–36064 Begutachtungen Beschädigter
            36069–36147 Kriegsbeschädigtenfürsorge
            36248–36255 Übergang des Versorgungswesens
            37011–37019 Fürsorge für Kriegsbeschädigten
R89 Reichsversicherungsamt
    Bd. 2 Kranken- und Invalidenversicherung
        Film 4555 Krankenfürsorge für Kriegsteilnehmer nach dem Kriege
            4922–49233 Gewährung der Invalidenrente und Beginn des Begriffs der Erwerbsfähigkeit
R1501 Reichsministerium des Innern
    Bd. 6 Medizinalpolizei
            9384–9385 Psychopathenfürsorge
            11803–11804 Hypnose und Suggestion

Bd. 13 Schutz der Republik
    9403–9410 Gesundheitliche Schäden der Kriegs- und Nachkriegszeit
    26033–26034 Kriegervereine
    26080 NSDAP und Kulturpolitik, Remarque Film

R8034 II Reichspressearchiv
    5718–5720 Sozialpolitik
    2320–2328 Kriegsinvaliden, Witwen- und Waisenfürsorge
    2330–2331 Kriegsbeschädigtenfürsorge
    2329 Arbeit für Kriegsbeschädigte
    2765 Flugwesens
    7038 Kriegervereine

R36 Deutscher Gemeindetag

R58 Reichssicherheitsamt
    Meldungen aus dem Reich (SD reports)

NS 5 VI Bd. 7 Deutsche Arbeitsfront

NS 6 Parteikanzlei

Bundesarchiv Koblenz (BAK)
Deutsche Kriegsopferversorgung, Zeitschriften, 1934–

Bayerisches Hauptaatsarchiv, Abteilung IV, Kriegsarchiv, Munich
Stv. Gen. Kdo I, Ak 159

Bundesarchiv mit Stiftung Archiv der Parteien und Massenorganisationen der
DDR, Berlin-Lichterfelde
Internationaler Bund – Organ der Kriegsbeschädigten Zeitschriften, 1919–1933

Deutsche Bücherei Leipzig
Krieg 1914–1918 Sammlung

Staatsbibliothek Berlin
Krieg 1914–1918 Sammlung

List of newspapers

Berliner Lokale Anzeiger
Berliner Tageblatt
Deutsche Kriegsopferversorgung—Nationalsozialistische Monatschrift
Deutsche Tageszeitung
Die Erziehung
Internationaler Bund der Kriegsopfer
Reichsbote Berlin
Der Stahlhelm
Der Reichsbund der Kriegsbeschädigten
Die Rote Fahne
Süddeutsche Monatshefte
Versorgung-Fürsorge-Zeitung
Vorwärts
Vossische Zeitung
Weimarische Zeitung
Westfälische Kriegsfürsorge

Published Primary Sources

Baumgarth, Hans-Georg, *Das Geschlechtsleben im Kriege – Eine Rechtfertigung für viele Unglückliche* (Berlin: Rosen-Verlag, 1920).

Binswanger, Otto, *Die seelischen Wirkungen des Krieges* (Stuttgart and Berlin: Deutsche Verlags-Anstalt, 1914).

Böhm, B., *Die Notwendigkeiten einer besonderen Versorgung und Fürsorge für Hirnverletzte Kriegsbeschädigte* (München: Druck von C.W. Rau, Buchdruckerei Und Verlag, 1927).

Dick, Alfred, 'Soldatenversorgung vor und nach dem Weltkrieg', *Deutsche Kriegsopferversorgung*, 4 Jahrg., Folge 8, May 1936.

Dix, Kurt Walter, *Psychologische Beobachtungen über die Eindrücke des Krieges auf Einzelne wie auf die Masse* (Langensalza: Hermann Beyer & Söhne, 1915).

Draeseke, J. and Herms, O., *Die Hilfschule im Dienste der Kopfschussverltzten – Beobachtungen in der vom hamburgischen Landesausschuß für Kriegsbeschädigte Eingerichteten Schule für gehirnverletzte Krieger* (Berlin: Vossische Buchhandlung Verlag, 1917).

Federmann, *Der Krieg und die deutsche Volksseele* (Berlin: Verlag des Evangelischen Bundes, 1915).

Fraatz, Paul, 'Die Bedeutung der Neuordnung der Reichsversorgungsrechts', *Deutsche Kriegsopferversorgung*, 2 Jahrg., Folge 12, September 1934.

Friedrich, Ernst, *Krieg dem Kriege!* (Berlin, 1924).

Fuchs, W. *'Weil wir nicht Kriegsbereit sind !' Eine psychologische Studie, gewidmet den deutschen Eltern, den deutschen Lehrern und der deutscher Jugend* (Berlin: Verlag C.A. Schwetschke und Sohn, 1914).

Gau, 'Kriegs-Invaliden-Heime', *Westfälische Kriegsfürsorge*, 15 June 1920.

Gaupp, Robert, *Die Nervenkranken des Krieges: Ihre Beurteilung und Behandlung* (Stuttgart: Evangelischer Presseverband für Württemberg, 1917).

Gonser, F., *Der Alkohol und der Krieg* (Berlin: Mäßigkeits-Verlag, 1915).

Grote, Hans Henning, ' "Im Westen nichts Neues" – Offener Brief an Fritz von Unruh', *Der Stahlhelm*, 1. Beilage, 'Die Bewegung', Nr. 11, 17 March 1929.

Haberland, 'Hysterie', *Deutsche Kriegsopferversorgung*, 2 Jahrg., Folge 6, March 1934.

Haffner, Paul, and Janssen, Johannes and Thillen, E., (eds) 'Planmäßiger Kampf gegen Würdelosigkeit im weiblichen Geschlecht', *Frankfurter Zeitgemäße Broschuren*, Band XXXV (Hamm: Breer & Thiemann, 1916).

Harnoß, Martha, 'Zur Heilbehandlung der Kriegerinterbliebenen', *Reichsbund der Kriegsbeschädigten*, 1 May 1926.

Hartmann, Karl Ernst, *Lehrbuch der Kriegsbeschädigten- und Kriegerhinterbliebenen-Fürsorge mit besonderer Berücksichtigung der neuen sozialpolitischen Maßnahmen Der Reichsregierung* (Westfalen: Selbstverlag des Verfassers, 1919).

Hirschfeld, Magnus, *Sittengeschichte des Weltkrieges*, Zweiter Band (Leipzig: Verlag Für Sexualwissenschaft, Schneider & Co., 1930).

— *Zwischen Zwei Katrastophen* (originally *Sittengeschichte der Nachkriegszeit*, Hanau am Main: Verlag Karl Schustek, 1966).

Hißfeld, Alma, 'Stellungsnahme der Hinterbliebenen zum nationalen Trauertag', *Reichsbund der Kriegsbeschädigten*, 1 April 1921.

Hoche, Alfred, 'Über Wesen und Tragweite der 'Dienstbeschädigung' bei nervös und psychisch erkrankten Fedzugsteilnehmern', *Monatschrift für Psychiatrie und Neurologie*, 39, 1916, 351–54.

— *Krieg und Seelenleben* (Freiburg: Speyer & Laerner, Universitätsbuchhandlung, 1915).

Hoffmann, H., 'Psychologie und Kriegsopfer', *Reichsbund der Kriegsbeschädigten*, 1 July 1926.

Jünger, Ernst, *Der Krieg als innere Erlebnis* (Hamburg: E.S. Mittler & Sohn, 1922).

— *The Storm of Steel* (New York: Howard Fertig, 1993).

Kahn, Eugen, 'Psychopathen als revolutionäre Führer', *Zeitschrift für die gesamte Neurologie und Psychiatrie*, 52, 1919.

Kaufmann, Fritz, 'Die planmässige Heilung komplizierter psychogener Bewegungsstörungen bei Soldaten in einer Sitzung', *Münchener Medizinische Zeitschrift*, 63, 1916, 802–4.

Keinau, Wilhelm, 'Im Westen Skandal! Wir fordern Verbot!' *Der Stahlhelm*, Nr. 50, 14 December 1930.

Koetzle, H., 'Gedanken zur Reform des Reichsversorgungsrechts', *Deutsche Kriegsopferversorgung*, 2 Jahrg., Folge 1, October 1933.

Kolb, *Die nervös Kriegsbeschädigten vor Gericht und Strafvollzug – Nach einem Vortrag für Richter, Ärzte, Strafanstaltsbeamte* (München: J. Schweitzer-Verlag, 1919).

Kügelgen, Carlo von, 'Nicht Krüppel – Sieger!' *Versorgung-Fürsorge-Zeitung*, Nr. 1, 16 January 1927.

Lewandowsky, M., 'Über den Tod durch Sinusströme', *Deutsche Medizinische Wochenschrift*, 43, 1917, 1169.

Lindenberg, Karl, *Der deutchen Kriegers inneres Erlebnis* (Stuttgart: Druck und Verlag von Greiner & Pfeiffer, 1917).

Lißmann, P., *Die Wirkungen des Krieges auf das männliche Geschlechtsleben* (München: Verlag der Aerztlichen Rundscau Otto Gamelin, 1919).

Loewy-Hattendorf, Erwin, *Krieg, Revolution und Unfallneurosen* (Berlin: Verlagsbuchhandlung von Richard Schoetz, 1920).

Mendel, Kurt, 'Die Kaufmannsche Methode', *Neurologisches Zentralblatt*, 36, 1917, 181–93.

Muche, Felix, *Wir müssen und werden siegen! Der Einfluß der Suggestion auf unser Nervensystem, 2. Die Macht der Suggestion im Weltkriege* (Leipzig: Verlag von Oswald Mutze, 1916).

Mühlberger, Max, 'Bedeutende Kriegsbücher – Vergleichende Betrachtung nach ihrer Weltanschaulichen Stellung', Nr. 23, December 1930.

Müller, Rudolf, *Ketten – Opfer der Inneren Front* (Leipzig: Anzengruber-Verlag Brüder Suschitzky, 1920).

Neter, Eugen, 'Die seelische Zusammenbruch der deutschen Kampffront', *Süddeutsche Monatshefte*, Heft 10, 22 Jahrgang, July 1925, 45–46.

Oberlindober, Hanns, 'Ein Jahr National-Sozialistische Kriegsopferversorgung', *Deutsche Kriegsopferversorgung – National Sozialistische Monatschrift*, 2 Jahrg., Folge 8, May 1934.

Oppenheim, Hermann, 'Der Krieg und die traumatischen Neurosen', *Berliner Klinische Wochenschrift*, 52, 1915, 257–61.

Pönitz, Karl, *Die klinische Neuorientierung zum Hysterieproblem unter Einflüsse der Kriegserfahrungen* (Berlin: Verlag von Julius Springer, 1921).

Pfändner, 'Zensurskandal – Der Streit um den Remarqueschen Film "Im Westen Nichts Neues" ' *Reichsbund der Kriegsbeschädigten*, Nr. 24, 24 December 1930.

Preiß, H.A., *Geschlechtliche Grausamkeiten liebestoller Menschen* (Frankfurt a.M.: Süddeutsche Verlagsanstalt, 1921).

Plaut, Paul, 'Psychographie des Kriegers', *Beiträge zur Psychologie des Krieges* (Leipzig: Verlag von Johann Ambrosius Barth, 1920).

Röhm, Ernst, 'Über den Frontsoldaten', *Deutsche Kriegsopferversorgung*, 2 Jahrg., February 1934.

Schlottau, Hans, 'Kriegsfurioso – Visionen eines Verewundeten', Vorwart Hermann Klamfoth, Erste Flugschrift, Friedensbund der Kriegsteilnehmer und Friedensfreunde (Hamburg: Pionier-Verlag, Carl Thinius, 1920).

Schneider, Carl, *Das Kriegsbeschädigten-Problem: Zur Frage der Sonderorganisation Der Kriegsbeschädigten* (Essen: Kray, 1918).

Schneider, Friedrich, 'Die Kölner Nervenstation für Kopfschüsse und ihre Bedeutung für die pädigogische Psychologie und Berufsberatung', *Kölnische Volkszeitung*, August 1918.

Schultz, J.H., 'Seelischen Krankenbehandlung', *Berliner Tageblatt*, 5 October 1921.

Schultze, Ernst, *Die Mobilmachung der Seelen* (Bonn: A. Marcus & E. Webers Verlag, 1915).

Schulze, Hans, *Starke Nerven* (St. Matthews in Stettin: Fischer & Schmitt, 1917).

Schweyer, Franz, *Die Ansprüche der Kriegsbeschädigten und Kriegshinterbliebenen Nach dem neuen Reichsversorgungsgesetze* (Berlin: Carl Heymanns Verlag, 1920).

Seldte, Franz, 'Der Stahlhelm – Das Bollwerk Deutschlands', *Der Stahlhelm*, 1. Beilage, 'Die Bewegung', 12 October 1930.

Toller, Ernst, *Eine Jugend in Deutschland* (Hamburg: Rowohlt, 1963).

Unruh, Fritz von, 'Im Westen nichts Neues – Erich Maria Remarques Roman', *Vossische Zeitung* (Berlin), in *Das Unterhaltungsblatt*, 5 February 1929.

Vogeley, Emil, 'Die Psychiatrie und Neurologie im Dienst der kapitalistischen Klasse', *Internationaler Bund – Organ der Kriegsbeschädigten, Kriegsteilnehmer und Kriegerhinterbliebenen*, Nr. 1, October 1928.

Weiler, K. 'Ein Jahr Kriegsneurotikerbehandlung im I. bayer. A.K.', *Münchener Medizinische Wochenschrift*, 66, 1918, 401–7.

Weinhausen, Friedrich, 'Die Kriegsbeschädigten und der Wiederaufbau', *Weimarische Zeitung*, Nr. 232, 25 August 1919.

Wilmanns, Karl, 'Die Behandlung der Kranken mit funktionellen Neurosen im Bereich des XIV A.K.', *Deutsche Medizinische Wochenschrift*, 43, 1917, 427–29.

Wulffen, Erich, *Der Sexualverbrecher: Ein Handbuch für Juristen, Verwaltungsbeamte und Ärzte* (Berlin: Langenscheidt, 1910).

— *Kriminalpsychologie des Täters* (Berlin: Langenscheidt, 1926).

Würth, Alma, 'Warum ist der Krieg – modern?' *Reichsbund – Organ des Reichsbundes der Kriegsbeschädigten, Kriegsteilnehmer und Kriegerhinterbliebenen*, Jahrgang 13, Nr. 19, 10 October 1930.

Young-Rißmann, 'Der verlorene Krieg und die Sittlichkeitsfrage', Vierte Auflage, als Vortrag von Frau Young-Rißmann gehalten zu Freiburg i.B. am 30 September 1923 Zur Tagung des Weißen Kreuzes (Dinglinen: St. Johannes Druckerei, 1930).

Secondary Sources

Bartov, Omer, *The Eastern Front, 1941–1945—German Troops and the Barbarisation of Warfare* (Oxford: Palgrave, revised edition, 2001).

Baynes, Norman H. (ed. and trans.), *The Speeches of Adolf Hitler*, vol. I, April 1922-August 1939 (Oxford: Oxford University Press, 1942).

Berger, Stefan, *Social Democracy and the Working Class in Nineteenth and Twentieth Century Germany* (London: Longman, 2000).

Berghahn, Volker, *Der Stahlhelm, Bund der Frontsoldaten, 1918–1935* (Dusseldorf: Droste, 1966).

Bessel, Richard, *Germany after the First World War* (Oxford: Clarendon Press, 1993).

Biess, Frank, *Homecomings: Returning POWs and the Legacies of Defeat in Postwar Germany* (Princeton: Princeton University Press, 2006).

Binion, Rudolf, *Hitler Among the Germans* (DeKalb: Northern Illinois University Press, 1976).

Binneveld, Hans, *From Shellshock to Combat Stress: A Comparative History of Military Psychiatry*, translated by John O'Kane (Amsterdam: Amsterdam University Press, 1997).

Blaßneck, Klaus, *Militärpsychiatrie im Nationalsozialismus – Kriegsneurotiker im Zweiten Weltkrieg* (Baden-Baden: Deutscher Wissenschafts-Verlag, 2000).

Bourke, Joanna, *Dismembering the Male – Male Bodies, Britain and the Great War* (Chicago: University of Chicago, 1996).

— *An Intimate History of Killing – Face to Face Killing in 20th Century Warfare* (New York: Basic Books, 1999).

Broszat, Martin, *Hitler and the Collapse of Weimar Germany* (Leamington Spa: Berg, 1987).

— *The Hitler State* (New York: Longman, 1981).

Browning, Christopher, *Ordinary Men – Reserve Police Battalion 101 and the Final Solution in Poland* (New York: Harper Perennial, 1992).

Brunner, Jose, 'Will, Desire and Experience: Etiology and Ideology in the German and Austrian Medical Discourse on War Neuroses, 1914–1922', *Transcultural Psychiatry* 37:3, 2000, 295–320.

Burleigh, Michael, *Death and Deliverance – Euthanasia in Germany, c.1900–1945* (Cambridge: Cambridge University Press, 1994).

Burleigh, Michael and Wippermann, Wolfgang, *The Racial State – Germany 1933–45* (Cambridge: Cambridge University Press, 1991).

Campbell, Joan, *Joy in Work, German Work – The National Debate, 1800–1945* (Princeton: Princeton University Press, 1989).

Canning, Kathleen, *Gender History in Practice: Historical Perspectives on Bodies, Class and Citizenship* (Ithaca: Cornell University Press, 2006).

Carsten, F.L., *War against War – British and German Radical Movements in the First World War* (Berkeley: University of California Press, 1982).

Chickering, Roger, *Imperial Germany and the Great War, 1914–1918* (Cambridge: Cambridge University Press, 1998).

— *The Great War and Urban Life in Germany* (Cambridge: Cambridge University Press, 2007).

Childers, Thomas, *The Nazi Voter: The Social Foundations of Fascism in Germany, 1919–1933* (Chapel Hill: University of North Carolina Press, 1981).

Cohen, Deborah, *The War Come Home, Disabled Veterans in Britain and Germany, 1914–1939* (Berkeley: University of California Press, 2000).

Cocks, Geoffrey, *Psychotherapy in the Third Reich*, second edition (New Brunswick: Transaction, 1997).

Confino, Alon and Fritzsche, Peter, *The Work of Memory – New Directions in the Study of German Society and Culture* (Urbana and Chicago: University of Illinois Press, 2002).

Crew, David F., *Germans on Welfare – From Weimar to Hitler* (New York: Oxford University Press, 1998).

— 'The Ambiguities of Modernity: Welfare and the German State from Wilhelm to Hitler', in Geoff Eley (ed.), *Society, Culture and the State in Germany, 1870–1930* (Ann Arbor: University of Michigan Press, 1996).

Crouthamel, Jason, 'Male Sexuality and Psychological Trauma: Soldiers and Sexual "Disorder" in World War I and Weimar Germany', *Journal of History of Sexuality* 17:1, January 2008 (Univ. of Texas Press), 60–84.

— 'Mobilizing Psychopaths into Pacifists: Psychological Victims of the First World War in Weimar and Nazi Germany', *Peace and Change: A Journal of Peace Research* 30:2, April 2005 (Blackwell Publishing), 205–30.

— 'War Neurosis versus Savings Psychosis: Working-Class Politics and Psychological Trauma in Weimar Germany.' *Journal of Contemporary History* 37:2, April 2002, 163–82.

Daniel, Ute, *The War from Within – German Working-Class Women in the First World War*, translated by Margaret Ries (Oxford University Press, 1997).

Davis, Belinda, *Home Fires Burning – Food, Politics and Everyday Life in Berlin* (Chapel Hill: University of North Carolina Press, 2000).

Dean, Eric T., *Shook over Hell: Post-Traumatic Stress, Vietnam and the Civil War* (Cambridge: Harvard University Press, 1997).

Decker, Hannah, *Freud in Germany: Revolution and Reaction in Science* (New York: International Universities Press, 1977).

Deist, Wilhelm, 'Der militärische Zusammenbruch des Kaiserreichs: Zur Realität Der "Dolchstosslegende"', in Wilhelm Deist (ed.), *Militär, Staat und Gesellschaft – Studien zur preussisch-deutschen Militärgeschichte*, vol. 34 (Munich: R. Oldenbourg 1991).

— 'Verdeckter Militärstreik im Kriegsjahr 1918?' in Wolfram Wette (ed.), *Der Krieg Des kleinen Mannes: Eine Militärgeschichte von unten* (Munich: Piper, 1992).

Diehl, James M., *The Thanks of the Fatherland – German Veterans after the Second World War* (Chapel Hill: University of North Carolina Press, 1993).

— *Paramilitary Politcs in the Weimar Republic* (Bloomington: Indiana University Press, 1977).

— 'German Veterans' Politics under Three Flags', in Stephen Ward, *The War Generation – Veterans of the First World War* (Port Washington: Kennikat Press, 1975).

Eckart, Wolfgang U., '"The Most Extensive Experiment that the Imagination Can Conceive": War Emotional Stress and German Mental Medicine, 1914–1918', in Roger Chickering (ed.), *Great War, Total War: Combat and Mobilization on the Western Front* (Cambridge University Press, 2000)

Eghigian, Greg, *Making Security Social – Disability, Insurance and the Birth of the Social Entitlement State in Germany* (Ann Arbor: University of Michigan Press, 2000).

— 'The Politics of Victimization: Social Pensioners and the German Social State in the Inflation, 1919–1925', *Central European History* 26, 1993, 375–404.

Ehrenreich, Barbara, *Blood Rites – Origins and History of the Passions of War* (New York: Owl Books, 1997).

Eksteins, Modris, 'All Quiet on the Western Front and the Fate of a War', *Journal of Contemporary History* 15:2, April 1980, 345–66.

— *The Rites of Spring* (Boston: Houghton Mifflin, 1989).

Elder, Sace, 'Murder, Denunciation and Policing in Weimar Berlin', *Journal of Contemporary History* 41:3, July 2006, 401–19.

Eley, Geoff, *Reshaping the German Right* (New Haven: Yale University Press, 1980).

— *Forging Democracy – The History of the Left in Europe, 1850–2000* (Oxford: Oxford University Press, 2002).

— (ed.) *Society, Culture and the State in Germany* (Ann Arbor: University of Michigan Press, 1996).

— 'How and Where is German History Centered', in Neil Gregor, Nils Roemer and Mark Roseman (eds), *German History from the Margins* (Bloomington: Indiana University Press, 2006).

Feldman, Gerald, *Army, Industry and Labor in Germany* (Princeton: Princeton University Press, 1966).

Ferguson, Niall, *The Pity of War* (New York: Basic Books, 1999).

Fischer, Suzanne Hayes, *Mother of Eagles – The War Diary of Baroness von Richthofen* (Atglen: Schiffer Military History, 2001).

Freud, Sigmund, *Beyond the Pleasure Principle*, translated by James Strachey (New York: Norton, 1961)

— *Civilization and its Discontents*, translated by James Strachey (New York: Norton, 1961).

Frevert, Ute, *Women in German History—From Bourgeois Liberation to Sexual Liberation*, translated by Stuart McKinnon-Evans (Oxford University Press, 1990).

Fritzsche, Peter, *A Nation of Flyers: German Aviation and the Popular Imagination* (Cambridge: Cambridge University Press, 1992).

Fussell, Paul, *The Great War and Modern Memory* (New York: Oxford University Press, 1975).

Gellately, Robert, *Backing Hitler – Consent and Coercion in Nazi Germany* (Oxford: Oxford University Press, 2001).

Geyer, Michael, 'Ein Verbote des Wohlfahrtstaates – Die Kriegsopfervorsorgung in Frankreich, Deutschland und Grossbritannien nach dem ersten Weltkrieg', *Geschichte und Gesellschaft 9*, 1983, 230–77.

Gilman, Sander, *The Jew's Body* (New York: Routledge, 1991).

Gregor, Neil, and Roemer, Neils, and Roseman, Mark (eds.), *German History from the Margins* (Bloomington: Indiana University Press, 2006).

Haeberle, Erwin J., 'Swastika, Pink Triangle and Yellow Star: The Destruction of Sexology and the Persecution of Homosexuals in Nazi Germany', in Martin Bauml Duberman, Martha Vicinus and George Chauncey, *Hidden from History: Reclaiming the Gay & Lesbian Past* (New York: Nal Books, 1989).

Hagemann, Karen and Stefanie Schüler-Springorum (eds), *Home/Front – The Military, War and Gender in Twentieth Century Germany* (Oxford: Berg, 2002).

— 'The Military, Violence and Gender Relations in the Age of the World Wars', in Karen Hagemann and Stefanie Schüler-Springorum (eds), *Home/Front – The Military, War and Gender in Twentieth Century Germany* (Oxford: Berg, 2002).

Harrington, Ralph, 'The Railway Accident: Trains, Trauma and Technological Crises in 19th Century Britain', in Mark Micale and Paul Lerner (eds), *Traumatic Pasts: History, Psychiatry and Trauma in the Modern Age, 1870–1930* (Cambridge University Press, 2001).

Haselbeck, Helmut, and Engelbracht, Gerda, '"Vom Aufbruch in eine andere Zukunft" – Bremer Psychiatrie zwischen 1945–1975', in Franz Werner Kersting (ed.) *Psychiatriereform als Gesellschaftsreform – Die Hypothek des Nationalsozialismus und der Aufbruch der sechziger Jahre* (Paderborn: Ferdinand Schöningh, 2003).

Herf, Jeffery, *Reactionary Modernism: Technology, Culture and Politics in Weimar and the Third Reich* (Cambridge: Cambridge University Press, 1984).

Hirschfeld, Gerhard, Krumeich, Gerd and Renz, Irena (eds), *'Keiner fühlt sich hier Mehr als Mensch ...' Erlebnis und Wirkung des Ersten Weltkriegs* (Frankfurt a.M.: Fischer, 1996).

Hirschfeld, Magnus, *The Sexual History of the World War*, translation of the 1941 edition (Honolulu: University Press of the Pacific, 2006).

Hofer, Hans-Georg, 'Nerven-Korrekturen: Ärzte, Soldaten, und die 'Kriegsneurosen' im Ersten Weltkrieg', *Zeitgeschichte* 27, 2000, 249–69.

Hoge, Charles W., *et al.*, 'Combat Duty in Iraq and Afghanistan, Mental Problems and Barriers to Care', *The New England Journal of Medicine* 351:1, July 2004, 13–22.

Hong, Young-Sun, 'World War I and the German Welfare State: Gender, Religion and The Paradoxes of Modernity', in Geoff Eley (ed.) *Society and Culture and the State in Germany, 1870–1939* (Ann Arbor: University of Michigan Press, 1996).

— *Welfare, Modernity and the Weimar State, 1919–1933* (Princeton: Princeton University Press, 1998).

— 'Gender, Citizenship and the Welfare State: Social Work and the Politics of Femininity in the Weimar Republic, *Central European History* 30:1, 1–24.

Hüppauf, Bernd, 'Schlachtenmythen und die Konstruction des "Neuen Menschen", in *'Keiner fühlt sich hier mehr als Mensch …' Erlebnis und Wirkung des Ersten Weltkriegs*, in G. Hirschfeld, G. Krumeich and I. Renz (eds), *Erlebnis und Wirkung des Ersten Weltkriegs* (Frankfurt a.M.: Fischer, 1997).

Joseph, Tiffany, '"Non-Combatant's Shell Shock": Trauma and Gender in F. Scott Fitzgerald's *Tender is the Night*', *NWSA Journal* 15:3, Fall 2003, 64–81.

Kaes, Anton, *M* (London: British Film Institute, 2000).

— *Shell Shock: Trauma and Film in Weimar Germany* (Princeton: Princeton University Press, forthcoming).

Kater, Michael, *Doctors under Hitler* (Chapel Hill: University of North Carolina Press, 1989).

Kaufmann, Doris, 'Science as Cultural Practice in the First World War and Weimar Germany', *Journal of Contemporary History* 34(1), January 1999, 125–44.

Kern, Stephen, *Anatomy and Destiny – A Cultural History of the Human Body* (Indianapolis: The Bobb-Merrill Company, Inc., 1975).

Kershaw, Ian, *The 'Hitler Myth'—Image and Reality in the Third Reich* (Oxford University Press, 1987).

— *Hitler, 1889–1936: Hubris* (New York: W.W. Norton & Co., 1998).

— *Hitler, 1936–1945: Nemesis* (New York: W.W. Norton & Co., 2000).

Killen, Andreas, *Berlin Electropolis – Shock, Nerves and German Modernity* (Berkeley: University of California Press, 2005).

Kienitz, Sabine, 'Der Krieg der Invaliden – Helden-Bilder und Männlichkeitskonstruktionen nach dem ersten Weltkrieg', *Militärgeschichte Zeitschrift* 60, 2001, 367–401.

Kocka, Jürgen, *Klassengesellschaft im Krieg: Deutsche Sozialgeschichte, 1914–1918* (Göttingen: University of Göttingen, 1973).

Kolb, Eberhard, *The Weimar Republic*, translated by P.S. Falla (New York: Routledge, 1988).

Kundrus, Birthe, 'Gender Wars – The First World War and the Construction of Gender Relations in the Weimar Republic', in Karen Hagemann and Stefanie Schüler-Springorum (eds), *Home/Front – The Military, War and Gender in Twentieth Century Germany* (Oxford: Berg, 2002).

Kruse, Wolfgang, 'Die Kriegsbegeisterung im Deutschen Reich zu Beginn des ersten Weltkrieges: Entehungszusammenhänge, Grenzen und ideologische Strukturen', in Marcel van der Linden and Gottfried Mergner (eds), *Kriegsbegeisterung und mentale Kriegsvorbereitung: Interdisziplinäre Studien* (Berlin: Dunker & Humblot, 1991).

Kühne, Thomas, *Kameradschaft: Die Soldaten des nationalsozialistischen Krieges und das 20. Jahrhundert* (Göttingen: Vandenhoeck and Ruprecht, 2006).
— *Männergeschichte, Geschlechtergeschichte: Männlichkeit im Wandel der Moderne* (Frankfurt: Campus, 1996).
— 'Gender Confusion and Gender Order in the German Military, 1918–1945', in Karen Hagemann and Stefanie Schüler-Springorum (eds), *Home/Front: The Military, War and Gender in Twentieth-Century Germany* (New York: Berg, 2002).
Large, David Clay, *Berlin* (New York: Basic Books, 2000).
Leed, Eric J., *No Man's Land: Combat and Identity in World War I* (Cambridge: Cambridge University Press, 1979).
Leese, Peter, *Shell Shock: Traumatic Neurosis and the British Soldiers of the First World War* (London: Palrave, 2002).
Lemmens, Franz, 'Zur Entwicklung der Militärpsychologie in Deutschland zwischen 1870–1918', in Winau and Müller-Dietz (eds), *'Medizin für den Staat – Medizin für den Krieg': Aspekte zwischen 1914–1945* (Husum: Mattiesen, 1994).
Lerner, Paul, *Hysterical Men – War, German Psychiatry, and the Politics of Trauma in Germany, 1890–1930* (Ithaca: Cornell University Press, 2003).
— 'An Economy of Memory: Psychiatrists, Veterans, and Traumatic Narratives in Weimar Germany', in Alon Confino and Peter Fritzsche (eds), *The Work of Memory- New Directions in the Study of German Society and Culture* (Urbana and Chicago: University of Illinois Press, 2002).
— 'Hysterical Men: War, Neurosis, and German Mental Medicine, 1914–1921', Dissertation: Columbia University, 1996.
— 'From Traumatic Neurosis to Male Hysteria: The Decline and Fall of Hermann Oppenheim, 1889–1919', in Mark Micale and Paul Lerner (eds), *Traumatic Pasts: History, Psychiatry and Trauma in the Modern Age, 1870–1930* (New York: Cambridge University Press, 2001).
— 'Psychiatry and the Casualties of War in Germany, 1914–1918', *Journal of Contemporary History* 35:1, January 2000, 13–28.
Leys, Ruth, *Trauma: A Genealogy* (Chicago: University of Chicago, 2000).
Linder, Ann P., *Princes of the Trenches – Narrating the German Experience of the First World War* (Columbia: Camden House, 1996).
Link-Heer, Ursula, 'Männliche Hysterie: Ein Diskursanalyse', in Ursula Becher and Jörn Rüsen, *Weiblichkeit in geschichtlicher Perspektive* (Frankfurt: Suhrkamp, 1988).
MacCurdy, Marian Mesrobian, 'Truth, Trauma, and Justice in Gillion Slovo's *Every Secret Thing*', *Literature and Medicine* 19:1, Spring 2000, 115–32.
Maser, Werner (ed.) *Hitler's Letters and Notes* (New York: Bantam, 1974).
Mendelssohn-Bartholdy, *The War in German Society: The Testament of a Liberal* (New Haven: Yale University Press, 1937).
Micale, Mark and Lerner, Paul (eds) *Traumatic Pasts: History, Psychiatry and Trauma in the Modern Age, 1870–1930* (New York: Cambridge University Press, 2001).
Mierzejewski, Alfred C., *The Most Valuable Asset of the Reich – A History of the German National Railway*, vol. 1, 1920–1932 (Chapel Hill: University of North Carolina Press, 1999).
Mosse, George L., *Fallen Soldiers – Reshaping the Memory of the World Wars* (New York: Oxford University Press, 1990)
— *The Image of Man: The Creation of Modern Masculinity* (New York: Oxford University Press, 1998).
— *Nationalism and Sexuality – Respectability and Abnormal Sexuality in Modern Europe* (New York: Howard Fertig, 1985).

— 'Shell-Shock as a Social Disease', *Journal of Contemporary History* 35:1, January 2000, 101–8.

Neumarker, K.J., 'Karl Bonhoeffer and the Concept of Symptomatic Psychoses', *History of Psychiatry* 12:46, 2001, 213–26.

Perry, Heather, 'Re-Arming the Disabled Veteran: Artificially Rebuilding the State and Society in World War I Germany', in Katerine Ott, David Serlin and Stephen Mihm (eds), *Artificial Parts, Practical Lives: Modern Histories of Prosthetics* (New York: New York University Press, 2002).

Peukert, Detlev, *The Weimar Republic: The Crisis of Classical Modernity*, translated by Richard Deveson (New York: Hill and Wang, 1989).

— *Inside Nazi Germany: Conformity, Opposition and Racism in Everyday Life* (New Haven: Yale University Press, 1987).

Poore, Carol, *Disability in German Culture* (Ann Arbor: University of Michigan Press, 2007).

Preller, Ludwig, *Sozialpolitik in der Weimarer Republik* (Stuttgart: Franz Mittelbach, 1949).

Radkau, Joachim, *Das Zeitalter der Nervosität – Deutschland zwischen Bismarck und Hitler* (München: Carl Hanser Verlag, 1998).

Remarque, Erich Maria, *All Quiet on the Western Front*, translated by A.W. Wheen (Boston: Little Brown & Co., 1929).

— *The Road Back*, translated by A.W. Wheen (Boston: Little Brown & Co., 1931).

Richthofen, Manfred von, *Der Rote Kampfflieger*, translated as *The Red Baron* by Peter Kilduff (San Diego: Aero Publishers, Inc., 1969).

Riedesser, Peter and Verderber, Axel, *'Maschinengewehre hinter der Front': Zur Geschichte der deutschen Militärpsychiatrie* (Frankfurt: Fischer Taschenbuch Verlag, 1996).

Roudebush, Marc, 'A Battle of Nerves: Hysteria and its Treatments in France during World War I', in Paul Lerner and Mark Micale (eds), *Traumatic Pasts: History, Trauma and Psychiatry in the Modern Age* (New York: Cambridge University Press, 2001).

Rürup, Reinhard, 'Der Geist von 1914 in Deutschland – Kriegsbegeisterung und Ideolisierung des Krieges im Ersten Weltkrieg', in Bernd Hüppauf (ed.), *Ansichten vom Krieg – Vergleichende Studien zum Ersten Weltkrieg in Literatur und Gesellschaft* (Königstein: Forum Academicum, 1984).

Schüler-Springorum, Stefanie, 'Flying and Killing – Military Masculinity in German Pilot Literature, 1914–1939', in Karen Hagemann and Stefanie Schüler-Springorum (eds), *Home/Front – The Military, War and Gender in Twentieth Century Germany* (Oxford: Berg, 2002).

Schmiedebach, Peter, 'Sozialdarwinisumus, Biologismus, Pazifismus— Ärztestimmen zum Ersten Weltkrieg', in Blecker and Schmiedebach (eds), *Medizin und Krieg: Von Dilemma der Heilberufe, 1865–1985* (Frankfurt a.M.: Fischer, 1987).

Shay, Jonathan, *Odysseus in America – Combat Trauma and the Trauma and the Trials of Homecoming* (New York: Scribner, 2002).

— *Achilles in Vietnam – Combat Trauma and the Undoing of Character* (New York: Maxwell Macmillan, 1994).

Shepard, Ben, *A War of Nerves—Soldiers and Psychiatrists in the 20th Century* (Cambridge: Harvard University Press, 2000).

Showalter, Elaine, 'Rivers and Sassoon: The Inscription of Male Gender Anxieties', in Margaret Randolph Higonnet, *et al.*, *Behind the Lines: Gender and the Two World Wars* (New Haven: Yale University Press, 1987).

— *The Female Malady: Women, Madness and English Culture, 1830–1980* (New York: Penguin, 1985)

Stark, Gary D., *Entrepreneurs of Ideology: Neoconservative Publishers in Germany, 1890–1933* (Chapel Hill: University of North Carolina, 1981).

Stone, Martin, 'Shellshock and the Psychologists', in W.F. Byum, Roy Porter and Michael Shepard, *The Anatomy of Madness*, vol. 2 (London: Tavistock, 1985).

Tatar, Maria, *Lustmord – Sexual Murder in Weimar Germany* (Princeton: Princeton University Press, 1995).

Theweleit, Klaus, *Male Fantasies*, vols 1 and 2 (Minneapolis: University of Minnesota Press, 1987).

Ulrich, Bernd, *Die Augenzeugen – Deutsche Feldpostbriefe in Kriegs- und Nachkriegszeit* (Essen: Klartext, 1997)

— '"als wenn nichts geschehen wäre" – Anmerkungen zur Behandlung der Kriegsopfer während des Ersten Weltkriegs', in Gerhard Hirschfeld, Gerd Krumeich and Irena Renz (eds), *'Keiner fühlt sich hier Mehr als Mensch ...' Erlebnis und Wirkung des Ersten Weltkriegs* (Frankfurt a.M.: Fischer, 1996).

Ulrich, Bernd and Ziemann, Benjamin (eds), *Frontalltag im Ersten Weltkrieg* (Frankfurt a.M.: Fischer, 1994).

— *Krieg im Frieden – Die umkämpfte Erinnerung an den Ersten Weltkrieg* (Frankfurt a.M.: Fischer, 1997).

Verhey, Jeffrey, *The Spirit of 1914: Militarism, Myth and Mobilization in Germany* (Cambridge: Cambridge University Press, 2000).

Wehler, Hans-Ulrich, *The German Empire, 1871–1918*, translated by Kim Traynor (Leamington Spa: Berg, 1985).

Weindling, Paul, *Health, Race and German Politics between National Unification and Nazism, 1870–1945* (Cambridge: Cambridge University Press, 1989).

Weitz, Eric D., *Creating German Communism, 1890–1990* (Princeton: Princeton University Press, 1997).

Welch, David, *The Third Reich – Politics and Propaganda* (New York: Routledge, 1993).

Wetzell, Richard F., *Inventing the Criminal: A History of German Criminology, 1880–1945* (Chapel Hill: University of North Carolina Press, 2000).

Whalen, Robert W., *Bitter Wounds – German Victims of the Great War, 1914–1939.* (Ithaca: Cornell University Press, 1984).

Widdig, Bernd, *Culture and Inflation in Weimar Germany* (Berkeley: University of California Press, 2001).

Winkler, Heinrich August, *Von Revolution zur Stabilisierung: Arbeiter und Arbeiterbewegung in der Weimarer Republik, 1918–1924* (Berlin, 1984).

Winter, Jay, 'Shell Shock and the Cultural History of the War', *Journal of Contemporary History* 35:1, January 2000, 7–11.

— *Sites of Memory, Sites of Mourning: The Great War in European Cultural History* (Cambridge: Cambridge University Press, 1995).

Witkop, Philipp (ed.), *German Students' War Letters*, translated by A.F. Wedd, foreword by Jay Winter (Philadelphia: University of Pennsylvania Press, 2002, originally published 1929).

Woollacott, Angela, *On Her Their Lives Depend – Munitions Workers in the Great War* (Berkeley: University of California Press, 1994).

Wright, Gordon, *The Ordeal of Total War, 1939–1945* (New York: Harper & Row, 1968).

Young, Allan, *The Harmony of Illusions: Inventing Post-Traumatic Stress Disorder* (Princeton: Princeton University Press, 1995).

Zweig, Stefan, *The World of Yesterday* (Lincoln: University of Nebraska Press, 1964).

Index